# RACE AND CULTURE

# RACE
## AND
# CULTURE

A WORLD VIEW

## THOMAS SOWELL

BasicBooks
*A Division of HarperCollinsPublishers*

*Designed by Ellen Levine*

LIBRARY OF CONGRESS CATALOGING-IN-PUBLICATION DATA
Sowell, Thomas, 1930–
  Race and culture : a world view / Thomas Sowell.
    p.  cm.
  Includes bibliographical references and index.
  ISBN 0-465-06796-4
  1. Ethnic groups.  2. Ethnic relations.  3. Culture.  4. Race.
I. Title
GN495.4.S69  1994
305.8—dc20                                       94-4748
                                                    CIP

94 95 96 97 ♦/HC 9 8 7 6 5 4 3 2

*. . . men are not blank tablets on which the environment inscribes a culture which can readily be erased to make way for a new inscription.*

—Oscar Handlin[1]

# CONTENTS

# PREFACE

This book challenges many dogmas of so-called "social science," as well as many underlying assumptions about racial issues and cultural differences. This challenge is based on more than a decade of research for this book, which in turn represents the culmination of more than twenty years of research and writing on issues of race and ethnicity in general. *Race and Culture* covers a wider range of subjects and issues than any of my previous writings in this area. It draws upon research, discussions, and observations in many countries visited during journeys that took me completely around the world twice and other journeys that took me twice around the Pacific basin.

These travels were not incidental. In addition to a large amount of literature collected and many discussions with scholars, officials, and others in various countries, these on-site observations made vivid what words or photographs could only begin to suggest. There is nothing like being inside the great mosque in Cordoba, seeing its grand design and the fine craftsmanship with which it was constructed a thousand years ago, to appreciate the achievements of the civilization from which it came. And to see, a short walk away, a bridge built another thousand years before that by the Romans—still carrying heavy traffic today—is to see another great civilization's cultural impact when Spain was part of the Roman Empire. To walk through a graveyard in an old village in Australia's Barossa Valley and see all the gravestones written in German, in this

English-speaking country, is to get a sense of the tenacity of the German culture, even when transplanted 10,000 miles from home. From the ancient walled city of Jerusalem to the ultramodern city-state of Singapore, each place told its own story in its own way.

Perhaps the best way to focus on the central theme of this book is by contrast with prevailing "social science" doctrines which make the surrounding environment the shaper of groups' behavior and institutional decisions the arbiters of their fate. While we can all agree on the influence of "environment" in some very general sense, there is a vast difference between (1) regarding groups as being shaped by immediate circumstances, including the people and institutions around them, and (2) regarding groups as having their own internal cultural patterns, antedating the environment in which they currently find themselves, and transcending the beliefs, biases, and decisions of others.

The vast migrations of peoples over the centuries have left many racial and cultural groups in settings radically different from the settings in which their own cultures evolved, facing challenges and opportunities undreamed of by their ancestors.

Group cultural patterns may indeed be products of environments—but often of environments that existed on the other side of an ocean, in the lives of ancestors long forgotten, yet transmitted over the generations as distilled values, preferences, skills, and habits. The outward veneer of a new society—its language, dress, and customs—may mask these underlying differences in cultural values, which are nevertheless revealed when the hard choices of life have to be made, and sacrifices endured, to achieve competing goals.

Where an analysis is confined to one society—racial and ethnic groups in the United States, for example—it can be difficult to establish which patterns are the result of the way particular groups were treated in American society and which are the results of their own internal cultural patterns. But where the analysis is international in scope, then the group patterns which recur in country after country can more readily be distinguished from historical differences in the group's experience from one country to another.

The fundamental conflict between the approach which focuses on group cultural patterns and that which attributes intergroup economic and social differences to differential treatment by "society" leads to other differences. These derivative differences include very different weights attached to political activity as a factor in group advancement. For exam-

ple, if a poorer group's fate is largely in the hands of contemporary outsiders, then political activity designed to persuade or pressure those outsiders is essential to the group's progress. But if a group's own culture,
and the skills, behavior, and performances derived from that culture are
the primary determinants of its economic and social fate, then groups
which rise from poverty to prosperity need not be particularly active
politically, nor particularly successful in whatever political activity they
engage in. History indeed records numerous groups rising from poverty to
prosperity, in many parts of the world, with no corresponding political
activity or political success.

Chinese, German, Japanese, Italian, and Indian immigrants have risen
to prosperity in many countries, often after harrowing beginnings, without
ever achieving any notable political success. Such political leaders as
have occasionally risen from such groups have typically come to prominence only *after* the group was already well established economically,
and have typically represented broader constituencies in the larger society, rather than being spokesmen for their own ethnic interests. By contrast, the Irish have been unusually successful politically at many levels,
including becoming prime ministers of Britain, Canada, and Australia,
and presidents of the United States. Yet it would be difficult, if not impossible, to argue from history that the Irish have risen more rapidly than
these other groups.

With all groups, important changes take place over time, so that neither their own cultures nor those of the surrounding societies in which
they live remain absolutely fixed. Economic and technological progress
alone require and ensure this. Nevertheless, existing cultural values have
much to do with which groups keep up with the advances of science,
technology, and organization, which fall behind, and which spearhead the
advancing frontiers of human knowledge. But, while time is often an
important variable in changing relationships among groups, nations, or
civilizations, time by itself accomplishes nothing. In particular, it is a
serious mistake, with dangerous consequences, to imagine that time itself
improves relations among racial and ethnic groups. History shows dramatic, tragic, and sustained retrogressions, as well as periods of progress,
in the relations among groups. For example, there was not a single race
riot between the Sinhalese majority and the Tamil minority in Sri Lanka
during the first half of the twentieth century, but mob violence and
ghastly atrocities between these two groups have become commonplace in
the last half of the century. In the United States, blacks living in various

northern cities in the last quarter of the nineteenth century experienced growing acceptance, exemplified by an absence of black ghettoes, but such ghettoes took shape among other signs of growing hostility to blacks in the early twentieth century. In Europe, Jews experienced less discrimination and violence during the first thousand years of the Christian era than in the second thousand years.

Culture, as the term is used here, will not be confined to what one scholar on ethnicity has called "real culture," such as "music and art."[1] On the contrary, the focus here will be primarily on those aspects of culture which provide the material requirements for life itself—the specific skills, general work habits, saving propensities, and attitudes toward education and entrepreneurship—in short, what economists call "human capital." That is not because of a "glorification of the practical,"[2] conceived of as an antithesis to higher culture, but because the material resources from which physical survival itself must come are also requirements for music, art, literature, philosophy, and other forms of higher culture. In general, it is precisely the more prosperous societies, and the more prosperous groups within given societies, which have a sufficient margin of time and resources to devote to higher culture, rather than to meeting survival needs. Moreover, in comparing groups and societies, matters of subjective taste and habitual conditioning are so intimately involved in evaluations of music and art that it is far more problematical to speak of one group or society as being more advanced or more effective in these realms than to say that one group or society is more advanced in industrial skills or medical care.

While the histories of many groups are fascinating in themselves, the ultimate purpose of this study is not description but analysis. It attempts to show some of the ways in which their cultures or "human capital" have affected the advancement of particular groups, the societies of which they were part, and ultimately the human race. Human capital has not been randomly distributed, being itself a product of circumstances that have varied widely in different parts of the world with different climates, geography, and histories. The purpose of this book is not to offer some grand theory explaining cultural differences. Its goal is to demonstrate the reality, persistence, and consequences of cultural differences—contrary to many of today's grand theories, based on the supposedly dominant role of "objective conditions," "economic forces," or "social structures."

This book deliberately offers little in the way of direct policy prescription, for its underlying premise is that what is most needed is an understanding of existing realities, the history from which the present evolved, and the enduring principles constraining our options for the future. There is seldom a shortage of people willing to draw up blueprints for salvation. What is important is that such people and those who judge their proposals both understand what they are talking about.

Lest the word "race" in the title of this book lead to misunderstanding, or to quibbling, the term is used in the same general sense in which it has been used in my earlier writings, dating back to *Race and Economics:* "The term 'race' will be used here in the broad social sense in which it is applied in everyday life to designate ethnic groups of various sorts—by race, religion, or nationality."[3] A more scientific definition of race is not attempted, for such a definition would have little relevance to the human beings currently inhabiting this planet, after untold centuries of racial intermixtures. In much the same way, "continent" is not always a strictly geographical term. Yet few people object because Europe and Asia are considered separate continents, despite being one continuous land mass. The real distinction between them is not geographical but biological— that racially different people originated on different sides of the Caucasus Mountains.

Because this study focuses more on social realities, rather than on biological realities, it defines racial or ethnic groups primarily in social rather than biological terms. Thus Adolph Plessy, of *Plessy v. Ferguson* fame, is defined here as "black" even though he was seven-eighths Caucasian and people with less Caucasian ancestry than that are considered "white" (*branco*) in Brazil. This is also in keeping with the cultural focus of this study, for Plessy was raised in the black culture of the United States and *brancos* with more African ancestry than Plessy were raised in the *branco* culture of Brazil. Similarly, we need not address the philosophical and legal question that is controversial in Israel: "Who is a Jew?" For our purposes, a Jew is anyone who is socially regarded as a Jew, whatever the religious or biological realities may be. Only in Chapter 6 (Race and Intelligence) will the focus shift to a more biological concept of race, when discussing issues of heredity and environment.

Race is one of the ways of collectivizing people in our minds. In some societies it is the most important way of separating people for differential treatment. In other societies, however, people are treated differently according to their religion, nationality, caste, or other characteristics. Each characteristic has its own mystique, and there is no reason to assume that the mystique of race is unique in its pervasiveness or its power, except in particular societies. In other societies, people may face oppression, humiliation, or even genocide, while being physically indistinguishable from the surrounding population. In many cases, special modes of dress, insignia, or other indicators of group membership have been imposed, precisely because there are no natural biological indicators to provide practical guidance in carrying out policies of differential treatment. Race is a biological concept but it is a social reality. How important it is in a given setting can only be determined empirically from an examination of that setting.

To all the usual difficulties of trying to understand any complex subject, there is an added dimension of difficulty in trying to analyze racial and cultural issues. Emotions are often high and sensitivities great on all sides. Conclusions that disturb comfortable or convenient visions, or the reputations or careers based on them, are certain to attract not only criticisms but denunciations, distortions, and even outright lies. No matter how many times in history myriads of individuals or groups have each claimed to have the one and only truth—and have subsequently been proven wrong—there are still new claimants who feel that any challenge to *their* particular view is not only intellectually invalid but also a moral outrage to be discredited and stamped out at all cost. However, the progress of the human race would not have been possible, and we would all still be living in caves, if there were not also other people willing to weigh new ideas and evidence, to take what they can from them, and to gain what insights they can, even from reasoning with which they cannot fully agree. It is for such people that this book is written.

# ACKNOWLEDGEMENTS

A book on a subject of this scope could not have been written without the help of many other people. In addition to the usual intellectual indebtedness to those whose specialized scholarship in a variety of areas made possible my synthesis and analysis, there are many more direct obligations incurred for generous help given to me personally by a multitude of scholars, librarians, journalists, and officials, scattered literally around the world. These obligations begin at home with the Hoover Institution, which has supported my work in many ways, including financing four lengthy international trips to collect information, publications, and data in 1984, 1987, 1988, and 1989. My assistant Na Liu deserves special praise and special gratitude for work above and beyond the call of duty, as she coped with integrating numerous drafts of numerous chapters and literally thousands of footnotes—not all of them cited correctly by me, as Na's great diligence discovered. The Institute for Educational Affairs in Washington has also been helpful in supporting my research trips.

My heartfelt gratitude goes to *all* those who helped, even though the frailties of my memory raise the painful possibility that some may be inadvertently omitted from the detailed list that follows, in alphabetical order: Professor Bernard Anderson of the Wharton School, Professor Reginald Appleyard of the University of Western Australia (Perth), Dr. H. Avakian, Australian Institute of Multicultural Affairs (Melbourne), Dr. Alexandre Bennigsen of the École des Hautes Études en Sciences

Sociales (Paris), Dr. André Bétéille, University of Delhi, Professor Rondo Cameron of Emory University, Dr. Suma Chitnis of the Tata Institute of Social Science (Bombay), Professor Gregory Clark of Stanford University, Professor Walker Connor, Trinity College (Connecticut), Professor John B. Cornell, University of Texas, Professor H. J. de Blij of the University of Miami, Mr. Suman Dubey of *India Today* (New Delhi), Dr. Peter Duignan of the Hoover Institution (Stanford), Professor James Fawcett, Director of the East-West Center, University of Hawaii, Professor James R. Flynn of the University of Otago (New Zealand), Dr. Lewis Gann of the Hoover Institution (Stanford), Mr. Hu Gentles of the Private Sector Organization of Jamaica, Mr. Petro Georgiou of the Australian Institute of Multicultural Affairs (Melbourne), Professor Margaret A. Gibson of California State University (Sacramento), Mr. Harvey Ginsberg of William Morrow Publishers, Professor Nathan Glazer of Harvard University, Professor Anthony G. Hopkins of Oxford University, Professor Donald L. Horowitz of Duke University, Professor James Jupp, Australian National University (Canberra), Professor Wolfgang Kasper of the Australian Defence Force Academy (Campbell), Professor Robert Klitgaard of the University of Natal (South Africa), Mr. Leslie Lenkowsky of the Hudson Institute, Mr. Greg Lindsay of the Centre for Independent Studies (Sydney), Professor Seymour Martin Lipset of Stanford University, Professor John McKay, Monash University (Australia), Dr. Ratna Murdia of the Tata Institute of Social Science (Bombay), Professor Charles A. Price of the Australian National University (Canberra), Dr. Alvin Rabushka of the Hoover Institution (Stanford), Mr. Sohindar S. Rana of the U.S. Information Service (New Delhi), Professor Peter I. Rose of Smith College (Massachusetts), Miss Claudia Rosett of the *Asian Wall Street Journal* (Hong Kong), Dr. Dominique Schnapper of the École des Hautes Études en Sciences Sociales (Paris), Dr. Sharon Siddique and Dr. Kernial Sandhu Singh of the Institute for Southeast Asian Studies (Singapore), Professor Sammy Smooha of the University of Haifa (Israel), Professor Leo Suryadinata of the National University of Singapore, Professor Malcolm Todd, University of Exeter (England), Mrs. Mary Lynn Tuck, American Historical Society of Germans from Russia (Nebraska), Professor Philip E. Vernon of the University of Calgary (Canada), Professor Henry Walker of Cornell University, Professor Myron Weiner and Mr. Steven Wilkinson of the Massachusetts Institute of Technology, and Dr. S. Enders Wimbush of Radio Free Europe (Munich).

# CHAPTER 1

# A WORLD VIEW

Racial, ethnic, and cultural differences among peoples play a major role in the events of our times, in countries around the world, and have played a major role in the long history of the human race. Both intergroup socioeconomic differences within a given country and larger differences on a world stage between nations or whole civilizations reflect large cultural differences that have pervaded history. The history of cultural differences among peoples enables us to understand not only how particular peoples differ but also how cultural patterns in general affect the economic and social advancement of the human race.

A particular people usually has its own particular set of skills for dealing with the economic and social necessities of life—and also its own particular set of values as to what are the higher and lower purposes of life. These sets of skills and values typically follow them wherever they go. Despite prevailing "social science" approaches which depict people as creatures of their surrounding environment, or as victims of social institutions immediately impinging on them, both emigrants and conquerors have carried their own patterns of skills and behavior—their cultures—to the farthest regions of the planet, in the most radically different societies, and these patterns have often persisted for generations or even centuries. The role of a particular people's cultural equipment or human capital is much clearer in an international perspective than in the history of one country. If our view is limited to one country, then it may seem

plausible, for example, to attribute the Jews' rise to prosperity and predominance in New York's garment industry to circumstances peculiar to
that period of American history when masses of Jewish immigrants
arrived in New York.[1] But if our vision encompasses an *international* perspective—a world view—then we see that Jews have been prominent, if
not predominant, in the apparel industry over a period longer than the
entire history of the United States, and in countries ranging from
medieval Spain to modern Australia, from the Ottoman Empire to the
Russian Empire, as well as in Argentina, Brazil, Germany, and Chile.[2]
Similarly, while a one-country analysis might make it seem plausible that
Chinese retailers were once predominant in Jamaica for reasons peculiar
to Jamaica,[3] a world view shows that they were also predominant in the
same occupation in the Philippines, Malaysia, Thailand, Indonesia, Vietnam, Panama City, and Lima, Peru.[4]

Much the same story could be told of the Germans who pioneered in
building pianos in colonial America, czarist Russia, France, Australia,
and England.[5] India's entrepreneurial Gujaratis have likewise been
prominent or predominant in business enterprises from Fiji to virtually
the entire eastern coast of the African continent, from Kenya to South
Africa.[6] Italian fishermen have plied their trade not only around the
Mediterranean from Greece to Spain and North Africa, but also in San
Francisco, Argentina, and Australia,[7] just as Italian architects have
designed structures ranging from the Kremlin to sewer systems in
Argentina.[8] Scots historically played a major role in the international diffusion of medical knowledge, having first established Europe's leading
medical school in Edinburgh in 1726 and subsequently sent its physicians to settle from Russia to Virginia, with Edinburgh graduates establishing the first medical school in the United States in Philadelphia, as
well as the medical school at King's College (later renamed Columbia
University) and at Dartmouth.[9]

Innumerable other groups have become prominent or predominant in
particular occupations in countries all over the planet. The even distribution or proportional representation of groups in occupations or institutions
remains an intellectual construct defied by reality in society after society.
Nor can this all be attributed to exclusions or discrimination, for often
some powerless or even persecuted minorities predominate in prosperous
occupations. Christians and Jews were explicitly second class under
Islamic law for most of the long history of the Ottoman Empire, but they
predominated in the commerce and industry of that empire, as well as in

medical science.[10] In Russia under the czars, the German minority—about one percent of the population—constituted about 40 percent of the Russian army's high command in the 1880s,[11] just as German generals had been prominent in the high command of the Roman legions,[12] and generals of German ancestry led the American armies in both World Wars of the twentieth century, as well as in the Persian Gulf war of 1991.

Group occupational patterns, repeated in country after country, are only one of numerous cultural patterns that follow racial or ethnic groups around the world. Viewing such groups internationally frees us from prevailing "social science" doctrines which presuppose that a given nation is causally—and hence morally—responsible for whatever occupational, economic, or other patterns, "disparities," or "imbalances" are found among the various groups within its borders. Differences among groups, and even among subgroups within a given people, are the rule rather than the exception, all over the planet—in matters within their control, as well as in matters influenced by decisions made about them by other individuals or institutions. Fertility rates, alcohol consumption, performance and behavior in school, suicide rates, and output per man-hour are just some of the indicators of behavioral differences among racial and ethnic groups, whether in the same society or in different societies. Even in mundane, manual occupations, large intergroup differences have been common. In colonial Malaya, for example, Chinese workers on the rubber plantations collected sap from the trees at more than twice the rate of Malay workers.[13]

Even when the larger society is oblivious to finer breakdowns of subgroups within a given group—when "all blacks look alike," for example—the differences among these subgroups are often as large as the differences between the whole group and the general population.[14] People of Scottish ancestry have long been among the more prosperous groups in the United States, but people of the same ancestry in the Appalachian region have also constituted one of the most enduring pockets of poverty among white Americans. As long as our view is confined to American society, it may be plausible to believe that "objective conditions" in Appalachia, or the way people were "treated" there, accounts for the anomaly. Indeed, prevailing social doctrines all but require that approach. Yet, if the history of the Scots is viewed internationally, then it becomes clear that the subgroup which settled in Appalachia differed culturally from other Scots before either boarded the ships to cross the Atlantic.[15]

Similarly sharp differences can be found in the history of those emigrants from Japan who settled in Brazil, as compared to those who settled in the United States. During World War II, the Japanese living in the United States were treated much more harshly than the Japanese in Brazil, who did not suffer mass internment during the war, just as they had not suffered the severe discrimination experienced by Japanese Americans before the war. Yet the Japanese in the United States remained loyal Americans while the United States fought Japan—and the Japanese in Brazil remained strongly, even fanatically, pro-Japan. This is virtually inexplicable by the approach which sees groups as being shaped by the society around them and how it treats them. Yet it is readily understandable in terms of the cultural differences which existed between the two groups of Japanese *before they left Japan*.[16]

Cultures are not erased by crossing a political border, or even an ocean, nor do they necessarily disappear in later generations which adopt the language, dress, and outward lifestyle of a country.

The cultural history of the human race is not simply the sum of the discrete histories of particular groups. Because groups interact in various ways—through trade, migration, or conquest, for example—the benefits of one group's cultural advantages spread to other groups. The most obvious way this happens is when products or services are interchanged. Sometimes the technology, or the knowledge behind the technology, also spreads. In addition, the interaction in itself tends to shatter cultural insularity, which can otherwise be stultifying. When the Moors conquered medieval Spain, for example, they brought not only the tangible products of Islamic civilization but also its science and philosophy, as well as their concerns for the purity of the Arabic language. Under their cultural influence, Spanish Jews then turned their attention toward science and toward a similar concern for the Hebrew language. While much that the medieval Spanish Jews did initially in science either repeated or derived from the science of the Islamic world, the longer-run consequence of this cultural encounter was a *reorientation* of much Jewish intellectual endeavor, which in later times produced quite different and original scientific discoveries of their own.[17]

Much of the advancement of the human race has taken the form of such cross-cultural borrowings and influences. However, even to say that mankind has advanced, if only in particular spheres, is to say that some ways of doing things—some cultures—are *better* in some respects than others, that they are more effective for particular purposes.

Plain and obvious as cultural differences in effectiveness in different fields should be, there has developed in recent times a reluctance or a squeamishness about discussing it, and some use the concept of "cultural relativism" to deny it. After archaeology and anthropology have revealed the cultural achievements of some groups once dismissed as "primitive," and especially after the ravages of racism shocked the world when the Nazi death camps were exposed at the end of World War II, there has been an understandable revulsion at the idea of labeling any peoples or cultures "superior" or "inferior." Yet Arabic numerals are not merely *different* from Roman numerals; they are *superior* to Roman numerals. Their superiority is evidenced by their worldwide acceptance, even in civilizations that derive from Rome.

It is hard to imagine the distances encountered in astronomy, or the complexities of advanced mathematics, being expressed in Roman numerals, when even expressing the year of American independence— MDCCLXXVI—takes up more than twice the space required by Arabic numerals, and offers far more opportunities for errors, because a compound Roman numeral either adds or subtracts individual numbers according to their place in the sequence. The Roman numbering system also lacked a zero, a defect of some importance to mathematicians. Numbers systems do not exist in a vacuum or as mere badges of cultural identity. They exist to facilitate mathematical analysis—and some systems facilitate it better than others. Other cultural features likewise exist to serve a social *purpose*, not simply to put a cultural label on people, and those purposes are often of enormous importance, sometimes matters of life and death. Early European settlers in Australia sometimes died of hunger or thirst in a wilderness where the Australian aborigines had no trouble finding food or water.[18]

Perhaps the clearest and strongest indications of cultural advantages in particular fields have been the willingness of peoples in other cultures to abandon their own products or practices in favor of cultural imports. Guns have replaced bows and arrows all over the planet, as books have replaced scrolls. Bearers of foreign cultures have been imported, temporarily or permanently, to impart new skills, and native youths have been sent abroad to acquire those skills in the lands of their origins. Both processes were used to create modern industry and technology in Japan,[19] for example, and both processes have been going on in other countries for centuries. So has industrial espionage, despite being legislated against as far back as 1719 in Britain.[20]

The effectiveness of particular cultures for particular things can be of the highest importance. Much—perhaps most—of human history cannot be understood without understanding such things as the conquest of ancient Britain by the Roman legions against a vastly larger British military force, simply because the legions were a militarily superior organization from a more advanced society. It is not necessary to claim that a particular people or a particular culture is superior in all things or for all time. On the contrary, world leadership in science, technology, and organization has passed from one civilization to another over the centuries and millennia of human history. But neither is it necessary to deny the greater effectiveness of particular cultures for particular things at particular times and places—even if other contemporary cultures may be superior for some other things.

Cultures are of course not spread randomly among the world's population but are concentrated separately in different peoples—different racial or ethnic groups. Neither the races nor the cultures are pure, but both biological and cultural differences can be discussed in general terms that correspond, at least roughly, to a recognizable social reality.

The term "race" was once widely used to distinguish the Irish from the English, or the Germans from the Slavs, as well as to distinguish groups more sharply differing in skin color, hair texture, and the like. In the post–World War II era, the concept of "race" has more often been applied to these latter, more visibly different, categories and "ethnicity" to different groups within the broader Caucasian, Negroid, or Mongoloid groupings. However, this dichotomy between race and ethnicity is misleading in its apparent precision. Neither race nor related concepts can be used in any scientifically precise sense to refer to the people inhabiting this planet today, after centuries of genetic intermixtures. The more generic term, race, will be used here in a loose sense to refer to a social phenomenon with a biological component, rather than make a dichotomy whose precision is illusory.

Whatever the biological reality, race as a social concept is a powerful force uniting and dividing people. Whether visible on the physical surface or simply felt in the emotional depths, race provides the cohesive groupings in which cultures have been concentrated, transmitted, and carried around the world. However, the erosion of both racial and cultural distinctiveness has been as real as their persistence. A world view of race and culture must encompass both. But it cannot regard any group as a tabula rasa on which a given surrounding society puts its own imprint, whether spontaneously or through social engineering. On the contrary, a world view of race and culture makes possible a closer and more critical look at the vague and ambiguous concept, "society."

Is *society* or the *environment* where people are currently living? Or does it include the influences of their ancestral lands, or perhaps other lands where they may have settled for centuries in between? Once environmental explanations of group behavior begin to take on this expansive concept of "society," then a given country's causal or moral responsibility for current economic and social conditions within groups is correspondingly reduced and hopes for major social changes in a short time through government policy become less realistic.

Groups may change on their own, even if outsiders cannot mold them to predetermined patterns. How and why groups change is one of the questions to which the history of races and cultures offers clues. In a sufficiently long view, these changes have been profound, both among groups living as minorities among others and groups living as separate nations. China was, for more than a thousand years, far more advanced than Europe in technology and organization, yet eventually Europe overtook China in these respects and has remained ahead for several centuries since. The history recorded is the history of peoples and nations, but the patterns that emerge are patterns of cultures.

Even in a technological age, the diffusion of technology as such is not as important as the cultural receptivity of different nations, peoples, and cultures to that technology—their ability to take the technology, make it their own, modify it to suit their own purposes and circumstances, and develop it further on their own. Some nations and peoples have done this to a far greater extent than others, many of the latter being content to consume the products of more advanced technology, or perhaps to imitate the machinery that produced these products, following in the wake of others who continue to advance the technological frontier. What a student of Asian social history said of that region of the world would apply far more broadly across the planet:

> Some groups have with seeming ease jumped straight from a primitive mode of life into an almost full participation in world thinking and world economy. Others, which for centuries have enjoyed a much higher culture, somehow fail to adapt themselves to new conditions.[21]

When British industrial technology was the leading technology of the world in the eighteenth and nineteenth centuries, not only the products of that technology but also the productive machinery in which it was embodied spread around the planet, as British railroads and British textile machinery, for example, appeared on every inhabited continent.[22] Yet some countries, such as the United States, seized upon this British technology and not only reproduced it but also developed it and eventually overtook the British themselves in its further elaboration and progress.

That this happened in the United States to a greater extent than in continental Europe, which also borrowed heavily from British technology, has been attributed to the fact that Americans not only spoke the same language as the British but were also heirs of the same intellectual traditions and cultural orientations. Yet Japan seized upon Western technology in much the same way and, after decades of being technological copiers and producers of shoddy imitations of Western merchandise and machinery, eventually forged to the forefront of technology and became the world's standard for quality in such fields as optics and automobiles. Neither similarities of race or culture can explain this Japanese receptivity to Western technology. Yet, clearly, not all of Asia was able or willing to make this transplanted portion of European culture their own. Nor has Japan been willing to imitate Western civilization in all things, and it has in many respects openly disdained many of the Western patterns of thought and behavior as social degeneracy.

When European technology has been seized upon by peoples so different as Americans and Japanese—one the clear heir of the European culture and the other from a radically different culture and race—then it is clearly the cultural *receptivity* of different peoples which is crucial, rather than simply their initial similarity to those in the technological vanguard. This suggests that the diffusion of technology is not simply a process of making information available or even transferring the embodied technology itself to other lands. Rusting Western machinery and decaying Western factories in many Third World countries, in the wake of massive international aid programs, are a monument to the fallacy of believing that technology transfer is simply a matter of access, rather than of cultural receptivity as well.

Nor is it enough that isolated individuals in less developed nations become highly trained, or even inventive, in the new technology. A substratum of workers skilled in mechanical, electrical, and electronic technologies is often needed in the modern world, just as skilled craftsmen were an essential support for those in the forefront of earlier stages of industrial advancement. Without these and other complementary conditions, many highly trained individuals are not as productive, and some simply relocate from their own Third World societies to more industrially advanced societies where their knowledge and talents find readier outlets, greater support, and fuller appreciation and reward. This "brain drain" from the less developed to the more industrialized world is neither inevitable nor inherent in societal differences in technology or living standards. When Americans were learning British industrial techniques or when the Japanese were learning Western techniques in general, this did not lead to a "brain drain" of Americans or Japanese to Europe but led instead to a buildup of a technological elite in the United States and in Japan, and that in turn led to the technological development of these societies. Whether those individuals who master the more advanced culture of other societies will remain in their own country, applying their knowledge to the development of their own economy and society, or migrate to other countries that are more receptive, depends upon the culture of the home country and the political and economic decisions which facilitate or stifle the use of the new knowledge.

In short, peoples are no more the creatures of the objective circumstances around them when it comes to international technological diffusion than in the case of domestic minorities. In both cases, the culture of the people themselves is a major factor in the outcome, even if the crucial feature of a particular culture is in some cases simply its receptivity to other cultures.

Technology is of course not the sole determinant even of economic progress. Differences in work habits, savings propensities, organizational skills, personal hygiene, attitudes, and self-discipline all influence end results, both economic and social. Differences in all these respects influence economic and social outcomes among different groups within a given country, as well as among the nations of the world. These differences, however, are not static. Cultures spread, whether by the assimilation of technology, the migrations of peoples, or the imposition of foreign cultures through conquest.

It would be enormously valuable to understand just why and how some cultures have seized the initiative at various periods of history and have lead the technological, scientific, or medical advancement of the human race. Unfortunately, at the current stage of "social science," it is a struggle merely to establish that some cultures are in fact more productive in various ways than others, whether we are comparing the cultures of different nations or civilizations or the varying cultural achievements of different racial and ethnic groups within a given society. Yet differences have been the rule, rather than the exception, in countries around the world,[23] though the magnitudes of these differences, and the reactions to them, have varied widely.

## GROUP DIFFERENCES

The most basic and straightforward attempts to understand the role that particular cultures have played in the advancement of particular groups, and ultimately of the human race, encounter formidable obstacles. A prime obstacle is the prevailing intellectual vision which not only insists on a cultural relativism that denies that some cultures are more advanced than others, but which also treats group progress as a function of the way those groups are treated by "society." While the actions of others have often had profound effects, whether on minority groups or on whole conquered nations, peoples are not mere creatures of other peoples—and their *long-run* fate, especially, is seldom determined by other peoples' policies. Influences from outside may indeed reshape a people, but seldom in a way directly controlled, or perhaps even predicted, by any particular individual or council of decision-makers. Despots may inflict enormous sufferings on a people without remaking them to the intended specifications. Even mass extermination can leave the survivors no more molded to the oppressors' desire than before, as the post-Holocaust Jews dramatically demonstrate, not least by the establishment of the modern state of Israel.

Cultures involve attitudes as well as skills, languages, and customs. Attempts to measure cultural differences between groups by attitude surveys, however, miss the crucial point that culture is expressed in *behavior*, not lip service. The values of a culture are revealed by the choices actually made—and the sacrifices endured—in pursuing some desired goals at the expense of other desired goals. The fact that many different groups may regard many of the same things as desirable does not mean that they will all exhibit the same patterns of trade-offs when actually confronted with the inevitable sacrifices of the real world, as distinguished from the costless choices of attitude surveys. Education and personal safety may be valued by a wide range of human beings in a great variety of cultures, but what they are prepared to do—to sacrifice—in pursuit of those goals varies enormously.

Cultural relativism may be especially pernicious when technological or other backwardness is simply defined out of existence, instead of being overcome concretely in the real world. The remarkable rise of Japan from technological backwardness in the mid-nineteenth century to the first rank of industrial nations by the late twentieth century was made possible by a painful awareness of their own backwardness by the Japanese of the Meiji era, and the determined and enduring efforts they made to overcome it in the generations that followed.[24] To have defined this backwardness out of existence would have been to remove the basis for their historic achievements.

## "Stereotypes"

One of the obstacles to understanding what behavioral characteristics follow each group around the world is the widespread use of the term "stereotypes" to dismiss whatever observations or evidence may be cited as to distinguishing features of particular group behavior patterns. But behavior has consequences, and when these consequences are the same for the same groups in disparate settings, that is an empirical fact not to be waved aside. It is understandable that Russians might wish to explain away the remarkable success of German farmers in their midst by citing special dispensations granted the German emigrants by the czarist government.[25] But when similar success is found repeatedly among German farmers in Australia, Mexico, Brazil, Honduras, the United States, Chile, and Paraguay,[26] then that theory cannot bear the weight of that history. Similarly, to explain Chinese predominance in retailing in Jamaica by factors peculiar to Jamaica[27] does not explain their predominance in retailing in numerous other societies on the opposite side of the planet.

Despite such evidence from countries around the world, it has become a common rhetorical fashion to refer to particular groups as having been placed (or forced) into particular occupational niches by the larger society. For example, it has been claimed by a well-known specialist on ethnic groups that "the position of middleman minorities is preordained by the relations of power and of production imposed by the ruling class."[28] Such groups are "ascribed to a niche,"[29] according to this view, and to attribute their position to their own cultural characteristics is "mere reiteration of prevalent stereotypes."[30] Yet, by some staggering coincidence, Argentina, Australia, the United States, Poland, Jamaica, Brazil, England, Curaçao, Russia, and other countries all chose to "assign" to Jews the role of middleman minority!

Even if one were somehow able to believe in this incredible coincidence for the Jews—and for a similarly long list of countries for the overseas Chinese, the Gujarati Indians, and the Lebanese—the question would remain: How does "society" also assign the *skills* necessary in the niches to which it assigns groups? If Germans were somehow "assigned" the niche of piano makers in Russia, France, England, Australia, and the United States, how did that assignment tell them how to make pianos? The same question could be asked regarding Italian architects, Scottish medical pioneers, or Irish politicians—all in country after country, which supposedly assigned them to their various respective professions. The thesis that groups are assigned to a niche is also confronted by the uncomfortable fact that groups too small to be noticed by the larger society—Albanians in Australia or Macedonians in Canada, for example—likewise end up concentrated in special occupations.[31] The small number of Koreans in the United States became noticeable only *after* they became concentrated in particular kinds of retail stores, in particular kinds of inner-city neighborhoods.[32]

Although the "assignment" thesis is a nebulous metaphor with no actual mechanism specified, and no empirical test of that thesis against alternative hypotheses, its survival may be explicable by its role as a buttress to the larger belief that observed patterns of group differences must be due to the surrounding society and that society's stereotypes. But the presupposition of an absence of distinguishing group values and traits is as arbitrary as any stereotype. Even where the evidence for distinguishing characteristics consists not of empirical facts about fields of specialization in work or studies, or rates of alcoholism or business ownership, but rather of local observations about the industriousness or honesty of the Germans, for example, dismissing such observations as mere stereotypes becomes progressively less tenable when these presumed stereotypes occur in numerous countries as far apart as Brazil and Russia, or Australia and the United States,[33] in an era before modern mass communications put these societies in touch with each other's stereotypes. Why would such distant and disparate societies have the same stereotypes about the same group, if these were *only* stereotypes?

Even within given societies, when the same beliefs about a given group appear among both insiders and outsiders, it is hard to explain this in terms of stereotypes based on ignorance. If the Chinese in Malaysia consider themselves "frugal" and the Malays consider them "stingy," both are denoting the same behavior pattern, though with different connotations. Conversely, a remarkable range of economically less successful ethnic groups in countries around the world—the Assamese and Maharashtrians in India, the Hausa-Fulani in Nigeria, Creoles in Trinidad, Malays in Malaysia, and Sinhalese in Sri Lanka—blame themselves for unprogressive attitudes and behavior patterns which handicap them in competition with more aggressive, education-minded, or business-oriented, groups in their respective countries.[34]

To cling to the "stereotypes" dogma, in the face of multiplying examples of parallel observations about the same groups' behavior in the most widely separated and diverse societies, is hardly a basis for claims of being scientifically fastidious. Clearly, not every belief about every racial or ethnic group is to be accepted as true a priori. Where the implications of a belief can be tested against empirical evidence, then that must be done and the belief rejected if it proves to be inconsistent with the facts. For example, the notion that middleman minorities cause prices and interest rates to be higher than they would be otherwise can be rejected for its inconsistency with such evidence as rising prices and higher interest rates after these minorities have been expelled.[35] But equally, when the empirical evidence reinforces the belief, that too is not to be ignored or dogmatically dismissed.

Even if all races all over the globe have identical innate potential, tangible economic and social results do not depend upon abstract potential, but on developed capabilities. The mere fact that different peoples and cultures have evolved in radically different geographical settings is alone enough to make similarity of skills virtually impossible.

The peoples of the Himalayas have never had an equal opportunity to develop the skills of great seafaring nations. How would Eskimos have acquired the skills needed to process raw materials found only in the tropics? The continent of Europe has had virtually every geographical advantage over the continent of Africa, whether in navigable waterways, more fertile soil, more ample and reliable rainfall, and a climate that does not support the devastating tropical diseases so deadly to man and animals in Africa.[36] The many deep and slow-moving rivers of Europe are a sharp contrast to the relatively few rivers in Africa, with the African rivers also being beset with rapids and waterfalls. Given the enormous importance of water transport, how could that fail to affect the economies and cultures of the two continents? Is it sheer coincidence that the poorer

parts of Europe have been areas lacking these geographical advantages—
regions more remote from the sea and with rivers frozen a substantial part
of the year (as in Russia), or regions with low-volume rivers and meagre
rainfall (like the Iberian peninsula), or regions culturally and economically fractured by mountain barriers (as in the Balkans)?

Geographical disparities are of course just one of the many influences
at work. But alone they are enough to make problematical any equality or
identity of skills, or any equality of natural resources or cultural development. Nor is there any reason to presume that the numerous other factors
at work, including accidents of history, are similar across the planet.
Every society and every era does not have a Genghis Khan, any more
than they all have the same deposits of petroleum, gold, or iron ore. All
the ramifications of these differences defy enumeration, much less trac-
ing in detail. But it would be a staggering coincidence if they all worked
out in such a way as to produce such a uniformity of capabilities that we
could confidently ascribe all observations of group differences to the bias
of the observers and dismiss them as "stereotypes."

## Economic Differences

Economic differences between peoples are the most demonstrable, not
only in terms of incomes or occupations but also, to a considerable extent,
in terms of productivity differences. As already noted, even among uneducated and unskilled rubber plantation laborers in colonial Malaya, those
who were Chinese produced more than double the output of those who
were Malay.[37] Not surprisingly, the Chinese earned more than double the
income of the Malays.[38] Chinese plantation workers were also preferred to
Indian plantation workers as far away as British Guiana.[39] When railroads first began to be built in nineteenth-century France, British laborers averaged three or four times as much earth moved as did the French
laborers.[40]

National comparisons tell much the same story as comparisons
between groups within the same society. Indeed, even the very large economic differences between nations may often *understate* the differences
between the economic effectiveness of different cultures. The economic
performance difference between the culture of Britain and the culture of
the Iberian peninsula, for example, cannot be assessed solely in terms of
the economic history of Britain versus the economic history of Spain and
Portugal, or even of transplanted British societies (such as Australia and

Canada) versus transplanted Spanish or Portuguese societies (such as Argentina or Brazil), for much of the economic development of such countries as Argentina and Brazil has been spearheaded by technology and people from non-Iberian sources—whether from Britain, Germany, Japan, or other nations more economically advanced than Spain and Portugal.[41]

Similarly, much of the industrial and agricultural development of nineteenth-century and early twentieth-century Russia was the work of people from outside the dominant Russian culture—domestic racial and ethnic minorities, such as the Germans and the Jews, as well as foreign capitalists and the technology they brought.[42] Much of the industrial and commercial development of southeast Asia has historically been largely the work of Europeans, Americans, and the overseas Chinese. In Africa, those newly independent nations which have driven out the Europeans, either by design or as a by-product of their policies, have suffered economically while those nations which have made efforts to retain Europeans, have generally advanced.[43]

An ideal test of the relative economic (or other) effectiveness of different cultures would be what they achieve in isolation, without the help of people or technology from other cultures. But no such laboratory test is possible with the nations of today, or of the past several centuries. What we can do is to recognize not merely the general complexities of history but also—and more importantly—that the net effects of these complexities have tended to understate, rather than overstate, the consequences of cultural differences.

The issue of cultural differences in economic effectiveness among various ethnic groups has been trivialized by some writers, by simply *defining* differences in skills and performance as "class" differences—thereby enabling them to say that ethnic differences have no significant influence on economic outcomes, once "class" differences are held constant.[44] In other words, when you remove all the differences in skills and performance between groups, their economic earnings differentials tend also to disappear. Who would have thought otherwise? Calling capability differences "class" differences is a meretricious use of words, since class is not defined by skills. A millionaire through inheritance, with no economically meaningful skills, is not in the same social class as someone who is poverty-stricken and who has no economically meaningful skills. Conversely, a surgeon and an engineer may be in the same social class, though their skills are quite different.

The incidence of economically valuable skills no doubt varies from class to class, but it likewise varies from ethnic group to ethnic group and from nation to nation. The difference is that ethnic groups and nations have an existence independent of arbitrary definitions based on skills. Moreover, some immigrant groups begin at a lower socioeconomic level than that of the surrounding population and eventually rise above them, due to their skills, work habits, or other economic performance differences. They have changed class precisely because of their skills, capabilities, or performance. Educationally, some ethnic groups achieve performance levels in certain fields exceeding the performance levels of higher class individuals from other ethnic groups. This is clear on various mental tests, for example, where Asian American students from families with low incomes scored higher on the quantitative portion of the Scholastic Aptitude Test in 1981 than did black American, Mexican American, and American Indian students from families earning several times as much.[45] These complex intergroup patterns cannot be reduced to simple "class" differences. The desperate expedient of redefinition suggests how difficult it is to evade the reality of ethnic differences—and how much some wish to believe otherwise.

Vast differences between the economic productivity of peoples from different cultures do not imply that these differences are permanent, much less hereditary. Early nineteenth-century Germans were clearly well behind the English in industrial technology, as demonstrated by their need to have the English not only build but even man the first railroads and steel mills in Germany. Yet, within a century, the Germans had surpassed the English in industrial technology. So had the United States, over the same span of time. Much the same story could be told of Japan, which moved from imitator to initiator over the same span of time. As just one example, the first Nikon camera, produced in 1948, was a blatant imitation of a German camera—the Contax—a camera later completely eclipsed, both technologically and commercially, by the further development of the Nikon by the Japanese.[46]

The normal tendency of economic processes is to disseminate technology, knowledge, and skills from their places of origin to where they are lacking. The law of diminishing returns means that the rewards of any factor of production tend to decline where that factor is abundant, and to be higher where it is more scarce. Like water seeking its own level, abundant factors tend to flow to where their scarcity makes their productivity and reward greater. Thus capital, skills, organization, technology, or hard-working labor tend to flow toward regions and cultures where they are especially scarce. But the very scarcity and value of these skills and traits mean that those who possess them are likely to become more prosperous than the indigenous people of the recipient countries. Political reactions to these economic realities have often been negative, and sometimes violent, as during the industrialization era in czarist Russia, when foreigners were hated, denounced, and sometimes physically attacked by Russians whose country they were developing.[47]

Among the myriad political responses to productivity differences have been measures to keep out or drive out the economically beneficial, but politically offensive, factors of production, even when that has meant brutal mass expulsions of peaceful human beings. This has happened on every continent and in many centuries, whether or not the resented people were physically different or indistinguishable to the naked eye. It has happened in affluent societies and in nations so poor as to be in desperate need of the very skills that are resented. The political mobilization of envy has led to legal restrictions on productive groups, preferential policies for those unable to compete with them, mass expulsions, confiscations, and mob violence. Such responses have been common in the most culturally diverse societies—whether directed against the Tamils in Sri Lanka, the Germans in Russia, the Japanese in Peru, the Ibos in northern Nigeria, the Chinese in Indonesia, the Jews in Germany, the Armenians in Turkey, or many other groups in many other places.

The political perception of economic differences has implications which reach well beyond the domain of race and ethnicity. High productivity may contribute greatly to the material well-being, physical health, and cultural opportunities of a nation, and yet those responsible for that productivity may be resented, hated, and attacked both politically and physically. Down through the centuries and around the world, the bearers of the skills and disciplines that bring economic progress have been viewed as people whose prosperity has come at the expense of others. The repeated history of economic losses suffered by nations that expelled them has yet to teach a permanent lesson to the contrary.

Those who have created economic enterprises are depicted politically as having "taken over" or "monopolized" economic activities that existed *somehow*. Their share in the additional output they created is depicted as a net loss to the economy, especially if any of it is spent in another country. Thus the Indians of East Africa have been said to have acquired a "stranglehold" on the commerce and industry of that region—as if that commerce and industry existed independently of the Indians and simply fell victim to their malign influence. Much the same vision has been applied to the work of the overseas Chinese, the Jews, the Armenians, and others. The economic benefits created have been taken for granted, while the special prosperity of particular classes, nations, or ethnic groups who have established the industry and commerce from which these economic benefits flow have come to be regarded as suspicious, or as demonstrably sinister.

## Technology Transfer

Transference of the productive advantages of other cultures may be less socially resented or politically resisted when it is a transference of inanimate technology from country to country, rather than a transference of flesh-and-blood people, whose very presence and prosperity raise troubling invidious questions. Yet cultures vary widely in their receptivity to technology transfers, and especially in the extent to which their own people master this technology and begin to develop it themselves. Similarities between the technologically more advanced society and the society which receives its technology can facilitate this transfer, but some culturally very different society may also be receptive. British technology, for example, took root in both the United States and Japan.

British textile-manufacturing technology spread rapidly to the United States in the late eighteenth century, and British iron-making and steel-making technology, and railroad technology, spread equally rapidly to the United States in the nineteenth century. In textile manufacturing, the first spinning mule was smuggled into the United States from Britain in 1783 and, a decade later, this and other textile machinery was being manufactured and sold in New York.[48] The revolutionary Bessemer steel-making process, introduced in Britain in the 1850s, was so quickly mastered and improved in the United States that by the late 1870s Americans were better steel producers than anyone in Europe.[49] It took even less time—about a decade—for American mechanical engineers to produce locomotives that could compete with British locomotives and begin to drive the latter from the American market.[50] Less than five years after the British produced pig iron with anthracite coal, Americans were doing the same.[51]

Technology transfer from Britain to the United States represented one end of a spectrum, where both nations spoke the same language and shared very similar cultural traditions and mental habits. Even so, a considerable movement of people was involved, with American railroad loco-motive production, for example, being due largely to a group of American engineers who had gone to Britain to observe and study British produc-tion methods.[52] Technicians and craftsmen from Britain also went back and forth across the Atlantic to the United States during the early indus-trial revolution, acting as conduits of technology.[53] Japan had a larger technological and cultural gap to overcome, but eventually it did so—and to a greater extent than some European nations, or European offshoot societies overseas, which had more in common culturally with the British. One indication of the gap between Japan and the West when Commodore Perry opened this closed society to the world in the mid-nineteenth cen-tury was the reaction of the samurai to whom he presented a gift of a scale-model train:

> At first the Japanese watched the train fearfully from a safe distance, and when the engine began to move they uttered cries of astonishment and drew in their breath. Before long they were inspecting it closely, stroking it, and riding on it, and they kept this up throughout the day.[54]

A century later, the Japanese "bullet train" would be one of the tech-nological wonders of the world, surpassing anything available in the United States. But before this happened, a major technological transfor-mation had to take place in Japanese culture, opening the country up to the leading technology of the West, especially British technology, which lead the world in the nineteenth century.

During the early stages of the industrial revolution, when much tech-nology developed out of practical experience rather than scientific under-standing, the transfer of technology involved the movement of individuals with that practical experience. But while practical knowledge and experi-ence were particularly important in the early phases of industrialization, with technicians and artisans playing a major role,[55] the later rise of more sophisticated, science-based technologies made formal education in these technologies, and in the sciences behind them, more important. This, in turn, made formal training a growing source of international tech-nology transfers, as students from less industrialized nations increasingly studied in the universities and technical institutes of the most technologi-cally advanced countries. These two methods of technology diffusion, as well as books, journals, and widespread industrial espionage, have long coexisted, but the proportions changed significantly over time. While formal training was expensive, trial-and-error learning was also expensive indirectly, whether in lesser efficiency or in outright damage to the equipment used.

In nineteenth-century Japan, for example, a technologically advanced cotton-spinning mill imported from Britain fared worse than two smaller and simpler British mills imported at the same time, because Japan at that point in history lacked people with sufficiently sophisticated skills to maintain the more advanced technology.[56] Japanese dyers who used imported dyes without the necessary scientific knowledge ruined fabrics, until the Japanese government sent students overseas to learn chemistry.[57] The incompetence of early Japanese engineers resulted in faulty designs for cotton mills, which required costly corrections after they were built.[58] Even the more modest skills required of workmen were sufficiently lacking to lead to damaged machinery and costly shutdowns for repairs.[59] With the passing years, however, Japanese skill levels began to rise. By 1880, most foreign engine drivers for locomotives in Japan were dismissed and replaced with Japanese who had mastered the craft. That same year a Japanese engineer constructed a railroad line from Kyoto to Otsu with no help from foreign engineers.[60] By the 1890s, a whole cadre of British-trained Japanese engineers had emerged and Japan was producing its own locomotives, which were comparable in quality to those manufactured in Britain or the United States.[61]

In the early stages of technology transfers, there has often been an accompanying transfer of people to install, operate, and maintain the equipment, as well as to train people in the country to which it is transferred. Thus, many technicians, workers, and foreman in nineteenth-century French, German, Danish, and Russian shipyards were British.[62] Czarist Russia's industrialization program of the late nineteenth and early twentieth centuries relied heavily on engineers, technicians, and workers from Western Europe and the United States, as did parts of the early Communist economy.[63]

The countries to which technology is transferred may respond very differently, ranging from passive acceptance of the products or technology to an active involvement in adapting and further advancing the techniques they have learned and the scientific analysis behind those techniques. Much of the Third World has remained a passive recipient of modern products or modern technology, while Japan seized upon Western technology in the nineteenth century and later overtook the West in many respects by the late twentieth century. The specific reasons why some cultures are more receptive and adaptive to various features of other cultures remain a question. What cannot be questioned seriously is that cultures vary greatly in this receptivity, as they do in many other ways. The issue is not one of "access" to technology, as has been naively believed even in responsible official circles,[64] but what is done with that access. Emphasis on access is another of many evasions of causal responsibility by a people for their own situation. In an age of worldwide mass communication, books translated into innumerable languages, international student exchanges, worldwide capital markets, and multinational corporations, access to technology is seldom the problem.

What is also clear is that some cultures have been far in advance of others at a particular juncture in history, not just in isolated processes but across a broad technological and intellectual front. Many centuries ago, Japan adapted from China not only the Chinese method of writing and Chinese philosophical ideas, but also such mundane things as the cultivation of cotton and the technology of its spinning and weaving.[65] Today, the technological positions of the two countries are clearly reversed, again across a wide spectrum. A gap in technology has been equally real, large, and important in both eras, though without the permanence that might suggest innate differences in ability. Similarly in Europe, Britain was largely a recipient of technological advances from the continent before the British became a net exporter of new technology toward the end of the seventeenth century and the beginning of the eighteenth.[66] Here too, the gap was not only large but also covered a wide range of technologies. In medieval times, European civilization as a whole learned much from the Islamic world, also across a broad spectrum, from astronomy to philosophy, mathematics, crafts, and agriculture[67]—and again, the direction of flow was reversed in later centuries. Sometimes a reversal takes place in a relatively short time, as history is measured: German engineers came to Britain to learn shipbuilding in the nineteenth century, but by the early twentieth century they came to teach.[68]

However varied the responses to technology from another culture, by and large technology transfers seem to have been more readily accepted than the permanent transfers of human beings from another culture, especially when these immigrants continued to remain distinctive groups, rather than assimilating. Put differently, there is less resentment of superior machinery than of people with superior skills. Yet even the machinery may be resented to some extent, when its foreign origins or foreign ownership is taken as invidious reflections on the capabilities of the local inhabitants. In Argentina, for example, a national celebration was declared when the British-owned railroads became Argentine-owned.[69]

## CULTURAL ATTITUDES

Cultures differ not only in their accomplishments but also in the attitudes which shape those accomplishments. These attitudes are much more related to economic outcomes, for example, than are such much-touted "objective conditions" as initial wealth or natural resources. Japan has prospered economically, despite being nearly destitute of natural resources, while many Third World nations languish in poverty on fertile land, well endowed with minerals and with potential for hydroelectric power. Argentina once imported wheat, even though it had some of the finest land in the world for growing wheat—as subsequently demonstrated by immigrants from other cultures, who turned Argentina into one of the great wheat-exporting nations of the world.

Among the cultural attitudes which influence economic outcomes are attitudes toward education, toward business, and toward labor, especially so-called "menial" labor.

### Education

Education is one of those things which is almost universally desired, across the most diverse cultures, and yet this deceptive universality conceals large differences between cultures as to what one is prepared to sacrifice in time, effort, and foregone pleasures to acquire what kind of education. In many Third World countries, desperately needed scientific, technological, organizational, and entrepreneurial skills tend to be neglected in favor of education in easier subjects. Culturally different minorities in these countries—the Tamils in Sri Lanka or the Chinese in Malaysia, for example—often supply a disproportionate number, sometimes an absolute majority, of the students in mathematics, science, engineering, or medicine.

Similar patterns are found in Latin America. A mid-twentieth-century study of students at the University of São Paulo showed that students of non-Brazilian ethnic origin were more heavily concentrated in engineering, economics, and similar "modern" fields, while those of predominantly Brazilian family backgrounds were in more traditional areas such as law and medicine.[70] Similarly, at the University of Chile, people of

German or Italian origin were prominent among the students in physics.[71] In much of Latin America, technical and scientific careers were long regarded with condescension,[72] with the result that a disproportionate amount of the industrialization of the region was done by immigrants and foreigners.

Agricultural science has likewise tended to be neglected, even in pre-dominantly agricultural nations of the Third World. In Nigeria, for exam-ple, more than 40 percent of the jobs for senior agricultural researchers were vacant at one time.[73] In Senegal, it was 1979—nearly two decades after independence—before agriculture was even taught at the univer-sity level, though the University of Dakar had thousands of liberal arts students.[74]

In Malaysia, the Malay college students have tended to concentrate in the liberal arts[75]—and many have ended up working for the government after graduation,[76] for they lacked skills that would have a value in the economy. Nor is Malaysia unique in this respect. A Cabinet member in Fiji declared frankly that the "only use" for the Fijian students coming out of their educational system was "in government service, to warm pub-lic chairs."[77] In India, three-quarters of the college graduates have gone to work for the government,[78] and a leading authority on Africa described African education as "a machine for producing graduate bureaucrats."[79] Indonesian youth have likewise turned after graduation toward bureau-cratic careers, despite the warning of Indonesian novelist Ananta Toer that "we must get rid of the silly idea of wanting to be government clerks."[80] Government employment remains a prime objective and a prime source of intergroup conflict in underdeveloped countries around the world.[81]

Formal education, especially among peoples for whom it is rare or recent, often creates feelings of entitlement to rewards and exemption from many kinds of work. In India, for example, even the rudiments of an education have often been enough to create a reluctance to take any job involving work with one's hands. In the 1960s it was estimated that there were more than a million "educated unemployed" in India, who demon-strated "a remarkable ability to sustain themselves even without gainful work, largely by relying on family assistance and support."[82] Nor is this social phenomenon limited to India. Other Third World nations have shown similar patterns.

Such attitudes affect both the employed and the unemployed. Even those educated as engineers have often preferred desk jobs and tended to "recoil from the prospect of physical contact with machines."[83] In short, education can *reduce* an individual's productivity by the expectations and aversions it creates, as well as increase it by the skills and disciplines it may (or may not) engender. The specific kind of education, the nature of the individual who receives it, and the cultural values of the society itself all determine whether, or to what extent, there are net benefits from more schooling. Blindly processing more people through schools may not promote economic development, and may well increase political instability. A society can be made ungovernable by the impossibility of satisfying those with a passionate sense of entitlement—and without the skills or diligence to create the national wealth from which to redeem these expectations. The role of soft-subject intellectuals—notably professors and schoolteachers—in fomenting internal strife and separatism, from the Basques in Spain to the French in Canada,[84] adds another set of dangers of political instability from schooling without skills.

It is understandable that Third World peoples who have been ruled for generations by colonial bureaucrats sitting behind desks, wearing collar-and-tie and shuffling papers, should seek to imitate that role when they get the chance. But the wealth and power of the imperialist nation that put the colonial bureaucrat there in the first place was not created by sitting behind desks and shuffling papers. The science, the technology, the organization, discipline, and entrepreneurship that produced wealth and power usually did so thousands of miles away, beyond the sight of the colonial peoples—and these fundamentals are not primarily what they seek to imitate.

Both in underdeveloped countries and among lagging groups in industrialized nations, there has developed a taste for easy, self-flattering courses such as Maori Studies in New Zealand, Malay Studies in Singapore, and a variety of ethnic studies in the United States. The claim is often made that the morale-boosting effects of such courses will enhance the students' academic performance in other fields, but this claim remains wholly unsubstantiated. What is clear is that easier courses, whether in ethnic studies or otherwise, prove attractive to students from lagging groups.

Such patterns are found in many countries. For example, college students in India from untouchable caste backgrounds specialize in the easier, less prestigious, and less remunerated subjects.[85] Similarly, just over half of those Soviet Central Asians who reached the higher educational levels specialized in the field of education.[86] A similar pattern of seeking easier subjects and easier institutions has been found among Middle Eastern and North African Jews in Israel,[87] as well as among Hispanics in the United States.[88] Irish Catholics in Northern Ireland likewise show less interest in science and technology than the British Protestants there.[89]

Subsequent generations may begin to move into more difficult fields as their preparation and confidence improve. In the United States those black, Hispanic, and American Indian college students whose parents attended college before them have specialized in mathematical and scientific fields to a much greater extent than other members of their respective groups—and to an extent not very different from that found among other American college students.[90]

## Occupations

Cultural attitudes toward commerce and industry have varied as much as attitudes toward education. A disdain for commerce and industry has, for example, been common for centuries among the Hispanic elite, both in Spain and in Latin America.[91] Similar attitudes have been prevalent in the Portuguese colonial empire.[92] Even those elites with vast wealth have tended to have that wealth in landholdings, rather than in industry or commerce. The result in much of Latin America has been an over-representation—sometimes an absolute predominance—of non-Hispanic, non-Portuguese, immigrants and their children among the leading commercial and industrial figures of various countries. Twentieth-century studies have shown that more than 40 percent of the business leaders in Mexico had foreign paternal grandfathers. Among Argentine businessmen prestigious enough to appear in that country's *Who's Who*, 46 percent were foreign-born, and many others were the sons of immigrants. In Brazil, a majority of industrial entrepreneurs have been either immigrants or the children of immigrants. Among the heads of large industrial enterprises in Santiago, Chile, about three-quarters were immigrants or the children of immigrants. Even in countries with relatively little immigration, such as Colombia and Peru, immigrants and their children have been heavily represented among industrial entrepreneurs.[93]

The disdain for commerce and industry at the higher social levels of Hispanic and Portuguese societies has been paralleled by an aversion to manual labor and hard work at the lower social levels. Such attitudes are not simple laziness, but reflect what one scholar writing on seventeenth-century Spain characterized as "a puerile pride in indolence" reflecting an aversion to the "stigma of social dishonor" associated with manual trades.[94] Similar attitudes could be found, centuries later, in Spanish and Portuguese offshoot societies in Latin America. Even intellectual work was viewed with disdain by the Brazilian aristocracy.[95] Paraguayans were bewildered by the unrelenting work of Japanese agricultural colonists who settled in their country.[96] Honduran farmers complained that it was unfair for them to have to compete with German farmers in their country, for the latter worked too hard.[97] Brazilian, Chilean, Argentinean, and Paraguayan governments deliberately sought out non-Iberian immigrants for the hard work and severe living needed to pioneer in opening up virgin wilderness in these countries.[98]

The point here is not that there is something peculiarly "wrong" with Iberian culture. What is peculiar is the extremely high productivity of a relative handful of northwestern European nations and their overseas offshoots, such as the United States and Australia, and their Asian counterparts who have borrowed and developed Western technology, Japan being the preeminent example. In an international perspective, it is these prosperous countries which are the exceptions rather than the rule. Beyond this small set of nations, output per capita is sharply lower.[99] Why and how just the right combination of the right factors happened to come together in this small group of nations, quite recently as history is reckoned, is a major unanswered question. Muting these differences with squeamish politeness, or waving them aside with cultural relativism, seems unlikely to uncover any of the answers. Not only Hispanic and Portuguese cultures, but also the cultures of much of the Third World make business and commerce far less attractive to the educated classes than government employment or work in the professions.[100]

The issue is not one of "ability" in the abstract, or even of concrete skills, nor simply a willingness to engage in economic activities. These activities have their own prerequisites, which are met to varying degrees by different cultures. Clearly these requirements are met less often, or less well, in cultures where there is a cultural resistance to contractual obligations,[101] where there is "a rather plastic sense of the truth,"[102] where hypersensitivity to status distinctions make cooperation difficult to achieve in the workplace,[103] where initiative and responsibility are rare,[104] or where notions of accuracy or of cause-and-effect are hazy.[105]

The whole process of scientific abstraction, which lies at the heart of modern technology, is foreign to the mental habits of much—perhaps most—of the human race. Mental testers in a number of countries have noted the difficulty of getting peoples from some cultures even to take abstract questions seriously.[106] The issue of innate "ability" can hardly even be raised in a context where *orientations* are so different. Even to test running speed in a foot race, people must first agree to run in the same direction at the same time.

Aversions to "menial" work have likewise varied widely from group to group and from society to society. Japan today is an exception to the common pattern among industrialized nations of importing foreigners to do their "menial" work. Japan has no difficulty in getting its own people to do such work, which carries no such stigma as elsewhere.[107] By contrast, many people in Sri Lanka continue to have extreme aversions to doing any work with their hands, complicating even the simplest economic tasks.[108]

Individuals or groups with values more consonant with the requirements of a modern industrial economy may exist within a given society, or enter it from abroad, but whether or not they will have an enduring effect can still be problematical. Where an indigenous and complacent elite is socially powerful enough to absorb dynamic new rising elements on its own terms—for example, to accept wealthy entrepreneurs only in so far as they abandon business for landownership—this may sterilize these dynamic elements as factors in the general progress of the society. A classic example is the Demidov family, which virtually created the Russian iron and steel industry in the eighteenth century, and supplied half or more of that country's total output for many years, as well as being the leading iron-producing enterprise in all of Europe. The Demidovs were ennobled by the czar and ultimately disappeared from commerce and industry into the landed aristocracy.[109] It was common for rising capitalists in czarist Russia or imperial China to aspire to become landed gentry or government officials,[110] and a similar process has marked the history of Spain and of Latin America. Much the same pattern existed in eighteenth-century France, where commercial success seldom lasted three generations in a given family, because wealth led to nobility or public office.[111] Predatory and corrupt government policies and practices toward businessmen—regarded as prey rather than assets—often hasten the transition of entrepreneurs to other roles in such societies.[112]

Societies which have historically lacked indigenous entrepreneurship have relied disproportionately on foreign elements who were outside the influence of the social forces which discouraged or diverted indigenous entrepreneurship. This was especially ironic in the case of later imperial and early republican China, whose modern industrial and commercial life were dominated by Europeans and Americans, while a vast overseas Chinese entrepreneurial class flourished elsewhere around the world, unencumbered by the restrictive social patterns of their native land. China was not, however, unique in relying heavily on foreigners for entrepreneurship, trade and crafts. Sixteenth- and seventeenth-century Spain was also heavily dependent on people from other parts of Europe, or from the Islamic world, to fill such occupations,[113] just as Spanish-offshoot societies in Latin America would later be dependent on immigrants from non-Hispanic Europe, Asia, or the Middle East to fill such occupations.[114] A similar pattern of heavy dependence on domestic minorities and on foreigners in many economic activities was characteristic of the Ottoman Empire,[115] as well as many countries in Southeast Asia and parts of Africa.[116]

## Cultural "Identity"

The question of distinctive behavioral traits, values, and ways of thinking is separable from the question of self-conscious "identity" as a member of a particular ethnic group. One may repudiate one's roots and still exhibit them unwittingly. The *conversos*, fifteenth-century Spanish converts to Christianity from Judaism, in many cases promoted anti-Semitic policies, but nevertheless worked in the same kinds of occupations and with the same kinds of success as when they had been Jews. Many overseas Chinese in southwest Asia who considered themselves patriotic Thais or Burmese nevertheless maintained work habits and values that were distinctively Chinese. So have many of the partly Chinese of southeast Asia, some of whom have been as notoriously anti-Chinese politically as the *conversos* of Spain were anti-Jewish.

Conversely, people who have in fact lost contact with their cultural roots, and who have shared little or none of the social experience of their group, may not only "identify" with their group, but even do so in a highly vocal and exaggerated form. It has, in fact, been a common social phenomenon around the world that those who have lost a culture have often been its most strident apostles. Africans educated in Europe and America, and thoroughly Westernized in their thinking and values, have been among the most extreme apostles of pan-Africanism. The concept of "negritude" originated in Paris, among Caribbean emigres.[117] The word "Pakistan" was coined in Cambridge, England, by Moslem students from the Indian subcontinent.[118] In Peru, it was the acculturated mestizos, rather than the American Indians living in indigenous communities, who lionized the ancestral culture of the Incas.[119] The promotion of Buddhist extremism and Sinhalese chauvinism in Sri Lanka in the 1950s was spearheaded by a Westernized, Oxford-educated, Christian Sinhalese who grew up unable to speak the language of his own people.[120] Not only have cultural revivals often been led by the most assimilated group members, in these and other countries;[121] so have revivals of historic grievances. While first- and second-generation Japanese in Canada, who personally suffered pervasive discrimination and then internment during the Second World War, showed little lasting resentment in the postwar era, the third generation became very emotionally involved in these events that they did not experience. Among their many laments about the older generation was this: "Why didn't they tell us what it was like to be a dirty Jap in Canada during the Second World War?"[122]

Genuine continuity of cultural identity is seldom as strident or as dramatic as artificial revivals. The speaking of Yiddish among many modern Jews has seldom occasioned as much public bombast as the speaking of Gaelic among a handful of modern Irish, or the speaking of Swahili among a handful of American Negroes. Groups such as the Amish in Pennsylvania, or the Mennonites in Canada, the United States, and Mexico, have preserved centuries-old ways of life—almost as in a time capsule—without striking any defiant public poses about it. The principle that a culture is most stridently defended when it is irretrievably lost applies beyond issues of ethnicity. In the United States, it was the generation of Southerners born after the demise of the Confederacy who glorified the lost cause of the Civil War era and its aftermath, as in the motion picture classic, *Birth of a Nation*, the scholarly but apologetic history of U. B. Phillips, and the grand glorification of all, the novel and movie *Gone With the Wind*.[123] Racial and ethnic cultural identities likewise tend to assume their most ideological form after they are "gone with the wind."

Exaggerated cultural "identity" is more than a foible. Among its more serious social consequences are (1) putting a dangerous leverage in the hands of extremist fringes within each group, and (2) stifling the cultural advancement of lagging groups by sealing them off from the cultural advantages of the larger society around them. The problem of putting leverage in the hands of extremists is the greater immediate danger, though cultural provincialism can take a heavy toll in the long run.

Even if 90 percent of both group A and group B consist of well-meaning people with no real animosity toward the other group, the way that they respond to clashes between their respective hostile fringes can differ greatly according to the degree of group identity and solidarity within each group. Where identity and solidarity are at fever pitch, every such clash can be seen as a sign of a larger threat by one group as a whole against the other group as a whole, whereas in quieter times both groups might see the same episodes as the work of hooligans or demagogues whom most members of both groups disdain. The social cost of exaggerated identity can be very high to the groups involved and to the whole society.

The long-run costs of exaggerated "identity" can be especially high to groups lagging behind their contemporaries in education, income, and all the social consequences that flow from these. Throughout history, one of the great sources of cultural achievement, both for groups and for nations and even civilizations, has been a borrowing of cultural features from others who happened to be more advanced in given fields at a given time. Medieval Jews in Spain copied the science and mathematics developed in the Islamic world, and only later began to make their own original contributions. Western civilization as a whole absorbed both technologies and science from China and the Islamic world (including parts of the Indian subcontinent) as the foundation for its own ascent to world leadership in these fields. In the twentieth century, Japan was long known for its cheap and shoddy imitations of European and American products, before it eventually emerged as a world leader—both quantitatively and qualitatively—in developing many products it had once copied.

Exaggerated group "identity" makes copying others akin to treason. Even groups already speaking a language common to a billion of their contemporaries on Earth (English) and encompassing a vast literature in science, philosophy, and other fields, have been urged to abandon that language for an ancestral tongue which most no longer speak, which is spoken nowhere else on the planet, and which has little or no literature. In the case of the Maoris in New Zealand, the argument has even been made that Maori should become the official language of the whole country.[124] In Malaysia, English has been abandoned as the language of higher education, even though it is a language so widely read there that the country's leading newspaper, *The New Straits Times*, is published in English.

Where separate group identities are government-subsidized—often under the general label of "multiculturalism" in Australia, Britain, Canada, and the United States—an artificial Balkanization is fostered, in utter disregard of the tragic historic consequences of Balkanization in many parts of Asia and Africa, as well as in the Balkans themselves.

# CHAPTER 2

# MIGRATION AND CULTURE

Migrations have transferred cultures across vast distances and thereby transformed whole regions of the planet, as new skills, new organizational patterns, new work habits, new savings propensities, new attitudes toward education and toward life, all have had their impact on the environments to which people moved. Cultures may be shaped by the environments in which they have evolved, but they are also capable of reshaping other environments to which they are transferred.

Human migrations take many forms. Whole peoples have moved together across whole continents, as with Genghis Khan's conquering hordes sweeping across Asia and deep into Europe. By contrast, Jews and Chinese have been expelled en masse from a number of countries at various periods of history, and millions of Africans were transported in bondage to the Western Hemisphere and to the Middle East. Around the world, vast numbers of refugees have fled the disasters of nature and of man. In addition to specific cultural differences between particular racial and ethnic groups who migrate, there are more generic differences between refugees and conquerors, or between emigrants who assimilate into the surrounding society and those who remain encapsulated in their own enclaves within the recipient societies. These various kinds of cultural differences, and their consequences, will be explored in turn, as will the larger question of the evolution of a modern culture shared to a degree by many peoples and cultures around the world.

# THE IMPACT OF IMMIGRATION

The voluntary emigration of individuals and families has been the largest source of international movements of people in recent centuries. Even a small country like Lebanon has sent hundreds of thousands of emigrants abroad in the course of a century, and 2.5 million Moslems emigrated from the Russian Empire to the Ottoman Empire in the last half of the nineteenth century.[1] However, Europe, as the major conquering force of this era, has supplied most of the world's emigrants. The United States has been the largest recipient of European emigrants and the most dramatic example of the economic and cultural changes they wrought. Of the 70 million people who emigrated from Europe over the past few centuries, nearly 50 million went to the United States[2]—and 35 million of these arrived in just one century, from 1830 to 1930.[3] However, other transplanted European societies, such as Australia, Argentina, Canada, or Brazil were also transformed and developed, not simply by the respective conquering peoples but also—and in some cases, primarily—by peoples from other parts of Europe. These have included not only immigrant settlers but also sojourning foreigners who have played a major role in the economic development of Latin America, for example.

Non-European emigrants have also played a major role in the modernization of many societies, including societies largely under the political control of European colonial powers. Emigrants from the Indian subcontinent, for example, created both retail and wholesale trade, as well as industries and international trade, across vast regions of East Africa, where the rupee was at one time the standard currency.[4] Chinese emigrants, often beginning as coolie laborers, likewise ended up as entrepreneurs who transformed the economic and social landscape of many countries in Southeast Asia.[5] Whether in East Africa or Southeast Asia, the transformation of whole economies by immigrants was often also an economic transformation of the immigrants themselves, if not from poverty to riches, at least to a modest prosperity by the standards of the times and places. Similar stories could be told of the Lebanese in West Africa, or the Japanese in southern Brazil or western Canada, where they were a major part of the pioneering phase of economic development. Such economic and social transformations did not end with the pioneering eras in these countries. Successive waves of immigrants from different sources often added new and different skills, attitudes, and resources, sometimes with dramatic effect.

Such transformations reflect substantial cultural differences between the existing population and the newcomers. For example, although the Portuguese inhabited and ruled Brazil for hundreds of years, they did little to develop a modern economy there, before the arrival of other European immigrants. In early nineteenth-century Brazil, even such basic items as doors, flour, salt, sugar, furniture, and books were imported.[6] German, Italian, and other immigrants created much of the industry of the country, beginning in the late nineteenth century, and their descendants continued dominant in these industries even in the middle of the twentieth century.[7] During the period from the late nineteenth century until the end of World War II, importers in São Paulo were almost invariably immigrants.[8] This was not due to a lack of wealthy Portuguese Brazilians. But those members of the Brazilian plantation-owning elite families who pursued nonagricultural careers tended to go into the professions, rather than into commerce or industry. As late as 1913, only 2 Brazilian-owned firms ranked among the top 15 exporters in the port city of Santos.[9]

Argentina, like Brazil, was profoundly changed by the changing composition of its people, brought on by immigration that was massive, relative to its existing population size. As of 1914, immigrants constituted 30 percent of the total Argentine population—about twice as high as the highest proportions ever reached in the United States during the peak of its mass immigration era.[10] The effect of the immigrants on the Argentine economy was far more than demographic, however. Little economic activity flourished in Argentina, except for cattle raising, before the era of large-scale immigration began. Both industry and agriculture in Argentina were created by immigrants.

In 1873, Germans in Buenos Aires owned 43 import-export businesses, 45 retail establishments, and about 100 artisan craft shops.[11] Italians, who have been the most numerous among Argentina's immigrants—in some years more than half—have been credited with turning the Argentine Pampa into productive agricultural land, both as farmers and as farm laborers.[12] The Italians' economic role was also large in the city, where their skills, muscle, and savings were major factors in the development of many trades.[13] As of 1895, foreigners constituted about three-fifths of Argentina's industrial workers and about four-fifths of the owners of industrial enterprises.[14] As late as the 1920s, it was said of Argentina that "if you want a shoe soled, a lock or kettle mended, a bookcase made, a book bound or a pamphlet printed, a roll of film developed or a camera repaired, you will go to an immigrant or the son of an immigrant."[15] In the middle of the twentieth century, more than three-fourths of all Argentine generals, admirals, and bishops—over a 25-year period—were either immigrants or (mostly) the sons of immigrants.[16]

In Mexico, in the early twentieth century, Yucatán went from being one of the poorest provinces in the country to being one of its most prosperous, as a result of industrial development led by immigrants, who constituted less than one percent of the province's population.[17] In Peru, most of the manufacturing firms not controlled by foreigners were controlled by immigrant families.[18] In Chile, German immigrant farmers turned a virtually barren wilderness into one of the agricultural showplaces of South America,[19] and Germans also established such industrial enterprises as tanneries, saw mills, soap factories, flour mills, distilleries, shoe factories, and shipyards.[20] Immigrants played such a large role in the industrialization of Chile that they and their children still owned three-quarters of the industrial enterprises in Santiago in the second half of the twentieth century.[21]

Seldom were these immigrants simply prosperous foreigners who brought their wealth with them. On the contrary, most of those who became middle class in Argentina were working class in origin.[22] The pioneering German farmers in Brazil and Paraguay were typically of peasant origins, and faced harrowing experiences in their early years, when it was a struggle merely to survive.[23] Italian farm laborers were initially poverty-stricken and brutally treated. To an even greater degree, so were the Chinese and Japanese indentured laborers brought into Peru, though their descendants went on to become prominent among Peruvian retail store owners.[24] What all those groups brought was not wealth but the ability to create wealth—whether on a modest scale or a grand scale, whether through specific skills or just hard work. They did not share the Spanish and Portuguese settlers' disdain for manual labor, or for commerce and industry, or for thrift.[25]

The work of European—largely non-Iberian[26]—immigrants in developing Latin America was supplemented by the economic activities of foreign businessmen, who did not necessarily settle permanently in the countries where they established businesses, but who nevertheless played a major role in the various economies of the region. Aliens tended to dominate commerce in general and international trading firms in particular. In Recife, one of Brazil's leading ports in the nineteenth century, only 22 out of 65 import-export merchants were Brazilian in 1841, and only 23 out of 77 in 1848. Of 27 export firms that shipped virtually all of the coffee from the port of Santos in 1885–1886, only 4 had Portuguese surnames. In Rio de Janeiro, not quite one-third of the members of the Associação Commercial from 1844 to 1902 were native Brazilians.[27] Such predominance of foreigners among international traders was common throughout Latin America in the nineteenth century.[28] In Valparaíso and Santiago, foreigners outnumbered Chileans in the import-export business by nearly two-to-one and owned four times as many firms. Foreigners also owned four times as many large-scale international trade, wholesale, and retail firms as the Mexicans did in Mexico City. In Montevideo, foreign importers outnumbered Uraguayans by seven to one.[29]

In Buenos Aires in 1888, less than 10 percent of all import-export, wholesale, and retail firms were Argentine-owned.[30] For the country as a whole, 81 percent of all industry was foreign owned in 1895 and 66 percent as late as 1914. Whether this decline in foreign dominance represented a rise of an Argentine entrepreneurial class or the naturalization of foreigners is not clear. Still, in 1914, foreigners owned, in addition to two-thirds of Argentine industry, nearly three-fourths of Argentine commerce.[31] Nor was this pattern unique to Argentina or to these particular economic sectors. British capital, skills, and entrepreneurship played major roles in developing railroads and public utilities in Latin America. Lima, Peru, was unusual among Latin American capitals because its municipal utilities were built without significant British investment.[32] Where Latin American businesses managed to succeed in competition with foreigners, this commercial success often lasted only one generation, as successful Latin American businessmen had their sons educated for the professions.[33] Partly this reflected a cultural preference for "gentlemanly" occupations like land ownership, the professions, or a government career.[34] Partly too, it reflected Spanish inheritance laws, which would prevent a business from being passed on wholly to one son.[35] Given that a business's viability with divided leadership was economically problematical, its prospects in the second generation might often be more precarious than in the first generation.

The stunning impact of immigrants in transforming whole economies was not a pattern peculiar to Latin America, nor to European immigrants. In various other parts of the world, modern economic development was largely the work of immigrants or foreign investors, with the indigenous population playing little or no role in the modernization process. In colonial Malaya, for example, Chinese immigrants provided much of the labor that developed that country's giant tin industry and immigrants from India manned the rubber plantations—both financed largely by European and American capital.[36] Similar patterns of European capital and non-European immigrant labor combining to create economic development could be found from Fiji in the South Pacific to countries on the east coast of Africa and in the Middle East. Yet, in these and other countries, the earlier or indigenous population has almost invariably come to resent those foreigners, whether sojourners or immigrants, who raised the economic level of their country. In a later period especially, after the actual origins of particular economic activities have faded into the mists of time, foreign groups have often been denounced for having seized control of the nation's industries and exploited its people. It is as if businesses and wealth came into existence *somehow* and foreigners happened to take possession of them.

The great era of European emigration and the establishing of European offshoot societies in the Western Hemisphere, Australia, and New Zealand has been succeeded by a large-scale emigration from less developed nations, especially in the twentieth century. By the 1980s, an estimated 50 to 55 million people were living outside the lands of their birth, about 60 percent of these being from less developed countries.[37] Nor were all of these migrants from the Third World simply unskilled laborers. India alone had more than a quarter of a million physicians, scientists, engineers, managers, administrators, and people in similar high-level occupations living in other countries around the world in the late twentieth century.[38]

Not all emigrations ended with the emigrants settling permanently. Whether economically successful or not, many emigrants re-emigrated to yet another country, and sometimes to a third or fourth. Historically, the Jews have wandered from country to country, often in search of nothing more than a respite from persecution. Most of the Germans who immigrated into Canada in the late nineteenth century came not from Germany but from Russia, where they had lived for generations, before conditions became intolerable.[39] Some of these Germans who were Mennonites migrated again from Canada to Mexico, and some of these migrated yet again from Mexico to Honduras.[40] Just over half the men who immigrated to Australia from the Greek mainland during the 1920s had lived in some other country before reaching Australia.[41] In the twentieth century, most of the Japanese immigrants to Bolivia came not from Japan but from Peru.[42] The story of emigration is also a story of re-emigration.

Emigrants are not always "minorities" in the labor force. During the 1980s, there were countries in the Middle East where foreign workers made up about half the total labor force (Saudi Arabia, Libya, and Bahrain), and others where foreign workers constituted about four-fifths or more of the total labor force (Kuwait, Qatar, and the United Arab Emirates).[43] Much of this labor came from Asia. An estimated 2.5 million migrant workers from Asia were in the Middle East in the 1980s. These Asian workers typically earned several times what they made at home.[44] They were usually young married men whose wives and children remained behind in their home country.[45] Their annual remittances from the Middle East totaled 7 billion U.S. dollars annually in 1980.[46] Nor was this predominance of foreign workers in the labor force unique to the Middle East. In Fiji and Guyana, immigrants from India and their descendants came to outnumber the Fijians and the Afro-Americans, respectively, and in Mauritius the Indians eventually constituted more than two-thirds of the total population.[47]

Cultures that migrate may or may not diffuse into the surrounding society. In Brazil, the zest for entrepreneurship and industrialization brought by immigrants eventually affected some of the offspring of the traditional planter elite who were trained at the São Paulo Polytechnical School.[48] However, there is little evidence of a diffusion of the transplanted culture of immigrants in Malaysia, Fiji, or the Middle East. Sometimes, perhaps because of sheer size differences between the immigrant and indigenous populations, the opposite happens—immigrants absorb the dominant culture around them. But the extent to which this happens, and the pace at which it happens, both vary greatly with the particular group and with the kind of societies to which they have migrated. Germans in Russia remained almost totally resistant to Russian culture for more than a century, re-immigrating in the late nineteenth century with virtually the same culture with which their ancestors had entered the country under Catherine the Great.[49]

Emigrants have often been described in national terms as Lebanese, Filipinos, or Yugoslavs. But they may think and act together in much different—and usually smaller—categories. Many of the immigrants in Southeast Asia have appeared to their host societies as simply Chinese, but they settled separately as Cantonese, Fukkienese, Hailams, etc., practiced different occupations, and often fought each other. Lebanese emigrants likewise often lived separately and antagonistically to one another in foreign lands, recreating the animosities between various factions which have divided Lebanon itself.[50] Among other groups as well, it has been common for small geographical concentrations of people from the same place in the country of origin to settle together in small geographical concentrations in the country of destination.

Immigrants do not settle at random in a new country. Towns and villages only a few miles apart in Albania, Italy, Greece, or Yugoslavia, for example, have sent their emigrants to very different parts of Australia, where they engaged in very different occupations.[51] Nor is this pattern peculiar to Australia. About 2,000 people from one Macedonian village lived in Toronto at one time—while only 500 people remained in that village back in Macedonia. Provincial and even village concentrations of Italians have remained together in the same neighborhoods in Buenos Aires, Toronto, and New York.[52] Similarly localized origins and destinations have been found among Swedish immigrants in South Dakota farming communities,[53] and among Lebanese immigrants in a number of countries.[54]

These clusterings of familiar people in a new country reflect the high costs and high risks of emigration in human, as well as in economic, terms and represent attempts to soften their impact. By following in the footsteps of a member of the family, or someone else from the same community, emigrants are not as lost, isolated, or devastated by unexpected events as if they had settled alone at random in a new country. This was particularly important when many emigrants had little money, education, or conception of life beyond their own traditional communities. The national labels that others put on these community-centered people sometimes had no relationship to their conceptions of themselves or to the way they formed social ties in their new countries. Many emigrants from villages in Italy only discovered, after reaching the Western Hemisphere, that they were Italians.[55] Emigrants from Yugoslavia set up Serbian or Croatian organizations in Australia far more often than they set up Yugoslavian organizations.[56]

Just as national labels may implicitly overstate the social cohesion of the groups under those labels, so may these national labels obscure the *international* ties among some groups whose cohesion extends across national borders. One of the reasons for the prominence of Jews in international trade, in various countries and various periods of history, has been their ties to other Jewish international traders in other countries.[57] Similarly, Lebanese emigrants to a number of countries could enter an international network of Lebanese textile traders, centered in Manchester, England,[58] even though they might not be able to associate with other factions of Lebanese immigrants in the same country. More generally, the labels put on any group by observers and analysts need not coincide with the lines of social cohesion or cultural loyalty respected by those people themselves.

The ratio of male-to-female immigrants can have a profound effect on the survival of the cultures which the immigrants bring with them. A lopsidedly male immigrant population, often characteristic of early or exploratory immigration, may lead to much intermarriage and a subsequent dilution or extinction of the particular immigrant culture. But where whole families immigrate together, or where the sexes are sufficiently balanced to permit new families to be formed within the immigrant group, the group itself can retain its cultural cohesion longer. Both patterns may occur with the same group of immigrants in the same country, where sex ratios vary substantially by region. German immigrants who settled together as families in South Australia's Barossa Valley, for example, recreated German communities that remained solidly German in language and culture for generations, while German men who settled in Australia as individuals in Victoria and New South Wales were relatively quickly absorbed into the Australian population.

The male:female ratio has varied enormously among immigrant groups, as well as within the same group over time. Spanish immigration to the Western Hemisphere was about 95 percent male at the beginning of the sixteenth century and declined to about 65 percent male by the end of that century.[59] Japanese, Italian, or Chinese immigration has often consisted of more than ten times as many men as women, while the Irish famine emigration to the United States was roughly sex-balanced, as refugee migrations tend to be, and in some years the Irish women outnumbered the men. Even among immigrant groups which are predominantly male in the early exploratory phases, it is not uncommon for more women than men to immigrate in later years, after the group has decided to settle permanently and form families. This has happened among Japanese, Italian, and Chinese immigrants in various times and places.

Emigration is not always over long distances, nor always intended to be permanent. A number of groups have developed a pattern of sojourning some years abroad, in order to make and save enough money to return home in prosperity. Land-hungry peoples, such as Italians or Poles, have historically followed such patterns in order to return home and become landowners. More commercial people, such as the overseas Chinese, have

also followed a similar pattern of living abroad during youth and returning home in more mature years—at least until China became Communist
in 1949. Some temporary migrations have even been seasonal, especially
among agricultural workers and particularly after the rise of the steam
ship sharply reduced the costs of overseas travel.

Sojourners have often played major economic roles, not only in the
societies to which they went, but also in the societies from which they
came. The impact of the sojourning overseas Chinese on the economies of
Southeast Asia is perhaps the most dramatic example, but British engineers and technicians, in smaller numbers, have had similarly dramatic
impacts on countries where they introduced the technology of the industrial age, including Russia, Japan, Germany, Argentina, and the United
States in the nineteenth century.[60] Conversely, some sojourners have traveled from less developed countries to more industrialized nations,
expressly for the purpose of acquiring knowledge to bring back to their
homelands. Japanese, Germans, Americans, Russians, and others made
such sojourns to eighteenth- and nineteenth-century Britain to acquire
the latest technology there.[61] In the late twentieth century, so many foreigners have traveled to the United States for advanced training in science and technology that more than half of all mathematics and engineering Ph.D.s awarded by American universities went to people who were
not American citizens.[62]

While much immigration has been across oceans or between continents, there has also been much regional migration within South America, Europe, or Africa. It has been estimated that 80 to 90 percent of
these migrations in South America are illegal,[63] so accurate statistics are
highly unlikely to be found. There are estimates of tens of thousands of
Salvadorans having migrated—temporarily or permanently—to Honduras,[64] and of as many as 100,000 Brazilians living in Paraguay in the
late twentieth century.[65] By and large, migrations in Latin America have
apparently been from the poorer to the more prosperous nations, notably
to Argentina and Venezuela.[66] Similarly, in Europe, "guest workers" have
come typically from the poorer countries of the continent and beyond.
Africa has also known large scale migrations—as well as expulsions and
mass refugee flight. The 50,000 Indians and Pakistanis suddenly
expelled from Uganda in 1972, and a similar number of Ghanaians
expelled from the Ivory Coast in 1983, were especially dramatic examples that captured world attention. But vast numbers of Europeans and
Indians have been gradually forced out of other African countries and

have fled in a steady stream over the years, especially since independence spread through Africa during the 1960s.

The positive contributions of immigrants need not obscure their negative impacts on the societies receiving them. This is especially important in an era when cultural relativism creates taboos against discussing any unfavorable aspect of any group or culture. Yet standards of sanitation, incidences of crime and violence, proneness to become a charge upon the state, and many other social characteristics vary as much from one immigrant group to another as they do among other groups of human beings. In a given country at a given time, there may be similarly important differences between the current immigrants as a group and the people of the host society.

When cholera swept through Irish immigrant neighborhoods in nineteenth-century Boston and Philadelphia, or spread among Italian immigrants in nineteenth-century London, that was not simply a matter of "perceptions" or "stereotypes" by the society around them. Neither were the corruption and violence of the criminal tongs among the immigrant Chinese populations in various Southeast Asian countries over a period of centuries, nor the Hong Kong immigrant organized crime ring in the San Francisco Bay area in the late twentieth century.[67]

The negative impacts of immigrants do not end with behavior that is clearly harmful in and of itself. The nature of their interactions with the existing population of a country can be affected by biological, linguistic, religious, and other characteristics which enable some immigrant groups to fit in more readily than others. Indeed, some immigrant groups desire to fit in moreso than others, and politically organized programs in some countries promote subsidized retention of foreign cultures, despite complaints of Balkanization.[68]

Immigrants from Britain have tended to blend in more readily in the United States than have immigrants of a different color from Asia or the Caribbean. However, Asians or Hispanics have tended to become culturally assimilated over time, and eventually have had substantial rates of intermarriage by the third generation in the United States, while Germans who settled in eighteenth-century Russia were far less assimilated a century later, and intermarriage remained very rare, despite a greater physical similarity between Germans and Russians than between Chinese and white Americans, for example. Koreans in Japan have likewise remained a very separate social group, notwithstanding similarities with the Japanese population in skin color, hair texture, and the like.

What matters is not how similar the groups may seem to outsiders but how different they seem to each other. At various times and places, differences in religion have been more important than differences in color or language, but at other times and places the order has been the reverse. There is no universally paramount criterion of difference, nor any given objective measure of dissimilarity. Yet, however subjective some group differences may be, their social costs are quite real and may be quite large. These costs may be paid economically, or in a reduced quality of life, or in bloodshed.

In addition to real costs entailed by immigrants, there are often also false charges that they are a burden to the native-born population, in situations where they are not. However, sometimes there are hidden costs which may be different from what is charged, but significant nonetheless. A common charge against immigrants, for example, is that they take jobs from native-born workers. But there is no fixed number of jobs, from which those going to immigrants can be subtracted. More producers coming into an economy mean more output and more demand, which in turn creates more jobs.

It is an empirical question whether the additional jobs created as a result of the immigrants' economic activities equals or exceeds the number of jobs the immigrants themselves take. It is by no means out of the question that native workers may have more jobs available after immigrants arrive. Studies of the large influx of Mexican immigrants into southern California, for example, showed no adverse impact on either the unemployment rate or the labor force participation rate of blacks in that region, who might be competing for similar jobs. In fact, job trends for blacks were more favorable in this area heavily impacted by Mexican immigrants than in the nation at large.[69] But while there has apparently been an increase in the total number of jobs, there has been a correspondingly lower pay scale, as the large influx of immigrants has lessened the need for employers to raise wages in order to attract sufficient workers.[70]

The economic consequences of immigration on the native population in the host country are much more complicated than the job displacement theory suggests. It is also more complicated than the defenders of immigrants usually admit when they say that immigrants take jobs that the natives would not accept anyway.

Where there are welfare-state benefits available to low-income citizens, this means that the wage and salary level needed to attract these citizens into the labor market is higher than otherwise. Given this situation, it may well be true that immigrants take jobs that natives reject *at existing low wage levels*. But this does not mean that those jobs would have been unfilled in the absence of immigration. Because there are very few occupations that can be dispensed with entirely, many jobs would have been filled with natives at higher wage rates, even if the total number of jobs were less than when abundant supplies of immigrants are available. It is a common pattern in welfare states to have such jobs as hotel maids or hospital orderlies held by immigrants from poorer countries, but this does not mean that there would be no maids or orderlies if there were no immigrants.

While immigrants bring demonstrable benefits to an economy, their hidden costs include the cost to the taxpayers of maintaining more native-born workers in idleness, whether as a permanent way of life or as a more lengthy average period of unemployment between jobs, as the natives search longer for work that pays sufficiently more than they receive from unemployment compensation or other welfare-state benefits. The more numerous and more remunerative the welfare-state benefits, the higher the cost to the taxpayers of having a large-scale immigration of working-class immigrants. Even if the immigrants themselves do not resort to the welfare state enough to offset their own tax contributions—and studies in Canada, Australia, and the United States suggest that immigrants pay more into the public treasury than they take out,[71] at least in these particular countries—their indirect effects in keeping more natives idle longer can still impose burdens on the taxpayers. Whether these additional burdens exceed the additional taxes paid by the immigrants themselves is an empirical question in each country. However, it may be worth noting that countries with large and wide-ranging welfare-state benefits, such as New Zealand, are especially resistant to large-scale immigration, even when the existing population is small, both absolutely and relative to the country's land and natural resources. Authorities in Denmark have cracked down on refugees seeking asylum, on grounds that they are in fact seeking to milk the welfare state there.[72] Germany, which has had both open borders and generous welfare-state benefits available to new immigrants, has also had some of the most bitter and violent anti-foreigner activities of any country in the world. On purely economic grounds, it should not be surprising that immigrants are less in demand, now that they are much more costly to the countries receiving them. In the era before the full flowering of the welfare state, immigration was much freer in many parts of the world, and a number of countries in the Western Hemisphere actually subsidized immigration.

The social consequences of immigration are even harder to estimate than their economic consequences. An influx of immigrant children into the schools may make it harder for young native-born children to learn to speak the native language of the country properly. Moreover, dogmatic attitudes among educators may discourage native parents from complaining, for fear of being labeled "racist" or the like.[73] Both crime rates and rates of childbearing may be higher among immigrants, simply because immigrants tend to be young adults, and young adults tend to commit more than their share of the crimes in all groups, as well as being more likely to produce children. Correcting the data for age differences between the immigrants and the native population may reveal that the immigrants are no more likely than natives of the same age to have children or to commit crimes, but these statistical "corrections" are socially meaningless to those who find their children's education compromised by an influx of students who do not speak the language, or who find themselves increasingly victimized by crime. Often, it is not only the native-born population, but even earlier waves of the same immigrant group who resent the newcomers, as, for example, acculturated Mexican Americans often resent the new immigrants from Mexico.[74]

Whether for social or for economic reasons, a majority of the people polled in Belgium, Britain, France, Germany, and Italy in 1991 declared that there were "too many" immigrants living in their countries.[75] Moreover, such feelings have led to political demands for restricting immigration in a number of European countries, as well as in the United States and Australia,[76] while Japan avoids the whole problem by keeping immigrants out.

How many of the objections to immigrants represent personal experience or valid inferences about the costs imposed on the society by immigration, and how many objections represent misunderstandings of the situation or intergroup prejudices, is a perplexing question. However, what is quite clear is that immigration often generates internal conflict and that such conflict is itself a serious cost, regardless of whether it is or is not based on true and legitimate concerns. Organized political efforts to promote retention of foreign languages and cultures add to the social cost of admitting immigrants, even when in fact the immigrants themselves are rapidly assimilating, because that assimilation may be far much less widely known than the strident separatist demands of group advocates with their own agendas.[77] Needless intergroup friction over illusory issues has very real costs to the whole society.

The chief focus here is not on such current immigration policy issues. Rather, the larger and longer-run question concerns the economic and social effects of enduring group cultures, as compared to the effects of more immediate surroundings and more immediate government policies, or the political activities designed to influence such policies. In short, with immigrants as with conquered peoples or middleman minorities, the question is the degree to which internal cultural patterns persist and shape the economic and social fate of a people.

There are many kinds of immigrants and these differ generically from one another, in addition to the particular cultural differences they have as racial or ethnic groups. Refugees, for example, differ generically from sojourners, in that the former tend to be relatively evenly balanced between the sexes, while the latter are often predominantly male, especially during the earlier or exploratory phases of migration to a new country.

People who are fleeing disasters or the impending threat of disasters tend to flee without regard to sex and without the selectivity of other kinds of migration. By contrast, those who migrate to accomplish some purpose abroad and then return home are likely to be a selective sample of the home population and are more likely to be men hoping to establish themselves financially and return to form a family or to be reunited with a family that was waiting and may now hope for a better life with the return of the father. Other kinds of immigrants also differ generically in other ways. Two such generic groups of immigrants are middleman minorities and encapsulated minorities.

## Middleman Minorities

In addition to sharing various economic functions and arousing similar political hostilities, middleman minorities have also tended to exhibit similarities in certain social traits, despite their great differences from each other in specific cultural features such as religion, food, dress, and language. The overseas Chinese and the Jews of the diaspora are obviously of different races and have different religions, food, and language. Yet they—as well as Lebanese, Armenians, and Gujaratis and Chettyars from India, among others—have been noted for such patterns as working long hours, thrift, peacefulness (sometimes equated with cowardice), commercial reliability, and "clannishness." Much of this pattern simply goes with the economic role they play.

Because small retail businesses are much more easily set up than giant industrial enterprises, the pressure of numerous competitors virtually ensures that profits cannot come easily to middleman minorities. Hours must be adapted to the convenience of the customers, which may mean being open before they go to work in the morning and after they return home at night. Very long hours of work have been the hallmark of middleman minorities around the world, whether Chinese in Southeast Asia,[78] Lebanese in West Africa and the United States,[79] Koreans in the United States,[80] Indians in South Africa,[81] or Jews, Armenians, or other middleman minorities in other countries. So has a pattern of living at very low levels of consumption and amenities, in order to survive on meagre profits and save to build up the business. It has been common for middleman minorities around the world to begin by living in the backs of their stores, and in Sierra Leone the Lebanese simply slept on the counters, which they also used to prepare their meals.[82] In many times and places, it has been necessary to work and save for years, often in hard manual labor, just in order to accumulate enough money to be able to set up a little business, which then required additional sacrifices. A study of Korean businessmen in Atlanta showed that they worked an average of nearly four years—sometimes two jobs at a time—before accumulating enough money to open their first business, and that they then worked an average of more than 60 hours a week in their stores or shops.[83] In an earlier era, Lebanese businesses in the United States were open an average of 16 to 18 hours a day.[84] Similar hours were worked by the overseas Chinese in the Philippines, seven days a week.[85]

In times and places where people were scattered or transportation difficult, the middleman's mobility as a peddler has been a substitute for the customer's mobility. This pattern was common among Lebanese peddlers in parts of the United States, Canada, Argentina, Brazil, the Caribbean, Australia, Senegal, the Ivory Cost, and Sierra Leone, for example.[86] Similar patterns were common among Jewish, overseas Chinese, Indian, and other peddlers in many other countries around the world, before these middleman minorities moved up to establish other commercial businesses (including Bloomingdale's department stores and Haggar clothes).[87] Such patterns faded over time after a more widespread availability of both public and individual transportation made the customers more mobile. Where customers have been poor, credit has been extended to them at high risk and correspondingly high interest—whether charged separately or included in the prices of goods. In peasant societies, considerable credit may have to be advanced to farmers to tide them over until harvest time, and considerable transportation, coordination, and storage may be required to collect numerous small crops and later dispense them in large shipments to urban or international markets.[88]

Because middleman minorities have typically operated with thinner profit margins per item than their indigenous counterparts, they have had to be very *calculating*, often with little room for error, and this characteristic may be particularly resented by others who tend to follow tradition or routine, or who seldom look far ahead or exercise much self-discipline. That is, middleman minorities may be most resented by those most dependent on them to supply the economic requirements which they themselves lack—for example, to save and supply credit for those who do not save.[89] Economic complementarity often means social difference and political antagonism.

One of the important roles played by middleman minorities is making credit available to people too poor or too unreliable to be considered good credit risks by others. Often this is possible only because the middleman minority takes the trouble to get to know many of the local people individually, and so can sort out the differing credit risks more accurately than a bank, a large corporation, or a government agency could. This pattern has been widespread, from the Lebanese in West Africa[90] to the Chinese in Thailand.[91] Yet equally widespread is the view that middleman minorities are charging "usurious" or "unconscionable" interest rates, whether charged separately or included in the price of the products. But government agencies set up to supply credit to prevent such "exploitation" have often lost money,[92] suggesting that the interest rates charged by middleman minorities were covering a very real risk. Moreover, the supposedly exploited peasants have been known to prefer dealing with the middleman minority, even after government alternatives have become available.[93]

Middleman minorities around the world are often accused of "taking advantage" of other people's "weaknesses," such as customers' buying things on credit that they cannot readily afford. Accusations of this sort were as commonly made against the Jews in eighteenth-century France as against the Chinese in Southeast Asia.[94] Both customers and social theorists thus displace responsibility and anger onto the middleman, and often cite his "exorbitant" prices as the reasons for the customer's difficulties in making the payments, when in reality the likelihood of default is the reason for prices being higher than in stores which either require payment in cash or more sweepingly exclude credit risks.

The very nature of the occupation restricts the kinds of personalities who can be middlemen. There is, for example, little room for a middleman who is rowdy, drunken, or who cannot be depended on to be open for business, or to pay his suppliers or employees. Reliability is a prerequisite for the economic survival of middlemen, and has long been their hallmark, whether they were Lebanese in West Africa,[95] Chinese in Southeast Asia,[96] or Koreans in the United States.[97] Moreover, insofar as middleman minorities live surrounded by people with very different values and lifestyles—many of which would be economically fatal to them—it is important to insulate their culture, and especially their children, from such influences; in a word, to be "clannish."[98] What was said of Lebanese immigrant storekeepers in the United States would apply to other middleman minorities in many other settings:

> School-age children, when not in school, were at their parents' elbows, waiting on customers, making change, stocking shelves, and imbibing the shrewdness of operating an independent business on meagre resources. They were inculcated with the parents' work and thrift ethics and the lesson that family unity and self-denial was essential to the family's goals. . . . With all of their attraction to America, Lebanese parents, however, disapproved of their children growing up "like American children" without the restraints of Lebanese values.[99]

In a later era, Korean businessmen in New York were found to be "contemptuous of the extravagant life styles of blacks and Puerto Ricans, from whom they want to maintain a social distance."[100] Even though Korean businesses have often been located in inner city and minority neighborhoods in various cities in the United States, the Koreans themselves have lived away from such neighborhoods, whether in New York, Atlanta, or Los Angeles.[101]

With clannishness often goes a sense of superiority, whether openly displayed or muted by politeness. This too may be an almost inevitable consequence of the social circumstances. It is a contradiction in terms to say that one values certain norms and yet remains indifferent to the fact that other people violate them. Moreover, differences in norms and habits are at the heart of the economic relationship between the middleman minority and the clientele they serve, whether in American cities or in the peasant communities of Burma, where Chettyars from India were the middleman minority:

> The main Chettyar business was to give credit to the paddy farmers. The Burmese peasant seldom had the instincts of a capitalist. When he harvested the paddy and sold his crop he liked to have a good time, make a contribution to the pagoda, buy clothes and jewels for his wife—and then just hang on till the next harvest. Chettyar credit ensured that he could hang on.[102]

Were the Chettyars to share the values and behavior patterns of the Burmese peasant, they would of course be of no use to the Burmese peasant. It is precisely their differences which creates economic complementarity. Yet the political effects of these differences may be far from beneficial.

Indigenous customers of the middleman minorities often resent both the attitudes and the values of the latter. Strongly held values that differ sharply between groups imply either antagonism or separation—each of which can take a variety of forms, or can be muted or concealed under a variety of polite practices or euphemisms—or else can explode into open hostility and violence. But to complain of "clannishness" or physical separation in this situation is to opt for the risk of open clashes. This situation is not a "problem" with a "solution," like academic exercises. Rather, there is a question of trade-offs under serious constraints and with serious costs either way.

Commercial transactions that require trust and reliability are more readily concluded among people who share not only certain traits, but whose possession of these traits can be verified more easily. An extreme example of this are the Hasidic Jews of New York's jewelry industry, who give each other consignments of precious gems to sell, without the need for contracts or other costly safeguards that would be absolutely necessary if dealing with strangers. Lebanese traders in the interior of Sierra Leone likewise have had to depend on the honesty and reliability of other Lebanese traders in the port city, who sold their consignments of produce in the international market and shared the proceeds.[103] The Chinese in Southeast Asia have also been noted for the large and complex transactions which they conduct among themselves without written contracts.[104] In medieval times, international credit operations and credit banking were initially family enterprises, among such trading groups as the Jews and the Indians, and risk pooling on long voyages originating in the Middle East was often practiced either within families or within the same ethnic group, whether among Jews, Indians, or the overseas Chinese.[105] The considerable economic advantages of this mode of doing business—beneficial both to themselves and to their customers, who get lower prices deriving from lower business costs—are made possible by "clannishness." It is a benefit with a cost, and either its acceptance or rejection involves a trade-off.

The Chinese in Southeast Asia, Indians and Lebanese in Africa, and Vietnamese and Koreans in America's black ghettoes, are often accused of not hiring local people for responsible positions. Such complaints against middleman minorities are long standing, as well as widespread. In Uganda, for example, the Young Baganda Association in 1919 complained that Indian firms did not hire enough Baganda clerks and shop assistants.[106] Similar complaints have been made in India's state of Assam, that the Marwari businessmen there did not hire enough Assamese.[107] In Senegal, a common complaint has been that Lebanese businessmen do not hire enough Africans.[108] Nor are such complaints limited to different racial groups. A Nigerian writer complained of the Nigerian middleman from another region "giving employment to people of his own ethnic group in preference to the employment or training of the local indigene."[109]

Despite the widespread nature of such complaints that middleman minorities seldom hire from the surrounding population or take them into business partnership, this view misses the crucial point—that the very prevalence of these middleman minorities in other people's communities indicates that differences in behavior and values are involved. Otherwise, indigenous middlemen would predominate among their own people. These differences cannot simply be talked away, and can be ignored only at risk to the survival of the businesses themselves. Sometimes there is an assumption that indigenous employees or partners of middleman minorities would acquire skills which would eventually enable them to function in similar roles. However, where middleman minorities have in fact hired or taken into partnership members of the local population they serve— often under political pressure—these middlemen's complaints about the locals have seldom been about a lack of skill, but rather about a set of attitudes and behavioral patterns detrimental to the business. In India's state of Assam, for example, Marwari businessmen complain that the

Assamese are lazy and unreliable employees.[110] Similar complaints have been made about local employees by Lebanese businessmen in the Ivory Coast,[111] and Korean businessmen in Atlanta.[112] Unreliability here includes both failures to show up for work and a pattern of thefts from the business. Attitude problems have included charges made by Indian businessmen that their African partners expected to share in profits without making any contribution toward earning them.[113] In Malaysia and Indonesia, where government policy pressures the overseas Chinese to take in indigenous partners, it is understood that only the Chinese will actually run the business and do the work, in what are popularly called "Ali-Baba" enterprises, where Ali is the local partner and Baba the overseas Chinese who does the work.[114] Nor can all these complaints from middleman minorities be waved aside as prejudices. In Malaysia, for example, the Malay government itself has been scathing in its criticisms of the Malays for lacking initiative and enterprise.[115] Similar criticisms have come from within other groups in countries around the world.[116]

Political leaders who pressure or threaten middleman minorities into hiring people they do not wish to hire, or even to give them responsibilities (including partnerships) that they would not have given them otherwise, may succeed in the short run in thus extracting additional benefits from those middlemen already doing business in the community, but they correspondingly reduce the attraction of locating new businesses in such communities or nations, in the same way as a surtax would discourage or deter new firms from entering. Even those minority middlemen already trapped, as it were, can redirect some of their economic commitment elsewhere by (1) cancelling plans for local expansion, (2) educating their children for different work, (3) reinvesting their profits elsewhere, (4) seeking opportunities to relocate themselves, or (5) retiring earlier than otherwise. In the increasingly hostile atmosphere of post-independence Senegal, for example, young Lebanese men with professional qualifications have left the country.[117] Malaysia's anti-Chinese policies have likewise led to an exodus of Chinese capital, as well as people.[118] Asians in Kenya transferred large amounts of capital out of the country during its transformation from British colony to independent nation bent on "Africanization."[119] Korean storekeepers in the United States often use the profits earned in black neighborhoods where they are harassed to move on to new stores in white neighborhoods.[120] Over the centuries, Jews have repeatedly left countries where anti-Semitic policies and mob violence had become intolerable.

Indigenous political leaders, well aware of such counterproductive economic consequences of their pressures against middlemen, nevertheless have every incentive to push such policies, which reap immediate political gains, whatever their long-run economic damage to the community or the nation. Indeed, these political leaders or community activists are often among the first to denounce middleman minorities because they "make their money and leave." Yet minority businessmen have often stayed for generations—or even centuries—before being subjected to pressures to meet politically determined goals.

Hostility toward middleman minorities is often explained in terms of features peculiar to a particular group, such as the religious role assigned the Jews by some Christians—"Christ killers," in its crudest form. But exactly the same general pattern of hostility, occupational restriction, ghettoization, expulsions, and sporadic mass violence have marked the history of the Chinese in Southeast Asia, even though religion has not been nearly as prominent a feature of Chinese culture, and the Chinese are assigned no such demonic role in the history of other religions in Southeast Asia. Envy and hostility that have been expressed in religious terms in Europe have simply been expressed primarily in secular terms in Asia. While some Southeast Asian Moslems denounce the overseas Chinese as infidels whose love of pork and gambling are offensive, these objections are hardly crucial, for non-Moslems in the region exhibit similar hostility toward the Chinese.

Among the many charges levelled at middleman minorities by their critics is that they are sojourners whose loyalties are to another nation, and that they drain away the resources of the host country to enrich their respective homelands. Indeed, sojourning has even been alleged to be a necessary part of the very definition of middleman minorities.[121] But the Jews, the classic middleman minority to whom others are analogized, had for many centuries no homeland to which they could return. To say that they had an emotional "attachment to an ancestral homeland"[122] is to say no more than could be said of Irish Americans, Germans in Russia, or Japanese in Brazil, none of whom have been regarded as sojourners or as middleman minorities.

The Chinese in Southeast Asia were in fact for many years sojourners—but not predominantly so since the 1930s, and especially not so since the Communists took control of China in 1949. Far from exhibiting the former pattern of an overwhelmingly male immigrant population characteristic of sojourners, the overseas Chinese in general became sex-balanced, family-based communities with local roots in countries around the world. The Jews have lived in that pattern for centuries. So have the Parsees in India, and so did the Armenians in the Ottoman Empire. Moreover, the ending of the sojourner pattern among the overseas Chinese, and a correspondingly drastic reduction of remittances to China, did not reduce the hostility to them or the discrimination against them in Southeast Asia. Similarly, anti-Semitism has been virulent in countries where the Jews were a stable, settled community for centuries. Genocidal levels of violence have been unleashed not only against the Jews but also against such other non-sojourning groups as the Armenians in Turkey and the Ibos of Nigeria—the attacks against those groups exceeding even the mass violence unleashed sporadically against the sojourning Chinese.

It is often claimed, not only by politicians but by scholars as well, that middleman minorities "monopolize" certain occupations or industries.[123] The fact that middleman minorities organize their own professional and business associations is hardly decisive evidence of this, because (1) both successful and unsuccessful groups do the same, and (2) middleman minorities were also organized in industries where they lost out in competition to others—as the Chinese were displaced by Europeans in highly capitalized industries in Southeast Asia—just as they were organized in industries where they prevailed. Loose use of words like "monopolize" confuses *exclusion* of others with *outperforming* them. Far from being able to exclude business competitors, middleman minorities have often found indigenous businessmen already well established in countries to which they immigrated, and only by offering lower prices, credit, longer hours, and the like, have middleman minorities replaced them in the economy. Even after having done so, middleman minorities represent no economically meaningful "monopoly," since they tend to be concentrated in highly competitive industries, whatever the racial composition of the competitors.

Characteristics that derive from the differentness or hostility of the surrounding population have often been included among the essential characteristics of middleman minorities—for example, living in separate enclaves, clinging to an alien language and culture, maintaining separate organizations, and a general social exclusiveness, especially as regards marriage. But these patterns have been equally characteristic of German farmers in Russia and Latin America, Russians living in Central Asia, and Japanese farmers in Brazil, not to mention the British of the colonial era in countries around the world. Where middleman minorities have been accepted by the host society, they have tended to assimilate both culturally and biologically. The Jews of pre-Nazi Germany were a classic example. So are the Chinese in the United States, as contrasted with the Chinese in Malaysia.

Some have tried to depict the cultural characteristics of middleman minorities as primarily a function of the constraints imposed upon them by the host societies in which they live, and only secondarily of the group's own cultural development.[124] In short, their economic activity has, in this view, been "more the consequence of what they were allowed to do, than of any 'traditional' proclivity" of their own. By arbitrarily restricting the range of examples to colonial societies, one can lend some credence to the idea that middleman minorities "were let in on sufferance, to fulfill a specific purpose."[125] However, even in colonial societies, middleman minorities were often present, and sometimes economically dominant, in some occupations before the colonial power arrived on the scene. This was certainly true of the Indians in Zanzibar or the Jews in parts of Poland annexed by czarist Russia. In other areas taken over by imperialist powers, middleman minorities were of course not exempt from the general heavy-handed economic control exercised by some colonial governments. But this is not to say that their concentration in retailing, money-lending, and other traditional middleman occupations was primarily a result of choices made by colonial officials—especially since these occupations were traditional among such groups in non-colonial societies as well. Often the colonial regime simply codified and rigidified existing economic patterns, or tried to manipulate them for the benefit of its home country or local members of the imperial race. Moreover, similar occupational patterns have been common in countries which were not colonies, and where no official policy existed on the occupations of individuals or groups.

In countries such as Australia, the United States, or Argentina, for example, no one chose the occupations of Jews, other than the Jews themselves. Once past Ellis Island, a Jewish immigrant to America was free to go wherever he chose, geographically, occupationally, or otherwise—and usually chose to locate in major metropolitan areas and in the same kinds of industries and occupations as Jews in Argentina or Australia. Meanwhile, the Irish in all three countries chose entirely different paths. The claim that denial of access to land forced middleman minorities into urban occupations is not without historical examples, but that claim can also be pushed too far, especially as applied to recent history. Wealthy

Jewish philanthropist Baron de Hirsch bought up large areas of land for Jews in a number of countries, in a vain attempt to change their urban concentration patterns. Yet often the Jews who settled on this land drifted back to urban occupations within a generation.

Attempts have been made to use the Indian farmers in Fiji, Guiana, and South Africa as evidence that the availability of land in these countries led them to an agricultural occupational pattern quite different from that of Indians who settled elsewhere and became middleman minorities.[126] But this ignores the crucial fact that Indians *from an agricultural background in India* were deliberately selected and transported to these places (and to Sri Lanka and Malaya) during the colonial era, while Gujaratis, Chettyars, and other middleman groups from India settled in East Africa, Burma, and elsewhere. Indeed, such groups as the Gujaratis continued to follow middleman occupations in Fiji, South Africa, and other countries where most Indians were farmers or farm laborers. It was precisely the traditional proclivity which reappeared in distant societies, despite the arbitrary dismissal of that possibility by intellectuals.

Whatever the race or culture of middlemen, they have aroused suspicions, resentments, and misunderstandings in the most disparate societies around the world. Even where they were not a distinct minority at all, the very functions they performed have been misunderstood and the people performing them condemned. Selling the same product for more than it cost the seller has been seen as morally objectionable, and requiring more money to be repaid than was lent originally has been condemned in both secular and religious laws. Merchants were held in low esteem in Confucian China and usury was outlawed in both the Christian societies of medieval Europe and the Moslem societies of North Africa and the Middle East. A common complaint among the colonial officials of West Africa during the imperialist era was that there was excessive petty trading going on among the Africans, who would be more productive if transferred into either industry or agriculture. Yet a noted economist who studied the economy of the region found that these African petty traders performed essential and valuable services, which he analyzed in detail and concluded: "If the traders were superfluous, and their services unnecessary, the customers would bypass them to save the price of their services, that is, the profit margin of the intermediaries."[127] Many of these supposedly redundant African petty traders camped outside European-owned stores, so the alternative of eliminating the middleman was readily at hand, had the African consumers chosen to buy in the standard quantities sold by European merchants, rather than purchase in the smaller quantities offered by African traders who would sell "a single drop of perfume, half a cigarette or a small bundle of ten matches."[128]

In the very different setting of a prisoner-of-war camp during World War II, very similar misconceptions arose regarding the role of middlemen. Some Allied prisoners of war circulated among their fellow POWs, exchanging various items from the standard Red Cross packages which they all received monthly, and trading also for items of personal belongings that some wished to swap for other things. In addition, these middlemen would lend cigarettes or chocolates from Red Cross packages near the end of the months to those who had already used up their own, charging interest by requiring a repayment of more cigarettes or chocolates from the next month's Red Cross packages. Here too, the middlemen were not racially distinct from their customers, and their flourishing business indicated to an economist among them that they were performing a valuable service, but that was not how public opinion in the POW camp saw them:

> Taken as a whole, public opinion was hostile to the middleman. His function, and his hard work in bringing buyer and seller together, were ignored; profits were not regarded as a reward for labour, but as the result of sharp practices. Despite the fact that his very existence was proof to the contrary, the middleman was held to be redundant. . . [129]

In short, misunderstandings of the middleman function occur in the most disparate settings, among the most disparate peoples, and have led to moral condemnations, legal prohibitions, and violence ranging from lethal mob riots to genocide. It is virtually impossible to explain this worldwide pattern, which goes back thousands of years, by the special characteristics of a particular middleman minority or a particular society in which they happen to be, though no doubt local variations add special features or special rhetoric. But, both the middleman minorities themselves and those opposed to them have responded to the constraints inherent in the circumstances, whether economic and social constraints in the case of the middlemen or the constraints of human understanding by those observers who misconceive the nature of the economic function being performed. A third element that has often proved to be decisive and disastrous has been the talented demagogue, whether local or national, who knows how to exploit the situation for his own ends.

One of the curious features of middleman minorities has been their affinity for the political left, despite being themselves almost textbook capitalists. Jews in Europe, the United States, Chile, Israel, Cuba, and South Africa have historically been prominent on the political left, whether moderate or extreme. American Jews have a long history of supporting very liberal candidates of both major political parties, and regardless of whether the candidate (or his opponent) was Jewish or not.[130] Many Jewish university students in Brazil have been so politically radical and anti-Zionist that they have cut their ties with their parents and the Jewish community.[131] Despite various attempts to explain this affinity for the political left in terms of Jewish traditions or Jewish history, this pattern is not confined to Jews, but has been common among other middleman minorities around the world. In postwar Malaysia, for example, the Communist guerrillas who plunged that country into civil war were almost all overseas Chinese.[132]

The overseas Indians have likewise been identified with the political left in various countries. Urban Indian voters in Malaysia supported left-wing parties.[133] In Fiji, the short-lived Indian-dominated government which provoked the military coup of 1987 was a left-wing government, bent on nationalization and income redistribution.[134] The Indian vote in the first elections held in Ceylon supported a number of Marxist candidates.[135] In South Africa during the era of white-minority rule, Indians were characterized as "more Communistic than the blacks."[136] Similarly, the best-known Indian politician in the Western Hemisphere has been Dr. Cheddi Jagan of Guyana, a Marxist with substantial political support from within his own East Indian community. [137]

Why middleman minorities, of all people, should be supporters of the political left is a large, unanswered question. Part of the answer may be that such groups often evolve toward non-entrepreneurial careers and lifestyles in the wake of entrepreneurial success. Children of prosperous businessmen often enter a university atmosphere that is politically left of center in countries around the world. Moreover, the prosperity which represents hard-won achievement by the older generation is, to the younger generation, merely a windfall gain and therefore a potential source of guilt. In addition, the remarkable achievements of the older generation of middleman minorities make them "a tough act to follow" in the same field, while political leftism offers the younger generation instant moral superiority. It may also be that middleman minorities, as groups with histories of being persecuted, cannot identify with conservative establishments, or are not fully accepted by them, despite having reached high economic levels.

The differing political orientations of the Middle Eastern Jews and the Westernized Jews in Israel lend support to the notion that it is the *evolution* of middleman minorities toward non-entrepreneurial roles which marks their susceptibility to the doctrines of the political left. Middle Eastern Jews, who largely remained middlemen in the Arab world before entering Israel,[138] have generally supported the more conservative parties,[139] while the Ashkenazic Jews of Europe and the Western Hemisphere, who were more likely to be intellectuals and professionals, have long supported socialism and the welfare state.[140]

Whatever the combinations of reasons, the tendency of middleman minorities to favor the political left is a striking phenomenon worthy of further research and analysis.

## Encapsulated Minorities

The Germans who lived in separate enclaves in czarist Russia for about a century, and then moved to the Western Hemisphere, represent an unusual and revealing social phenomenon. Cut off from their original culture for generations, and yet virtually unaffected by the culture around them, they preserved a way of life that had changed in Germany itself— so much so that they appeared strange to other Germans whom they encountered in passing through Germany, or after reaching the United States or Brazil. The Volga Germans and Black Sea Germans had been isolated in both time and space, encapsulated as it were, in the eighteenth century, while the rest of the world moved on. Over time, some Russian words might infiltrate the German language they spoke, but nevertheless, it was still German being spoken, on into the twentieth century.[141] Even more striking examples of being encapsulated were those German religious sects whose withdrawal from the world and its "progress" was very deliberate—the Amish and the Mennonites, for example, whose language, dress, and farming techniques remained in the eighteenth century in many ways. Neither the Germans in Russia nor the Amish and the Mennonites in the United States remained literally 100 percent unchanged, but what is remarkable is how few were their concessions and adaptations to a world which changed radically around them, over a period of two centuries.

Jews in the Islamic countries of North Africa and the Middle East showed a similar pattern, though not so much by choice as by centuries of isolation among Moslems, while their contacts with the Western world grew tenuous. The historic reversal of the relative positions of Sephardic and Ashkenazic Jews, painfully apparent later in Israel, reflected the encapsulation of many Sephardics in an Islamic world which had not matched the dynamism of European civilization in recent centuries.[142] Where the Sephardic Jews were *not* encapsulated—as in the United States or in Curaçao—no such dramatic reversal of position took place, even though Ashkenazic Jews advanced rapidly in these places. Moreover, within Ashkenazic Jewry, the historic differences between German and Eastern European Jews reflected the encapsulation of the latter among the Poles and Russians. Once this isolation was ended, after the massive migrations from Eastern Europe to the United States, the gap began to close.

There are varying degrees of encapsulation, as with most social phenomena. Overseas Indians have tended to live in relative isolation from surrounding cultures and cut off from the culture of India as it has developed since they or their ancestors left the subcontinent. Yet their degree of isolation from the host culture, the stability of the original culture, and their isolation from cultural changes in India have not been as great in most countries as with the Volga Germans of the nineteenth century, for example. Travel back and forth to India has maintained contact with the homeland for Indian communities in Asia and Africa, and modern communications (including movies) have supplemented this, especially for overseas Indians in the more distant Western Hemisphere.

Encapsulated groups are more than a social or historical curiosity. They represent one test of the effects of genetic and environmental factors. The historic reversal of the relative cultural and economic positions of the Sephardic and Ashkenazic Jews, for example, undermines any argument that either was genetically superior to the other, even though differences in physical appearance indicate that they are indeed genetically different. Economic and social gaps that opened between Reich Germans and Russian Germans in nineteenth-century Europe, and narrowed in twentieth-century America, likewise illustrate the effects of large environmental differences.

# CHAPTER 3

# CONQUEST AND CULTURE

*Now, if there be a fact to which all experience testifies, it
is that when a country holds another in subjection, the
individuals of the ruling people . . . think the people of
the country mere dirt under their feet. . .*

—John Stuart Mill[1]

The history of conquest constitutes much of the history of the human
race. The conquerors of one era are often the conquered of another.
Ancient Rome imposed its yoke from Britain to North Africa and the Middle East, yet Rome itself has also been conquered many times by foreigners, its treasures looted, its people tortured, its women raped, and the
defenseless slaughtered. Much the same story could be told of the rise
and fall of the great Chinese dynasties, the Islamic empires, the vast
domains of Genghis Khan, and other ancient and modern conquerors.

Conquest and subjugation are among the ugliest aspects of the human
experience. Pyramids of the heads of the slain were regularly presented
as gifts to the sultans of the Ottoman Empire—these heads sometimes
numbering in the thousands and representing defenseless prisoners[2]—
while ordinary Ottoman soldiers divided among themselves the women
and boys of the conquered peoples for their own sexual amusement.
Among the conquering Bemba tribe in pre-colonial Africa, it was common for chiefs to have singers and drummers whose eyes had been
gouged out, to prevent their running away.[3] In the Western Hemisphere,
the Aztecs used thousands of prisoners of war for human sacrifices,[4] some
having their hearts torn out and others being burned alive.[5] The sadistic
tortures of the Romans included skinning people alive, boiling them in
water or oil, and applying red-hot metal to various parts of their naked
bodies.[6] During the infamous Bataan death march of World War II, Japan-

ese soldiers forced captured American soldiers to kill each other, sometimes by burying their friends alive. Yet, with all the horrors of conquest,
the world we live in today is a world shaped by historic conquests and
their cultural consequences.

## CULTURAL DIFFUSION

The very words we use and the framework within which we think are
shaped by cultural patterns spread by force in centuries past. Much of
modern Europe is a cultural heir of the Roman Empire, and its languages
offshoots of Latin. Other European languages, such as German and
Slavic, prevail in a geographic pattern established by conquests of the
fifth and sixth and centuries.[7] The Islamic conquests during Europe's
"dark ages" were an important source of light, bringing advances in
mathematics, science, and philosophy to Europe from a vast domain that
reached from the Indian subcontinent to the Atlantic Ocean. So-called
Arabic numerals originated in fact among the Hindus of India, though the
misnomer reveals the source through which this numbering system
reached Western civilization. The conquest of Spain by the Moslems in
the eighth century was especially important, as Spain became for centuries thereafter a center of diffusion into Northern and Western Europe
of the more advanced knowledge of the Mediterranean world and of the
Orient in astronomy, medicine, optics, geometry, printing, and geography.
Even the philosophy of ancient Greece often reached Western Europe in
Arabic translations, which were in turn retranslated in Spain into Latin or
into the vernacular languages of Western Europe.[8]

The later rise of Northern and Western Europe to world preeminence
in science and technology built directly on these cultural foundations,
brought to them by Moslem conquerors. In modern times, the most
advanced science and technology has been spread by Europe's own conquests throughout the world, as well as by migrations and other means.
Half the planet—the Western Hemisphere—is a cultural product of four
centuries of European imperialism. The great Chinese empire lasted far
longer but, for understanding today's racial and cultural relationships, the
European impact is of more immediate concern, not only in the Western
Hemisphere, but in Asia and Africa as well.

Not all conquests have been culturally meaningful, however, much less
culturally beneficial. At one extreme, there have been wars of extermina-

tion, such as that of Rome against Carthage, in which cultural consequences were minimal and confined to those few who somehow managed
to survive. Other conquests, for the more usual goals of extracting wealth
from the conquered peoples, may not have lasted long enough to be culturally meaningful. When the Nazis occupied much of France for four
years during World War II, that had little or no permanent impact on the
French way of life after the war was over. Neither French cuisine nor the
particular fields of endeavor in which Frenchmen excelled was changed
by this painful period in the history of France. Many other conquests
have likewise had little or no cultural effect, whether because of the brief
duration of the conquest, or because the conquerors had only limited
aims, such as control of a strategic port, establishing military bases,
extracting minerals, or extorting tribute in various ways that left the cultural life of the conquered peoples largely untouched. It must also be recognized that some conquests have done more to destroy an existing culture than to spread a new one. In ancient times, especially, conquests by
mounted barbarians had ruinous impacts on early, agriculturally based
civilizations.[9] Later in history, wanton destruction of great libraries in
conquered lands was especially devastating in an era of handwritten
scrolls, many of them irreplaceable. The conquering Vandals have left
their name as a generic term of disgrace, but many other conquerors have
also delighted in destruction, quite aside from those who deliberately
sought to stamp out the cultures of the conquered peoples, when they had
nothing better with which to replace it.

If one looks far enough back through history, virtually all peoples have
been conquered peoples. But a study of race and culture is concerned
with those conquests which have made a cultural difference in the lives
and history of the conquered and the conquerors.

Before ancient Britain was invaded and conquered by the Roman
legions, not a single Briton had ever done anything to leave his name in
the pages of history.[10] It was only after the coming of the Romans that
buildings were constructed for the first time in Britain.[11] Roads were also
built by the Romans, towns developed, agricultural methods advanced,
and sculpture and representational art in general spread.[12] In Churchill's
words, "We owe London to Rome."[13] The contributions of Roman civilization to Britain were perhaps even more dramatically demonstrated by the
consequences of the withdrawal of the Roman legions in the fifth century
A.D., to return to the continent to defend the declining empire against its

enemies there. By the beginning of the sixth century, British towns were crumbling, with buildings and statues in ruins. Roadways and waterways fell into disrepair, and in some places wild vegetation, including forests, began to reclaim what had been human settlements.[14] The dead began to be buried more crudely than before, often without coffins, and in shallower graves.[15] The governmental structure, which had unified most of the island under the Romans, now fragmented into tribal domains, too weak and disorganized to withstand marauders and invaders from continental Europe. Britain was not unique in its retrogressions after the decline and fall of the Roman Empire. On the continent as well, cities declined and in some places disappeared.[16] Such goods as pottery, cloth, and metal products were more poorly made than in Roman times.[17] An estimated one thousand years passed before the material standard of living in Europe rose again to the level achieved under the Romans.[18] As late as the early nineteenth century, no city in Europe had as dependable a water supply as many European cities had had in the days of the Roman Empire.[19]

Where cultural transfers occur as a result of prolonged subjugation of peoples less advanced than their conquerors, ambivalence has been one of the dominant notes of such conquests. More advanced conquerors have been hated, admired, imitated, and killed. Often the ambivalence has been present within given individuals, as well as representing widely differing reactions among different groups among the conquered peoples. British rule in India produced much ambivalence on both sides, continuing long after independence.[20] Some Puerto Ricans have made desperate, terrorist efforts to gain their island's independence from the United States—a goal resoundingly defeated at the polls by their fellow Puerto Ricans, both in a plebiscite on that specific issue, and in regular elections among political parties advocating various statuses for Puerto Rico.[21] In Wales, even home rule has been rejected at the polls by the Welsh, though Welsh nationalists have engaged in vandalism and sporadic terror in opposition to the union with England, and some Welsh intellectuals have complained bitterly of English political and cultural hegemony.[22] During the colonial era in Africa, many Africans who saw European civilization as a liberating advance over traditional indigenous culture, nevertheless resented the racism that came with it:

> To be called "boy," to have to stand in queues and let any white person go ahead, signs "for whites only," these things scarred and angered Africans, especially the educated ones.[23]

Similar, and sometimes worse, things happened to many other conquered peoples, whether they were racially distinct from the conquerors or physically indistinguishable. Cromwell's slaughters and mass confiscations of land in Ireland, and the oppressive and degrading laws which fastened second-class status on the Irish for more than a century thereafter, were all too typical of what other conquerors have done. The oppressions of various indigenous peoples in the Western Hemisphere by other indigenous peoples preceded the arrival of Columbus and may help explain many American Indian tribes' decisions to join with the new race from Europe in attacking their erstwhile oppressors.[24]

To attempt to add up a total of the net advantages and disadvantages of conquest would be a staggering task. Two learned authorities on the history of colonialism declare: "It is hard to make general statements with regard to even a single territory under the sway of any one colonial power."[25] When another scholar referred to the Germans as having produced in their colony in the Cameroun "numerous public works" and "numerous acts of brutality,"[26] he was saying something that could be said of many colonial powers, from ancient to modern times.

What is somewhat clearer is that those peoples conquered longer and more thoroughly subjected to the cultural hegemony of more advanced societies have tended themselves to excel in the economic and cultural realms in which the conquerors have had an advantage. It was precisely the southeastern part of Britain—England—that was conquered earliest and most thoroughly incorporated into the Roman Empire, which developed into the most advanced part of the British Isles. Centuries later, during the colonial era in India and Ceylon, members of the same racial or ethnic groups developed very different levels of skills, education, and economic initiative, according to whether they lived for long under the direct rule of the British, or in regions that held out as independent regions. Even after India achieved independence, the Andhras who had lived under British rule proved to be overwhelming competition for the Telanganans who had lived under Indian princes, though racially and in most cultural aspects they were the same people.[27] Similarly, in Sri Lanka, those Sinhalese who lived in regions conquered earlier by the British continued, generations later, to outperform their fellow Sinhalese from the Kandyan highlands that remained independent longer.[28] Other highlands, from Scotland to Southeast Asia, allowed indigenous upland peoples to hold out longer in independent—and backward—enclaves.

*Cultural Receptivity*

Even where various groups within a conquered country have all been subjected to, or given access to, the culture of the conquerors, their receptivity to that culture has often varied radically. Sometimes there has been a deliberate decision to remain removed from the new culture, as when Moslem groups in various African and Asian countries under European colonial rule refused to become involved in the schools and other institutions set up by Christian missionaries there. In many cases, missionary schools were the only schools, so that those outside the missionary school system were permanently handicapped in all competitions requiring skills and education, whether in clerical occupations, the medical or legal professions, in the military officer corps, or in scientific or engineering fields. Throughout the colonial era in Nigeria, for example, the vast majority of the Western-educated Nigerians were from the southern region of the country, while the majority of the population lived in the predominantly Moslem north. As of 1912, for example, there were fewer than a thousand students in elementary school in northern Nigeria, compared to more than 35,000 in the rest of the country. A quarter of a century later, there were still fewer than a hundred secondary school students receiving Western education in the northern region, compared to more than 4,200 in the rest of Nigeria.[29] Such educational disparities had enduring consequences. Of 160 Nigerian physicians in the country in the early 1950s, only one was from the Hausa-Fulani people who were dominant in the north, while there were 49 Ibos and 76 Yorubas from the southern regions of the country.[30] In the army, three-quarters of the riflemen were Hausa-Fulani, while four-fifths of the officers were southerners. As late as 1965, one half of Nigeria's officer corps were Ibos,[31] a historically less prosperous group[32] which had seized upon Western education to advance themselves. Even within northern Nigeria, southern Nigerians dominated many occupations requiring education, skills, or entrepreneurship.[33]

Nigeria was by no means unique in such disparities—or in the rearrangements of group rankings in the wake of cultural transformations wrought by colonial rule. In colonial Ceylon, the Tamil minority located in the less fertile northern tip of the island seized upon Western education to a far greater extent than the Sinhalese majority who, as Buddhists, were resistant to Christian missionary education. As of 1921, there were more physicians from the Tamil minority than from the Sinhalese majority.[34] As of 1942, the Ceylon Tamils, who were 11 percent of the population, were more than 30 percent of all the students in Ceylon University College.[35] In 1945, on the eve of independence, the Tamils were 30 percent of the civil servants and held 40 percent of the judicial posts in the country.[36] The superior educational achievements of the Tamils continued on into the post-independence era. As of 1969, in what was now the independent nation of Sri Lanka, the Tamil minority provided 40 percent of all university students in the sciences, including 48 percent in engineering and 49 percent in medicine.[37]

Both in Nigeria and in Sri Lanka, the success of upstart minorities provoked political backlashes, group quotas, mob violence, and ultimately civil war. All except civil war have also resulted from similar situations in Malaysia, Fiji, and several states in India. In other countries as well, different groups among the conquered have responded very differently to the new cultural and economic opportunities created by incorporation into a larger or more advanced nation. Wales, Ireland, and Scotland all advanced economically after being incorporated into the United Kingdom, but only Scotland developed its own entrepreneurial and technological class, rather than having Englishmen fill these roles in its economy. In the Soviet Union, Russian technical experts were sent into various republics to run the more advanced parts of their economies, but Armenia used its own technical experts and even exported some to other parts of the USSR.[38] What was said of the ancient Britons in Roman times was much more widely applicable, that these Britons "learnt from Rome not the lessons she was able to teach but the lessons their previous training enabled them to learn."[39] In short, conquered peoples are not a blank slate on which the conqueror's culture writes its message. The receptivity of the receiving culture is a vital part of the cultural transfer.

Conquest has not only brought more advanced technologies and more sophisticated modes of thought to some new areas; it has expanded the cultural universe in general. More has been involved than a transfer of things and ideas: *Cultural insularity has been shattered.* Any belief that existing ways of doing things are the only ways becomes palpably untenable. All within the expanded domains become players on a larger stage. Less advanced peoples within this larger cultural universe have not only acquired the benefits of a more sophisticated culture but also, in many cases, have eventually become contributors to its further development. Thus the peoples of the Yangtze River valley contributed to the development of the Chinese civilization which had begun earlier in the Yellow River valley.[40] In a later era, after the conquest of Scotland by the English and the English language and culture, the Scots did not simply imitate the English but themselves eventually forged to the forefront of British culture and world civilization in many fields in the eighteenth century, producing such landmark figures as David Hume in philosophy, Adam Smith in economics, Joseph Black in chemistry, and James Watt, who developed the epoch-making steam engine. More broadly, the Scots forged past the English in industrial engineering[41] and created one of the leading medical schools of the world, whose graduates created some of the earliest medical schools in colonial America, where Scots were also two-thirds of the colonial governors.[42]

Conquerors as well as conquered have been culturally transformed. When Arabs transmitted the cultures of Asia, of Hellenistic Greece, and of Persia a millennium ago, they not only transformed those cultures, but were themselves transformed.

Conquest has spread more advanced cultures, not just to those peoples directly conquered, but also to independent peoples in the same geographical regions, to which the cultural advances have been further diffused by trade, migration, and the general transmission of knowledge, whether by formal education or through informal contacts. Artifacts of Roman civilization reached Britain, for example, well before the Roman conquest of the island,[43] and also reached other countries and regions which Rome never conquered, such as Poland, Scandinavia, and the Baltic.[44] In a later era as well, cultural artifacts were spread by conquest beyond the borders of the lands actually conquered. In other ways, the cultural consequences of conquest have not been limited to direct transfers from conquerors to the conquered. Often the conquerors have been conduits for cultural advantages that originated with other peoples or in other lands.

Much of the culture spread by the Arab conquests, for example, did not originate with people who were themselves Arabs. Many of these cultural features were the material or intellectual products of other societies encompassed by the vast Islamic empire, or were the products of individuals and groups, including Christians and Jews, within the orbit of the Arab conquests.[45] The cultural artifacts diffused by the Arab conquests also included products known within the empire which originated outside the empire, such as paper and printing from China, which were transmitted through the Islamic world to Western Europe, enabling mass-produced books to replace costly handwritten scrolls, with revolutionary implications for the wide diffusion of knowledge.

The Arabic language created a common medium facilitating the transmission of culture across vast distances and throughout an enlarged cultural universe, promoting new advances. Much the same story could be told of the modern era, when European empires brought not only the fruits of European culture—much of its beginnings borrowed from other civilizations—but also European languages that spanned the globe and reached back in time for thousands of years for the thoughts of both European and non-European thinkers, all now available in modern translation.

Conquest has not only expanded the universe through which ideas, products, and technologies could move, but has also led to massive redistributions of the peoples of the world. Nor has this redistribution of peoples been limited to the conquerors themselves, historic as such invasions have been, whether of the Mongols and the Turks into Europe and the Middle East or of Europeans into the Western Hemisphere and Australia. Both the ravages of war and the subsequent benefits of pacification have spread other populations—neither conquerors nor conquered—far from their lands of origin. The havoc and chaos of war raging through ancient China sent refugees fleeing to adjoining lands, where they spread the Chinese culture.[46] In other instances and in other eras, the pacification of large regions under the conquerors' hegemony has enabled other peoples to settle in places where they would never have dared to settle before, among indigenous peoples whose wrath or spoilation they could not have risked before. While there was some movement of immigrants from China or India into Southeast Asia before European imperialists established colonies there, the vast majority of such immigration of Chinese and Indians into regions inhabited by Malays and Indonesians occurred after European hegemony was established in the region. Likewise, in parts of sub-Saharan Africa, it would have been fatal for members of some tribes to go settle in regions inhabited by other tribes until after the Europeans had established control over them all. Much of the commerce and industry of whole regions of the planet was created by these large-scale migrations—whether of Chinese into Southeast Asia, Indians into East Africa, Germans and Italians into Brazil and Argentina, or other groups whose international movements were facilitated by the prior conquests of others.

## Cultural Effects on the Conquerors

The cultural consequences of conquests have not been limited to the effects of the conquerors on the conquered peoples. Nor have the conquerors always had a more advanced culture, as they themselves sometimes recognized by absorbing the cultures of those they subjugated. Sometimes they were biologically absorbed by the conquered people, as the Normans were eventually absorbed by the English and as various conquerors were absorbed by the Chinese.

While conquering peoples have sometimes brought a more advanced technology, or more highly organized economic, political, and social systems than those known to the conquered peoples, at other times the conquerors have prevailed by sheer force of numbers, or by military skill, over peoples otherwise more advanced than themselves. This was true of many conquerors who came out of Central Asia—most famously the hordes of Genghis Khan, but also the founders of the Ottoman Empire, among others[47]—to conquer more civilized societies around them, whether in China, the Middle East, or Eastern Europe. While the conquest of ancient Britain by the Romans was clearly the triumph of a people more advanced in every way, the conquest of China by the Manchus marked the rise to power of a people who themselves acknowledged Chinese cultural superiority, and who strove to acquire and preserve that culture. Likewise, the Roman Empire both absorbed and spread the culture of the Greeks it conquered.

While barbarians repeatedly encroached militarily on civilized societies over a period of millennia, culturally it was civilization which encroached upon barbarian society, as the products of civilization and the comforts of civilized life seduced many of the barbarian conquerors into settling down into a new way of life and these products and this way of life to some extent diffused outward towards others who still led primitive and nomadic existences. Like other cultural diffusions, this one was selective. Many of the agricultural techniques of civilizations that developed in river valleys were inapplicable in the steppes and deserts of Central Asia. But even where various aspects of civilization were available to be adopted, not all were equally attractive to peoples from another cultural background. Metal weapons, cloth, and gold, for example, were far more likely to be appealing than mathematics.[48]

Sometimes the very military success and political overlordship of the conquerors lead to preoccupation with military prowess, to the detriment of other kinds of achievement and to a general arrogance which blinds them to the growing achievements and growing power of others, ultimately to their own detriment. Where a conquering people has long channeled its energies into military prowess and into the skills and talents of rule, including the petty dominion of bureaucratic functionaries, its attitudes toward the more mundane economic activities left to the subject peoples can also be affected. These economic activities—which ultimately feed, clothe, and house everyone, as well as providing economic support for military conquest—have often been disdained by the conquering people, as among the Spaniards and the Portuguese, both in Europe and the Western Hemisphere, and among the Ottoman Turks.[49] The conquering Mongols in Asia likewise left commerce and production to the conquered peoples.[50] It is not simply that vital economic activities may be left to others, but that such activities are actively disdained by the conquering people, even those of modest means. Among the Ottomans, for example, whole occupations were stigmatized as the occupations of infidels[51] and the development of such fields was correspondingly neglected, to the ultimate detriment of the empire. In medieval and early modern Spain, a similar disdain countenanced the expulsions of whole peoples—hundreds of thousands of Moriscos,[52] as well as hundreds of thousands of Jews,[53] both of whose lost skills were a blow to the economy. "Who will make our shoes now?" asked the archbishop of Valencia, after the Moriscos had been expelled—despite his own support of the expulsions.[54]

The arrogance so often accompanying conquest has likewise led conquering peoples to disdain and underestimate the achievements of other nations, including rival powers and rival civilizations. For centuries, the armies of the Ottoman Empire had repeatedly defeated and routed the armies of Europe on the battlefields, had spread their power up through the Balkan peninsula to the very gates of Vienna and had comparable cultural advantages over Europe in various fields. After centuries of such preeminence, the Ottomans and the Islamic world in general disdained to learn enough about or from the rising civilizations of Europe to prevent Europe's eventual turning of the tide against them and subsequent European subjugation of Moslems.

One small but common example of the arrogance of conquerors has been their refusal to learn the languages of the conquered peoples, while forcing the latter to learn their language. It was more than two centuries after the Norman conquest of England before there was a king of England who spoke more than a few words of English.[55] Laws and parliamentary proceedings were in French, which was also the language of social discourse among the aristocracy, while the English language and culture remained that of the masses and of the lesser gentry. In other societies as well, the elite among the conquered people have often adopted the language and culture of the conquerors in order to become part of the new elite, even as junior partners. Thus, in a later era, English spread around the world as the language of the educated classes among the conquered peoples in the British Empire—continuing as the world's most widely spoken language, long after the empire itself had disappeared. Similarly, French became the language of the elites, and eventually of the masses, in the French empire in Africa and the Caribbean, while Spanish and Portuguese became the dominant languages in Latin America. In the Soviet Union, only 3 percent of Russians spoke another language, and even among the millions of Russians living in the Central Asian republics, fewer than 10 percent spoke one of the Central Asian languages.[56] Yet more than half of all the non-Russians in the Soviet Union spoke Russian,[57] usually in addition to their own native language.

Because absorption of the language and culture of the conquerors typically begins with the elite among the conquered peoples, this has created or widened divisions among the indigenous population. Sometimes the division has been not so much by social class as by geographical location, with those located near the foreign cultural centers or spheres of military or economic concentration being the first to absorb the foreign language and culture, with those in the hinterlands continuing the older speech and customs. Thus, in Africa during the era of European colonialism, Africans located in and around the colonial capital, or in the principal ports, would tend to begin speaking English or French, as the case might be, and to become Christians, while those back in the interior bush country retained their indigenous languages and indigenous religions. Similarly, people living in the Scottish lowlands became anglicized long before the highlanders, among whom Gaelic continued to predominate in the eighteenth century and had still not completely died out in the early nineteenth century.[58] However, just as a conquering people can be biologically absorbed when they are greatly outnumbered by the conquered, so the culture of the conquerors can be absorbed in the local culture, which then moves up the social ladder. Thus the English language absorbed many French words during the era of the Norman domination of England, but English ascended the social scale at the same time, with Chaucer's

*Canterbury Tales* being a landmark as the first literary classic written in the English language. The country's laws and parliamentary proceedings began to be written in English in the next century. The intermarriage of the Normans with the English also began at the lower levels and rose up the social scale, until eventually even kings of England began to marry English women.[59]

In short, there has been no single pattern for the cultural diffusions which occur as a result of conquests. Sometimes it is the conqueror's culture which prevails, sometimes that of the conquered, but seldom does either prevail unmodified. What is clear, however, is that such diffusions are common, widespread, and historic in their consequences. One small sign of how thorough these cultural consequences can be is that few, if any, words survive in the English language today from the language of the ancient Britons whom the Romans conquered, while words of Latin, Germanic, and French derivation abound in English.

## Economic Consequences

The economic consequences of conquest have been both intentional and unintentional, as well as both positive and negative. The physical destruction and loss of life inseparable from conquest are one obvious cost to the economy. The turmoil of protracted wars imposes further costs in the form of reduced economic activities in places subject to military operations and reduced investments in general when the unknown outcome of military conflicts makes returns uncertain and hoarding wealth in the economically unproductive form of gold or jewels more and more attractive. Yet successful conquests that put an end to years—or generations—of sporadic marauding across a vulnerable borderland can make a major contribution to economic activity in places where no one would have dared to farm or build before. Thus, even after the European conquerors in Rhodesia took over large amounts of the best land for themselves, the Africans nevertheless had more land to use than before,[60] since they could now live in places where it would have been suicidal to settle when intertribal hostilities raged.

Conquests have been undertaken to exploit the natural resources of other lands, to extort tribute (including slaves) from the conquered peoples, to settle part of the conqueror's population in conquered lands, to establish strategic military bases abroad, or for a variety of other reasons. While economic objectives have long figured among the principal causes for conquest, the reductionist notion that economic motives can be automatically inferred behind conquests of the modern capitalist era is ironically applied to a period—the nineteenth and twentieth centuries—when noneconomic influences were especially strong, particularly in the case of the conquest of much of sub-Saharan Africa.

European officials responsible for the public treasury were often opposed to the development of a colonial empire in Africa,[61] which they correctly saw as having little capacity to repay the cost of conquest—except in unusual situations, such as the Congo or South Africa, with their valuable mineral resources.

Europe's economic impact on Africa was far greater than Africa's economic effect on Europe. Contrary to various economic theories of imperialism, Africa was not a major outlet for European investment or exports. In the early twentieth century, Britain's investments in Canada alone were larger than its investments in Africa and India put together[62]—and more British money went to the United States than to Canada.[63] France and Germany were likewise reluctant to sink much of their money into Africa.[64] Commercial trade with Africa was similarly trivial for the economies of the European imperial powers. On the eve of the First World War, Germany exported more than five times as much to a small country like Belgium as to its own colonial empire,[65] which was larger than Germany itself. France likewise exported ten times as much to Belgium as to all its vast holdings in Africa. Out of Germany's total exports to the world, less than one percent went to its colonies in Africa.[66]

Africa was somewhat more significant to Europe as a source of imports, though most of these imports to Europe from Africa came from relatively few places, such as the South African gold mines and diamond fields, or West Africa's cocoa and palm oil regions. Over all, Britain received less than 7 percent of its imports from Africa—less than from any other continent, including thinly populated Australia.[67] Nor were African colonies usually important sources of profit to European investors, or of revenue to European governments. German colonies, for example, in the years leading up to World War I, consistently absorbed expenditures greatly exceeding the revenues raised within the colonies, with taxpayers in Germany having to make up the difference. In the private economy, of 19 firms owning sisal plantations in German colonies, only 8 paid dividends. Only 4 out of 22 firms with cocoa plantations paid dividends, as did only 8 out of 58 rubber plantations and only 3 out of 48 diamond mining companies.[68]

Viewed from Africa, however, the situation looked quite different. While trade with Africa was a small part of the total international trade of the European colonial powers, trade with these powers was a substantial proportion of the total international trade of the African colonies.[69] Moreover, African exports and imports grew substantially during the colonial era. In German East Africa, for example, exports of peanuts, rubber, cocoa, coffee and sisal all grew several-fold in the relatively brief period from 1905 to 1913.[70] Similarly dramatic increases in exports from British, French, and Belgian colonies in Africa occurred between 1938 and 1958.[71] Correspondingly, Africa had rising imports, as well as more consumption of locally produced goods, both raising the living standards of Africans. Real consumption in the Belgian Congo, for example, rose 77 percent between 1950 and 1958.[72] In addition, the European impact on colonial Africa included creation of virtually the whole modern industrial and commercial sectors of many African countries. Europeans also introduced new agricultural crops and new farming techniques,[73] as well as creating the modern infrastructure of roads, harbor facilities, rail lines, telegraphs, motor transport, and the like.[74] One small indication of what this meant economically is that a single railroad boxcar could carry as much freight as 300 human beings—the usual method of transport in much of Africa—and could cover in two days a distance that would take a caravan two months.[75]

These benefits were by no means without high costs. In addition to deaths from military action during the initial conquests, and often later bloody suppressions of uprisings, there were numerous abuses, injustices, and even atrocities committed against Africans by the conquerors. Forced labor was one of the most widespread and most deeply resented of the chronic abuses to which conquered Africans were subjected. The conditions of this forced labor, like everything else, varied greatly from colony to colony and from time to time. However, even among contract laborers, conditions could be dire. In the Portuguese colony of Angola, during the closing decades of the nineteenth century, no contract laborer who went to São Tomé was ever known to have returned alive.[76] After an uprising of the Herero people in German Southwest Africa in 1904 had begun with a massacre of 123 Europeans, a German general ordered his soldiers to kill every Herero, armed or unarmed, whether men, women, or children. An estimated 60,000 out of 80,000 Herero were in fact killed before the general was recalled to Berlin.[77]

Many factors went into the decisions to acquire colonies in Africa, with

the economic factor not necessarily being dominant in either the acquisi-
tion or maintenance of those colonies. Particular individuals such as
Cecil Rhodes might make fortunes in the colonies—and represent their
gains as gains to the nation, even if the taxpayers back home lost more
than the European entrepreneurs in the colonies gained. In the case of
Africa, powerful missionary lobbies in London pushed the British government into more and more involvement in African affairs, often over the
opposition of colonial and treasury officials, and initial attempts at limited involvement often led to being drawn deeper and deeper into unfore-
seen circumstances requiring wider and wider military and political commitments. What made all this possible, not only for Britain but for other
European colonial powers as well, was that the resources required to take
over large areas of Africa were relatively small compared to what was
available to the European governments. As one historian of warfare has
noted: "One month of a European war cost more than a year of colonial
war."[78] When maintaining control of African colonies became more costly
as independence movements there gained momentum after World War II,
the continent was abandoned as swiftly as it had been conquered. In the
relatively few cases where a sustained and determined effort was made to
hold onto a colony seeking independence, or to maintain a local European hegemony in the face of indigenous uprisings, it was typically where
a substantial expatriate European community in the colonies was unwilling to leave or reluctant to share power, as in Algeria and Rhodesia. In
short, there was little to suggest that African colonies had sufficient economic value to the imperial nation as a whole to put up a real fight to hold
onto them.

The impact of Europe on Africa, for good and evil, was relatively brief
as history is measured—about three generations, as compared to the centuries in which the Romans ruled Britain or imperial China ruled parts of
Southeast Asia or the Moslems ruled parts of Europe. Just as the 1880s
saw the beginning of the European "scramble for Africa," so the 1960s
saw their massive withdrawal. This withdrawal began in the northern tier
of Moslem states in the 1950s, when Libya, Morocco, and Tunisia became
independent, then spread rapidly southward over the next two decades as
Nigeria, Tanzania, Uganda, the Congo, Kenya, and other black nations
achieved their independence.[79] Much as the withdrawal of Roman rule
from Britain led to widespread retrogressions, so in many parts of Africa
the departure of the European rulers was followed by technological breakdowns, failing economies, and political chaos marked by military coups.

Although the modern capitalist era might seem to be one in which economic motives for imperialism would predominate, in fact the imperialism of this era was more fleeting and less culturally penetrating than that of medieval or ancient times. One reason was that the modern capitalist era coincided with the rise of democratic politics in the leading European powers, opening the government to a variety of conflicting influences and interests. Moreover, a purely capitalist view of the costs and benefits of conquest would make most conquests simply not worth the money. It was, after all, Adam Smith—the father of laissez-faire economics—who urged his fellow Britons to abandon the American colonies and any other colonies that would not pay their own way.[80]

Such noneconomic motives as national glory, political power, ideological struggles, and religious crusades have promoted conquests that could not have been sustained on the basis of economic cost-benefit analysis alone. Enormous costs have been imposed on the subject peoples—and to some extent on the economy of the country as a whole—in pursuit of political objectives. Stalin's deliberately created famine in the Ukraine in the 1930s cost the lives of millions of human beings[81] who, even aside from humanitarian considerations, could have been contributing to the Soviet economy. Yet this operation was a political success in terms of breaking the back of Ukrainian opposition to the Soviet program. As one Soviet official explained at the time:

> A ruthless struggle is going on between the peasantry and our regime. It's a struggle to the death. This year was a test of our strength and their endurance. It took a famine to show them who is master here. It has cost millions of lives, but the collective farm system is here to stay. We've won the war.[82]

Politically motivated behavior can ignore costs much more readily than economically motivated behavior. Subjugation is not free, even to those who subjugate, quite aside from its costs to the victims. Thus the imperialism of the modern era, though able to span the globe because of unprecedented wealth and technology, was almost ephemeral by comparison with the empires of earlier times, when Rome ruled the subject peoples of Western Europe for centuries and China ruled its subjects in Southeast Asia for more than a thousand years. The speed with which modern colonies were abandoned when they became troublesome is much more characteristic of the capitalist era than the fact that such colonies were

acquired in the first place. The rise of democratic and humanitarian principles may also have reduced the ability of imperialist powers to suppress
their subject peoples in the way that Stalin suppressed the Ukrainians.

## Biological Consequences

The consequences of conquest are not only cultural, political, and economic, but genetic and epidemiological as well. Vast numbers of men
moving through a new area tend to leave behind large numbers of women
pregnant with biologically mixed babies, and to exchange diseases with
the general population. Diseases have often killed far more soldiers than
warfare. Typhus, for example, killed 17,000 of the 20,000 Spanish soldiers lost in the siege of Granada in 1490, and more than ten times as
many French soldiers died of exposure and deprivation during Napoleon's
campaign in Russia as died in combat.[83] The indigenous population of
the Western Hemisphere was all but exterminated by their sudden exposure to the diseases of Europe and Africa—far more so than by the military campaigns which occupy so much of history. It has been estimated
that the U.S. Army killed a grand total of approximately 4,000 American
Indians in more than two decades of fighting in the middle of the nineteenth century.[84] Diseases had a far more devastating impact. Smallpox,
malaria, influenza, and other diseases brought from Europe and Africa
decimated the indigenous population within a few generations, before
their surviving remnants acquired biological immunity.

The nineteenth-century American Indian population of the United
States was only about one-fourth of what it had been before the white man
arrived,[85] and only in the twentieth century has it regained the numerical
level of pre-Columbian times.[86] The vulnerability of American Indians to
the diseases of Europe and Africa produced even more extraordinary devastation in other parts of the hemisphere. The indigenous population was
virtually annihilated in the Caribbean.[87] The indigenous Indian population of Peru declined by approximately 90 percent after the Spanish conquest.[88] In Brazil, the present-day American Indian population is estimated at less than 5 percent of the Indian population when the Europeans
arrived.[89] This was part of a more general pattern of a devastating impact
of European diseases on indigenous populations during the era of European colonization around the world, as well as the impact of local diseases on the European conquerors.[90]

## INDEPENDENCE AND ITS AFTERMATH

Conquest, whatever its benefits, has seldom been a condition relished by the conquered. The struggle for freedom has been as pervasive throughout history as conquest itself. Conquered peoples have acquired their freedom in a wide variety of ways. A fundamental distinction must be made between those countries which wrested their freedom from a determined and vigorous colonial power, as the Americans did, and peoples to whom freedom came largely as a by-product of political decisions made by others elsewhere. The latter was the pattern of Roman Britain, of various central and southeastern European nations after World War I, and of many Third World nations who received their independence after World War II. It is one thing for a colony to achieve nationhood as a result of its own internal economic development, military strength, and political cohesion. It is another for it to find itself free without these achievements.

While Britain was clearly one of the most developed and advanced nations in the world at the time of the American revolution, there was no huge cultural gap between Britons and Americans, who were at that point largely transplanted Britons. Americans were quite capable of maintaining both the economic and political structures inherited from the colonial era, and eventually of developing both in new directions. No such capability had existed in fifth-century Britain when the Romans withdrew to defend the threatened empire on the continent, nor in many Third World countries that were freed in the post–World War II era. The inability of the early Britons to maintain the economic and cultural level left by the Romans was paralleled by their inability to maintain a national government, or to maintain a strong military defense against successive waves of marauders and invaders from continental Europe.

A number of nations in eastern, central, and southeastern Europe likewise achieved independence after the First World War as a by-product of the dismemberment of the defeated Austro-Hungarian Empire by the victorious Western allies, rather than as a result of their own strength or cohesion. While able to survive economically, often largely as a result of the skills of German, Jewish, and other minorities, they were far less viable militarily, and later ended up being picked off—one by one—by Hitler in the late 1930s. Austria and Czechoslovakia were taken over by military threat and internal subversion, even before World War II started, and Poland collapsed almost immediately after the attack which began that worldwide conflagration. Any such threats or attacks on the Austrians or the Czechs in an earlier era would have encountered the formidable Austro-Hungarian Empire, rather than a series of small and individually vulnerable nations.

Those sympathetic to the plight of conquered peoples have often tended to idealize them. But this tendency to idealize conquered peoples sometimes has had the dangerous consequence not only of over-estimating their economic, political, or military viability, but also of under-estimating their capacity for oppression and violence against their own minorities. The history of newly independent nations formed from the dismembered Austro-Hungarian Empire after World War I showed a general pattern of escalating anti-Semitism.[91] The escalating discrimination and oppression against the Chinese in Southeast Asia, the Indians in East Africa, and the Lebanese in West Africa after post–World War II independence swept through these regions repeated a similar pattern, as have later outbreaks of savage ethnic violence and civil war in territories once part of the Soviet Union or of Yugoslavia. Often it has been claimed that a divide-and-conquer strategy of the imperialist power is responsible for intergroup antagonisms. But in many cases these antagonisms antedated the arrival of the imperialists and burst forth with renewed fury after their departure.

A related claim is often made, that national boundary lines drawn by conquerors have not coincided with cultural and ethnic lines, but have artificially divided peoples from their brethren who reside in adjoining territory made part of another nation. In much of the world, however, there are no lines that could possibly have been drawn that would have coincided with "natural" ethnic, linguistic, or cultural divisions. Centuries of migrations, conquests, and the emergence of widely scattered ethnic enclaves, interspersed among one another, as well as varying degrees of assimilation, have produced such a cultural maelstrom as to defy unscrambling. What a distinguished historian said of the Balkans could be said of many other parts of the world—that drawing political boundaries "through this ethnic confusion, with fragmented peoples and uncertain loyalties, would have been a matter of the gravest difficulty even if there had been goodwill on all sides"—which "there never was."[92]

For better or worse, conquests have shaped much of the cultural and racial history of the world.

# CHAPTER 4

# RACE AND ECONOMICS

Race does not change the fundamental principles of economics. However, the application of economic principles in a racially and culturally heterogeneous population introduces complications beyond those found in the analysis of economic transactions in homogeneous populations. Cultural differences between groups are reflected in their roles as workers, consumers, entrepreneurs, tenants, or other economic transactors. As the history of various racial and ethnic groups has shown repeatedly, such groups differ greatly in their specific job skills, general work habits, occupational preferences, business traditions, educational backgrounds, thriftiness, and many other factors affecting economic results.

The study of economic results is a study of *cause and effect*. Philosophical observations, moral lamentations, or political rhetoric are not economic analysis. What economics can contribute to an understanding of the incomes, occupations, and general material well-being of racial and ethnic groups is a systematic analysis of the incentives existing under different market conditions. The consequences of such incentives follow general economic principles which have emerged over a period of centuries of study of markets, prices, incomes, profit rates, and other such variables. The economics of race is essentially the application of those principles to heterogeneous populations.

The markets in which individuals and groups transact are also heterogeneous—some highly competitive and others under various forms of control by government, labor unions, business cartels, and the like. Add to this the sweeping range of things that are bought and sold—from bread to stock options and from clothing to oil wells—and the possible combinations of heterogeneous groups and heterogeneous markets are virtually limitless. However, the general principles of economics, as applied to racial and ethnic groups, can be illustrated in three broad kinds of transactions—those involving employment, housing, and the sale of consumer goods and services.

## EMPLOYMENT

Employment is obviously a crucial economic factor, whether for individuals or groups. The kind of occupation in which someone is employed affects not only current earnings and the way of life that this makes possible, but also future prospects for the individual and the individual's children, including their education and careers. Occupations differ not only in current rates of pay but also in the likelihood of future unemployment, both of which affect the level of prosperity of individuals and groups. However, despite the great importance of occupations and earnings in setting upper limits to current living standards and to the rate of saving for the future, history repeatedly shows how mistaken it is to regard those limits as tightly constricting over time, and how completely misleading it is to label particular occupations "dead-end jobs" or particular wage levels as "subsistence."

In country after country, immigrants from China, Italy or Japan, for example, have begun at the bottom of the occupational ladder, in arduous, unskilled, "menial," and low-paid work, often in jobs disdained by the local population. Yet, with the passing years and generations, these immigrant groups have typically risen above the average incomes and occupational levels of those around them. Current earnings did not predetermine future earnings, as "vicious cycle of poverty" theories claim. Some poverty is indeed persistent across generations, but the differences between those individuals and groups who remain mired in poverty and those who advance must be sought in other factors besides their initial earnings. Likewise, people working for what others characterized as "subsistence" wages have often saved a significant part of their incomes and used it to establish small businesses, buy homes, or otherwise contribute to their own advancement. Similarly, so-called "dead-end jobs" do not predetermine the future. Italians once predominated among people shining shoes in New York and in such Brazilian cities as Rio de Janeiro, São Paulo, and Santos[1]—and such an occupation epitomizes the "dead-end job" which has no promotional ladder attached to it. Yet Italians rose from such jobs, probably no less rapidly than people working in civil service or other jobs with preset promotional ladders.

The Chinese in colonial Malaya often began as unskilled laborers on the rubber plantations or in the tin mines. The savings from their earnings on such jobs later enabled them to begin small, precarious businesses which eventually prospered. At the beginning of the twentieth century, Japanese immigrants in the United States were agricultural field hands and domestic servants to an even greater extent than their black contemporaries.[2] Yet the Japanese rose from such occupations within the lifetime of the first generation, and the second generation began at higher levels, in wholly different sectors of the economy, largely as a result of education. In short, while occupations are an important influence on the immediate economic prospects of an individual or group, these occupations are hardly all-determining in the long run, even for a given individual.

In some cases, immigrants' rises from humble beginnings have simply reflected a return to higher positions held before immigrating. Immigrants who had been professionals in pre-Castro Cuba often began in much lower occupations in the United States, in order to support themselves until they could reestablish their professional careers. In an earlier era, Jews from Eastern Europe brought with them needle-trade skills and entrepreneurial experience which took some time to turn into business ownership in America's garment industry. These situations must be distinguished from the situations of Chinese, Italian, or Japanese immigrants, who more usually brought with them neither skills nor entrepreneurial experience. In both sets of circumstances, however, neither the initial occupations nor the earnings levels in those occupations were the determining factor in the long-run economic results.

In racially and culturally heterogeneous societies, employment prospects for individuals and groups often vary not only with their own skills and work patterns, but also with their acceptability to co-workers, customers, or employers. Where particular groups are less acceptable to others, that can lead to their being segregated, either in particular business establishments or in different business establishments in the same or other industry. This job segregation may or may not be accompanied by discrimination in earnings received. Racially and culturally heterogeneous groups are also affected differently by wage controls, occupational licensing laws, or other governmental policies, whether or not these policies explicitly or intentionally make racial distinctions.

## Employment Segregation

As with other uses of the term "segregation," employment segregation as a policy or act of employers must be distinguished from the mere existence of a pattern in which different groups choose different occupations, or have qualifications for a different set of jobs. The dearth of Japanese Americans or Hispanic Americans among professional basketball players has seldom, if ever, aroused charges of group segregation or discrimination, for the unusual tallness of professional basketball players makes it unlikely that groups with below-average height would be well-represented there. Nor is the under-representation of whites in professional basketball attributed to anything other than the unusual interest and skill in basketball among blacks.

A group once well-represented in basketball, the Jews, no longer is, as alternative employment opportunities in other fields have attracted them away over the years. The exodus of Irish Americans from boxing, where they once dominated, has likewise followed their rise in alternative careers. In short, segregation as an employer policy cannot be inferred from group-representation statistics, which are readily influenced by the varying skills and choices of the groups themselves. This is not to deny that deliberate group segregation by employers has existed and continues to exist, but rather to point out that mere numbers do not define or demonstrate its existence.

Group segregation as a deliberate policy or action by employers is a very old and widespread phenomenon. During the era of mass immigration to the United States, American employers discovered that putting Irish and Italian immigrants in the same work crew produced a high probability of violence, especially if these were jobs that required the workers to live together for long periods of time—in crews constructing railroads or canals, for example. Indeed, employing Italians whose origins were in different parts of Italy created the same potential for violence. Migratory agricultural laborers have likewise tended to be racially or ethnically homogeneous groups spending months living together as they work. Often they have been recruited and managed by someone of their own racial or ethnic background, whether that be Mexican, Italian, West Indian, or other. Differences of language, as well as intergroup animosities, can lead to such segregation policies, whether or not the employer himself has any antipathy toward any of the groups in question. Moreover, such segregation does not in itself imply that one group is paid more or less than others, or is used for higher or lower occupations. That is a separate question, and one with varying answers according to circumstances.

What job segregation of this sort does imply is that there are higher costs of employing mixed groups of incompatible workers than in employing more homogeneous groups of workers, whether those costs originate in language differences, lifestyle differences, or intergroup animosities. In other words, *the higher costs are inherent.* There are no "solutions" to this "problem" that will make it disappear, without incurring other costs. Looked at another way, intergroup incompatibilities can raise production costs, whether through interruptions of work by arguments or fights, through mistakes in communication because of workers' misunderstanding each other's language, or because an atmosphere of tension in the work place lowers morale in general or causes a firm to lose its best workers, who are more likely to have job alternatives available elsewhere, in less tense surroundings.

In some cases, the higher costs of mixed workforces are due to different groups of workers wanting different working conditions. In an earlier era, for example, Jewish immigrants from Eastern Europe often did not want to work on Saturdays (their Sabbath) in American factories. Because factories of that era typically operated six days a week, the cost of having mixed Jewish and Christian work crews would have been to have part of the workforce absent on each of two days a week instead of having everyone absent when the business closed down on Sunday. The costs entailed by such scheduling difficulties would vary from industry to industry and would be complicated by changing ratios of Jews to Gentiles with normal labor turnover over time.

In any event, under these conditions, there were lower production costs when Jews and Christians were employed in separate business establishments, whether in the same or different industries. Because this was in fact a cheaper way to produce output, the pressures of economic competition in the product market would favor the survival of firms with either all-Jewish or all-Gentile workforces, whether or not the owners of these firms were Jews or Gentiles, whether or not these owners and employers had any animosity toward the other group, and irrespective of whether Jews or Gentiles were better workers. Both in czarist Russia and on the lower east side of New York during the immigrant era, it was common for Jewish workers to have Jewish employers.[3] In such situations, however, there is no economic reason to expect one group of workers to be paid more than the other for the same work, performed with the same efficiency.

In places where there were few Jews and work schedules were geared to the Christian majority's preferences for having Sundays off, it would be difficult for Jewish workers to find a full range of jobs open to them, consistent with Saturday religious observances. Again, this was not a "problem" with a costless "solution." However such a dilemma might be resolved, higher costs would result, whether to the business or to Jewish individuals. Over time, after rising productivity made possible two-day closures of businesses on the weekend, both Jewish and Gentile employees could be off at the same time, observing their respective Sabbaths, and so could be employed in the same business establishments without such costs.

While employment segregation does not, in itself, necessarily imply different earnings for different groups, there are circumstances which can lead to such pay differences—and other circumstances that do not. To the extent that different groups have, each within itself, the full range of complementary economic factors—management as well as labor, skilled as well as unskilled workers—alternative businesses can be set up to accommodate the lower costs of segregated employment, without either labor or management earning any less than in other firms producing the same output. However, to the extent that one group lacks one or more complementary factors required to create a whole business establishment—if they lack management or skilled labor, for example—then they may either face poorer prospects of being hired or have to accept lower rates of pay to induce others to employ them.

Those workers and managers who belong to the majority, or to other minorities with a full range of entrepreneurial and job skills, cannot be paid less than their compatriots elsewhere or they will go elsewhere themselves. Therefore any costs associated with unsegregated employment—whether due to differences in language or religion, or to antipathy—will tend to fall on those groups without the alternative of establishing their own businesses. To establish by law the principle of "equal pay for equal work" increases the likelihood of the minority's not being hired at all, and to establish group hiring quotas where they live increases the chances that employers will locate away from where they live, whether in other parts of the country or overseas. This is because the costs are real—

not simply a matter of "perceptions" or "stereotypes"—and such laws do not reduce these costs.

The extent to which there are additional costs associated with unsegregated hiring is an empirical question, and no doubt varies from place to place and from time to time. However, even during the Jim Crow era in the American South, blacks were seldom paid less by an employer for doing the same job as white employees. Rather, blacks were excluded from certain higher-paying jobs that would have put them on the same plane as whites. In the South especially, the resistance of whites was not so much to physical proximity to blacks, but rather to associating with them on a plane of equality. Blacks were welcome to live in white homes as servants, even by whites who would refuse to sit down at the same table with blacks to discuss business, for the latter implied equality while the former and more intimate association did not.

## Employment Discrimination

Discrimination is easier to define in concept than to determine in practice. Numerous demonstrable differences between groups—in skills, education, and experience, for example—make it difficult to tell whether intergroup differences in pay or occupations reflect these productivity differences or instead represent arbitrarily lower pay to different groups performing similar tasks with similar efficiency. Moreover, discrimination against a group as a whole must be distinguished from discrimination against particular individuals within a group. Group discrimination might imply, for example, that the average Maharashtrian in Bombay is paid less than the average Gujarati or South Indian is paid for performing the same work with the same degree of efficiency. This kind of discrimination, however, is usually very costly to a private employer in a competitive market. Where the victimized groups can form their own businesses, they can sell the resulting output in the product market, where consumers seldom care who produced the products they buy. The fact that other employers refuse to pay what their productivity would otherwise command only means that they earn the same wages, profits, interest, etc., by forming their own businesses. This, however, is not the only way in which attempted discrimination can fail. Moreover, it is not merely that the targeted victims can escape discrimination under these particular conditions; those attempting to discriminate in this way incur needless costs in a competitive market.

The costs of employment discrimination take many forms and vary with many factors. If two groups of equal productivity are paid significantly different wage rates for doing the same job, then employers who hire the lower-paid group stand to make more profit and, over time, to displace their business rivals who have imposed higher labor costs on themselves by hiring labor at pay rates above what is necessary to get the work done. Given that businessmen are in business to make money, rather than to promote particular social views, even highly prejudiced employers seldom persist in this costly kind of discrimination. Indeed, the entire social history of white-ruled South Africa was a history of white employers resisting and evading government policies mandating employment discrimination against blacks.[4] There is no compelling reason to believe that these employers had radically different racial views from those of other South African whites of that era. What was different was that employers would incur large costs in carrying out the kind of employment discrimination which the South African government sought to impose. The net effect was that blacks were often hired in larger numbers and in higher occupations than permitted by law, even during the era of apartheid.[5]

Where groups differ in their productivity, pay differences which exceed those productivity differences are still discriminatory. So obviously is a refusal to hire qualified applicants because they simply belong to the "wrong" racial or ethnic group. Either kind of discrimination is costly to the employer. In the first case, discriminating employers pay more than necessary, whenever they hire someone from the group they prefer. In the second case, when they refuse to hire applicants from other groups, they must either take longer to fill their vacancies, or accept less qualified people, or pay more to attract a larger pool of applicants from which to select fully qualified people solely from the preferred group.

Meanwhile, those competing employers who are either less prejudiced or more aware of the costs of discrimination get their work done cheaper. These employers with lower production costs can afford to undersell the discriminating firms in the product market, while still making a profit— and in fact earning that profit on more units sold, because of cheaper prices. If discriminating employers choose simply to let the job vacancies remain unfilled longer, rather than resort to higher pay rates, then this either leads to delays in filling customers' orders—implying slower sales and perhaps a loss of impatient customers—or resorting to overtime work (at premium pay) to get the work done on time with a short-handed workforce. The particular choices made may vary with the employer or the industry, but the costs of discrimination remain inescapable in a competitive marketplace, and vary only in the form they take.

A very different kind of discrimination occurs—and can persist, even in a competitive market—when a particular group is less productive than others but individuals within that group are just as productive as anyone else. Here the cost of discrimination must compete with the cost of knowledge. If the average Irish immigrant in nineteenth-century America was more beset with alcohol problems affecting his work performance, or was otherwise more troublesome or less productive, then many employers would be reluctant to hire the Irish for jobs where such deficiencies could prove costly. At the same time, there were also Irishmen who did not drink at all, who were productive, cooperative, and were otherwise desirable workers. The cost of sorting out such individuals from their compatriots was not always negligible, and the smaller their proportion the less likely was the sorting to be worth the effort. For certain demanding kinds of jobs, it was cheaper to use the stock phrase of the time: "No Irish need apply."

It is bitter medicine to the fully qualified individual to be denied employment because of the racial, ethnic, or other group to which he belongs. It is economically fallacious, however, to say that the below-average earnings of the group as a whole are due to such discrimination. Were the whole group's average productivity under-estimated, the opportunities for less prejudiced or more profit-minded employers would be too great for gross misperceptions to survive the competition of the marketplace. This conclusion is not simply an expression of optimism but of empiricism. Even when markets are not fully competitive, but have elements of collusion, the pressures of the marketplace can still be formidable. In the period after the American Civil War, whites in the South organized cartels designed to hold down the earnings of blacks who worked for them, either directly as employees or as sharecroppers on their land. But, as long as the cartel-set earnings of blacks understated their actual productivity, it was profitable for individual white employers to hire blacks away from their competitors at higher pay, or to allow black sharecroppers a higher percentage of the crop. The net result was that these white cartels collapsed all across the South, amid bitter recriminations among whites.[6] Later organized attempts of California employers to hold down the wages of Japanese immigrants in the early twentieth century likewise collapsed under the stress of employer competition for labor.[7]

Though not an economist, W. E. B. DuBois recognized the distinction between underpaying a group as a whole and underpaying particular individuals who were more productive than the average of their group. In 1899 DuBois wrote, "the individual black workman is rated not by his own efficiency, but by the efficiency of a whole group of black fellow workmen which may often be low."[8] If white people were to lose their racial prejudices overnight, he said, this would make very little immediate difference in the economic condition of most blacks. According to DuBois, "some few would be promoted, some few would get new places" but "the mass would remain as they are," until the younger generation began to "try harder," until the "idle and discouraged" were stimulated and the whole race "lost the omnipresent excuse for failure: prejudice."[9] Whatever the degree of accuracy of DuBois' observations, the important conceptual point is that he distinguished discrimination against an individual from discrimination against the group. The former could not explain why one group earned less than another.

Clearly, an end to racial discrimination would have made an enormous difference in the career of DuBois himself. Initially an academic scholar, he was barred by race alone from teaching at the leading universities. Similarly, such multitalented individuals as Paul Robeson were greatly handicapped by racial barriers. Eventually, both DuBois and Robeson became embittered Communists. In other countries as well, individuals far in advance of their own respective racial or ethnic groups have been so galled at being denied economic opportunities or social acceptance that they became leaders of movements to overthrow existing authorities and the existing social and economic order. Such political responses have not been the only responses, however.

A common economic response to being individually undervalued because of sorting costs has been for those with lower sorting costs to employ the undervalued individuals. Other members of the same group often can sort their compatriots at lower costs, either because of specific knowledge of the individual or his family available within the group or because of a greater facility in reading cultural cues peculiar to the group. The simplest case is when employers within the group hire workers from their own racial or ethnic background. However, labor contractors from within the group may also take on the sorting role, supplying workers whom they have selected to employers in the larger society, and in some cases coming along with them as supervisors, and as arrangers of their housing, transportation, and food in the case of migrant work crews, agricultural or industrial. This comprehensive role for labor contractors was once common among Italians and other Mediterranean immigrants, whether in Australia or the Western Hemisphere.[10]

Yet another way in which undervalued individuals can be sorted out is self-employment—the individual's own cost of knowledge of his capability and conscientiousness being less than anyone else's cost of acquiring the same knowledge. Self-employment need have no large initial capital requirements, as bootblacks, ragpickers, hawkers, and others demonstrate. Although such occupations have been labelled "dead-end jobs," they have often provided not only immediate subsistence but also stepping stones to other occupations, through money saved, experience acquired, and reputation built. It was not uncommon for a Jewish peddler, beginning with either a backpack or a pushcart, eventually to open a small shop, which could later grow into a larger store, sometimes even a department store, and in a few instances eventually a nationwide chain of department stores. Jews went through this progression in societies as far apart as Australia and the United States. On a more modest level, Italian immigrants in Britain, France, Australia, Argentina, and the United States often worked as street musicians, a form of self-employment that could, for the more talented, lead to careers in music. In these and many other ways, undervalued individuals escaped limits set by outsiders' lack of knowledge and high sorting costs.

A special form of self-employment that was once prominent during the era of mass immigration to the United States was performing work on assignment in the home. Clothing manufacturers, for example, would supply material to be sewed together in workers' homes, paying on a piece-rate basis for the completed work. Jews on the lower east side of New York were prominent among both workers and employers in the garment industry. Working at home minimized problems of language differences, Sabbath observances, finding kosher food, avoiding intergroup friction, or prior determination of productivity by employers. Groups such as the Italians, who did not want women to be working outside the home, also found the homework system fit their cultural values. Work at home often involved the whole family, including children young enough that parents were reluctant to send them out to work among strangers, or to leave them to roam the streets while their parents were away. None of these advantages came free. With so many poor immigrants flooding into the United States, their competition for work at home drove the rates of pay so low that a family had to supply many hours of work from its members to earn a living. Labor in the garment industry, whether performed at home or in factories, was often worked long and hard at relatively low rates of pay per piece or per hour. It was "sweatshop" labor.

Social critics and reformers often referred to sweatshop labor as "exploited." Yet the more candid, like journalist-reformer Jacob Riis, admitted that the sweatshop employer himself often received a thin and precarious profit margin, and bankruptcies were not uncommon in this highly competitive industry.[11] The real beneficiaries were the masses of ordinary consumers, who were enabled to buy new, mass-produced clothes within the limits of their own wealth-generating capacity. The benefits of affordable clothing have become so much taken for granted in later times that it is easily overlooked that this widespread availability of new clothes was a social revolution in the last quarter of the nineteenth century.

Before, even in a relatively prosperous country like the United States, many of the clothing needs of ordinary, working-class people were met by homemade clothes, or by second-hand clothes acquired through the marketplace, or hand-me-down clothes received from older family members. New store-bought clothes were rarer and all clothing was worn longer before being discarded. Second-hand clothes were health hazards that spread diseases as they changed hands, so that the growing availability of new, cheap, mass-produced clothing represented an advance in disease control, as well as in the general standard of living.

The historical picture of sweatshop conditions in the poverty-stricken slums of the nineteenth century has often been invoked in the twentieth century to bar homework of a sort bearing no resemblance to such conditions. Both nineteenth-century sweatshop workers and nineteenth-century consumers were severely limited by the much smaller wealth-generating capacities of that era. It was not the banning of sweatshop labor but the enormous increase in wealth-generating capacity that raised American workers to higher levels of prosperity over the years, while enabling consumers to buy their products around the world.

### "Cheap Labor"

It has become an oft-repeated statement, among scholars as well as journalists, that employers have sought or directly imported "cheap, unskilled labor" from abroad, often members of a different racial or ethnic group. While this has in fact happened in some countries, it has also often been the case that the labor imported has been no cheaper than the labor locally available—especially when transportation and other costs borne by the employer are counted—but has been imported for its greater productivity or reliability. In East Africa, for example, workers were imported from India, at considerable expense, to build the railroad from Mombasa to Lake Victoria, in preference to using the local Africans.[12] Even when the work is simple, unskilled labor, it may be performed with enough difference to lead to significant differences in pay. In colonial Malaya, Chinese laborers were paid substantially more than Indian laborers for doing the same work, simply because the Chinese produced more output.[13]

What is salient in cases like these is not that the labor is "cheap," in terms of payment per unit of time, but that the cost of getting the work done is lower because the workers are more diligent, reliable, skilled, or careful. In short, the "cheap labor" cliché confuses earnings per unit of time and production costs per unit of output. Differences in productivity mean that the two are neither identical nor necessarily correlated. Cheaper local workers may in fact be more expensive, in terms of what it costs to get a given task accomplished, even if their low pay causes observers to think of them as "exploited."

Differences in worker productivity do not imply differences in specific skills. Even so-called "unskilled" labor is far from homogeneous. In addition, much technically skilled labor has also been imported at considerable expense, from the days of colonial America to the time of Soviet industrialization under Stalin. Workers are imported for their assets— whether skills or diligence—and not for such liabilities as being "unskilled." "Cheap, unskilled labor" may be an attractive phrase for writers but historically such workers have not been nearly as attractive to employers.

## Government Policy

In addition to market responses to the underlying constraints which produce such phenomena as employment segregation or sweatshop labor, there have also been political responses to such labor market phenomena. A variety of government policies have evolved over the years in many countries to set minimum wage levels, outlaw discrimination, ban homework, and in general regulate the labor market politically. The rationales and intentions of such policies are a matter of social or political philosophy. The actual consequences of such policies, however, are a matter of economics. These consequences may be racially disparate, even when neither the rationale nor the intention has any racial aspect.

Minimum wage laws are an example of government policy usually imposed with no racial or ethnic purpose, but which nevertheless has major racial or ethnic effects. Economics, as applied to homogeneous groups, predicts that raising wage rates artificially above their market level, whether by a minimum wage law, a labor union contract, or otherwise, tends to reduce the amount of labor demanded by employers, while simultaneously increasing the amount of labor supplied by workers at the higher and more attractive wage rate. The net result is a surplus of job applicants—unemployment. Numerous empirical studies by economists have confirmed this tendency of minimum wage laws, for example, to reduce employment among those affected.[14] These studies differ on the magnitude of the effect, which varies with the time period covered and the research methods used in particular studies.

The economics of heterogeneous groups takes this analysis a step further. Where a group is less in demand (whether because of lower skill levels, less energetic or less conscientious work, or because of others' aversion to associating with them), an artificially imposed wage-rate increase tends to increase their unemployment rate more than the unemployment rate of the general population, or of other workers in the same affected sectors or wage brackets. When an employer has a surplus of job applicants, those considered less desirable (for whatever reasons) are likely to be over-represented among the rejected applicants. Thus, for example, when inexperienced teenage workers are covered by the same minimum wage as experienced older workers, the resulting unemployment is likely to be higher among the teenagers.[15] When there are racial or ethnic differences as well, those teenagers from the group less in demand will tend to be especially over-represented among the unemployed. Black teenagers in the United States were especially hard hit by minimum wage rates which escalated after 1950.

The American minimum wage law, the Fair Labor Standards Act of 1938, remained essentially unchanged until 1950. By that time, the inflation that began during World War II had in effect repealed the law by raising wage rates for even unskilled workers above the level specified in the Act. As of that time, teenage unemployment was not appreciably higher than that of older workers, and black and white teenagers also had very similar unemployment rates. Beginning in 1950, however, Congress passed a series of minimum wage increases over the years, while also spreading the coverage of the law to new low-wage sectors that had been exempt previously. Over the next three decades, teenage unemployment rose relative to the unemployment of older workers and black teenage unemployment rose far above white teenage unemployment. By the 1970s, black teenage unemployment had risen to several times what it had been in 1950. At no time during the three decades after 1950, not even in the most prosperous years, was black teenage unemployment as low as it had been in 1949—a recession year.[16]

Although economic consequences of this sort do not depend on an intention to affect different groups differently, in some countries and at some periods of history minimum wage laws have in fact been instituted for the express purpose of causing one group to lose jobs which another group gains. In South Africa during the 1920s, a minimum wage law was passed as part of a wider program of deliberately displacing black workers for the benefit of white workers.[17] In Canada, at about the same time, a minimum wage law was passed for the purpose of displacing Japanese workers for the benefit of white workers.[18] During the era of the British Empire, British manufacturers were vocal advocates of government imposition of higher wage rates in India,[19] ostensibly out of humanitarian concern for Indian workers, though the clear self-interest of British manufacturers was in making India's labor artificially more expensive, to the benefit of British businesses competing with Indian businesses.

It might seem that groups less in demand would be employed less, whether or not there was a minimum wage law. However, as the earlier pattern of black teenage unemployment showed, groups that are less in demand can be employed as much as other groups. In fact, every U.S. Census from 1890 to 1950 showed blacks to have a higher labor force participation rate than whites.[20] As with many other economic phenomena, the crucial factor here was price—in this case, the price of labor. Where wage rates are free to vary with the productivity of workers, a worker with half the productivity is just as employable (at a lower wage) as a worker with twice the productivity (at a higher wage).

The widespread nineteenth-century practice of paying piece rates based on output, rather than wages based on time at work, further facilitated the hiring of people with differing productivities. The later increased use of wages based on hours worked, and still more so of annual salaries not closely tied to hours or output, has moved pay and productivity farther apart. Both tendencies, often promoted by those wishing to help workers, create incentives for employers to establish productivity levels below which workers become "unemployable," even though these same workers would have been perfectly employable in the era of piece-rates.

The structuring of jobs in a sequence, leading to promotion from one to another, likewise increases "unemployability" among workers unlikely to meet the requirements of the higher jobs in the sequence, even when they are perfectly capable of handling the job at the bottom that is actually vacant. Were the vacant job not part of such a sequence—if it were a so-called "dead-end job"—then a wider range of workers would be employable. Of these, some who might not have seemed promotable at the beginning may turn out to be so after being observed at work, and after acquiring new skills and experience.

Even those not promotable in the particular prearranged sequence may nevertheless move up in some other line of work—partly on the strength of experience and recommendations for conscientious work in the so-called "dead-end jobs." Vast millions of ill-educated, unskilled immigrants from around the world—many speaking little or no English—were readily absorbed into the nineteenth-century American economy, in "dead-end jobs" which in fact led upward to economic progress. In medieval England, servant girls in the homes of the rich often went on later to become owners and operators of their own inns,[21] utilizing their knowledge of food, manners, people, and organization acquired in their previous work. Blacks similarly became prominent among caterers in eighteenth- and nineteenth-century America: George Washington's farewell dinner for his officers after the Revolutionary War was held in a tavern owned by a free black man.[22] Conversely, the spread of job-promotion ladders in the twentieth century, whether in civil service or in corporate bureaucracies, has been accompanied by the spread of "unemployability."

While government policy may intentionally or unintentionally increase racial discrimination, some government policies are intended specifically to reduce discrimination. Here again, intentions or rationales do not determine actual outcomes. Economic incentives are crucial for understanding economic results. For example, if the government had passed an antidiscrimination law during the era when Jews and Gentiles both worked six-day weeks but had different Sabbaths, what incentives would this have created? The inherent costs of a mixed workforce would in no way have been reduced by the law. Clearly, the incentives would be to evade and violate the law.

New businesses opening up, or existing businesses opening new branches, would have incentives to locate away from communities with mixed Jewish and Gentile populations, to minimize the likelihood that there would be job applicants from the "wrong" group. Both Jewish and Gentile employers would have this incentive. This might lead to hiring patterns not much different from what would exist without an antidiscrimination law—or even to worse employment segregation than would have existed without the law. In the absence of an antidiscrimination law, employers primarily concerned about costs, rather than having any personal animosities toward one group or another, might hire workers from the "wrong" group in particular jobs where either a five-day week was feasible or where the work that was not done on Saturday, for example, could just as easily be made up on Sunday, or vice versa. Once an antidiscrimination law was in place, however, with government officials scrutinizing statistics for *all* occupations and examining promotions as well as hiring, then hiring people for special niches would expose the employer to costly litigation over charges of discrimination.

Clearly, under these conditions, there would be even more incentives than before to have all-Jewish or all-Gentile workforces, if the cost of locating away from concentrations of either group were not prohibitive. Given the extreme concentration of Jews during this era—more than half the Jews in the country lived on Manhattan's lower east side—it would not be difficult at all for a Gentile employer to locate where he was unlikely to have Jewish job applicants. An antidiscrimination law would have provided additional incentives to do so. In a later era, after the antidiscrimination laws of the 1960s, there were charges that more businesses were locating away from concentrations of black populations. If so, the antidiscrimination laws themselves may have contributed to such actions. Whether, on net balance, such laws reduce or increase discrimination, is an empirical question—and the empirical evidence is by no means unambiguous.

Government itself may also discriminate on the basis of race, religion, or other group characteristics. This includes employment discrimination, housing discrimination, and discrimination in the provision of a whole range of government services, from education to garbage collection, as well as government-mandated discrimination imposed on employers, landlords, or others in the private sector. The government has, in fact, been a major discriminator in countries around the world. Central Asians in the 1980s still encountered pervasive patterns of racial discrimination in the Soviet military forces, reminiscent of discrimination patterns encountered by blacks in the U.S. military services in the 1940s.[23] South Africa became notorious throughout the world because of apartheid. Numerous black African nations have discriminated against Asians and forced them out by the tens of thousands. Government discrimination has been built into laws from the tropical South Pacific islands of Fiji to the North Atlantic island of Ireland.

One of the crucial areas of discrimination by government has been in the quantity and quality of education made available to different groups, for this can have lasting effects on their productivity and career potential in the private sector as well. This kind of discrimination has occurred at many places and at various periods of history. For much of the history of Southeast Asia, the only education available to the Chinese has been that provided by the Chinese community, not by the local public education authorities.[24] In South Africa during the era of white rule, blacks began to be educated only after education was established for whites, and only to lower levels than whites, and with only a small fraction of the expenditure per student that whites received.[25] East Indians in Guyana were specifi- cally excluded from the first compulsory attendance laws in that coun- try.[26] In the United States, there have been not only large racial dispari- ties in educational expenditures for much of American history, but also—during the antebellum period in parts of the South—criminal penalties for educating blacks, even at private expense.[27]

These examples—by no means exhaustive—suggest that governmental discrimination in education may so handicap particular racial and ethnic groups as to make private discrimination difficult to detect or estimate, because groups end up with such different productivities as a result. Gov- ernment discrimination in the provision of various other public ser- vices—police protection, garbage collection, public health services, etc.—has had similarly disparate impacts on different racial and ethnic groups.

The government's economic impact on particular groups is not simply a question of what specific policies it follows but also—and perhaps more important—whether it follows any policy at all. Whether government plays a relatively minor role in the economy or is a pervasive influence can have important economic and other effects on racial matters. For example, policies designed to maintain white supremacy, in the economy as elsewhere, were common to the American South during the Jim Crow era and to South Africa throughout the era of white minority rule. Yet the constitutional and ideological limits on the role of government in the United States left vast areas of discretion to the private marketplace, with the net result that racist policies were less effective in stopping the economic rise of blacks in the United States as compared to South Africa. Private discrimination, even when organized into employer and landowner cartels, proved far less effective than discrimination by government, with its ultimate monopoly of force.

In both countries, those white political leaders most bent on suppressing blacks were also most opposed to the operation of a free market—not simply in racial matters but more generally. The Jim Crow era in the American South was dominated by the rise of radical populist politicians who railed against Wall Street as well as against blacks.[28] In South Africa too, socialist and statist thinking in general were the hallmarks of those who promoted first the "color bar" policies against blacks and later apartheid.[29]

In the United States outside the South, racial and ethnic antagonisms were by no means absent, but the dominant nineteenth-century American political philosophy of leaving the marketplace relatively free of government restrictions allowed these racial and ethnic interactions to sort themselves out—usually with less racial discrimination than in the South. That this was a market phenomenon, rather than a purely regional phenomenon, was indicated by a notable exception—the greater opportunities for black skilled craftsmen in the South. Northern crafts became unionized long before unionization caught on in the South. In the freer labor market for skilled craftsmen in the South, blacks fared far better than in the North.[30]

More generally, countries with active government controls and participation in their economies have tended to have more intergroup discrimination and strife than those countries in which government plays a lesser role in economic transactions. Many colonial countries, especially in the British Empire during the era of laissez-faire, had less discrimination and strife among their own peoples than in a later era of independence, when there was a much expanded government role in their respective economies. This pattern can be found from Sri Lanka to Nigeria, Trinidad, Uganda, Guyana, Malaysia, Kenya, and other countries once ruled by the British. In many colonies, whether ruled by Britain or by other European colonial

powers, there was far less enthusiasm for independence among minority
groups than among the majority population. In the exceptional case where
the British colonial authorities intervened massively to transfer vast economic resources—notably land ownership—in Ireland under Cromwell,
they created the same discrimination, intergroup bitterness, and enduring
strife as in other countries with similar policies.

The kinds of institutions through which discrimination is attempted
profoundly affect the degree to which it is likely to be carried out and
continued. Because arbitrary discrimination against groups is inherently
costly to the economy, these costs may be shuffled around in various ways
but do not disappear. Insofar as the marketplace remains free to convey
these costs to decision-makers, it creates a deterrent whose impact has
been manifest in even the most racist societies. Conversely, merely to call
some other social phenomenon "discrimination" and outlaw it does not
necessarily benefit the intended beneficiaries and may in fact reduce
their employment opportunities.

## HOUSING

### Quantity and Quality

Housing is a very heterogeneous product, ranging from hovels to man-
sions, so the supply and demand for this product in a culturally heterogeneous population offers highly varied possibilities, as does the perception
of the outcomes by heterogeneous observers. Many observers have been
appalled by the housing inhabited by people of a different class, race, or
national origin. Sometimes this has reflected simply a difference in
income between the observers and the inhabitants, the latter being
unable to afford anything better. At other times, however, the housing
choices have reflected different goals, or different trade-offs among goals.

Italian men living as immigrants or sojourners, whether in Europe,
the Western Hemisphere, or Australia, have been among the more
extreme examples of a group with minimal demands for housing, both
quantitatively and qualitatively. During the era of mass emigration from
Italy, it was not uncommon for several Italian men overseas to share a
single room,[31] when they were saving to take money back home or to
bring their families over to join them. This did not mean that housing
was unimportant to Italians. On the contrary, once the family was
reunited in a new country, housing often became such a high priority

that extraordinary efforts and sacrifices then went into buying their own homes. This might include children as well as adults working, and all living within very strict limits, so as to accumulate a down payment on a family home.[32]

Middleman minorities overseas, such as the Chinese in Southeast Asia, the Lebanese in West Africa, or the Indians in East Africa, have likewise often had an initial demand for housing that was minimal in quantity and quality, as the men saved for both business and family reasons. While the mass emigration of Jews, such as transferred the center of world Jewry from Eastern Europe to the United States, was often a refugee flight of whole families, their initial housing demands too were often limited not simply by income but also by high savings propensities found, for example, in the run-down neighborhoods on the lower east side of Manhattan.[33] In short, for these groups as for the Italians, housing choices as of a given time reflected long-run plans as well as short-run trade-offs. All this tended to be ignored by observers shocked at these groups' housing conditions, and especially by social reformers determined to do something about it.

Seldom have the crusades of social reformers been directed toward enlarging the set of options available to the groups whose housing the reformers disapproved. More commonly, housing reform efforts have *reduced* the existing options, whether by "slum clearance" programs that destroyed lower quality housing, by building codes that forbad construction of housing without amenities prescribed by reformers, or by other regulations limiting the number of persons living in a given space to what reformers found acceptable. In all these ways, less fortunate groups were forced to pay more for housing than they themselves chose. Their incomes could no longer be used to maximize their own satisfactions, according to their own values, goals, and trade-offs, but were partially diverted to making observers feel better.

Reformers often found it sufficient justification to point out the objective fact of improvement in average housing quality in the wake of their reforms. However, this improvement—paid for by higher rents charged the tenants—was equally available *before* the reforms, *if* the tenants valued the improvements as much as they valued alternative uses of the same money. Nor should it be imagined that housing quality today would be at the low levels of a century ago without housing reforms. Rising incomes tend to produce rising housing quality, whether or not there is government intervention in housing markets.[34] This applies not only to changes from one era to another, but also to changes within the lifespan of given individuals, as among groups who achieve eventual home owner-ship by initially paying low rents for lower qualities and smaller quanti-ties of housing. Other groups, such as the Jews or the overseas Chinese, have tended to invest such savings in business or in the education of their children.

Looked at more generally, in a world where people have multidimen-sional goals, all constrained within the limits of their wealth-generating capacity, government intervention can always improve *one* dimension and document that improvement objectively as a "success," ignoring the other dimensions sacrificed. Housing is only a special case of that general prin-ciple. As with other special cases, the dimension chosen for enhancement is typically one visible to observers, while those dimensions sacrificed are less visible. The future, being necessarily invisible, is often sacri-ficed, as is the present inner satisfaction of working toward a goal of hav-ing home ownership, business ownership, higher education for one's chil-dren, the independence of having some savings put aside, or the capacity to send for parents or other relatives or to help them get established in a new setting.

All such goals are retarded or destroyed when third parties are able to force tenants to pay higher rents for amenities chosen by third parties, at the expense of goals chosen by themselves. Such impositions of outsiders' values and preferences have been especially prevalent when reformers have come from a different cultural background and have had little understanding of, or respect for, the choices of the people involved. This in turn has been especially common where reformers have had more years of formal schooling and could therefore feel justified in dismissing the choices of others as uninformed and unintelligent. The most danger-ous kind of ignorance is the ignorance of the educated.

One of the leading advocates of social reform during the late nine-teenth century in New York was journalist Jacob Riis, who detailed the overcrowded and squalid living conditions in various immigrant neigh-borhoods. Yet Riis also noted in passing the collusion of tenants with their landlords to evade the new housing reform laws—and, indeed, the tenants' sometimes violent resistance to being evicted by the authorities from housing officially condemned as substandard and marked for demo-lition.[35] Such observations did not lead Riis to reexamine his own assumptions but were presented in passing as anomalies or perversities. Similar attempts to evade "benefits" chosen for them by others were

apparent earlier, in the mid-nineteenth century, when the British government passed laws mandating better living conditions on ships carrying
emigrants overseas. The conditions on the ships of that era were truly
appalling, by all accounts. Yet Irish emigrants rushed to get on those
ships *before* the deadline for improvement,[36] indicating that the lower
fares were more important to them than the improvements in the conditions under which they would be housed during the voyage.

## Housing Segregation

It is a common pattern in many countries around the world for different
racial and ethnic groups to concentrate in different communities or neighborhoods, or even on particular streets. German emigrants created whole
German towns and villages overseas, from Hermann, Missouri, in the
United States to Blumenau in Brazil and Hahndorf in Australia. The
Welsh in Bryn Mawr, Pennsylvania, or the Scots in Dunedin, New Zealand,
are among other groups that have done the same. A more usual pattern is
for particular groups to concentrate in particular sections of a town or
city—Chinatowns from Melbourne to Toronto being perhaps the best
known examples of this residential pattern. Often there has been still further differentiation within the ethnic ghetto. Within Jewish neighborhoods
on the lower east side of Manhattan during the immigrant era, for example,
Hungarian Jews concentrated in different sections from the Polish Jews—
and German Jews tended to live far from this whole Eastern European
Jewish settlement. Italians living in Buenos Aires, New York, or Toronto
have likewise concentrated residentially according to their own or
ancestral regional origins in Italy.

Most of these pervasive housing segregation patterns, including minute
subdivisions within ethnic enclaves, have not been visible to the naked
eye as, for example, black-white housing segregation is in the United
States. There has been a tendency to refer to the latter racial residential
segregation patterns as if they were unique, when in fact they are
uniquely visible. The pattern known as "white flight"—the exodus of
whites from a neighborhood when blacks begin moving in—is likewise
part of a much larger, if less visible, phenomenon. Jewish immigrants at
particular levels of acculturation have moved out of Chicago neighborhoods as less acculturated Jews moved in.[37] Native-born Americans have
moved out as Irish immigrants moved in.[38] Indeed, middle-class blacks
have moved away as lower-class blacks moved in—or have left neighbor-

hoods in Detroit to get away from Polish immigrants and left neighborhoods in Manhattan to get away from the Irish.[39]

Such residential "flight" patterns are not peculiar to the United States.
In the Caribbean, the same pattern can be seen between descendants of
people from India (called "East Indians" in the Caribbean) and people of
African ancestry (called "Creoles"). As a scholarly study found, "where
East Indians settled, Creoles generally departed."[40] In Australia, influxes
of Southern European immigrants into residential neighborhoods have led
to an exodus of Australians of British ancestry.[41]

People sort themselves out residentially around the world, not only by
race and ethnicity but also by income, education, lifestyle, and other
characteristics. The degree or severity of housing segregation differs from
group to group, as well as for the same groups in different cities of the
same country, and varies from one era to another. Residential segregation
also differs in whether it represents a chosen clustering or an exclusion
maintained by others, whether by custom, agreement, or law. Observers
who presuppose that a random distribution of people is desirable often
see residential sorting as a "problem" to be "solved," usually by governmental action. Often this view is accompanied by an assumption that
housing segregation is irrational or can only be an expression of prejudice
or animosity toward other groups.

In reality, there can be very high costs associated with a random distribution of people, in housing even more than in employment. Indeed, some
of the most pervasive and enduring *employment* segregation has occurred
where workers have been *housed* together for long periods on railroad or
canal construction projects, or as migrant agricultural laborers. The benefits of housing segregation are obvious in the case of groups who speak a
different language from that of the surrounding society. If literally distributed randomly across a large country such as Australia, Canada, or
the United States, non-English-speaking individuals could find themselves virtually isolated from the rest of the human race. Residential segregation allows such individuals to enjoy not only the company of compatriots but also a pooling of knowledge, often slowly or even painfully
acquired, about the larger society to which they are all adjusting.

There are of course costs as well as benefits from residential segregation. Insularity, delayed acculturation, and delayed understanding of
other groups are among these costs. It is as unnecessary as it is impossible to determine the net balance of these costs and benefits, for they vary

from individual to individual, and even for the same individual at different stages of development.

Government policy, expressed in a law, cannot of course take all these differences and nuances into account—whether or not that policy is to promote or reduce housing segregation. Governments around the world have done both and in some cases—in the United States, for example— the same government has followed opposite policies at different times. The federal government explicitly promoted housing segregation by law during one era and then banned it by law less than half a century later.

In a free market, the costs and benefits of housing segregation are conveyed to individual transactors in economic terms. To the individual landlord, the cost of discriminating against particular groups can be a longer vacancy period, during which idle units earn no rent, as otherwise qualified tenants are turned away for belonging to the "wrong" group. Alternatively, the landlord can reduce the vacancy periods by reducing rents, so as to keep his housing units fully rented with tenants from the "right" groups. Either way, the landlord must pay a price for his own discrimination. Particularly when the landlord himself does not live in the housing he rents, these costs are likely to be borne only when alternative courses of action would create even greater costs—whether because the excluded groups are more destructive than average toward housing or are sufficiently unpopular that other tenants tend to vacate when they move in. Seldom, however, is either the behavior of one group or the reactions of the other group completely uniform. This opens the way to the kinds of incremental adjustments common in a marketplace, as distinguished from the categorical policies of government.

Where different portions of each group differ culturally from the other group to varying degrees, or have different levels of tolerance toward others, those portions of each group most similar to one another tend to have the lowest costs of living near each other. For example, in the later colonial era in Ceylon and during the early years of its independence, educated Tamils and educated Sinhalese both spoke English and lived a Westernized lifestyle, which made it easier for them to live near each other and for both to live apart from their respective ethnic groups, who spoke separate languages and followed separate traditional lifestyles.[42]

For some racial and ethnic groups in the United States, the expansion of the ethnic enclave has tended to be led by individuals and families more acculturated to the norms of the larger society, and who "pioneer" in moving into neighborhoods formerly off limits to the group in question. Blacks, Jews, and others have exhibited this pattern. Studies of ethnic enclaves in various American cities have shown different residential zones within each enclave, corresponding to different economic and cultural levels, with the more prosperous and most acculturated zones being on the periphery of the enclave.[43] The enclave's expansion into the wider society thus tends to be led by those likely to encounter the least resistance—although in some cases, even the least resistance may be formidable, especially if the existing residents sense an entering wedge, behind which far more people of far less acceptability will ultimately arrive.

By contrast, government promotion of residential integration of groups tends to be both cruder and more costly. Either an unsorted collection of people from different groups will be put together in public housing, for example, or the less-educated, lower-income, members of different groups—people with disintegrating families and higher levels of vandalism, crime, and violence—will be concentrated in housing projects set in the neighborhood of a different group. This can be a costly process for both groups, in terms of the enduring animosities (and sometimes violence) generated.

Social reformers, seeking to unsort people who have sorted themselves, often assume that housing segregation patterns will endure indefinitely, through inertia, without outside intervention. History as well as logic undermine that belief. As individuals and families acculturate, they tend to move residentially to be with others of similar values or lifestyles. These moves may be within a given ethnic enclave, or series of enclaves, or may involve moving out into the larger society.[44] Similarly, as whole groups change culturally over time, their acceptability as neighbors changes as well. Irish immigrants to the United States in the nineteenth century were notorious for fighting, for alcoholism, for keeping farm animals in city neighborhoods, and for garbage and filth that made their communities prey to disease. Cholera was unknown in Boston until the Irish settled there in the mid-nineteenth century and cholera epidemics also concentrated in Irish neighborhoods in New York.[45] At that juncture in history, the cost of having the Irish immigrants dispersed at random in American cities would have been an even wider ruin of neighborhoods and an even greater spread of deadly diseases. With the passage of the years, and with internal improvement efforts by the Irish themselves, led by the Catholic church, the Irish began to rise from this condition—a whole class of "lace curtain Irish" separating themselves from the "shanty Irish." Eventually, the Irish as a whole group were widely accepted residentially and socially, and became largely dispersed among the general population.

Similar adjustments of residential patterns to social realities have occurred across the color line. Even before the American Civil War, free blacks began to move out of the South and into northern urban communities, though in small numbers compared to the mass exodus of the late nineteenth and early twentieth centuries. As a people brought into Western civilization at the bottom, many of these blacks required years of acculturation to new circumstances and new requirements of urban living as a free people. The reaction of the white population to their presence was largely negative and even antagonistic. One of many consequences of this was residential segregation. However, by the late nineteenth century, there were many indications that a culturally changed black population faced changed social attitudes, now expressed in wider access to residential housing.[46] In New York, Philadelphia, Detroit, and Chicago—and in cities outside the South in general—there were many relaxations or eliminations of previous racial restrictions. Greater access to housing was just one of these changes, which included greater access to public accommodations, as well as more voting rights, and more social acceptance across racial lines.[47] The period from 1870 to 1890, especially, has been called "an unprecedented period of racial amity and integration" in the North.[48] In short, blind inertia did not prevent changing realities, such as the growing acculturation of blacks, from being reflected in economic transactions as well as in social interactions. However, a mass exodus of blacks out of the South, beginning in the 1890s and accelerating in the early twentieth century, not only greatly increased the black urban population numerically but also changed its character culturally.

The new mass exodus of blacks from the South represented far less acculturated people—people whose behavior was widely decried within the black community, as well as by whites.[49] In the wake of this migration, the previous racial progress, in housing and other areas, not only halted but reversed. Where all-black neighborhoods had once been rare or nonexistent in various cities—Chicago, New York, Washington, Philadelphia, or Detroit, for example—the familiar black ghettoes of the twentieth century now took shape.[50] In short, where social realities have substantially changed the costs of intergroup residential integration—whether positively or negatively—the market has responded accordingly.

With housing segregation as with employment segregation, the crucial question is whether the situation involves real, substantial, and inherent costs or mere "perceptions" and "stereotypes." Where the costs of association are real—whether based on language differences or behavioral differences—these costs cannot be made to disappear by fiat. Where spontaneous sorting processes are free to operate, they tend to minimize these costs and where preconceived patterns of unsorted housing are imposed, as in government housing projects, the higher social costs tend to be manifested in heightened intergroup hostility and violence. Real costs must be paid, whether in money or in other ways, including bloodshed.

## GOODS AND SERVICES

Markets for consumer goods and services are typically competitive markets. Yet in racially heterogeneous societies there are often charges of "monopoly" or "exploitation" in such markets, often due to economic phenomena which are an expression of that heterogeneity.

### *"Monopoly"*

The harmfulness of monopoly is well established in elementary economics. Politically, however, the term "monopoly" is often used quite loosely to describe a wide variety of situations, including highly competitive markets. For example, the Lebanese were once said to "monopolize" the textile trade in parts of West Africa, because they were the most prominent businessmen in that trade, even though they competed actively against one another in the marketplace.[51] In much the same way, the Chinese have often been said to monopolize various economic sectors in a variety of countries, even though others remained free to enter those sectors and compete. Indeed, monopoly has even been alleged as a general characteristic of middleman minorities.[52] But where there is no power to exclude, there is no economically meaningful monopoly, even if the sellers are all of the same race or nationality.

Political use of the term "monopoly" may in fact produce policies that reduce competition. Ethnic minorities said to monopolize particular sectors of the economy may be restricted in immigrating into the country or in setting up new businesses—the net effect of which is to insulate existing businesses from competition and permit higher prices at the expense of consumers. While such policies may be imposed in hopes of permitting others, especially indigenous majorities, to set up businesses, it by no means follows that they will do so, or that this will result in more indigenous businesses overall if they do. Where less efficient indigenous businesses survive under the protection of such restrictions, the goods and services they provide cost consumers more, leaving less to spend on other purchases that could support other businesses, indigenous and otherwise.[53] In short, loose use of the word "monopoly," in a political sense quite different from its economic meaning, often leads to policies reducing competition and thus producing the very monopolistic results so loudly denounced.

The real hallmark of a genuine monopoly—enduring profits above the earnings level of competitive enterprises—is seldom shown in situations where particular groups, foreign or domestic, are said to have a "monopoly." The initial investors, or even the initial wave of investors in a newly developing economy, may earn above-average profits for a time, as they did in the early stages of foreign investment in czarist Russia, but the sharp decline in profits there—from 17.5 percent per annum to under 3 percent in just eleven years[54]—suggests something of the power of competition.

## "Exploitation"

Where sellers, moneylenders, or other economic transactors are predominantly of one group and the buyers, borrowers, etc., are from another group, charges of "exploitation" are common, though not commonly supported by evidence. In a heterogeneous population, credit availability and interest rates may vary with the repayment prospects of individual borrowers or groups of borrowers. Where those less likely to repay find credit less available, or available only at higher interest rates, that is not exploitation but higher charges to offset higher rates of default. The problem is to distinguish this situation from a situation where one group simply colludes to charge another group interest rates higher than those of a competitive market. The "power" of moneylenders in poor peasant societies has been a common refrain. However, the evidence does not fit this picture.

Often such moneylending groups as the Chinese in Southeast Asia, the Jews in Europe, or the Indians in Burma have simply lent, at high interest rates, to people whom others would not lend to at all—or would lend to only at even higher interest rates, or only with collateral that the borrowers did not possess. If the problem were in fact one of extortionate gains by existing lenders with "power," then alternative lenders would find the field profitable. But when the government of Burma, for example, attempted to prevent "exploitation" of Burmese peasants by Indian moneylenders, by itself extending credit to the peasants, the government suffered great losses on these loans.[55] In Malaysia, where the government likewise established a bank to provide alternative sources of credit to Malays supposedly exploited by the Chinese, this bank in fact extended credit primarily to the Chinese, the Indians, and foreigners—all of whom were rated better credit risks than the Malays.[56] Where Malaysian government loans have been made to indigenous borrowers, the incidence of bad debts has been high.[57] In short, the interest rates previously charged in a free market had conveyed an economic reality, not some mysterious "power" of Chinese or Indian moneylenders.

In some cases, interest is not charged separately, but is included in the prices of goods purchased on credit. In a heterogeneous population, that can mean different prices charged for the same item when purchased by individuals from different racial, ethnic, or other backgrounds. When such practices were discovered in American multiethnic neighborhoods by sociologists, there were claims that (1) "the poor pay more" and that (2) pricing was racially discriminatory.[58] This situation is not, however, fundamentally different from the charging of different interest rates to groups with different repayment records.

The relevant question is whether in fact the repayment prospects of different groups are the same or different. The question actually asked in research on this issue has been quite different—whether matched *individuals* from different groups are charged different prices. This presupposes a negligible cost of knowledge in determining whether individuals vary from their group average in the repayment of credit. Even in the absence of an empirical test of the hypothesis of group "exploitation" in interest rates, it is clear on general economic principles that an overcharged group, or a group denied credit on terms that their repayment prospects would justify, provide an especially profitable opportunity for other lenders. Once again, the question is: What is the actual reality, as distinguished from "perceptions" or "stereotypes"?

Knowledge cost may make lending seem more risky to given lenders than the reality would reveal. During the era of mass Italian immigration to the United States, for example, American bankers may well have been unaware of both the high saving propensities and the reliable repayment patterns of the Italian immigrants. However, those within the Italian

American community were well aware of these facts and created their own institutions to profit from that knowledge. A bank established in California called itself The Bank of Italy, in order to attract the business of the Italian immigrants. It became so successful that its branches spread across the state, attracting business far beyond its initial clientele, and ultimately becoming the largest bank in the world under a new name—The Bank of America.[59]

While it is possible for those within a given ethnic group to recognize the economic realities of the group faster than outsiders can, it is not necessary for the group to have its own bankers (or other economic transactors) for that reality to make itself felt in the marketplace. Initially poor Lebanese immigrants established such a reputation for creditworthiness in Sierra Leone that they were able to get merchandise on credit from European businesses there,[60] thereby facilitating their success as retailers. Similarly, the reliability of Germans from Russia in repaying loans caused them to be able to get farm mortgages on very favorable terms from American banks.[61] Conversely, where repayment prospects are less favorable, that reality too can make itself felt in the marketplace, both to lenders inside and outside the ethnic group. Black-owned banks in the United States have tended to have high rates of failure and the surviving black banks have tended to invest *outside* their community even more than white banks.[62]

When a study of lending institutions in the United States showed that black applicants for mortgage loans were turned down at a significantly higher rate than white applicants, this was widely regarded as proof of racial discrimination, even though this study did not control for previous credit history or existing debt levels among the applicants.[63] It also did not take into account differences in net worth between blacks and whites, though whites tend to have a larger net worth than blacks in general, or even blacks in the same income bracket. Indeed, blacks in the highest income bracket do not average as much net worth as whites in the second-highest income bracket.[64] As with so many studies of statistical disparities between groups, this study did not examine the disparities in the underlying factors behind the results. Moreover, the underlying reasoning ignores the fact that lending is not done as a favor by lenders to loan recipients, but as a way for lenders to make money for themselves.

Although goods and services can vary in price because of differences in the implicit interest charged to groups with different credit risks, sometimes the prices of goods and services vary with the neighborhood, rather than with the individual or group. Here too, often "the poor pay more" because they live in neighborhoods with higher costs of providing those goods and services. Higher than average rates of crime or vandalism obviously increase the costs of doing business, including not only the losses directly suffered but also the costs of more security devices needed to control losses—iron grates for store fronts, or security guards in and around the stores, for example.

There are other and more indirect costs, but costs that are very real and very consequential nevertheless. Both labor and management tend to be less willing to work in unpleasant neighborhoods, meaning that stores and other businesses there must either pay higher wages and salaries to attract the same quality personnel as work in other neighborhoods or (more likely) be content with poorer quality personnel offering poorer service to the customer at higher prices—and with no additional profit to show for it. Many large chains of supermarkets, department stores, and other businesses may simply not maintain stores in less desirable neighborhoods, rather than face these problems or compromise their general reputation for quality.

Economically, these are not mere questions of "perceptions" or "stereotypes." Where an underlying reality differs from the general perception, there are more lucrative profit opportunities for those with more accurate knowledge. But where the reality does not differ substantially from the perception, then different prices, interest rates, or credit availability can persist indefinitely, or until the reality itself changes. Exploitation theories in general imply that higher rates of profit are obtained than those found in competitive markets. The normal fluctuations of prices, sales, and costs can produce transiently high or low profits, even in a competitive market. Exploitation implies *persistently* higher than average profits—but evidence of persistent profits above the norm is seldom offered to support the exploitation thesis.

Slum landlords or sweatshop operators during the American mass immigration era apparently did not make particularly high profits.[65] By the late twentieth century, many businesses were moving out of black ghettoes, an action hardly suggesting special profitability. Internationally, the relatively hasty withdrawal of European imperial powers from their colonies in Africa and Asia during the 1950s and 1960s—in many cases, with no armed uprisings by the colonial peoples—likewise suggests that there were no vast profits being made to justify a real struggle to maintain control. Where there were bitter armed struggles, as in Algeria or Kenya, for example, it was often because of a large expatriate European community, born and raised in the colonies, and unwilling to give up its protected and privileged status there—not because of huge profits going to overseas corporations.

## IMPLICATIONS

Economics often assumes a homogeneous population, simply in order to keep the analysis from becoming needlessly complicated. This assumption, however, is not fundamental to the analysis. When applying economic principles to racial and ethnic groups, the heterogeneity of the population cannot be ignored and is in fact fundamental to the situation. Behavioral differences between groups can impose costs on either or both. If one group is more prone to crime or disease, that imposes costs on any other group in contact with them, whether at work or living in the same neighborhood. Where there are language differences, costs are imposed on both groups. Such costs are real and do not depend upon perceptions or stereotypes, nor do they necessarily entail prejudice or animosity.

People tend to try to minimize their own costs in various ways—such as job segregation, residential segregation, or the offering of different credit terms to different groups. The competitive pressures of the marketplace not only reflect these cost differences but also respond to behavioral changes that raise or lower the costs of intergroup transactions. Government policies which attempt to produce a homogeneity of results, despite a heterogeneity of behavior, have the net effect of creating incentives for private transactors to reduce economic transactions. This reduction can take the form of fewer employment opportunities in the wake of minimum wage laws or less credit available after interest-rate ceilings are imposed by usury laws, for example. The impact of such reduced economic opportunities tends to fall disproportionately on the initially less fortunate group, which is to say, the group whose reality differs most from the implicit assumption of homogeneity behind the policy.

A special case of attempts to produce homogeneous results in heterogeneous populations are "affirmative action" policies which a number of countries have initiated under various labels, such as "positive discrimination" (India), "standardization" (Sri Lanka) or "reflecting the federal character of the country" (Nigeria). The actual impact of such policies has been highly disparate as between the initially more fortunate members of the officially preferred groups, who have gained the lion's share of the benefits, while less fortunate members of these groups have sometimes actually fallen further behind the general population under policies designed to benefit them.[66] Such results are far less surprising when seen in the perspective of economics, as a study of incentives and their consequences, rather than rationales and their goals.

Economics is a study of cause and effect, not intentions and hopes. Those who judge policies by their good intentions, or who presuppose that unhappy economic situations are a result of bad intentions, often see economic adjustments to real differences as simply racial discrimination. However, for the concept of racial discrimination to have either analytical or moral significance, it must be distinguished from the mere economic reflection of actual differences among groups. That distinction often gets lost in political discussions of discrimination—and sometimes even in scholarly discussions. If all differences between the earnings, occupations, and employment rates of different groups are simply *defined* as "discrimination," then it is circular reasoning to say that discrimination *causes* these differences, and compounded meaninglessness to quantify these "effects" of discrimination.[67] The reiteration of assumptions in the midst of statistics does not constitute evidence.

Once the possibility of economic performance differences between groups is admitted, then differences in income, occupational "representation," and the like do not, in themselves, imply that decision-makers took race or ethnicity into account. However, in other cases, group membership may in fact be used as a proxy for economically meaningful variables, rather than reflecting either mistaken prejudices or even subjective affinities and animosities. A study in the United States, for example, found that black landlords as well as white landlords preferred white tenants.[68]

The familiar linking of group prejudice to economic discrimination and that, in turn, to income disparities assumes away both behavioral or performance differences among groups and the economic cost of indulging unfounded beliefs in a competitive market. The effectiveness of economic competition does not depend on any employer's awakening to his own enlightened self-interest. Even if some employers are incapable of changing their minds, the marketplace is not incapable of changing which individuals can continue to survive as employers. The same is true for landlords, moneylenders, and other economic transactors. Being wrong may be a free good for intellectuals, judges, or the media, but not for economic transactors competing in the marketplace.

The cost of group discrimination explains why it is not generally as prevalent as a mere listing of economic disparities might suggest—and also why its prevalence varies greatly in different kinds of economic markets. Conversely, the less any enterprise's survival depends upon economic efficiency, the less is the inefficiency of discriminatory behavior an effective deterrent. Government agencies, which derive their support from the national treasury, clearly do not depend upon economic efficiency for their survival. The costs of discrimination to society as a whole may be just as high when done in a government agency as in a private enterprise, but the actual income of decision-makers who discriminate is unaffected in a government agency, however much it may cost the taxpayers. On the simplest economic principles, more discrimination would be expected where its costs are less—and that is what is found empirically. In many countries, governments have long been the most discriminatory employers, whether ordinary discrimination or "reverse discrimination" under affirmative action.[69] For similar reasons, government-regulated public utilities have likewise been very prominent among discriminatory employers—again, whether ordinary discriminators or practitioners of "reverse discrimination."

While privately owned utilities earn profits, their *rates* of profit are limited to levels determined by government regulatory agencies. As an unregulated monopoly, a utility company supplying electricity, for example, might be able to charge $5 for a given quantity of electricity and earn a 20 percent return on its investment, operating at maximum efficiency. But if a regulatory agency has determined that 8 percent is the limit of what the company will be permitted to earn, then the corresponding price of the same electricity might be $4—again, operating at maximum efficiency. Under regulation, however, there is less incentive to operate at maximum efficiency.

Prejudices of the company's management or labor can be indulged, even if this increases costs, for these costs will then "justify" higher prices to consumers, as long as the profit rate does not rise above 8 percent. If the same amount of electricity that would cost $4 under maximum efficiency now costs $6 with group discrimination, the utility company has lost nothing, even though the public may lose millions of dollars. Given these economic incentives, it is hardly surprising that American telephone companies were in one era among the most discriminatory employers toward blacks and, just a few years later, among the employers with strong preferential hiring of blacks.[70] Neither policy was costly to them.

Non-profit organizations such as universities are likewise under less pressure to maintain maximum economic efficiency, for their higher costs are treated as showing a "need" for the donations which keep them going or can politically justify dipping into their endowments. Similarly, foundations can use more of their money for meeting their own internal "needs" when costs are higher, as they are with discriminatory hiring. Like regulated public utilities, universities, foundations, and other non-profit organizations were once especially notorious for their discrimination against blacks[71] and—no more than a generation later—became especially prominent among practitioners of preferential hiring of blacks under "affirmative action."

Not all interactions among different racial and ethnic groups are economically motivated. These interactions often are, however, economically constrained. Understanding the nature and principles of these economic constraints means adding a new dimension to an understanding of racial and ethnic issues.

# CHAPTER 5

# RACE AND POLITICS

Few mixtures are more volatile than race and politics. The normal frictions and resentments among individuals and groups seldom approach the magnitude of frenzy and violence produced by the politicization of race. The twentieth century, which has seen the spread of mass politics and mass ideologies to vast new regions of the globe, has also been the century of resurgent new racial persecutions, reaching new heights—or depths. The political ideal of "the right of self-determination of nations" has created new nations which used their newfound power to persecute their own minorities, first in Europe after World War I, then in much of Asia and Africa after World War II, and in the Balkans and the Caucasus after the respective breakups of Yugoslavia and the Soviet Union. The twentieth century has also seen the need for a new word—genocide—to describe what happened to the Armenians during the First World War and what happened to the Jews during the Second World War. A world shocked by the deaths of 6 million people during the Holocaust has been much less aware of the deaths of an estimated 10 million people killed in various parts of the world since World War II for belonging to the "wrong" racial or ethnic group.[1]

The direct role of politics in shaping racial and ethnic attitudes and policies is only one facet of political influences on race and culture. Many policies not intended as racial or ethnic nevertheless have disparate impacts on different groups. Public utility regulation, occupational licensing, or minimum wage laws can have profound—and usually adverse—economic effects on poorer minorities.[2] Some political arrangements, however, can ameliorate racial frictions and help defuse racial tensions, while other political circumstances can transform harmonious group relations into mutual bloodletting in the streets, within a few years' time. Political power, political institutions, and political ideologies have had both short-run and long-run effects on the economic and cultural fate of racial and ethnic groups, as well as on their ability to survive at all.

Political systems, like economic systems, need to be examined in terms of the incentives they create, rather than simply the goals they pursue or the philosophies or ideologies which shape those goals. Moreover, it would be a serious mistake to think of "the blacks," "the Jews" or "the Chinese" as unified entities consistently pursuing group self-interest. Leaders, as well as those striving for leadership within these and other groups, have their own agendas and their own personal career goals, and they respond to the political incentives which affect these agendas and goals, whether or not their responses advance the well-being of the groups in whose name they speak. This is not to say that all political leaders are cynical manipulators. It is to say that those most likely to survive and thrive in political competition are those more attuned to the exigencies of the political process, whether by intention or happenstance.

## POLITICAL INSTITUTIONS

Political systems are essentially systems of *power* and their relative effectiveness for different purposes reflects that central fact. Government may use its power to forbid, coerce, confiscate, punish, or expel. Goals achievable by these means are well within the effective control of government. Goals which depend upon the creativity, skills, thrift, work habits, organizational abilities, and technological knowledge in the population at large are much less within the power of incumbent officials to achieve within a politically relevant time period. In the short run—within the term of office of elected officials, for example—government can do little to increase substantially these sources of economic prosperity. It can also do little to change the people's traditions, attitudes, wisdom, and tolerance (or intolerance) inherited from the past—all of which constrain the options of existing power holders and determine the stability and viability of the governmental structure itself.

Political leaders in some countries—Malaysia, the Philippines, Nigeria, Sri Lanka, and Guyana, for example—have exhorted their own people to develop the dynamism exhibited by envied minorities in their midst.[3] There is, however, little evidence that these exhortations have been effective. Where the power of government has produced immediate effects has been in *reducing* existing productive capabilities by excluding, restricting, or expelling the groups possessing those capabilities. From the expulsions of the Jews from Spain in 1492 to the expulsions of Indians and Pakistanis from Uganda in 1973, this has been a way to achieve immediate political goals, though at lasting economic costs.

Government may also use its power to confiscate the wealth of some and transfer it to others, but this too is usually only a short-range benefit to the recipients and an overall loss to the country, as the plundered group usually reduces its production of wealth, whether because of the lack of incentives or because their wealth is hidden or sent abroad, or because they themselves leave for more hospitable countries. The negative consequences of political persecution and plunder are not limited to economic losses. Medical, cultural, and even military losses may be sustained by the country at large. After expelling the Jews, Spain later complained that its Moslem enemies had been able to put to military use the knowledge obtained from Jewish refugees from Spain.[4] Similarly, in the twentieth century, Jewish refugees from an increasingly anti-Semitic Europe—notably Albert Einstein and Edward Teller—helped make the United States the first nuclear power. In short, the ability to exert political power does not imply an ability to achieve what one wishes to achieve with that power, or even an ability to avoid overwhelming negative repercussions.

Control of political power can, however, sometimes be used to enlarge the options of society at large in two very different ways. In relations between governmental units, the more powerful unit can reduce the counterproductive activities of the less powerful units. Thus, in mid-twentieth-century America, the federal government of the United States eliminated extensive racial discrimination laws in the Southern states. Independent political units may also voluntarily agree to mutual reductions of their counterproductive activities. For example, when Germany was a fragmented collection of states and principalities, tariff and other barriers to trade among these numerous political entities severely handicapped the economic development of the whole region. By agreeing to remove many of these barriers when they formed the *Zollverein* or customs union in the early nineteenth century, these states and principalities freed the peoples of that region to develop the great human and natural resources already present.

With the essential resource of government being power, its essential mode of operation is the use of that power to constrain the options of people and organizations within its jurisdiction. All too often in history, government has constrained the options of racial and ethnic minorities much more so than it has constrained the options of the majority population. That has been true of independent republics like the United States, colonial regimes like those in Malaya or Australia, dynastic states like Japan, or the Ottoman, Russian, or Habsburg empires. In addition to such deliberate racial differentiation in the application of power, the general functioning of government and politics often has a racial impact, even when the intentions and explicit laws and policies are not racial.

Among the political institutions which greatly affect the fate of racial and cultural groups are (1) law and order, (2) democracy, (3) political parties, (4) the military, and—sometimes—(5) foreign governments in the homelands of particular racial or ethnic groups. These all have the potential for both positive and negative effects.

## Law and Order

One of the most important ways in which government's ability to reduce people's options can be used to *increase* other options is by maintaining the general conditions of law and order. This reduces everyone's options to inflict violence or to practice theft against others, but law and order is more than a zero-sum process, because the increased security it produces increases people's options to do things other than spend vast amounts of time and resources safeguarding their own belongings and personal safety. It is only because virtually everyone prefers losing the first set of options, in order to have the second, that law and order represent a clear social gain. Even criminals do not want *general* lawlessness or anarchy, for that would mean that each criminal would have to barricade himself in his home before daring to fall asleep and could not enjoy his ill-gotten gains in peace.

The economic importance of law and order is enormous, in a wide variety of contexts. Land subject to marauding raids is less likely to be farmed, regardless of its fertility. Such insecurity caused much land to lie idle in parts of Scotland and in parts of Africa, before outside conquerors subjugated the local combatants or raiders in both places, imposing peace under foreign hegemony.[5] The great overland routes through Central Asia that allowed medieval Europe to trade with the Orient varied greatly in their usability, according to whether each route was all under one political hegemony, as in the days of Genghis Khan, or whether trade through the region was subject to lawless raids and numerous local extortions.[6] Parts of southeastern Europe were virtually unpopulated during the era of Turkish raids there, and then became densely populated after the late eighteenth century, when those raids ceased. The new security permitted crops to be grown where before there were only a few herdsmen who could flee with their animals in the face of danger, whereas immobile crops in the field would have been burned by marauders.[7]

Law and order are not necessarily just. Their economic benefits depend more on their stability and predictability than on their even-handedness. Groups clearly given second-class status in the law have nevertheless prospered in stable societies, where that law has protected their persons and property. Often they have prospered more so than those with higher legal status. Obvious historical examples include the overseas Chinese in Southeast Asia, the Jews in Eastern Europe, and non-Moslems in general in the Ottoman Empire.

Law and order must be contrasted, not only with anarchy or with military insecurity, but also with a regime of arbitrary power, whether expressed in the extortions of individual officials or the unbridled confiscations of government. Pervasively corrupt or arbitrary governments inhibit economic development as much as a lawless frontier. It was only after the Romans established law and order over large parts of Britain that commerce and industry flourished there. It was only after modern imperialist powers established law and order over large areas of Southeast Asia that vast numbers of people from China and India migrated there, contributing to the economic development of the region.

Law and order directly foster investment. Britain's pioneering role as the first industrial nation was greatly facilitated by its ability to raise large amounts of capital cheaply, under stable laws securing property. People were willing to invest their savings in long-term ventures, including those which built railroads, canals, and other infrastructure, at very low rates of return because (1) those returns were protected by property law and (2) the stability of the currency meant that even modest rates of return would not be wiped out by inflation. By contrast, countries in which investments are jeopardized by the extortions of officials and the confiscations ("nationalization") of government find it difficult to attract needed capital, either from their own people or from foreign investors, except for projects having high and quick returns. In turn, these high and quick returns to foreigners are likely to provoke a political hostility to "exploitation" which inhibits the inflow of longer-term investments, in sufficient quantities to allow competition to reduce profit rates to more modest levels.

The huge investments of international capital which helped spread the industrial revolution throughout the world went primarily to countries where law and order were already established, such as the nations of Europe or European offshoot societies like those of North America, Australia, or South Africa. These massive investments dwarfed European investments in those less developed regions of the world where law and order were less firmly established, either by indigenous rulers or by colonial powers.

Just as the establishing of law and order facilitates investment, so the mere threat of a breakdown in one aspect of law and order—property rights, for example—can send capital fleeing the country. When anti-Asian sentiment surfaced as Kenya approached its transition from colony to independent nation in the middle of the twentieth century, Asian capital was sent abroad in large amounts—not to India or Pakistan, but to London.[8] Capital is cosmopolitan.

In many countries—perhaps most countries—the establishment of law and order over large regions was a long and arduous process. Yet those who today advocate that government's economic role is to preserve the essential framework of law and order, leaving more specific economic decisions to the marketplace, are accused of saying that government should "do nothing"—even though (1) it took centuries to accomplish what is today called "nothing" and (2) that "nothing" has brought widespread economic benefits to great numbers of human beings.

The economic importance of law and order is demonstrated not only by the differing facility of attracting capital and immigration into areas where it is less established or better established, but also by comparisons of the economic performances of different groups in the same society, when unusual circumstances cause some groups to be more subject to a reliable framework of law and order than are other groups. A militarily powerful nation may, for example, obtain unilateral "extraterritoriality" privileges for its citizens operating in a weaker foreign country. These citizens of the more powerful country then carry on their economic activities within their own framework of law and order, unhindered by the caprices or extortions of local authorities, who may continue to stifle the economic activities of the local people.

While the special extraterritoriality of diplomatic personnel is widely accepted as a reciprocal arrangement between nations, the unilateral imposition of extraterritoriality for one country's nationals operating in another country has been bitterly resented as humiliating infringements of sovereignty. However, the Ottoman Turks, after their historic conquest of Constantinople established their empire, *voluntarily* extended extraterritoriality to selected countries who were in no position to impose such a demand on them. This clearly suggests that there can be benefits to the host country in such special arrangements for law and order. More international trade and investment can be attracted when foreign traders and investors are shielded from the uncertainties, inefficiencies, caprices, extortions, or confiscations of local authorities.

In later centuries, during the declining phase of the Ottoman Empire as an international power, more and more European powers sought a special legal status, not only for their own respective nationals operating on Ottoman territory, but also for Ottoman subjects operating as agents for European governments or businesses. These agents were typically Christians—notably Armenians and Greeks—or Jews, rather than the Moslems who made up a majority of the empire's subjects. While these privileges conferred an advantage on foreign economic enterprises and domestic ethnic minorities competing with the majority of Ottoman subjects, this arrangement was not simply a zero-sum transfer of benefits. Much of the economic development of the empire's modern sectors was the work of these foreigners and domestic minorities, who had the benefit of a more reliable framework of law and order.[9] The Ottoman Empire was not unique in voluntarily extending to foreigners the right to live within its borders under their own laws. German farmers were encouraged to settle in other central European nations in the eighteenth century by being allowed to live under their own laws and customs in these new lands, which sought the advantage of the more advanced German farming methods.[10]

Those who focus on the justice or injustice of a given law and order, especially as regards racial and ethnic minorities, sometimes regard the undermining of that law and order as beneficial to oppressed groups. Yet, as law and order become less effective, often the least fortunate suffer more than others from its breakdown. In a city where crime is rampant, the poor suffer not only the full brunt of its physical dangers, but also the indirect costs of higher prices in neighborhoods plagued by theft and vandalism.[11] More fortunate groups can live in buildings with security systems and security personnel, and in neighborhoods located strategically away from the worst areas. Historically, the lawlessness of a frontier society, the collapse of an empire, or the disruption of civil government by the vagaries of warfare, have all unleashed violence against vulnerable minorities.

The Chinese were victims of such mob violence during the vigilante era in San Francisco and during the interregnum between the withdrawal of Japanese forces from Indonesia after World War II and the reestablishment of Dutch rule. The Volga Germans became targets of violence and looting by their neighbors during the anarchic period when Red and White armies contended for supremacy after the Bolshevik revolution. Jews suffered repeatedly from the breakdown of law and order in medieval Europe. The great increase in violent crime in the United States that began in the 1960s claimed a disproportionate number of black victims, with more blacks than whites being murdered in some years,[12] even though blacks have been less than one-eighth of the population of the country.

## Democracy

The apparently simple concept of democracy—majority rule—becomes not only complicated but confused when various desirable goals such as freedom, equality, or the dignity of the individual are made part of the definition of democracy. Whether majority rule will in fact lead towards such things is an empirical question rather than a foregone conclusion. A painfully large amount of evidence indicates that majority rule can lead in the opposite direction, especially in multiracial or multiethnic societies. It does not inevitably or invariably do so, but the extent to which democracy promotes or negates these goals, and the conditions under which it has one effect rather than the opposite, are questions that need investigating. Settling the matter by definition preempts such an investigation.

In numerous colonial nations which emerged into independence after World War II, racial, ethnic, and religious minorities were unenthusiastic about independence, if not positively opposed to it, because they foresaw that majority rule would mean a trampling on their rights. The Karens in Burma, Africans in Zanzibar, Moslems in the Philippines, Chinese in

Indonesia, Maronites in Lebanon, and Tamils in Sri Lanka[13] were only some of the minorities with such fears—all too often justified, as subsequent events proved. For such groups, democracy did not mean freedom, equality, or the dignity of the individual. It was precisely their concerns over the prospective loss of such things that led them to prefer living under autocratic colonial rule.

Analogously, the rule of semicolonial state governments, supported by the bayonets of an occupying army, provided more protection of the rights of American blacks in the immediate post–Civil War South than this minority was to have when such governments were later superseded by governments more democratically elected and more broadly representative of the white Southern majority. It was precisely these latter Southern governments which instituted pervasive segregation and legalized discrimination, as well as devising new means of political disfranchisement, and which tolerated extralegal vigilante violence, including widespread lynchings of blacks.

Democracy is, of course, also capable of protecting the rights of minorities, or even of making special provisions for their advancement. In the second half of the twentieth century, such roles were assumed by democratic governments in the United States, New Zealand, Israel, India, Britain, and Canada, for example. Political parties representing ethnic coalitions also attempt to mute intergroup conflicts and moderate differences—the Alliance Party in Malaysia in the late twentieth century and the multiethnic political machines in American cities during the European immigrant era being examples of this. Democracy alone, however, is not enough to indicate which way political action and governmental policy will affect racial and ethnic groups. For that, it is necessary to look more closely at the nature of political parties, or of military forces, or sometimes the political actions of various groups' countries of origin.

## Political Parties

Political parties in ethnically diverse societies may play either a moderating or a polarizing role, depending upon the nature of the political competition. In democratic political systems, with all groups franchised and none able to organize a majority on purely ethnic issues, the competition to maximize electoral support requires mollifying the various ethnic groups and—where egalitarian principles or fear of national divisiveness are widespread concerns among the electorate at large—observing at least outward decencies, even toward ethnic groups that vote overwhelmingly for an opposing party.

In the United States, for example, the fact that most Jews vote for liberal Democrats does not mean that the Republican party can run for office on an anti-Semitic platform, which would repel Gentile voters as well as Jews, and Republican voters as well as Democrats. No Republican politician can proclaim himself a champion of Gentiles in the way in which a politician in Sri Lanka can proclaim himself a champion of the Sinhalese or a politician in Trinidad or Guyana can proclaim himself a champion of the Indians. Nor is this merely a matter of personal conviction, morality, or ideology. Politicians in all these countries are preoccupied with getting elected. The differences must be explained in terms of the political conditions which promote moderation and those that promote polarization.

For ethnic polarization to be a politically viable and attractive policy for office-seekers, it is not sufficient that particular groups vote overwhelmingly for one party while other groups vote overwhelmingly for another party. If ideology, economic self-interest, candidate charisma, party loyalty, and other such considerations provide the basis for a substantial proportion of the votes, then the parties are not ethnic parties, whatever the ethnic composition of their voters. The emergence of ethnic political parties, as in Nigeria, Sri Lanka, Trinidad, or Guyana, requires not only that particular groups give their voting support to particular parties but also that (1) those parties are dependent for their voting support almost exclusively on an ethnically defined constituency, that (2) their chances of gaining significant political support outside that ethnic constituency are virtually nil, and that (3) open appeals to ethnicity, including explicit antagonism to other groups, does not cost them votes within their existing constituency or in the general population.

All these are different ways of expressing the same condition—that major ethnic political parties are viable only where ethnic issues have *already* superseded class, ideological, charismatic, and other considerations, and where offending one group does not offend others outside that group. In short, such a society already exhibits ethnic factionalism. The question here is whether political parties moderate or accentuate existing antagonisms under these conditions.

Without all three prerequisites for a truly ethnic party, the tendency of political competition is to moderate rather than to accentuate existing ethnic conflicts. The percentage of black Americans who voted for Democratic party presidential candidates during the 1980s was similar to the overwhelming vote of particular ethnic groups for particular parties in Trinidad, Guyana, Ghana, Nigeria, and the Congo Republic[14]—but this did not make American political parties ethnic. Only the ability to gain political control of the government with an appeal *on ethnic grounds* to one ethnic group alone makes increased ethnic polarization a viable policy for politicians. Whether or not polarization promotes the long run viability of the country is another question entirely—and one often ignored by those seeking office and power.

The gaining of control of government power in South Africa by the Afrikaaner-dominated Nationalist Party in 1948 did not merely reflect existing racial and ethnic divisions, but significantly added to them through apartheid policies. Similarly, the gaining of regional political power *on an explicitly racial basis* by whites in the Southern United States after the Reconstruction era not only reflected but accentuated racism through Jim Crow laws. Whites were, of course, just as politically dominant in the rest of the United States, but the fact that that dominance was organized along ideological, economic, and other lines meant that there was no racial or ethnic party, as such, in the North and therefore no comparable incentives to exacerbate existing racial or ethnic conflicts. On the contrary, the role of American political parties representing multiethnic constituencies has historically been to mollify, reconcile, or at least paper over ethnic conflicts. For decades the same political party—the Democrats—played this moderating role in the North while playing a polarizing role in the South.

There were both racial and ethnic conflicts outside the South, but none of the ethnic groups was large enough to produce an electoral majority, and while whites as a whole were a clear racial majority, the relatively small black population of the North was not of sufficient concern to make racial politics preemptive over class, ideological, economic, and other issues. Thus, the United States outside the South developed a two-party system with multiethnic parties, while in the South a single race-based party—the Democrats—reigned supreme from before the Civil War until well after World War II. The coexistence of these diametrically opposite political tendencies in different regions of the same country, at the same time, and in the same national party, highlights the different effects of ethnically organized political parties and of political parties organized on various other nonethnic bases, even when the actual racial composition of the two kinds of party voters and leaders is quite similar.

Even more dramatic examples of the difference between ethnic and multiethnic parties in their effects on existing racial or ethnic conflicts can be found in the post-independence history of Sri Lanka and Malaysia. Initially, at independence, relations between the Sinhalese and the Tamils in Sri Lanka were nowhere near as hostile as those between the Malays and the Chinese in Malaysia, where a long civil war pitted Chinese Communist guerrillas against Malay troops and Malay villagers. Yet, over the years, the Malaysian multiethnic coalition government has generally managed to moderate potentially explosive resentments. By contrast, the relative amicability of relations between the Sinhalese and the Tamils at the time of national independence[15] has been turned into ever more bitter hostility by ethnic political parties outbidding each other for the support of one group or the other, with moderates on both sides being forced to ever more extreme positions by rivals for the same ethnic votes.[16]

The transition from the initial condition of mutual tolerance in Sri Lanka to the threshold level of group antagonism necessary to create ethnic-issue parties was produced in a few years by the skilled political demagoguery of Sinhalese political leader S. W. R. D. Bandaranaike, as part of his campaign to become prime minister in 1956. Once ethnic issues became preemptive for parties of all ideological leanings, ever more extreme demands from both the Sinhalese and the Tamils followed. Moreover, this political polarization has in turn increased cultural polarization, even among the cosmopolitan elements of both groups. Whereas highly educated Sinhalese or Tamils once spoke English in their homes, and spoke their respective group languages only to servants or other lower-class people, that changed after political polarization:

> Persons in these strata today, although English remains their first language, can read and write Sinhala or Tamil, increasingly speak to their children in one of those languages, and generally are educating their children in the Sinhala or Tamil medium.[17]

In short, the highly educated, cosmopolitan, elements of both Sri Lankan groups—once looked to hopefully as a bridge between the two communities, in part because they literally spoke the same language[18]— have themselves joined in the general polarization, now cultural as well as political. While this has been characterized as "a triumph of primordial identification and loyalty over the new identifications based on class, urbanization, and Westernization,"[19] it was in fact a product of a set of political incentives which has produced the same result in both Western and non-Western societies alike.

Although the threshold level of group antagonism necessary for ethnic-issue parties can be produced by a single political demagogue, the logic of ethnic-issue competition then acquires a life of its own, independent of the demagogue who initiated it. In the case of Sri Lanka, Bandaranaike's attempt to defuse ethnic tensions, after they had served his purpose by gaining him the prime ministership, led only to his being assassinated by one of the extremists on his side. Racial or ethnic polarization is not a readily reversible process, once the prerequisites for ethnic-issue parties have been created.

In some countries, such as Kenya and Zambia, the political polarization process was ended only by establishing one-party authoritarian government.[20] Malaysia dampened ethnic politics by making it a crime to question publicly the government's ethnic policy.[21] Nigeria recovered from an even more bitter and bloody civil war than that in Malaysia, changing its political system to require national electoral support for its president, which meant multiethnic support in a country whose various regions were dominated by different groups. While Nigeria continued to have strong ethnic voting patterns, the new policies did achieve the desired effect of de-escalating ethnic tensions, which had been at literally murderous levels, in direct contrast to the opposite trend, created by opposite political incentives, in Sri Lanka.

Even minority politicians with no real hope of achieving national power have every incentive to contribute to polarization, despite the fact that their outnumbered people will probably end up the losers, if their opponents have already made ethnicity an overriding issue. In such an atmosphere, the individual career prospects of the minority politician are enhanced as he assumes the role of defender of his beleaguered people.

Not everyone chooses to join in polarization, but the systemic effect may be the same as if they did. Parties and individuals ideologically opposed to ethnic polarization have suffered devastating political losses in such circumstances—in Sri Lanka, Guyana, and Trinidad, for example—leading some to do abrupt about-faces, in order to save their political careers.[22] Others have simply disappeared from the political scene, for lack of electoral support.

In the American South, during the era of one-party racial politics, there was no racial minority political party because Negroes were disfranchised. The erosion of racism within the region and the national imposition of voting rights for black Americans in the 1960s combined to destroy, very rapidly, the one-race, one-party system that had persisted in the region for more than a century. Given that whites were still a substantial majority in most Southern states, enfranchisement alone would have been insufficient to end racial polarization politics. Enfranchisement could simply have allowed black minority parties to emerge and to coexist alongside the white majority party, as single-group majority and minority parties exist in Sri Lanka, Trinidad, Guyana, and other places. Had race remained preemptive over all other political issues combined, for virtually the entire white population of the South, such a situation would have been politically viable in the region, with all the continuing potential for escalating polarization. What was necessary to break the back of the old racial politics of the South was at least a substantial minority of white voters responsive to other issues—including racial peace—to split the white vote, and so make it politically impossible for any party to antagonize the entire black electorate and expect to win. This was in fact the political situation in the South in the wake of the enfranchisement of blacks.

Two-party politics with biracial appeals spread rapidly through the South, with the strident "white supremacy" rhetoric of more than a century suddenly becoming taboo. Again, politics did not simply reflect public opinion. Under these circumstances, the incentives created by multiethnic, multiparty politics ran ahead of public opinion in moderating group antagonisms, just as single-party, single-race politics had exacerbated these antagonisms in the region for generations. The abruptness of the political change exceeded any likely pace of change in public opinion. In politics as in economics, there does not need to be an end to all racism for the effective power of racism to be broken. Competition is the crucial factor in both the economic and the political system.

In short, the rise of ethnic political parties—or the transformation of existing multiethnic, ideological, or interest-group parties into ethnic parties—is not only a response to ethnic divisiveness but also contributes to it, turning divisiveness into polarization. Conversely, competition among nonethnic parties has a moderating effect, as each party tries to entice additional voters from those beyond its own core supporters. In nonethnic, two-party systems, such as those in the United States, Britain, or Australia, both parties may crowd toward the center of the political spectrum in an attempt to compete for uncommitted votes. By contrast, ethnic political parties—as in Ghana, Sri Lanka, Trinidad, Guyana, or the Punjab—cannot compete effectively for voters beyond their own ethnic boundaries, and so have little incentive to moderate their ethnic claims and much reason to maximize their image of uncompromising dedication to the most sweeping forms of such claims.[23]

Even in situations where some groups have no political party because they are disfranchised—blacks in South Africa during the era of white minority rule, for example—political incentives can still have effects. Among the incentives to political moderation among disfranchised groups is the hope of gaining concrete concessions, even of a limited sort, which political moderates may then exhibit as trophies of their success and therefore as reasons for their constituency to support them and their approach. But, in situations where moderate demands are no more likely to be met than extreme demands, the extremists have the advantage of being able to politically outbid the moderates in rhetoric, without the corresponding disadvantage of being less able to deliver. In the early days of the African National Congress in South Africa, for example, the ANC demands were very moderate, but the refusal of the ruling whites to make even minor concessions enabled more militant and extreme elements to replace the moderates in the leadership of the ANC over the years.

By contrast, the very moderate leadership of Booker T. Washington was more successful in the United States, at least in the political sense that his approach retained the support of an important constituency (whether or not a majority) within the black population until his death and even beyond. Washington and his supporters could point to the fact that he was able to deliver, in terms of white financial support for the development of Tuskeegee Institute and other social ventures, even though Southern blacks remained during his lifetime almost as completely disfranchised as blacks in South Africa.

The original leaders of the African National Congress in South Africa were, in fact, conscious followers of Booker T. Washington, but his strategy failed politically there because South African whites were more intransigent, leading to a black leadership in South Africa that ultimately became much more extreme than the leadership of American blacks. Some observers have regarded the original demands of the ANC—such as token representation of blacks in the political councils of the nation—as demands quite acceptable to most South African whites by the 1980s, but of course these were no longer the ANC demands by then, in part because of the political incentives created by the unresponsiveness of an earlier generation of whites.[24]

## Military Politics

Military forces are seldom ethnically representative of their respective societies.[25] At one time, half the officers in the Malaysian air force were Chinese and only one-third were Malay—just the reverse of their proportions in the population of the country.[26] More than half the noncommissioned officers in the Soviet military were Ukrainians.[27] It has been common in many African and Asian states for minority ethnic groups to form a majority of the armed forces, or of the officer corps.[28] Whether these ethnic disparities represent conscious policies or the consequences of social patterns, they often have political implications, especially in newly established states vulnerable to military coups. However, ethnically motivated intrusions of the military into civilian politics is often preceded by ethnically motivated intrusions of civilian politicians into the internal military chain of command.[29] Ethnic polarization and military politics have made an explosive mixture in countries around the world.

Just as political careers are relatively more attractive to groups with less favorable economic alternatives, so are military careers in the lower ranks. Accordingly, in many colonial countries, the less modernized of the indigenous peoples—often from rural hinterlands—have supplied a disproportionate share of the ordinary soldiers in the colonial armies. This pattern existed in colonial Burma, Iraq, Nigeria, Somalia, and Indonesia, among other places.[30] Where the colonial power was deliberately selective on an ethnic basis, the groups sought for military service were often those noted for martial qualities, combined with political reliability—the Sikhs and Gurkhas in India being examples of such deliberate recruitment.

When colonial peoples were eventually allowed into the commissioned officer corps, often very different ethnic groups supplied officers than those which supplied the enlisted soldiers. This was especially so when becoming a commissioned officer required education at military academies, rather than promotion from the ranks. An educated officer corps has tended to draw upon the more modernized indigenous ethnic groups, whereas the enlisted men have come from more traditional ethnic or tribal regions. Thus, while the enlisted ranks of the Nigerian colonial army had a substantial majority of Hausa riflemen, more than half of its first African commissioned officers were Ibos. In Ceylon, Ghana, and Iraq, indigenous officers were trained at European military academies. But where officers were primarily promoted from the ranks, as in Kenya or Togo, their ethnicity was of course that of the enlisted ranks—which is not, however, to say that it was that of the general population. In colonies where both methods of commissioning officers were used, as in Uganda or Guinea, the officers promoted from the ranks were ethnically different from those commissioned out of military academies.[31]

The change from colonial status to national independence has also often affected the ethnic makeup of the military. Where the ethnic composition of the military, and especially of the military officers, has differed greatly from the ethnic composition of the ruling civilian politicians, ethnic polarization in the society has often led to political intervention designed to change the ethnic composition of the military, or to military intervention designed to change the ethnic composition of the civilian government—or to both. Ghana, Uganda, and Libya are examples of mutual interference of this sort.[32] Election results in ethnically polarized societies have been reversed by military coups when the ethnic group achieving political power through the ballot was hostile to the ethnic group in charge of the military, as in Sierra Leone or in Fiji.[33] But military power, with or without coups, has put ethnic minorities in political power from Uganda to Surinam.[34]

The suspicions and threats inherent in polarized societies with civilian and military power centered in opposing ethnic groups often make it nearly impossible for the line of demarcation between military and political institutions to be respected and maintained. Political attempts to forestall coups have included ethnic favoritism in military recruiting and promotion, sometimes extending to purges of military officers for political reasons, and sometimes assignment of top officers to either sensitive or inconsequential command posts, according to their ethnicity (and therefore presumed loyalties). This political violation of the integrity of the military in turn generates hostility even among nonpolitical career officers, and may itself promote or precipitate a coup. But failure to take such precautions against a coup can also be disastrous. In short, ethnic polarization creates military as well as political and social tensions that may often be virtually impossible to resolve.

In some situations, where there is an external threat felt by all, the military can become a source of moderation of ethnic tensions. Men of different ethnic backgrounds, living side by side on a daily basis in military units and in some cases being dependent upon each other for safeguarding one another's lives, often develop a better trust and understanding than they would have had in civilian life, where they lived in separate enclaves or in different social strata. The role of Irish soldiers in the British army in two world wars helped ease ethnic differences in the post-war eras.[35] The exemplary military record of Japanese American fighting units during World War II caused a virtually overnight change in other Americans' attitudes toward them.[36] The role of the Middle Eastern and North African Jews in defending Israel against military attack likewise helped bridge the gap between them and the European and American Jews in Israel.[37]

Where the external enemy is of the same race or ethnicity as one of the internal ethnic minorities, however, that group may well suffer from the animosities generated in warfare. Germans in Russia, Australia, and Brazil, for example, suffered from Germany's warfare against these countries during both World Wars.[38] But this is not inevitable. In the United States, the anti-German feelings of the First World War were not repeated in the Second, and hostile feelings against Japanese Americans were very quickly turned around by their own proofs of patriotism at home and abroad.

As an organization with a vital mission and a powerful set of traditions and codes of its own, the military can in many cases moderate ethnicity by its own overriding imperatives involving life and death. But the ability of strong ethnic feelings to endanger the military's role and effectiveness has led numerous nations to segregate different groups serving on military duty, whether in peace or war. Some ethnically segregated units existed in the American military from the Revolutionary War to the Civil War—Germans, for example, serving in German-speaking units—and racially segregated units were common as late as World War II. Imperial armies in the era of European colonialism often assigned segregated troops far from their local areas, whether in the colony or abroad, and the Soviet military continued this practice.

No single outcome can be predicted from the complex interaction of ethnicity, polarized politics, and the military, but many coups and much bloodshed indicate that all are powerful forces whose clashes can be catastrophic. But, while military coups have been a way of life in parts of Latin America and in many Third World countries emerging into national independence since World War II, the threat of military coups has long been remote in northwestern European nations and in their offshoot societies around the world, such as the United States or Australia. Perhaps it is the exemption of these latter nations from military intervention in civilian government which requires explanation, rather than the susceptibility of so many other nations to it. As in other fields, the mere copying of the institutions of stable societies cannot create the historically evolved traditions and attitudes that make those institutions work.

## Homeland Politics

The relationship between an ethnic minority community and its foreign homeland can produce a variety of political patterns. These have varied from group to group, and from time to time and place to place with a given group. Homeland politics include (1) efforts of a particular ethnic group to have its country of residence and citizenship adopt more favorable policies toward the ancestral homeland; (2) efforts of the homeland to get another country to adopt more favorable policies toward emigrants from the homeland and their descendants; and (3) homeland efforts to use its compatriots in other countries to advance its own national self-interest.

The relationship between cultural ties and political ties with a homeland is by no means simple and direct. Italians, for example, have tended to retain some cultural patterns from Italy, even after living for generations in other countries, but they have seldom exerted much political pressure for their respective countries of residence to behave more favorably toward Italy. Likewise, Germans in czarist Russia were, for generations, a highly separate and self-conscious enclave of German culture, while loyally serving the Russian Empire, even during the war against Germany in 1914–17. However, during the Second World War, hundreds of thousands of Germans defected from the Soviet Union to follow the German armies in retreat. Years of brutal treatment by Soviet authorities had much to do with the change.[39]

As far back as the nineteenth century, organizations within Germany attempted to maintain ties and wield influence with Germans in foreign lands, with and without the help of the German government. But Germans in Bohemia and in the Baltic long maintained their local political loyalties and were cosmopolitan in their willingness to welcome rising indigenous individuals into the dominant German culture. Yet the emergence of indigenous Czech chauvinism ultimately provoked German counter-chauvinism. In Czechoslovakia, the Germans in the Sudentenland became the

focal point of an international crisis in 1938 that led to the dismemberment of the Czech state. German governments have used, or attempted to
use, Germans in other countries as instruments of national foreign policy,
even before the rise of Hitler and the Nazis. These efforts have repeatedly
operated to the detriment of German communities in other lands, such as
Australia, Brazil, or the United States—all countries where nativist backlashes were particularly strong during the First World War.

International ethnic politics need not originate in the ancestral homeland or involve the homeland at all. For centuries, Jews in various countries have attempted to help one another, even when there was no ancient
or modern state of Israel. Mennonites have likewise maintained international ties with one another, unrelated to national governments. In the
later and declining Ottoman Empire, various European governments
assumed a protective role toward various Ottoman minorities who were
neither citizens nor descendants of citizens of these particular European
powers. These were typically Christian minorities. Russia, for example,
assumed a protective role toward members of the Orthodox religion,
France was protective toward Catholics, and Britain and Prussia toward
Protestants.[40] On an individual basis, members of these and other groups,
including Jews, might be extended diplomatic status by one of these protective governments for whom they were working in one capacity or
another, or were affiliated with as trading partners.[41] Many of the phenomena associated with homeland politics appeared in these relationships, notably divided loyalties by the protégés and a hostility toward
them by the surrounding populace during periods of strife or tension with
their foreign protectors.

Just as an ancestral link to a foreign country is not essential for some
of the social and political phenomena associated with homeland politics,
so the foreign link need not be a government. The Missouri Synod of the
Lutheran church in the United States has operated as an independent
center of influence on German communities in other countries, competing
with Lutheran organizations from Germany in intellectual and financial
support for affiliated religious bodies and their schools abroad. In Brazil
and Australia, for example, Lutheran organizations affiliated with American and German organizations differed in their respective responses to
Germany's military aggressions in Europe.[42]

The maintenance of a homeland culture in foreign countries is neither
a necessary nor a sufficient basis for political ties with the country of ori-

gin. Irish Americans have long been thoroughly acculturated in the United States, differing in no essential way from the general American population economically, socially, or politically. Yet Irish Americans have also long been a major source of the financial support that has kept the violence going in Ulster County. Jewish Americans have likewise become thoroughly Americanized, and yet they are the crucial source of the financial and political support from the United States that makes Israel a viable nation in the Middle East. Black American voters have been, to a lesser extent, a factor in American foreign policy toward African nations in general and South Africa in particular. Yet cultural affinities between Afro-Americans and Africans are tenuous at best.

The homeland can, in some cases, be a source of protection for their ethnic offshoots in other lands. Successive governments in China, under both the Kuomintang and the Communists, have asserted some form of protection for the overseas Chinese, though with highly questionable effectiveness in many cases, especially prior to World War II. During the same era, a more powerful Japan was much more effective in championing the cause of Japanese living overseas. The United States, for example, peremptorily cut off all immigration from China in 1882, leaving vast numbers of Chinese men stranded in the United States without their wives and children, often eking out pathetic existences in isolation for the rest of their lives.[43] Japanese immigrants were spared this fate because of the military power of Japan, which could not be insulted with such impunity. The face-saving "gentlemen's agreement," arranged between the United States and Japan, meant that Japanese families could be reunited in America, or new brides brought over to join husbands they had married by proxy, while Japan itself stopped further emigration to the U.S.

Japan took an active interest in overseas Japanese communities throughout the Western Hemisphere, not only negotiating government-to-government agreements regarding them, but also in some cases actively participating in the creation of Japanese colonies in other countries. In Asia, overseas Japanese became sources of military intelligence useful to Japan in its lightning conquests in the region following destruction of the American fleet at Pearl Harbor. While the reaction to potential Japanese espionage and sabotage threats were extreme in the United States, Canada, and Peru, such potential threats were not imaginary. Government officials in the United States would have needed to know much more about the cultural history of Japanese Americans than they did to realize that they were a group very loyal to the United States, in contrast to the Japanese in Brazil, who remained fiercely pro-Japan throughout the Second World War.

Remittances to the homeland from abroad have also, in some cases, been major economic factors within the homeland or in its international balance of payments with other nations. Remittances of Chinese Americans made the localities of their origins in China notably more prosperous.[44] Similarly, remittances from Japanese Americans contributed to the development of Hiroshima,[45] with the ironic and tragic result of making it a prime military target in World War II. By the late twentieth century, remittances from Asian workers in oil-rich Middle East nations were similarly substantial contributors to the economic well-being of their families back home and, in some cases, to their homelands' international balance of payments.[46]

While the homeland may, in some cases, help a branch of its people in a foreign country, often it will not even attempt to do so, when that would conflict with some other foreign policy objective. Despite the gruesome horrors perpetrated against the overseas Chinese (among others) under the Pol Pot regime in Kampuchea, China not only failed to protest publicly but remained an ally of the Kampuchean regime, as part of its foreign policy strategy of building regional alliances to offset the power of the Soviet Union and the United States in Asia.[47] Yet, under much less horrible conditions, the Chinese government dispatched ships to Indonesia to take Chinese refugees back to China after anti-Chinese riots in Indonesia, and opened its borders to many refugees from Vietnam at the time of the "boat people" exodus.[48] In both the latter cases, China's government was already at odds with the governments concerned, over other issues, and used the plight of the overseas Chinese in these countries as part of its propaganda campaign.

During the British colonial era in India, the Indian government often interested itself in the vicissitudes of Indians—especially Indian coolie labor—in foreign countries, publicly protesting, negotiating with other governments for better treatment of the Indians, or forbidding emigration from India to countries where conditions were deemed unsatisfactory. Nor was the colonial government in India deterred by the fact that the offending recipient country was almost invariably another member of the British Empire. Yet, ironically, after India became an independent nation, the Indian government has been far less assertive in such matters.[49] The foreign policy of India in the post-independence era has been directed toward achieving international stature as a leader among nonaligned Third World nations, and these have often been nations in which overseas Indians were oppressed or persecuted. In 1953, Indian Prime Minister Jawaharlal Nehru told the overseas Indians in Africa that they were "guests" of the Africans, "and if they do not want you, out you will have to go, bag and baggage."[50] Such prior acquiescence in the expulsions of people born and living in a country for generations was perhaps unique for any government. Certainly it did nothing to discourage African nations from forcing out native-born "guests" of Indian ancestry. In the most flagrant case, the summary expulsion of 50,000 Indians and Pakistanis from Uganda, stripped of their property and virtually destitute, it was the British rather than the Indian government which led the protests and pressured the Amin regime to moderate its brutal policies. In the case of discrimination against Indians in South Africa during the era of white minority rule, however, the government of India tried to intervene,[51] even though India had been quiescent when there was much worse treatment of Indians in Third World countries.

By contrast, Israel has interested itself in the fate of Jews in foreign countries, even when these were Jews whose Diaspora long antedated creation of the present Israeli state, and even when they were of a race never before resident in Israel—ancient or modern—such as Ethiopian Jews. The worldwide solidarity of Jews promoted by the Holocaust makes it politically impossible for the Israeli government to treat Jews in other countries as expendable, as so many other nations do their foreign offshoots, even for relatively modest foreign policy objectives.

## SOCIAL EFFECTS

If political institutions are inherently constrained in what results they can produce, political ideologies are not constrained in what they can promise. To maintain the plausibility of what they promise, however, they must first establish and then maintain a particular vision of social processes that will define a "solution" within the scope of political action. Whatever the real complex of social forces at work or the relative weights of various factors creating social difficulties for a particular group, political leaders tend to emphasize—sometimes exclusively—those factors for which a law or a government policy can be formulated, and those factors which lend themselves to the moral condemnation of other groups.

Factors such as intergroup differences in demographic characteristics, geographical distribution, skill levels, or cultural values tend to be ignored, however demonstrably important they may be in a cause-and-effect sense.[52] Thus, while the black population in late twentieth-century America suffered greatly from soaring rates of violent crime, from having much of its newborn generation raised by teenage mothers, and from widespread drug addiction, its political leaders have focused their efforts on correcting the failings (real and presumed) of the white population—racism, discrimination, and the like. Programs to reduce white peoples' wrongdoing have been not only more psychically and politically acceptable among black leaders; the correction of such wrongdoing can more plausibly be represented as being within the effective scope of government. This is wholly different from saying that investments of time and effort in this direction will more effectively raise the level of well-being among black Americans.

The attempt to project a group's ills or embarrassments onto other groups takes many forms. Even where other groups have created much of the economic development of a whole society—Indians in Uganda, Kenya, and Tanzania, the Chinese in Southeast Asia, non-Hispanic immigrants in Latin America—they have often been politically condemned for allegedly *lowering* the economic conditions of others, through "exploitation," the sending of wealth back to their homelands, or by other means. Their role in raising the economic level of the whole society tends to be ignored or downplayed politically, while they are depicted as *appropriating* a disproportionate share of the wealth that existed *somehow*. The widespread prevalence of this political pattern in highly disparate societies suggests common incentives rather than common cultural responses.

## Symbolism

Political "solutions" are often long on immediate symbolism and short on lasting results. This has happened too often, in too many parts of the world, to be accidental or mere failures of particular leaders. By its very nature, politics cannot create the skills, attitudes, and habits required for lasting economic achievement. What it can create instead are the tokens and symbols of such achievement. For example, politics cannot cause India's Assamese people to overtake its Bengalis or Marawis in work habits, skills, initiative, or entrepreneurship. Nor was that what the Assamese demanded:

... the Assamese increasingly demanded that Bengalis acknowledge the exclusive legitimacy of Assamese symbols in public life—not only the Assamese language, but Assamese cultural holidays, Assamese historic heroes, and recognition of the great events in Assamese history.[53]

These were not mere pious hopes. Violence, arson, and looting have backed up such demands on numerous occasions. When a university in Assam allowed Bengali students to take examinations in their own language in 1972, riots erupted in many towns in Assam and troops had to be called out to restore order.[54] Symbolic demands for cultural obeisance have been prominent in Indonesia as well. Pressure on the Chinese to change their names to Indonesian names and bans on such innocuous Chinese cultural manifestations as the colorful dragon processions,[55] which are common in many Chinese communities in other lands, exemplify a demand for politically imposed cultural victories over people whose economic achievements cannot be matched within any time period that is politically relevant. French separatists in Quebec have likewise made language and culture explosive issues in more than the figurative sense. Bombs were often their means of communicating frustration and anger against the more prosperous English-speaking Canadians. Pierre Trudeau emerged in Canada's Quebec province in the 1960s crying "French power,"[56] and having no substantive policy other than bilingualism and biculturalism.[57] He exemplified the symbolic substitute for economic achievements among a people historically less successful in the world in which they lived.

Preoccupation with political symbolism may be unlikely to produce either substantive achievement or the respect which such achievement brings. But if substantive advances are in fact achievable only after long enough time for major transformations of a whole people's productivity, then symbols, trinkets, and tokens may be all that are possible within a time horizon that is politically relevant.

## Group Polarization Patterns

Political anger and demands for privileges are, of course, not limited to the less privileged. Indeed, even when demands are made in the name of less privileged racial or ethnic groups, often it is the more privileged members of such groups who make the demands and who benefit from policies designed to meet such demands. These demands may erupt suddenly in the wake of the creation (or sharp enlargement) of a newly educated class, which sees its path to coveted middle-class professions blocked by the competition of other groups—as in India, French Canada, or Lithuania, for example.[58] While it is politically easier for the advantaged to seek further advantages in the name of the disadvantaged, they can also do so without such disguise, where they have sufficient political cohesion to make their raw power felt. Afrikaners in South Africa and Southern whites in the United States are extreme examples of a process in which nationalism, race, or religion are among the rallying cries around which to claim political privilege.

Sharp group differences in race, culture, or history may or may not exist in these political struggles. Such differences will be utilized politically when they do exist, but where the differences are small and even trivial to an outsider, they will simply be magnified for political purposes. India provides a number of examples of this, as a scholarly study has noted:

The nativist movement in Bombay opposes Tamil migrants but pays little attention to the more numerous Telugu-speaking migrants, though both are equally alien people from the south. The local population of the city of Hyderabad is hostile to migrants from the eastern part of the state with whom they share a common language, culture, and religion, but there is little resentment against Marathi, Kannada, and Tamil-speaking migrants from other states, with whom the cultural differences are far more substantial.[59]

Similar patterns have existed thousands of miles away in West Africa:

An instructive instance is provided by the vocal opposition in the Oyo and Ondo provinces of western Nigeria to the operations of produce buyers from Ijebu-Ode. For some years past Jebu traders from Ijebu-Ode have been operating in the neighboring districts of Oyo and Ondo purchasing cocoa and palm kernels. The Jebus are racially closely related to the population of Oyo and Ondo; ethnically and linguistically they are almost identical; moreover, the Jebus frequently engage local agents and lorry drivers to act on their behalf. These traders have secured supplies by outbidding the local produce buyers, and their activities have aroused opposition which is led by certain influential Yoruba chiefs. It is clearly unconnected with racial animosity and is a straightforward attempt by the local produce buyers to curtail competition which obviously benefits the local farmers. This is a particularly clear-cut example of the economic basis of ostensible xenophobia.[60]

Economics is often the key to such anomalies—and the implications reach well beyond India or Nigeria. Those cities in India with strident political nativist movements demanding preferential treatment for local groups have generally been cities where (1) most of the lower-middle-class positions were held by outside groups and where (2) there were growing numbers of the educated unemployed locally.[61] Such movements tend to be disproportionately staffed by, and appeal to, those who are part of the first generation of their family to be educated.[62] Ironically, it was such people who made Indians their target and prey in East Africa.

A rapid expansion of education is thus a factor in producing intergroup conflict, especially where the education is of a kind which produces diplomas rather than skills that have significant economic value in the marketplace. Education of a sort useful only for being a clerk, bureaucrat, or school teacher—jobs whose numbers are relatively fixed in the short run and politically determined in the long run—tend to increase politicized intergroup strife. Yet newly emerging groups, whether in their own countries or abroad, tend to specialize precisely in such undemanding fields. Malay students, for example, have tended to specialize in Malay studies and Islamic studies, which provide them with no skills with which to compete with the Chinese in the marketplace, either as businessmen, independent professionals, or technicians. Blacks and Hispanics in the United States follow a very similar pattern of specializing disproportionately in easier fields which offer less in the way of marketable skills. Such groups then have little choice but to turn to the government, not only for jobs but also for group preferences to be imposed in the marketplace, and for symbolic recognition in various forms.

Intergroup competition is, in one sense, inevitable in a world without unlimited resources, but the nature and intensity of this competition may be either moderated or accentuated, depending upon the institutions through which it takes place. The marketplace provides incentives for groups to moderate their competing demands upon the resources and output of the economy, because prices serve as an impersonal mechanism to cause self-rationing. Ethnic politics has just the opposite effect. Although politicians do not create economic benefits, they can transfer them, usually below cost and often free to the recipients. Just as prices force self-rationing, freeness permits self-indulgence. Competing demands readily escalate beyond what is available, without the constraining effect of price to convey the scarcity and production cost of what is demanded. The inherent constraints of economic life are not removed by political intervention. Rationing among individuals and groups is as much an inherent necessity as ever. The rationing must simply be done by other means, such as political struggles, violence, or the threat of violence.

Politics is not simply a mechanism for resolving existing differences among racial and ethnic groups. Politics can also generate and magnify such conflicts. Groups with little racial or cultural difference, such as the Andhras and the Telanganans in India,[63] may exaggerate what small differences there are, in order to compete for political favors as more or less artificially created social groups. Similarly, more or less "natural" social groups such as the Italians and Greeks in Australia, may make little or no effort to organize politically until *after* group-based benefits have been proffered by national political parties.[64] There is no such group as "Hispanics" anywhere in the world except in the United States, because only in the U.S. do government programs recognize such a category, thereby leading to political ethnic coalitions to capitalize on government grants and appropriations. In short, political favors are not simply responses to existing groups. The groups themselves may be artifacts created by political favors—and, even when not created by these favors, their degree of self-consciousness, politicization, or polarization may be functions of the availability of government largesse.

However detrimental polarization may prove to be to particular groups, or to the society as a whole, it may still be beneficial to those in official positions at various levels. In Thailand, for example, the abortive attempt to drive the Chinese out of the rice-exporting business by establishing a government monopoly did not achieve its goal, but did succeed in diverting profits to Thai soldiers, police officials, and politicians, whose cooperation became necessary to allow the Chinese entrepreneur to continue performing a function which only he could perform.[65] Much the same story of corruption and quasi-corruption could be found in Malaysia and Indonesia.[66] It is not at all uncommon for policies to be, simultaneously, politically effective and economically counterproductive. In Uganda, the expulsions of the East Indians were so popular that political pressure developed to do the same in neighboring Kenya, even though the economic consequences proved disastrous for Uganda.

While economic interests are sometimes significant in explaining political decisions, they are by no means universally valid explanations. Educated elites from less advanced groups may have ample economic incentives to promote polarization and preferential treatment policies, but the real question is why the uneducated masses from such groups give them the political support without which they would be impotent. Indeed, it is often the less educated masses who unleash the mob violence from which their elite compatriots ultimately benefit—as in Malaysia, Sri Lanka, or parts of India, Africa, or the United States, where such violence has led to group preference policies in employment, educational institutions, and elsewhere. The common denominator in these highly disparate societies seems to be not only resentment of other groups' success but also fear of an inability to compete with them, combined with a painful embarrassment at being so visibly "under-represented"—or missing entirely—in prestigious occupations and institutions. To remedy this within a politically relevant time horizon requires not simply increased opportunities but earmarked benefits directly given on a racial or ethnic basis.[67]

## Political Leadership

Politics is in large part a merchandising of "leadership"—not only particular leaders, movements, or parties but in addition the general *concept* of political leadership and its importance. It is not enough to represent oneself as the best leader, if in fact political leadership makes relatively little difference in many of the things that matter. The implicit agreement of contending leaders that leadership is important is too inherently self-serving to prove very much, but the most diverse political leaders share a common interest in exaggerating the importance of political leadership. Even ethnic minority leaders, with no realistic hope of acquiring decisive national power, have an incentive to join in the general promotion of the "leadership" concept, as that offers them individually their best chance of gaining whatever political positions may be available to them.

If ethnic political leadership were of major importance in economic advancement, then the more prosperous ethnic groups should exhibit higher quality leadership. It is by no means clear that they do. Prominent political leadership has been rare to nonexistent among the overseas Chinese in various countries where they rose from poverty to affluence. Such leadership as has emerged has tended to be the opposite of charismatic—to maintain low profiles personally and low profiles for the Chinese as a group. Much the same story could be told of the Jews in many countries over the centuries. Jews in Argentina resented even favorable attention from the political powers,[68] for heightened public awareness of Jews as a group could be dangerous in the long run.

Quality and prominence are, of course, very different aspects of leadership, so that little-known leadership might be wise and effective leadership in some circumstances. Even so, it is by no means clear that the leadership of more successful groups has been noticeably or consistently of better quality than the leadership of less fortunate groups. Part of the leadership of the overseas Chinese has historically been tong leadership. The tongs' clandestine and often criminal activities have generally brought increased resentments and repressions upon the Chinese from the authorities of their respective host societies. Ethnic political leadership has been slow to develop at all among Germans in a number of countries, the most notable exception being during the Nazi era, when such leadership among Germans abroad served largely to bring resentments, and in some cases repressions and violence, upon Germans as a whole.

Less successful ethnic groups are often richly endowed with leaders. Any well-informed American can readily name half a dozen black leaders, current or from U.S. history, but would probably have difficulty naming a similar number of Jewish or Japanese American ethnic leaders. Similarly, it is doubtful if they could name as many prominent Italian American ethnic leaders as prominent American Indian chiefs. Irish Americans have historically produced a number of notable ethnic leaders, but more so during their nineteenth-century poverty than during their twentieth-century rise to prosperity.

## Group Unity

The promotion of group unity has been one aspect of political leadership, but here again it is doubtful whether economically successful groups have been any more unified than less fortunate groups. Chinese communities in Southeast Asia have historically been fragmented according to their regional origins in China, and even among the small Chinese communities in the Caribbean, the Cantonese have remained residentially and socially separate from the Hakkas. Internal regional, caste, and religious separation among the peoples of India remain significant in overseas nations. Jews are divided into many groups that maintain separate synagogues and separate cemeteries, and have little or no intermarriage with one another. Mutual aid organizations among Italians overseas often run into the hundreds in a given country, because Italians from different provinces (or even cities or villages) maintain separate organizations and resist consolidation, even when this would produce better risk-spreading for insurance purposes. It is doubtful if internal divisions among American Negroes, for example, have historically been as severe as divisions among more economically successful groups—and certainly not more severe, either socially or politically.

The kind of idealized unity projected by political leaders and intellectuals has seldom existed among any racial or ethnic minority anywhere. Nor has the economic progress of racial or ethnic groups been much correlated with their closeness to, or remoteness from, such unity. The very attempt to enforce unity behind a particular political agenda can itself generate greater internal strife than would exist otherwise. Moreover, the history of ideas—both social and scientific—shows again and again that even the most brilliant thinkers typically grasp only part of the truth, and a fuller understanding comes only after a clash of ideas with others, even when those others are fundamentally mistaken on the whole. Those who insist on a monolithic group ideology are gambling the group's future on being able to achieve such an understanding without this process.

## Group Talents

All individual and group achievements require social preconditions, and therefore vary with the particular culture. But literary and verbal achievements—including political leadership—require much less social foundation than science, mathematics, or engineering. Even relatively backward peoples can produce clever politicians, shrewd demagogues, and masters of intrigue. It was not countries in the forefront of scientific or economic progress that produced Potemkin villages or the monumental corruption long characteristic of parts of the Middle East, the Far East, Latin America, and Africa.

Among the obstacles to economic development is often highly developed political corruption, and an attraction of native talent toward mutually thwarting and socially counterproductive activity, including political intrigue, military coups, and terrorist movements. The transfer of scientific and organizational knowledge from one society to another can be accomplished in a relatively short time, as history is measured. Japan is perhaps the classic example of that. In less than a century, it moved to the forefront of science and technology. But to create the whole range of social preconditions for receiving and applying cultural advances is a more formidable task, especially where the values of the culture are either unreceptive or tend to point people in entirely different directions.

In societies or among groups without the skills required for economic productivity and economic organization, politics is, if not "the only game in town," then at least one of the few games for which players have the necessary skills. As the main focus of talents and ambitions, politics can readily become both intricate and desperate. Preoccupation with politics may become a *substitute* for productivity, for either individuals or groups. An Idi Amin or an Adolf Hitler could hardly expect to acquire enough economic skills to rise from unpromising beginnings to anything resembling the prominence they achieved in politics. Groups or nations that are generations behind others in economic skills may also seek political shortcuts to importance, whether through ideology, symbolism, confiscations, terrorism, or war.

The issues they raise may be highly effective for political mobilization purposes, without being either the real causes of the problems their groups experience or the means of solution to the malaise they feel. However real the social suffering that has catapulted individuals to charismatic leadership, what they offer may represent only illusory solutions to illusory problems. Rationalistic attempts by others to reach compromise solutions with such political leaders may only escalate their demands or breed intransigence on demands that are already unreasonable. The turmoil, which others seek to end in rationalistic ways, may in fact be the very basis of the power held by political leaders. For example, India's attempt to bring peace through intervention in Sri Lanka produced murderous resistance, on both sides, by factions which have much more power to gain by continuation of the conflict than by its cessation.

## Ideological Visions

Beliefs, attitudes, ideals, and emotional loyalties have long been part of the glue that holds societies together. They have also facilitated or hampered the functioning of government, and fueled political movements. More specifically formulated and articulated political ideologies have played a larger and growing role in the two centuries since the French Revolution—first in Europe and in European offshoot societies, and then in other regions of the world to which European ideas were exported. These ideologies have affected race and culture, as they have affected all other aspects of human existence.

Among intellectuals especially, ideology can turn facts and morality upside down. For example, one scholar writing of the expulsions of Indians and Pakistanis from the newly independent nations of East Africa wrote:

> The crowning disgrace in the treatment of East African Asians came when the United Kingdom refused entry to Asian holders of British passports who had been booted out of Kenya. At least South Africa does not prevent its own citizens from entering its borders. If the Mother of Parliaments and the cradle of Western democracy behaved more badly than the most racist tyranny in the world, what do Asians have to look forward to?[69]

The ideological pattern of this kind of reasoning extends far beyond this particular episode or this particular intellectual, and so is worth examining more closely for its broader implications. The whole thrust of the attack is not against those in Africa who persecuted the Asians, who forcibly uprooted them from the land of their birth, and who expelled them from countries where their families had roots going back for generations. Moral indignation was not directed towards African governments that virtually confiscated all that the Asians had worked for and saved over several lifetimes, sending them destitute to new lands that most of these Asians had never seen. Instead, the thrust of the attack was against the country which provided them a haven and received them by the tens of thousands—more so than their own ancestral lands on the Indian subcontinent did.

Britain was singled out for condemnation as having "behaved more badly than the most racist tyranny in the world" simply because it eventually judged that it had reached the limits of its absorptive capacity for a foreign people who had never before lived in Britain, despite their possession of British passports from colonial days. In short, the sins of the Third World were glided over as silently as the humanitarianism of the West, in order to depict the limitations or imperfections of the West as peculiarly vicious.

Classic examples of such double standards and selective indignation can also be found in a vast literature on the history of slavery—a literature devoted almost exclusively to slavery in the Western world, with only a relative handful of writings on the larger number of slaves in the Islamic world.[70] Thus the institution of slavery, existing on every continent and going back thousands of years, is often discussed as if it were peculiar to Western civilization when, in fact, even the African slave trade was carried on by Arabs for centuries before Europeans took part, and continued for at least another century after the European slave trade to the Western Hemisphere ended. A scholarly—or at least academic—study of slavery has claimed that "legal barriers against manumission" were among the "distinctive characteristics" of "slavery in North America,"[71] when in fact legal barriers to manumission existed in Southeast Asia,[72] ancient Greece,[73] the French Antilles,[74] Surinam, and Curaçao.[75] Reports of how mild slavery was in Islamic countries, and how happy and contented the slaves were there, have been uncritically repeated by writers who would never accept such statements at face value when coming from the white slave society of the antebellum South in the United States.

Neither the enormous mortality rates of the trans-Saharan slave routes, nor the virtual absence of an African diaspora in Islamic countries which took more slaves from Africa than the West did, seems to arouse skepticism about the Middle Eastern version of the story of happy and contented slaves.

The biggest story about slavery—how this ancient institution, older than either Islam or Christianity, was wiped out over vast regions of the earth—remains a story seldom told. At the heart of that story was the West's ending of slavery in its own domains within a century and maintaining pressure on other nations for even longer to stamp out this practice. Instead, the West has been singled out as peculiarly culpable for a worldwide evil in which it participated, when in fact its only real uniqueness was in ultimately opposing and destroying this evil. Yet intellectuals have engaged in desperate attempts to discredit or downgrade the West's long moral crusade which ultimately destroyed slavery. These attempts have ranged from crude dogmatism about Western "economic interests" behind the abolition of slavery[76] to elusive insinuations along the same lines.[77]

A vast literature exists in which this same general ideological pattern is pervasive, whether the issue is slavery, racism, sexism, or other evils. In this literature, the sins and shortcomings of the human race are depicted as evils peculiar to the Western world, even when such evils have been demonstrably more prevalent or demonstrably worse in regions of the world ignored during outbursts of selective moral indignation. The reasons for such ideological patterns are a large and complex question. What is relevant here is that such ideologies are themselves a political force to be reckoned with. How successful these ideologies will prove to be in undermining the legitimacy of Western civilization, or in polarizing its races, is a question which only the future can answer.

## Ideological Vocabularies

Much of the vocabulary in which racial and ethnic issues are discussed and debated is a vocabulary less suited for clarification than for preventing consideration of factors embarrassing to those who hold a particular ideological vision. For example, performance differences among racial and ethnic groups are ideologically embarrassing to those who wish to present group differences in income or occupations as reflecting differential treatment of groups by "society," particularly when it is Western society. The whole issue of performance differences is often verbally preempted by confounding them with differential treatment, or initial good fortune, through the use of such words as "advantage" or "privilege," on the one hand, or "opportunity" or "access" on the other to characterize empirical differences in outcomes. This vocabulary transmutes all performance differences *ex post* into externally imposed "disadvantages" *ex ante*. Any group "under-represented" in desirable occupations or institutions is thus said to be "excluded"—regardless of what the facts may be.

While this pattern of verbal preemption has been widely used in discussing minorities in Western countries, such mental habits have become sufficiently general and automatic to be applied in other contexts as well—confusing differential results *ex post* with differential opportunities *ex ante*. The whole distinction between the internal characteristics of a group and the external circumstances it faces is thus verbally obliterated. Even without any immediate ideological purpose or intent, such ideologically based mental habits spread confusion, if not tendentiousness. For example, Koreans selling wigs in the United States have been said to face a "barrier" consisting of "their lack of a necessary combination of American business sophistication and capital."[78] Conversely, the success of Lebanese small businessmen in competing with European businessmen in colonial West Africa has been attributed to various Lebanese "advantages":

> The success of the Lebanese in outdistancing their European competitors is based on several factors. Firstly, the Lebanese had lower personal consumption levels than the Europeans. Besides, they had the advantage of having members of the family work in their shops and thus be an economic asset instead of a liability as was the case with the Europeans. In a situation where Lebanese skill was at least as good as their rivals, they could win over a gradually increasing share of the business by price com-

petition. In addition, the Lebanese skill was in some respects superior to that of the Europeans. The former had many more contacts with the African clients, were willing to talk and bargain with them at length, and therefore had closer knowledge of them. As a result, they could grant credit to the Africans with less risk than the European, could have earlier indication of shifts in consumer demand or crop prospects, and could manage the repayment relationship more skillfully. Another advantage of the Lebanese, in the early days at least, was that little of his profit had to be diverted to the amortization of fixed capital because there was little fixed capital. Thus, successful price competition by the Lebanese merchant was based on the advantages of both lower business and personal costs.[79]

Not one of these "advantages" was in fact an advantage. Each was a difference in performance, whether based on skill or sacrifice. At no point in this process did the Lebanese have any options available that were not equally available to Europeans. The Europeans simply did not choose to subject themselves to many of the conditions which the Lebanese endured. The *end result*—a supplanting of European businessmen by Lebanese—cannot be described by words which imply *an initial condition*, without ignoring the key intervening factor of performance. For example, if owning "little fixed capital" was an "advantage," why was it confined to "the early days" when the Lebanese, according to the same author, "started, practically penniless, as peddlers"?[80] In short, why would the Lebanese peddler later choose to relinquish his "advantage" of owning almost nothing, if that was in fact an advantage? Obviously, it would have been foolhardy for a poor Lebanese immigrant to have taken on the financial burden of buying or renting a shop at a time when he could barely survive as a peddler. But the fact that the Lebanese eventually did begin to own shops and other fixed capital suggests that there was no disadvantage to doing so.

The point is much more general than this particular example. Around the world, initial conditions are repeatedly confounded with end results by the use of words like "advantage" and "privilege," or "opportunity" and "access," to describe situations in which there are different performances. Negative words and phrases like "discrimination" and "denial" of "access" are likewise defined to include end results. Groups are said to be denied "access" to educational institutions, for example, when they simply fail to meet the same performance standards applied to others. Whenever group A outperforms group B, in any given set of circumstances, those cir-

cumstances are said to "favor" group A, according to the prevailing ideological vocabulary. Discussions of colonial Malaya, for example, abound in
statements that British policy there "favored" the Chinese, who in fact had
fewer rights and less government-provided education available than did
the Malays. The issue here is not facts, about which there is little dispute,
but rather about the ideological vocabulary in which facts are conveyed—
or obscured and distorted beyond recognition.

Only one step removed from this purely definitional obscuring of performance differences is the practice of explaining differential business
success by saying that one group had greater "access" to credit than
another. When the probability of repayment differs, whether between
individuals or groups, those who are better credit risks receive more
credit on better terms. To call this better "access" is again to confuse an
end result with an initial condition, ignoring intervening differences in
behavior.

In the United States, it is common to refer to groups as "segregated,"
not only when there have been special legal or other barriers confronting
them but also where there have not been, if they end up "under-represented" relative to their percentage of the population. Discrimination and
segregation are and have been among the ugly facts of life in various
countries around the world. These facts need to be confronted where they
exist—not trivialized by having the terms applied by redefinition to situations where they do not exist, and where very different factors need to be
confronted.

"Perceptions" and "stereotypes" are other words in the prevailing ideological vocabulary that serve the very similar purpose of obscuring
behavioral differences among groups. Like discrimination and segregation, unfounded perceptions and stereotypes are an important reality in
the history and current experience of some racial and ethnic groups. But
again, such a condition cannot be assumed a priori, merely because of an
unfavorable end result. Groups said to be dirty, loud, violent, etc., cannot
be arbitrarily assumed to be different, so that all adverse characteriza-
tions can be condemned. If the facts are not available, then such charac-
terizations remain unfounded charges, which prove nothing about either
the group or their accusers. Yet Cicero's warning to ancient Romans not to
buy British slaves because of their stupidity has been cited as
"racism"[81]—even though there was no counter-evidence against Cicero
and what evidence there is about the ancient Britons suggests that they
were in fact far behind their Roman contemporaries culturally.

One of the most used and least defined words in the contemporary ideological vocabulary is "racism." The most straightforward meaning of
racism is a belief in the innate inferiority of some race or races. This is
the sense which conjures up the image of Hitler and the Holocaust. But
the word "racism" is often applied in other, very different, senses to
wholly different situations. To some, every adverse judgement about any
aspect of the behavior or performance of any racial or ethnic group is
"racism." To others, it is only adverse judgements on the behavior or performance of a selected list of racial or ethnic groups which is "racism."
Thus, even sweeping denunciations of whites, "Anglos," or perhaps Jews,
may be exempted from the charge of racism.

More generally, those particular groups whose historic treatment is
part of a general ideological indictment of Western civilization cannot be
criticized in any way without risking the charge of "racism." Conversely,
verbal (or even physical) assaults originating within such groups are often
exempted from condemnation as racism—sometimes by an explicit redefinition which requires *power* as an essential ingredient in racism, so that
blacks for example cannot be called racists in American society. If this
kind of reasoning were followed consistently, then Hitler could not have
been considered a racist when he was an isolated street corner rabble-
rouser, but only after he became chancellor of Germany.

With varying degrees of explicitness, these tendentious ideological
redefinitions of racism have become so intermingled with the straightforward meaning—a belief in innate racial inferiority or superiority—that
the word may be irretrievably lost as a specific, meaningful concept. The
social phenomenon it originally referred to may continue to exist, in varying degrees and with varying effects, but empirical assessments of its
existence or importance are unlikely to be clarified by the use of such a
chameleon-like word. Indeed, the political overuse of the word may
destroy its effectiveness as a warning against a very real danger.

Many assume that racism is a prerequisite for discrimination, or is virtually synonymous with it. However, a generalized hostility or specific
discrimination may be directed against a particular racial or ethnic
group, without any belief that they are innately inferior. A political movement organized to ban Japanese immigration to the United States was
quite clear about this at their first meeting in 1905:

> We have been accustomed to regard the Japanese as an inferior race, but
> are now suddenly aroused to our danger. They are not window cleaners
> and house servants. The Japanese can think, can learn, can invent. We

have suddenly awakened to the fact that they are gaining a foothold in every skilled industry in our country. They are our equal in intellect; their ability to labor is equal to ours. They are proud, valiant, and courageous, but they can underlive us. . . . We are here today to prevent that very competition.[82]

Other groups have aroused resentments in other countries, without any suggestion that they were racially inferior. Often this resentment has been based on acknowledged superior performance. In Honduras, for example, the claim was that the Germans worked too hard for others to be able to compete with them.[83] In India's state of Andhra Pradesh, a leader of the Telanganans admitted that the rival Andhras were "better qualified for many of the jobs than we are" but asked: "Are we not entitled to jobs just because we are not as qualified?" With varying degrees of explicitness, many people in many lands have recognized the capabilities of the Jews, the Chinese, the Lebanese, and others—as reasons to discriminate against them. If "racism" is the appropriate label for such behavior, then clearly the word is no longer being used in the sense of a belief in innate inferiority. Sometimes a *superiority* has been conceded to the group targeted for discrimination. In Nigeria, for example, discriminatory policies were advocated on grounds that otherwise "the less well educated people of the North will be swamped by the thrusting people of the South."[84] In Malaysia, it was likewise argued: "Malaysia has far too many non-Malay citizens who can swamp the Malays the moment protection is removed."

The fundamental problem with an ideologically defined vocabulary in discussions of racial or ethnic issue is not that those with such a vocabulary may be right or wrong on this or that issue. The more fundamental problem is that we forfeit our ability to examine such issues empirically, and allow important social questions to be obscured, or the conclusions to be preempted, by mere tendentious words. The painful history of racial and ethnic relations is a sobering reminder of the high stakes which make clarity imperative and obscurantism dangerous.

# CHAPTER 6

# RACE AND INTELLIGENCE

Few subjects are so difficult to discuss as race and intelligence—much less to discuss unemotionally, logically, or empirically. Even if the emotional or ideological aspects can be put aside, formidable analytical difficulties remain. Race is an elusive concept to apply in practice, in today's genetically mixed populations, and intelligence is even more elusive. But because a discussion must proceed carefully and within limits does not mean that it cannot proceed at all.

Among the questions to be addressed are: (1) the existence, magnitude, and persistence of mental performance differences among racial and ethnic groups; (2) the reasons behind such differences, as these can be inferred from available evidence; (3) the reliability and validity of the instruments used to measure differences in mental performance; and (4) the social implications of these issues.

## GROSS DIFFERENCES

Questions of group differences in mental performance have existed long before IQ tests or other modern devices appeared. Cicero warned his fellow Romans not to buy British slaves, for he found them unusually difficult to teach. While some would consider such an assessment as mere evidence of bias or racism,[1] there is no a priori reason to dismiss Cicero's firsthand observations, on the strength of general presumptions among those 20 centuries removed from the facts. Indeed, much of what is known of the cultural and technological gulf between the tribal Britons of that era and the more advanced civilization existing on the continent of Europe would tend to support Cicero's conclusion of differences in mental performance, at that time. Whether those differences were genetic is another question entirely.

Despite much controversy over what specifically constitutes intelligence, it is generally agreed that it has more than one dimension. Various kinds of mental performance can therefore be compared among nations and groups—each performance being considered a facet of intelligence. This is sufficient for a discussion of gross differences, even if it does not identify which elements are central or essential to intelligence. Results on a variety of tests, for example, may therefore be indicative, without pretending to be definitive. For purposes of gross comparisons, these can include tests usually called "achievement" tests, as well as others conventionally labelled "aptitude" or "intelligence" tests. The question as to how different, and how sharply demarcated, these tests are from one another need not be debated here—nor the larger question as to how well the results of any of them correspond in practice to what they are designed to measure in theory.[2] For present purposes, they are all simply attempts to measure various aspects of mental performance—"intelligence" in a very general sense.

## International Comparisons

Modern international patterns of differences in mental test performance tend to follow patterns already noted in economic and demographic areas. Just as northern European societies and their offshoots such as Australia or the United States, together with Westernized Japan, tend to form one group with similar incomes and fertility rates, so they are also clustered together on mental test results. Traditional Latin American, Asian, and Middle East societies tend to differ significantly from them in mental test results, as in income and fertility. The science test scores of fourteen-year-olds around the world illustrate this:[3]

| MODERN OR WESTERNIZED | MEAN SCORE |
|---|---|
| Australia | 24.6 |
| England | 21.3 |
| Japan | 31.2 |
| Sweden | 21.7 |
| United States | 21.6 |
| West Germany | 23.7 |

| TRADITIONAL ASIAN, MIDDLE EAST, LATIN AMERICAN | MEAN SCORE |
|---|---|
| Chile | 9.2 |
| India | 7.6 |
| Iran | 9.4 |
| Thailand | 15.6 |

No one has to believe that an understanding of science is hereditary in order to believe that it is economically and socially significant. It is one of a number of cultural differences that have consequences.

There are both international and intergroup differences on other mental tests, including IQ tests. This is hardly surprising, since results on various standardized mental tests tend to have significant correlations with one another, whether these are called achievement tests or intelligence tests. For example, the Japanese population as a whole scored higher on one mathematical test than did any other population, as they did in science:[4]

| COUNTRY | SCORE |
|---|---|
| England | 19.3 |
| Finland | 24.1 |
| Japan | 31.2 |
| United States | 16.2 |

## Intergroup Comparisons

Intergroup differences in mental test performance within a given country can also be substantial. A 1981 study of Scholastic Aptitude Test score differences among American ethnic groups showed a range of more than a hundred points in average verbal scores among half a dozen groups, and a range of more than a hundred and fifty points in average mathematics scores among the same groups.[5] Differences were especially dramatic at the higher levels. More Asian American students scored above 700 on the mathematical portion of the SAT than all the black, Mexican American, Puerto Rican, and American Indian students put together, even though more than three times as many students from these latter groups took the same test.[6] Nor did these intergroup differences represent simply differences in socioeconomic background. Asian American students from families with incomes of $6,000 or less scored higher on the mathematics portion of the SAT than black, Mexican American, or American Indian students from families with income of $50,000 or more.[7] Such patterns are not peculiar to the United States. In the British colony of Hong Kong, Chinese school children outperformed the English school children on nonverbal tests, despite the higher socioeconomic level of the English in Hong Kong.[8] The Chinese also outperformed the Malays in Singapore[9] and the Indonesians in Indonesia.[10]

If intergroup differences on test performances cannot be explained away simply by socioeconomic factors, neither can they be wholly attributed to educational differences. An international survey of scores on the Porteus Maze test among illiterate adults showed striking differences among various groups, whether living at home or abroad. Among Indians in colonial Malaya, for example, Tamils had higher scores than Gurkhas, and both had higher scores than Bengalis in Bengal. The same study also included African bushmen, Chinese, and others. Although this survey was conducted entirely among illiterates, so that differences in quantity or quality of education are not a factor, the differences between the average scores of the top group and the bottom group—both from India—was even greater than the equivalent IQ differences between blacks and whites in the United States,[11] where large educational differences between the races have long existed. The question here is not whether these differences are cultural or genetic in origin. The point is that they are *real* and that their consequences are real.

All differences between groups that are genetically different are not genetic differences. Some groups have more children than others, for example, and children from large families generally tend to score lower on mental tests than children from smaller families. There are, of course, numerous other non-genetic differences between groups who differ genetically.

One of the first massive exercises in group mental testing was conducted among soldiers in the U.S. Army during World War I. Many were immigrants, and their average test scores varied according to their respective homelands. The proportions of soldiers with different ancestries who exceeded the American national norms were as follows:[12]

| | |
|---|---|
| English | 67 percent |
| German | 49 percent |
| Irish | 26 percent |
| Russian | 19 percent |
| Italian | 14 percent |
| Polish | 12 percent |

Civilian mental tests in the U.S. from the same period tended to show intergroup differences very similar in ranking and magnitude. While the English and Germans in the United States tended to equal or exceed the national IQ norm of 100, Americans of Italian, Slovak, Greek, Portuguese, Polish, Croatian, Spanish, and Lithuanian ancestry all averaged in the 80s. In these studies of civilians, black Americans' average IQ was in the same range as these latter European groups, and above some of these European groups, but blacks scored below all the Europeans on the U.S. Army mental tests. The civilian tests were conducted primarily in the Northern cities, where the various immigrant groups were concentrated, and Northern blacks have historically had higher IQs than Southern blacks.[13] The U.S. Army sample was more representative of the national distribution of blacks at that time—overwhelmingly Southern. This also illustrates the difficulties of trying to separate hereditary and environmental influences. Northern Negroes at this period of history differed both genetically and culturally from Southern Negroes.[14]

Substantial intergroup IQ differences have been common in other countries. The black-white IQ difference of about 15 points in the U.S. has been matched by the IQ difference between Sephardic and Ashkenazic Jews in Israel[15] or between Catholics and Protestants in Northern Ireland.[16] Nor are such IQ differences limited to different racial or ethnic groups. Some Appalachian Mountain communities have had average IQs in the mid-80s in the United States, as have some canal boat communities in Britain. So have inhabitants of the Hebrides Islands off Scotland.[17] In Indonesia, residents of Java score higher than Indonesians living in the outer islands, and women score higher than men.[18] In China, low-income and rural youngsters score lower on examinations.[19] Firstborn children in general tend to score higher on mental tests and to do better in school than later children in the same families.[20] Moreover, mental test patterns within a given race vary considerably when the environments are quite different—blacks in rural Georgia, for example, as compared to blacks in California.[21]

## Selectivity Bias

A complicating factor in both intergroup and international comparisons is that different proportions of each group and nation receive different quantities and qualities of schooling. In underdeveloped countries, less than 5 percent of the eligible age cohort received higher education in 1975, compared to 23 percent in the more developed countries—and there were further large variations within each of these broad categories. Nearly half the relevant age cohort in North America was enrolled in higher education, compared to 17 percent in Europe, 6 percent in Asia and Latin America, and less than 2 percent in Africa.[22] Therefore, tests given at a particular age or point in the educational process may be testing a more highly selected sample in one country or group than in another. However, the large test score differences among illiterates from different groups suggest that educational selectivity can by no means be considered a sufficient explanation. Moreover, groups "under-represented" in higher education, such as blacks, Hispanics, or American Indians in the United States, often score lower than groups "over-represented," such as Asian Americans, though the selectivity factor alone would suggest the reverse.

A long decline of American students' scores on the Scholastic Aptitude Test, from the mid-1960s to the early 1980s, has sometimes been attributed to an increase in the number of minority or "disadvantaged" children taking such tests, corresponding to their increased representation at American colleges during the 1960s and 1970s. Changing selectivity is thus blamed for lowering the average performance statistically when the performance may not have been lowered in fact among those previously taking such tests. In reality, however, the number of scores in the top brackets declined absolutely—and substantially. About 12,000 American youngsters scored 750 or higher on the mathematics SAT in 1976, but this declined to about 6,500 by 1981. Similar declines occurred on biology, French and German tests, and even more drastic declines occurred among those scoring in the top bracket on English composition.[23] In short, changing selectivity cannot explain the decline in

American SAT scores, which occurred at the top as well as in the rest of the distribution. Ironically, the small upturn in test scores in the 1980s was due largely to small improvements among black and other minority students.[24]

## Implications

A definitive study of intergroup or international differences in mental test performance would have to take into account not only selectivity bias but also many other factors—perhaps too many to be manageable. What is sufficient at this point is to establish that such differences are real, that they are common, that they are large, and that they are consequential. In this respect, they are like other behavioral differences in family patterns, eating patterns, work patterns and other cultural traits. The implications of international and intergroup differences in mental test performance for the heredity-environment controversy can be analyzed after first considering the internal patterns of mental test scores, as distinguished from their general levels, and after considering the degree to which mental test score differences between groups persist or change over time.

## PATTERNS OF DIFFERENCES

Intergroup differences exist not only on overall mental test scores, but also on internal patterns of strengths and weaknesses on different parts of mental tests. Questions involving three-dimensional conceptions of space, for example, tend to be especially difficult for African youngsters[25] and also for Jamaicans.[26] By contrast, these are the kinds of questions on which Hong Kong Chinese children outperformed the English children in Hong Kong, and outperformed children in such other places as Scotland or India. But Eskimo youngsters did even better than the Chinese on such questions.[27] In the United States, the Chinese did better than either Jews or blacks on spatial conceptions.[28] Differences in spatial perceptions have been linked empirically to differences in body chemistry.[29] Whether these in turn are linked to genetic differences, and whether these differ significantly by race, are separate questions. Considering how relatively recently in its long history Western civilization acquired its current conception of three-dimensional perspective,[30] it can hardly be surprising that similar concepts are not uniformly perceived within or between other cultures.

Regardless of whether this difference in three-dimensional perception is genetic or cultural, it is real. For some purposes, its genetic or cultural origin may not matter. For others, it may. Jews obviously do not suffer unduly because the profile of their abilities dips in the spatial conception area. But what is central here, as elsewhere, is that groups have their own distinctive patterns. Chinese, Puerto Rican, Negro, and Jewish young-sters in New York have each had different profiles of mental test strengths and weaknesses, quite aside from different levels of overall test scores. Very similar patterns were found among children from the same respec-tive groups in Boston. Moreover, those from families at higher socioeco-nomic levels had essentially the same test score patterns as poorer mem-bers of their respective groups, but at higher levels.[31]

Low overall test scores for particular groups are often blamed on "cul-tural bias" in the tests, and in particular on the use of words or informa-tion more likely to be familiar to some groups, such as white, middle-class test takers in the United States. Examples of such material are not difficult to find on some tests—including both "achievement" and "intel-ligence" tests. But most critics who argue this way often fail to ask whether in fact it is these kinds of questions which account for the low overall scores of groups who do poorly. Almost invariably, low-scoring groups do their worst on *nonverbal* questions, on abstractions that do not require middle-class vocabulary or information. This does not prove that cultural bias is not present, but it does indicate that any such bias must take a very different form from what is usually assumed or portrayed.

The pattern of low-scoring groups doing their worst on abstract ques-tions is neither new nor limited to today's low-scoring groups. A 1917 study of various immigrant groups tested at Ellis Island as they arrived in the United States showed the low-scoring groups among them doing par-ticularly poorly on abstract questions.[32] This confirmed an earlier (1913) observation by noted psychologist H. H. Goddard, who had tested such groups there: "These people cannot deal with abstractions." A similar judgement was voiced by L. M. Terman (creator of the Stanford-Binet IQ test), who studied low-scoring racial minorities in the southwestern United States and concluded that these groups "cannot master abstrac-tions."[33] A 1932 study of white children in isolated mountain communi-ties in the U.S. showed that they not only had low IQ scores over all, but were especially deficient on questions involving abstract comprehen-sion.[34] Black-white mental test score differences are likewise greatest on abstract questions.[35]

Similar patterns have been common in other countries and cultures as well. A study in England, for example, showed that rural working-class boys trailed their urban peers more on abstract questions than on other kinds of questions.[36] In the Hebrides Islands, where the average IQ of the Gaelic-speaking children was 85—the same as among blacks in the United States—the Gaelic-speaking youngsters did well on informational items but trailed their English-speaking classmates most on items involving such abstractions as time, logic, and other nonverbal factors.[37] In Jamaica, where IQs average well below normal, the lowest performance was on the least verbal test.[38]

In short, despite the verbal and informational biases of many mental tests, low-scoring groups tend to do their worst on nonverbal and noninformational (i.e., abstract) questions. This seems to hold true across racial lines, though of course the incidence of low-scorers differs from one racial or ethnic group to another.

Nonverbal questions are not necessarily less culturally biased. On the contrary, cultures seem to differ greatly in their reaction to abstractions. Indian children being tested in South Africa were reported as showing a "lack of interest in nonverbal materials."[39] West African boys "obviously became bored" with abstract questions, according to observers, and their scores *fell* when retested on such items,[40] reinforcing the inference that boredom was a factor in the results, since greater familiarity would otherwise tend to raise scores on the second testing, while boredom would tend to be worse on a second attempt. American Negro soldiers tested during World War I tended to "lapse into inattention and almost into sleep" during abstract tests, according to observers.[41] Lower-class youngsters in Venezuela were described as "non-starters" on one of the well-known abstract tests used there.[42] Inhabitants of the Hebrides likewise gave evidence of not being fully oriented toward such questions.[43]

In short, there is reason to doubt whether various groups apply themselves equally to abstract thought. If there is a significant difference in interest and application, then differences in results do not carry the same weight as evidence of underlying potential. Moreover, even if it were possible to galvanize everyone to the same pitch of effort on a given occasion for testing, this would still not eliminate the effects of prior years of differences in interest in the development of their abilities in that direction.

For many practical purposes, however, it makes no real difference whether poor performances in abstract thinking are due to neglect or to lack of capacity. In either case it has serious ramifications in a scientific and technological society.

## PERSISTENCE OF DIFFERENCES

Thus far the discussion has made no attempt to distinguish between hereditary and environmental causes of the differences between groups in the level or pattern of their mental test scores. The persistence of these levels and patterns over time may also be either hereditary or environmental. However, to the extent that intergroup rankings change over time, without significant changes in the genetic composition of the respective groups, such changes are more readily reconcilable with environmental rather than hereditary causes.

While international comparisons make it possible to see the persistence of group patterns under a wide variety of circumstances at a given time, it is more difficult to make comparably wide comparisons over time, because mental tests themselves are only about a century old in most of the world (though civil service examinations are many centuries old in China), and the era of mass testing has been only a few decades long. Nevertheless, within these limitations, it is possible to investigate what has happened.

The massive mental testing of American soldiers during the First World War provides one starting point for measuring persistence and change in mental test results. A similar massive mental testing of American soldiers in the Second World War permits a rare comparison at an interval of a quarter of a century, during an era when there were significant social and educational changes in the United States, not the least of which was the ending of large-scale immigration and the consequent acculturation of existing immigrant groups. The amount of schooling also rose for the general population. The differences observed after these social changes were striking.

The mental test scores of American soldiers during World War II averaged higher than in World War I by the equivalent of from 12 to 14 IQ points.[44] While such an IQ difference between two individuals would not be startling, this is a very substantial difference between averages for large groups. It is comparable to the difference between the IQ norm of

100 and the average IQ of various low-scoring groups around the world. Moreover, a very similar pattern of substantial test score increases has occurred in other countries, such as Holland, Japan, West Germany, Australia, and France.[45] Clearly, the average mental performance of millions of people can change significantly over time.

A more directly relevant question, in the context of heredity-environment issues, is that of the relative rankings of particular groups, and how these persist or change over time. World War I soldiers in the U.S. Army who had immigrated from Russia, Italy, and Poland had the three lowest mental test score averages among European immigrant groups, and not appreciably higher than the mental test scores of American Negroes.[46] Because most immigrants from Russia and Poland during this era were Jews, the distinguished mental test specialist Carl Brigham (creator of the Scholastic Aptitude Test) concluded that the results "disprove the popular belief that the Jew is highly intelligent."[47] Yet, within a decade, Jewish IQ scores were above the national average, where they have remained.[48] Brigham later recanted the general conclusions of his earlier study as being "without foundation."[49]

This was an era of rapid socioeconomic rise for Jews and of their rapid acculturation to American society. But it was *not* an era of large-scale intermarriage of Jews with other groups in the United States. The dramatic changes among American Jews were environmental, not genetic.

Italian Americans and non-Jewish Polish Americans likewise experienced significant changes in mental test scores over the years. A survey conducted by this writer, with samples of more than 10,000 from each group, showed the following median IQ scores over a period of six decades:[50]

|            | ITALIAN AMERICANS | POLISH AMERICANS |
|------------|-------------------|------------------|
| *Decades*  | *Median I.Q.*     | *Median I.Q.*    |
| 1920s      | 92                | 91               |
| 1930s      | 93                | 95               |
| 1940s      | 95                | 99               |
| 1950s      | 99                | 104              |
| 1960s      | 103               | 107              |
| 1970s      | 100               | 109              |

The rise in the IQs of Italians and Poles in the United States was even more dramatic than these data indicate. Both groups had average IQs of about 85 in civilian tests conducted around the time of the First World War.[51] Their total rise in IQ from that time to the 1970s was 15 points or more. These were also groups with relatively low rates of intermarriage during the period of their IQ rise, so that this again largely represents a change in environment rather than genes.

As in other areas, time in itself guarantees no progress. Nor are trends always continuous. One of the most mixed pictures in mental test results is that among American Negroes. Black soldiers in World War II scored further behind white soldiers than in World War I.[52] Yet a more recent study shows black orphans adopted by white families to have an average IQ of 106.[53] Moreover, regional differences in IQ have been significant and persistent among blacks—those in the South averaging about 80 and those outside the South averaging about 90.[54] Regional differences also cut across racial lines. During World War I, for example, black soldiers from Ohio, Illinois, New York, and Pennsylvania scored higher on mental tests than white soldiers from Georgia, Arkansas, Kentucky, and Mississippi.[55]

While the test scores of whole nations may rise over time, they may also decline over time. Scholastic Aptitude Test scores dropped steadily for nearly two decades in the United States.[56] A similar decline in academic standards occurred in China during the so-called "cultural revolution" of the 1960s.[57] Despite large overall ideological differences between the two countries, some similar changes in educational practices occurred in both countries during their declines, notably a disavowal of objective standards, an emphasis on "democratization" of education, and a decline in the authority of teachers.[58]

The common practice in the United States of comparing blacks in isolation with "the national average," or with whites lumped together, creates an illusion of group uniqueness that will not stand up under closer scrutiny, since the average IQ of American Negroes has been the same as that of a number of other groups, with differing ancestries, in countries around the world. The concentration of recent and bitter IQ controversies on black-white differences[59] has led to a banning of group IQ tests in some American cities, and to a widespread reluctance to publish such data. This has occurred at a time when a rising socioeconomic level among black Americans might lead to an expectation of a rise of IQ levels. The test scores of black students on the Scholastic Aptitude Test have in fact begun to rise[60] and, since standardized test results tend to correlate with one another, an inference might be made about a corresponding rise in black IQs. But the ban on IQ testing, and pressure against publication or discussion of interracial IQ differences, make it unlikely that this inference can be tested in the near future. Ironically, black political leaders and spokesmen are among the strongest supporters of this suppression of evidence.

The taboo against discussing race and IQ has not left this an open question. On the contrary, it has had the perverse effect of freezing an existing majority of testing experts in favor of a belief that racial IQ differences are influenced by genetics.[61] No belief can be refuted if it cannot be discussed. Nor can any individual or society get the benefit of the clarification which often follows an attempt at refutation, whether that attempt proves to be successful or not.

## HEREDITY AND ENVIRONMENT

The relative influences of heredity and environment cannot logically be discussed in categorical terms, though this often happens in the heat of controversy. Just as the hereditary organization of the body is the mechanism by which food is converted into weight, at a given level of physical activity, so the hereditary organization of the brain is the mechanism by which environmental stimuli are converted into intellectual results. To argue categorically as to which is more important is like arguing whether $f$ or $x$ is more important in the equation $y = f(x)$. The term $f$ stands for the process by which $x$ changes $y$.

In short, neither side can deny the effect of either factor, certainly not at the individual level. The real question is the incremental effect of a change of heredity or environment—*given* their existing combination—when comparing two groups. If the existing environment is intellectually stultifying, then an improvement in environment should improve intellectual performance more than if we began with a very stimulating environment. Conversely, individuals with very different hereditary potential should respond differently to the same environmental improvements. Because outcomes in both cases depend upon where we are to begin with, the effect of heredity and environment cannot be answered once and for all. The answer may be very different for the general society than for particular groups who begin with different combinations of environmental or hereditary factors.

## Policy Issues

What the controversy over heredity and environment is trying to get at is whether existing differences among individuals and groups are due more to the hereditary or environmental differences between them. To this cognitive issue is often added the policy issue, whether socially feasible changes can effect some desirable educational outcomes. These same two questions have dominated those on both sides of the issue.

The article by Professor Arthur Jensen, of the University of California at Berkeley, that set off the current controversy in 1969 was entitled: "How Much Can We Boost IQ and Scholastic Achievement?"[62] His answer, long since lost in the swirl of controversy, was that the school performance of disadvantaged minorities could be raised considerably above their existing levels, that there were "great and relatively untapped reservoirs of mental ability in the disadvantaged,"[63] which could be developed by using different teaching methods,[64] but that he expected no comparable changes in IQ scores. It was the latter issue on which the battle was joined, and which has largely submerged the rest of the discussion.

The enormous complexities of the issues involved require that both the cognitive issues and the policy issues be approached very carefully and systematically. What is at issue is *not* whether some races are good only to be "hewers of wood and drawers of water," or not even good for slaves, as Cicero said of the Britons many centuries ago. What is at issue is (1) whether there are important differences in the level or pattern of mental capabilities between racial groups, and (2) whether these differences are imprinted by differences in genes or differences in cultures.

It seems difficult to deny the very existence of differences in levels or patterns of developed capabilities, whatever one's views on innate potential. When the Chinese tested in Hong Kong, Singapore, Boston, New York, and San Francisco repeatedly show a superior sense of spatial conception, it is difficult to deny that there is something there, whatever its origin might be. Professor Jensen believes that the origin is genetic, but his policy conclusions do not depend on that. When he urged that "we further explore different types of abilities and modes of learning, and

seek to discover how these various abilities can serve the aims of education,"[65] he was urging a course of action equally compatible with purely
cultural differences in styles of thinking. In short, the issues are narrower
in policy terms than in emotional or ideological terms.

However many philosophic, political, or other overtones the heredity-
environment issue has acquired, it is ultimately an empirical question.
Evidence rather than preferences are decisive. It is a question as to what
sorts of evidence would be observed if one theory were correct, compared
to what would be observed if the opposite theory were correct.

## Empirical Evidence

If each group has a similar distribution of hereditary intellectual
potential (something not directly observable), what is there that would be
observable—and which would *not* be observable if groups differed in
their respective distributions of genetic intellectual potential? There are a
number of phenomena that would be observed in the one case, but not in
the other. None of these is sufficiently ironclad as to be definitive, but if a
significant number of them all point in the same direction, that may be
indicative.

If the differences between two groups are environmental rather than
hereditary, then members of one group raised in the culture of the other
should have an intellectual performance level more like their adopted
group, rather than their biological group. This is a pattern already noted
in the case of black orphans raised by white families in the United States.
A somewhat similar result has been found in the case of many children of
unwed mothers in early postwar Germany, children sired by American
soldiers in the army of occupation after World War II. There were no significant differences in the IQs of those sired by black soldiers from those
sired by white soldiers.[66]

If substantial changes in mental performance are observed without corresponding genetic changes, this too would suggest environmental causes
for the original differences—at least as regards those particular groups.
This pattern has already been noted in the history of Jews, Poles, and
Italians in the U.S, as well as in the substantial rise of raw test scores of
whole nations around the world.

One of the logical conclusions drawn by many early scholars, who
believed in the overwhelming role of genetics in determining intelligence,
was that the greater fertility of low-IQ classes and races would mean a

declining national IQ over time, as such groups became a rising proportion of the total population. Such predictions were made in Europe as well as America—and were falsified by the subsequent course of events in both places. Indeed, mental test norms have had to be adjusted upward to maintain national IQ averages at their definitional level of 100 points. This re-norming has concealed some of the very large IQ test performance changes that have in fact occurred over time.[67]

Some research findings indicate that females are less susceptible to environmental influences than males are.[68] Given that there are differences between groups in mental test performance, if these differences are environmentally caused, then the males of the low IQ group might be expected to have lower IQs than the females, who are less affected by environment. Conversely, if the differences between groups are hereditary, then the females of the low-IQ group would be expected to have lower IQs than the males of the same group. Research findings have consistently shown black females to have higher IQ test scores, and most other test scores, than black males in the United States.[69] The same was true among Jews when they scored low on mental tests in the past.[70] However, among white-raised black orphans with an average IQ of 106, there was *no* female advantage,[71] suggesting that the striking predominance of females among high-IQ blacks[72] is an environmental rather than a racial phenomenon.

All these results suggesting environmental reasons for intergroup mental test differences conflict with a very large body of research findings for the general population. Studies of individual and social class variations in mental test results suggest just the opposite—that hereditary differences account for much more of the average IQ variation among individuals than do environmental differences in society at large.[73] There is, however, no contradiction in the proposition that heredity may account for more variation *within* the general population, and environment for more of the variation *between* the general population and particular subgroups—especially when these subgroups are known to live under very different environmental conditions and to have a different cultural history as well. That is, incremental variations may be quite different in their effects on groups that are in very different environmental circumstances to begin with.

There is no a priori reason why there must be a single answer as to the relative effects of heredity and environment. Moreover, the very general concept "environment" covers many specific things, not all of which have the effects attributed to them. For example, while test scores usually correlate with family income or parental occupations in the general population, such socioeconomic indicators do not explain many intergroup differences. The Chinese children tested in Hong Kong came from families less affluent than those of the English children whom they outperformed on nonverbal tests.[74] In the United States, blacks of above-average socioeconomic status have not averaged as high IQ as whites of lower socioeconomic status,[75] and neither blacks, Mexican Americans, nor American Indians from families with incomes of $50,000 and above scored as well on the quantitative portion of the Scholastic Aptitude Test in 1981 as Asian Americans from families with incomes of $6,000 or less.[76] The environment that matters for this purpose may be cultural rather than economic.

"Environment" is not so much an answer as a gateway to further questions. It is a catchall phrase for any of a vast number of unspecified, nongenetic factors. In particular, "environment" cannot be confined to immediate surroundings, whether home, school, or neighborhood. Immigrant youngsters from various racial and cultural backgrounds, living in the same American neighborhoods and sitting side by side in the same schools, have had group IQ differences as great as those between residentially and educationally segregated blacks and whites in the Southern United States.[77] To salvage the environmental theory of IQ differences would require a much broader conception of environment, including cultural orientations and values going far back into history. But this broader conception of environment, reaching well beyond immediate circumstances, offers correspondingly less hope of substantial change by social engineering, such as remedial programs or the racial integration of schools.

## TEST BIAS

Many of the leading tests used for selection purposes, whether in employment or in admissions to college or postgraduate education, have been challenged on the ground that these tests are invalid in general, or are invalid for socially disadvantaged racial or ethnic groups. More specifically, such tests are said to underestimate the true ability of the disadvantaged, and therefore to predict a lower future performance than will in fact occur. Such charges have been brought against IQ tests, the Scholastic Aptitude Test, civil service examinations, and many others.

Long-continued and heated controversy over the predictive validity of mental tests is remarkable, because (1) this is fundamentally an empirical question, whose answer can be determined by a review of readily available facts, and (2) innumerable studies have been done over the years, testing the predictive validity of a wide variety of well-known tests. Moreover, those who have the responsibility for making selections—and who have to live with the consequences of the selections they have made—usually have a choice as to whether or not to use mental tests, which ones to use, and how much weight to give them. Alternative criteria and methods are also usually available to them, to use as complements to, or substitutes for, mental tests. Nevertheless, the predictive validity of mental tests has become a political issue reaching to the highest levels of government in the United States and a legal issue fought out again and again in the U.S. Supreme Court.[78]

## Empirical Evidence

There has been a huge accumulation of evidence on the correlation between test scores and subsequent performances, not only for the general population but also for particular racial and ethnic minorities. Repeatedly it has been demonstrated that the standard mental tests do *not* underestimate the subsequent performance of low-scoring minorities.[79] They have in fact a slight tendency to do the opposite—to predict for low-scoring minorities a higher subsequent performance than that actually achieved.[80] This pattern has been persistent over time and is international in scope.

In the Philippines, for example, students from low-income and rural backgrounds have not only had lower than average test scores, but have also done worse academically at the University of the Philippines than other students with the *same* low test scores.[81] In Indonesia, where men have averaged lower test scores than women, men with the same test scores as women have done poorer academic work than women at the University of Indonesia.[82] Numerous studies show similar patterns between blacks and whites in the United States. Blacks tend to score lower than whites on a variety of aptitude, academic achievement, and job tests, but even when comparing blacks and whites with the same test scores, the subsequent performance of blacks tends to be lower, whether academically or on the job. This includes academic performance in colleges, law schools, and medical schools, and job performance in the civil service and the Air Force.[83]

Faced with massive evidence that applicants who score low on entrance examinations generally perform less well as students, some critics of standardized tests claim that this is still no indication as to the ultimate criterion—performance in later life. Almost never are such assertions accompanied by empirical evidence of greater predictability of later life performance from alternative measures of ability.

Neither for minorities nor for the general population is there a perfect correlation between test scores and future performance, so anecdotal examples of exceptions abound. Moreover, there is no scientific way to determine whether a given correlation is "high" or "low." The relevant decision-making question is: Higher or lower than what alternatives? Assessing the prospects of human beings has never been a science. Nor is politicizing it likely to add to its precision.

Most of the controversies are not even conducted in empirical terms. From the cultural bias of particular questions—the use of words, or assumption of information, more likely to be known by middle-class members of the larger society—it is often concluded that such tests *must* underestimate the true ability of disadvantaged groups. The plausibility of this reasoning is often used as a substitute for empirical verification of the conclusion. The nebulous concept of "real" ability is seldom specified as to whether it means (1) innate potential (which is unknowable) or (2) developed capabilities existing at the time of testing, but incorrectly assessed by the test. If the latter, then the empirical basis of the correct assessment need only be specified and the greater predictive validity of alternative methods demonstrated by a higher correlation with subsequent performance. Nothing of the sort has been done.

In both political and legal processes, merely casting doubt on mental tests can create huge costs for those who use them. The cost of a relatively simple validation study under favorable conditions has been estimated at between $40,000 and $50,000.[84] Differential validation for separate racial or ethnic groups could cost much more. The imposition of such costs in turn becomes an incentive for the institution using tests to abandon the tests or to set aside their results in the case of particular groups. This is of course precisely the result desired by many group activists. With such large rewards available merely for producing plausible and vehement objections to tests, it is hardly surprising to find what one leading authority has called "endless" streams of "counterarguments, quibbles, and debating points."[85]

What is crucial to this process is that (1) the burden of proof is put on the accused, at very high cost, that (2) without sufficient sample sizes in all the relevant categories, nothing can be proved, and that (3) some American judges accept the premise that disparate results by group imply institutional discrimination. These political and legal circumstances have more to do with the persistence of the controversy than any ambiguity in empirical evidence.

## Group "Representation"

Political pressures for increased "representation" of academically low-performance groups in institutions of higher learning has existed in Communist nations like the USSR and China, as well as in democratic nations such as India or the United States, and in fact in countries scattered around the world, from Nigeria to Fiji to England. Sometimes the low-performance group is the majority population, as in Malaysia or Sri Lanka. Sometimes it is some minority group—untouchables in India or blacks in the United States, for example. Usually the low-performance group seeks out the less demanding colleges or universities, and then the less demanding fields within given institutions. Untouchables in India do both, as do Mexican Americans in the United States,[86] Sephardics in Israel,[87] and many others.

When top-level institutions seek greater numerical "representation" of low-scoring groups, they face severe problems in trying to get students at all comparable academically to their regular student body. This is especially so at elite institutions. When one group has a higher mean test score than another, the disparity between the representation of the two groups becomes progressively more extreme at higher and higher test score levels.[88] Even *within* the black American population, for example, a relatively minor difference of a few points in average IQ score between men and women translates into a several hundred percent over-representation of black women, relative to black men, at high IQ levels.[89] A similar pattern can be seen between blacks and whites, or between other groups. While the average Asian American student in 1981 scored a modest 30 points higher than the average white student on the mathematics portion of the Scholastic Aptitude Test (513 versus 483), more than twice as high a proportion of Asian Americans as whites had mathematics SAT scores of 700 and over.[90]

At the extremely high test score levels prevailing at elite American academic institutions, blacks are very rare. For example, many leading American colleges have student bodies whose average Scholastic Aptitude Test scores—verbal and quantitative combined—add up to 1,200 points or more. These include not only the obvious examples like Yale, Stanford, or Chicago, but also numerous lesser-known colleges like Davidson, Pomona, St. John's, Middlebury, Harvey Mudd, Carleton, and many others. However, blacks who meet these standards are relatively rare. There were fewer than 600 black students in the entire country with combined SAT scores of 1,200 in 1983, compared to more than 60,000 whites.[91] The eight Ivy League colleges alone could absorb every black undergraduate in the United States who scored over 1,200 and still have blacks statistically "under-represented" in the Ivy League.

Statistics are at least equally grim for the minority pool of applicants available to leading American engineering schools. There are about a dozen engineering schools in the United States where the average mathematics score alone on the Scholastic Aptitude Test is over 700 out of a possible 800. There were fewer than 200 black or Mexican American students who scored at that mathematics level in 1985, fewer than 100 Puerto Ricans, and fewer than 50 American Indians. Even if all the students at the 700 mathematics level applied to engineering schools, all four groups would still be grossly "under-represented" in engineering schools, for together their pools included fewer than 500 students—compared to more than 3,600 among Asian Americans.[92]

Similar patterns are found in postgraduate education. A score of 650 or above on the quantitative portion of the Graduate Record Examination is common at top-rated American graduate schools, in either the physical or the social sciences, but there were fewer than 150 black students in the entire country who met this standard in 1978–79. For top American law schools, a common threshold was a score of 600 on the Law School Aptitude Test in the 1970s and a college grade-point average of 3.25. Only 39 black students in the country met those standards in 1976.[93] Yet, in order to get a visible statistical "representation" of black students, far more blacks than this were admitted by these law schools. The net result, at ten top-rated American law schools, was that blacks constituted 7 percent of the student body, had LSAT scores averaging 144 points lower than those of their white classmates, entered law school with lower college grades than whites, and their law school grades were, on average, at the 8th percentile.[94]

The negative academic consequences of admitting particular groups of students on the basis of "representation" rather than qualifications is not confined to elite institutions or to black students. Elite institutions tend to take the lead in such policies, perhaps because of their visibility or because of their vast federal research grants (hundreds of millions of dollars at some institutions) which could be jeopardized by any charge of racial discrimination based on "under-representation" of minorities. But once these elite institutions begin to siphon off minority students who would otherwise qualify for admission to institutions at the second or third tier in terms of academic quality, these second- and third-tier institutions may end up with a conspicuous lack of minority students, unless they in turn also begin to admit minority applicants who fall below their normal admissions standards. In a climate of opinion in which statistical "under-representation" is equated with discrimination, both in political and legal discourse, each tier of schools may in self-defense admit minority students it knows to be unable to keep up academically.

Even if most minority students are able to meet the normal standards at the "average" range of colleges and universities, the systematic mismatching of minority students begun at the top can mean that such students are generally overmatched throughout all levels of higher education. Youngsters who could have succeeded at San Jose State University may be failing at Berkeley, while youngsters who could have succeeded at a community college are failing at San Jose State. Alternatively, a student who could have successfully carried out his plans to major in chemistry or physics at San Jose State may be forced to major in sociology in order to survive at Berkeley. In neither case does this imply that the students are "unqualified" in some absolute sense. They are mismatched institutionally.

## Prediction vs. "Ability"

There remains the curious question as to why tests whose cultural bias is apparent nevertheless do not underestimate the later performances of disadvantaged applicants, whether in school or at work. Performance involves much more than either innate ability or developed capacity, and there is no reason to expect these other factors to be evenly distributed among groups who behave differently in innumerable other aspects of life. If the degree of familiarity with middle-class words and information, for example, is a proxy for some of the attitudes, behavior, and experience affecting performance, then such questions may have predictive validity, even if the knowledge they test is as irrelevant as critics claim.

More generally, the predictive validity of any criterion—whether mental test scores, a criminal record, or marital status—does not depend upon the direct or obvious relevance of the criterion in question. If married men generally make significantly better insurance salesmen than single men, then this empirical generalization may be useful in employment selections, whether or not anyone knows why, and even if the marriage of existing single men for the sake of their careers would not improve their salesmanship in the slightest. If there are general differences in attitudes or behavior between those men who get married and those who do not, then some of these differences may affect their salesmanship—whether or not anyone knows specifically what such differences are. The predictive validity of a given criterion is an empirical question, not a question of plausibility or of demonstrated causation.

Many who express great misgivings at leaving decision-makers free to use tests as they see fit overlook the fact that these are seldom unconstrained decisions. Competition imposes powerful penalties for being wrong and offers high rewards for being right. The variation in decision-making processes among competing institutions subjects all standards to competitive stress and weeding out. Yale University cannot simply give in to inertia or fads in its admissions policies, if that gives Harvard a competitive edge in recruiting from the same pool of students. Still less can the Chrysler Corporation become capricious or self-indulgent in its hiring standards and hope to survive in competition with General Motors or with Japanese or European automobile manufacturers. The only people who can afford to make decisions without fear of consequences beforehand, and without being forced to correct mistakes afterwards, are precisely those third party observers whom critics turn to: judges, politicians, and bureaucrats.

Those who criticize tests as culturally biased often argue for the creation of "culture-free" tests or "culture-fair" tests. But if cultures are particular ways of accomplishing important human functions, then it would be an incredible coincidence if all cultures were equally efficient in all things. Massive cultural borrowings throughout history and around the world suggest that they are not. Moreover, since there are no culture-free societies, all performances will be performance in some given culture, so that attempts to predict performance are therefore attempts to predict what will happen within a particular cultural context. For a "culture free" test to do this seems almost a contradiction in terms.

To be culturally "fair" seems even more nebulous, a confounding of prediction and morality. Presumably, a culturally "fair" test would produce a similar distribution of results from peoples of different cultures. However much this might conform to the beliefs, desires, or philosophy of observers, it is not at all clear what practical purpose it would serve.

Where the purpose is not to predict consequences, in education or employment, but to assess innate potential, then "culture-free" test results might have some value as pure information, or for psychological, political, or ideological purposes. However, culture "fair" tests would lack even this effect, if their very construction and validation were based on creating a preconceived distribution of results. The same objection applies to tests designed to cause disadvantaged minorities to outscore the general population.

If the purpose of such tests is to demonstrate that any results desired can be produced by a change of questions, then such tests successfully accomplish this trivial purpose. However, tests do not exist for their own sake, but for what they attempt to predict about behavior outside of tests. The relevant standard for alternative tests—or for non-test criteria—is a better record of prediction. Few critics seem to want to meet that standard and few alternative criteria (interviews, recommendations, etc.) demonstrate as high a predictive validity as tests.

Some of the empirical correlations between test scores and subsequent performance may seem quite modest. However, once again the relevant comparison is not between the actual and the ideal, but between one predictive device and its alternatives. Moreover, test score correlations are complicated by the fact that many studies of correlation are based on samples drawn from institutions with a relatively narrow range of scores. There is little (if any) data on how well students with below-average mathematics scores perform at the Massachusetts Institute of Technology, for example, because such students are unlikely to be admitted to MIT in the first place. Whether MIT students who score 775 on the mathematics SAT do appreciably better than those who score 750 (the school average) is not a crucial indicator of predictive validity, just as measuring the performance of basketball players who are 7 feet tall against that of players who are 7 feet 2 inches tall will not prove whether height is important for basketball players.

Some critics of standardized tests have, however, seized upon modest correlations in such settings to argue that tests are "irrelevant." This argument is analogous to concluding that, because 7-foot 2-inch basketball players may not perform substantially better than those an even 7 feet tall, it shows that people of normal height (or, in principle, midgets) can generally play basketball as well as anyone, because height has little correlation with performance.

Where such reasoning has been put into effect by lowering admissions standards for some lower scoring groups, the fallacy has often been exposed in ways painful to the individual and to the institution. At the University of the Philippines, for example, when students from rural and low-income backgrounds were admitted with somewhat lower qualifications than other applicants (1) nearly half shifted out of their originally chosen majors or were forced out by poor performance, (2) four-fifths eventually dropped out of the university entirely, and (3) the remaining fifth averaged lower grades than their classmates.[95] Similar results have been found for untouchables in India[96] and for blacks in the United States.[97]

Viewing standardized tests instrumentally, the relevant criteria are the costs and benefits of such tests compared to alternative selection methods. If a modest correlation between test scores and grades increases the proportion of students who complete a given college from 80 percent to 95 percent, then saving the costs wasted on the 15 percent who would otherwise have dropped out may repay the costs of testing, several times over. Additional benefits include a higher proportion of top achievers.[98] Whatever the figures may be in a particular case, the question is not whether tests produce "high" or "low" correlations, but whether whatever correlation it has is sufficient to produce savings sufficient to cover its costs. These savings and these costs may be in money terms or in broader terms, but the basic trade-off remains the same in principle.

## The Special Case of "Orientals"

The spectacular rise of Japan from wartime devastation to economic and technological eminence in the postwar era, the similar upsurge of South Korea, Hong Kong, Singapore, and Taiwan in recent years, and the remarkable achievements of Chinese, Japanese, Korean, and Vietnamese students in the United States, have all served to revive genetic theories of intelligence. These racial theories now ascribe genetic superiority to "Orientals," defined as people indigenous to the region north of the Himalayas and east of the Caucasus, rather than to "Asians," defined in broader geographical terms to include Indians, Malays, or Indonesians as well. Among the evidence cited have been higher IQ or other test scores in Japan or among people of Chinese, Japanese, or other Oriental or Asian ancestry in the United States.

Such claims have been carefully examined in detail by Professor James R. Flynn of the University of Otago in New Zealand, in a way which is very revealing, not only as regards this particular issue, but also as regards the elusive and treacherous nature of statistics in general, when used uncritically. A closer examination of national IQ data, which seemed to show Japan to have the highest IQ of any nation in the world, turned up problems in the selection of tests and in the selection of individuals tested, which were enough to cause the principal advocate of Japanese superiority to concede that the test scores reported should be revised downward.[99] Moreover, since the issue raised was one of genetic or racial superiority, the relevant comparison was not simply between Japan and the United States, but between people of Japanese ancestry and white Americans. Here the advantage of the Japanese in Japan over whites in the United States shrank to 3 points in IQ score, which is considerably less than the increase in IQ experienced by a number of nations over time, while those nations' racial composition remained more or less unaltered.

If international IQ comparisons lent little support to the genetic theory of achievement differences, comparisons between Orientals and Caucasians within the United States dealt a real blow to the theory—and to the whole relationship between IQ and achievement. Some of the test results which seemed to show higher IQs among Chinese Americans and Japanese Americans than among white Americans turned out, upon investigation, to be tests using obsolete norms giving inflated IQ scores or tests normed on a substandard local white population.[100] A comprehensive survey of IQ studies over a period of several decades turned up no instance where Chinese or Japanese (or Asian or Oriental) Americans scored higher than the national average of white Americans. Often the racial differences in IQ were no more than one or a few points, but they invariably favored white Americans, often with the Orientals outperforming the whites on the nonverbal portions of the tests and the whites out-performing the Orientals on the verbal portions.[101]

What makes these results in the United States momentous in their implications is that Chinese and Japanese Americans do in fact outperform white Americans, both academically and in the economy. Orientals or Asians as a group have higher grades in school and higher scores on such achievement tests as the widely used Scholastic Aptitude Test. They also have higher incomes and are much more highly represented in high-level occupations than are white Americans.[102] In short, what has been claimed, erroneously, for blacks and other low-income minorities in the United States, is in fact true for Asian Americans: Their subsequent academic and job performances exceed what their IQ test scores would predict.

Among Chinese American and Japanese American school children born between 1945 and 1949, only half as high a proportion as among whites lagged behind the grade level appropriate for children their ages. Although a higher proportion of the students from these two groups ended up taking the Scholastic Aptitude Test than among whites, the Oriental students matched the scores of the white students, who were a smaller and presumably more select portion of the white student population as a whole.[103] As for performance in later life, the average Chinese American and Japanese American earned an income earned only by white Americans with higher average IQs than their Oriental counterparts.[104] Orientals in the United States were also better represented in high-level occupations than were white Americans—and the white Americans who reached these same occupational levels had higher average IQs than the Orientals who reached these levels.[105]

The general relationship between IQ and achievement, whether in school or in later life, has been well-established by a number of studies.[106] However, this *general* relationship does not apply to all groups, as the achievements of Chinese Americans and Japanese Americans demonstrate. But this general relationship cannot be simply waved aside whenever politically convenient, for the groups for whom it has been waved aside—notably blacks and other low-income minorities—are not the groups who demonstrate an ability to achieve beyond their IQ or other test score levels. Moreover, the remarkable achievements of people of Japanese ancestry, whether in Japan or in the United States, are clearly not due to racial superiority demonstrated on IQ tests, for that IQ advantage is very small in the case of the Japanese in Japan and nonexistent for Japanese Americans. Clearly, there are very large environmental factors at work, perhaps better described as cultural factors, to distinguish them from features of the immediate surroundings, as measured by conventional indices of socioeconomic conditions.

Although these cultural advantages do not apply today to low-income minorities, the large impact of cultural factors argues against any claim that low-income groups are doomed to remain where they are. Moreover, the importance of cultural factors, expressed in such mundane things as longer hours devoted to homework, points in the direction from which improvement can come.

## IMPLICATIONS

Among the innumerable capabilities which all human societies require, many are mental capabilities. If all these developed mental capabilities were, at all times, evenly distributed among all racial and ethnic groups, it would be a remarkable exception to the striking differences found among these groups in almost every other aspect of their behavior. But to say that there are intergroup differences in particular mental skills at a given time is not to say that groups that excel at some skills excel at all skills, so as to create general "superiority" or "inferiority," much less that skill levels or patterns remain fixed over time or are genetic in origin.

Although the discussion of intelligence has been almost exclusively in terms of mental tests, this has been a matter of convenience rather than importance. It is by no means established that mental tests have been devised for all (or most) of the vast spectrum of human skills. Even activities normally thought of as physical have mental dimensions that can make major differences in outcomes.

Farming, for example, has long been thought of as a physical activity with no mental dimension, and the peasant has often been depicted as an utterly stupid creature—"a brother to the ox," in one classic poem.[107] Yet groups with striking success in intellectual activities have often floundered or failed in agriculture, not from inability to meet its physical demands, but because of damaging errors or ineptitude in managing farms. Baron de Hirsch's far-flung agricultural colonies for Jews in the Western Hemisphere experienced many such difficulties,[108] as did the farms of nineteenth-century German immigrant intellectuals, derisively called "Latin farmers" in the United States[109] because they often knew that ancient language but understood little about farming.

Like farming, sports are often thought of as having only physical demands. But the importance of the mental dimension of most sports is indicated by the fact that few athletes reach their performance peak at their physical peak, around age 18, but more usually 5 to 10 years later, when they are more seasoned and experienced—smarter, in a word. The kind of split-second decision making—often in midair—required of a basketball player, in the midst of frantic efforts by opposing players and team mates, is obviously quite different from the kind of scholarship which may take years to produce a book. But to be an outstanding basketball player means to out-think opponents consistently in these split-second decisions under stress. Is it coincidence that the fields dominated by black Americans—basketball, jazz, running backs in football—all have this improvisational decision-making, with numerous factors being decided in an instant under emotional pressure? Perhaps—and perhaps not. Whether it is genetic or a cultural style is even more problematical.

Existing knowledge of the structure and nature of intelligence is far too preliminary to answer many of the questions raised about race and mental potential. The more immediate, practical use of mental tests as aids to prediction raises fewer and more limited questions. The relevant issue is not how accurate the predictions are on some absolute scale, or even relative to predictions in other fields, such as economics or weather forecasting. The question is whether alternative means of accomplishing the same tasks as mental tests have as good a record. The evasion of this crucial empirical question has been a consistent pattern among critics of mental testing.

Among American colleges and universities, the range of institutional test score averages is enormous. Scores on the quantitative portion of the Scholastic Aptitude Test, for example, range from an average of 750 at the Massachusetts Institute of Technology and the California Institute of Technology to less than 300 at Cheyney University.[110] Tests are used not merely to determine who is "qualified" to go to college—almost everyone is, somewhere, in the vast range of American colleges—but to attempt to match the level of performance of individuals and institutions.

The variance of test scores at a given institution may be relatively small, compared to the variance among college students as a whole. This means that predictions of individual performance rankings at given institutions can be quite difficult, when most of the students fall within a relatively narrow range. Factors such as attitude, discipline, and emotional state may become very important among students closely matched on mental test scores. In such a context, relatively modest correlations between score rankings and subsequent performance in college have caused some to dismiss the tests as "irrelevant," and to advocate opening admissions to applicants with far lower scores, especially when these students come from disadvantaged groups. Such practices have often led to disaster for both the individuals and the institutions.[111]

The many unanswered questions regarding race and intelligence do not mean that there are no answers at all. There are some important things already known, which at least limit the range of disagreement over empirical issues. Perhaps more significant, there are systematic analytical approaches which yield a measure of understanding, even if they do not yield the emotional satisfaction of categorical pronouncements.

# CHAPTER 7

# RACE AND SLAVERY

*Slavery until recently was universal in two senses. Most settled societies incorporated the institution into their social structures, and few peoples in the world have not constituted a major source of slaves at one time or another.* —David Eltis[1]

Although slavery in the United States was referred to as a "peculiar institution," slavery was in fact one of the oldest and most widespread institutions on Earth. Slavery existed in the Western Hemisphere before Columbus' ships appeared on the horizon, and it existed in Europe, Asia, Africa, and the Middle East for thousands of years. Slavery was older than Islam, Buddhism, or Christianity, and both the secular and religious moralists of societies around the world accepted human bondage, not only as a fact of life but as something requiring no special moral justification.[2] Slavery was "peculiar" in the United States only because human bondage was inconsistent with the principles on which this nation was founded. Historically, however, it was those principles which were peculiar, not slavery.

Although slavery has come to be identified with the enslavement of Africans, that too ignores the long history and vast scope of the institution. The very word "slave" is derived from the Slavs,[3] who were enslaved on a massive scale and were often sold into bondage all across the continent of Europe and in the Ottoman Empire. The Arabic word for slave likewise derives from the Arabic word for Slavs,[4] as did the word for slave in German, Dutch, French, Spanish, and Italian.[5] Nor were the Slavs the only Europeans enslaved. In just one raid on the Balearic islands off the east coast of Spain, the famous pirate Barbarossa carried off thousands of Christians into slavery,[6] and after a later raid on Venice, the booty he brought back included, in addition to such things as cloth and money, a thousand girls and fifteen hundred boys.[7] Europeans living in vulnerable coastal settlements in the Balkans were likewise raided by pirates and were carried off by the tens of thousands, to be sold in the slave markets of North Africa and the Middle East.[8] Russians by the hundreds of thousands were sold into the international slave trade by Turkic raiders, before a strong Russian state, and then empire, was consolidated and able to resist these incursions.[9]

Slavery was at one time common all across the continent of Europe and, as late as 1776, Adam Smith wrote that slavery still existed in Russia, Poland, Hungary, and in parts of Germany—indeed, that Western Europe was the only region of the world where slavery had been "abolished altogether."[10] In the sixteenth century, peace terms imposed by the Ottoman Turks required the defeated Hungarians to send them 10 percent of their population each decade as slaves.[11] It was common for the Ottomans to requisition a certain number of boys from among conquered European populations, these boys to be taken into the service of the imperial government.[12] In the eighteenth century, immigrant German farm communities on the lower Volga were raided by Mongol tribesmen and the captured Germans taken off to be sold in the slave markets of Asia.[13] In the 1820s, 6,000 Greeks were sent to Egypt as slaves and, half a century later, a report to the British Parliament noted that both white and black slaves were still being traded in Egypt and Turkey,[14] years after blacks had been emancipated in the United States.

Slavery was likewise common in Asia. The Manchus raided China, Korea, and Mongolia for slaves.[15] Raiders from the Sulu Archipelago, in what is now the Philippines, conducted large-scale expeditions to capture people as slaves across wide reaches of Southeast Asia. [16] Slavery of various kinds was also common in India, where the original *thugs* often murdered parents in order to get their children and sell them into bondage.[17] Organized slave markets and international shipments of slaves were also common in Asia. Slaves from India were shipped to Java and Indonesian slaves were shipped as far away as South Africa.[18] Despite its reputation as an island paradise, Bali lost many thousands of its people as slaves, most being shipped off to other parts of Southeast Asia.[19] Smaller or less advanced groups were set upon by marauders in many parts of Asia, as they were in other parts of the world—hill tribes, nomadic peoples, bands of hunters and gatherers, or primitive slash-and-burn agriculturalists being set upon by those who had reached more advanced stages of development and who had more advanced weapons. This pattern was common for centuries in Cambodia, Malaya, the Philippines, Burma, or the islands of Indonesia or New Guinea.[20]

Many peoples around the world—Christians, Jews, and Moslems, for example—exempted themselves from enslavement, while engaging in the enslavement of others. This left as prey those peoples in societies too small or too weak to defend themselves. Many such societies remained in sub-Saharan Africa—often in small, isolated villages—after most of Europe, Asia, and the Middle East had been consolidated into nations too powerful to be victimized in this way. In Africa as well, people from powerful warrior tribes, such as the Masai, were rarely enslaved.[21] Sub-Saharan Africa was unique only in remaining vulnerable longer. Where black Africans were themselves powerful, they often used that power to enslave their weaker neighbors, both for their own use and for sale to Europeans.[22] Conversely, in regions of Europe where there were vulnerable peoples without the military protection of strong nation states—as on the Adriatic coast, for example—these peoples were raided and enslaved for at least twice as long as the 300 years of slavery in the United States.[23] Only after the consolidation of political power in that region and the Catholic Church's intervention after the peoples of the Balkans had accepted Christianity for centuries did the enslavement of Bosnians and others stop[24]—and the Europeans then turn their attention toward Africa as an alternative source of supply.

Over the centuries, somewhere in the neighborhood of 11 million people were shipped across the Atlantic from Africa as slaves, and another 14 million African slaves were taken across the Sahara Desert or shipped through the Persian Gulf and other waterways to the nations of North Africa and the Middle East.[25] Significant proportions of both massive streams of slaves did not live to complete the journey.[26] Mortality rates were even higher among those who were walked across the burning sands of the Sahara than among those subjected to the horrors and dangers of the Atlantic crossing. On the Saharan route, several Africans were enslaved for every one who reached the Mediterranean alive.[27] Nor were these 25 million human beings the only victims of slavery. Africa itself used large numbers of slaves in all sorts of agricultural, domestic, military, and even commercial and governmental enterprises.[28]

Numbers never reached the same magnitudes in Southeast Asia, for example, where there was simply not the large demand for slaves that existed in the Ottoman Empire or in the Western Hemisphere. Supply alone cannot explain the existence or magnitude of slavery. There also had to be a demand from other societies wealthy and powerful enough to have a use for large numbers of people to work in its fields, mines, homes, or other places. Although North African and Middle Eastern nations dominated the slave trade from Africa for centuries before the Europeans appeared on the scene, the latter's insatiable demand for slave labor for their Western Hemisphere colonies caused the slave exports across the Atlantic to exceed during its era even the massive shipments of human beings from Africa into the Islamic world. During this era of European domination of the slave trade from Africa, about four times as many Africans as Europeans arrived in the Western Hemisphere in the centuries from the time of Columbus' voyages until 1820.[29] It was only the fact that the slave trade to the Islamic countries began earlier and continued longer that made the Middle East and North Africa the largest absorber of black Africans as slaves over the centuries. Moreover, it is only the existence of a vastly greater literature on slavery in the Western world than in the Islamic world[30] which creates the myopic illusion that slavery, or even African slavery, was a predominantly European phenomenon.

For slavery to be understood as a global phenomenon, it must be analyzed beyond any particular national background—and yet in the light of numerous real national and historical settings, rather than as an abstract model. To explain slavery as being a consequence of certain European ideas leading to bondage for Africans[31] is to ignore the glaring fact that slavery extended in time and space far beyond Europeans and Africans, and far beyond those who shared particular European ideas. Nor can a certain crop, such as sugar, be regarded as some kind of key to understanding slavery,[32] even in the Western Hemisphere, where millions of slaves worked on sugarcane plantations in South America and the Caribbean, for other millions toiled in the cotton fields of the southern United States. Worldwide, still more vast numbers of slaves worked in an enormous range of occupations, from the harems and military units of the Middle East to the clove plantations of Zanzibar, the coffee plantations of Yemen, the pearl fisheries of the Red Sea, and in mines from Egypt to Burma, as well as in high government posts in the Ottoman Empire, where enslaved eunuchs especially could acquire fearsome power.[33]

To make some sense of this chaotic complexity, it is necessary to recognize that the stark dichotomy of freedom and slavery concealed degrees and varieties which must be understood, in order to understand the phenomenon as a whole.

## GRADATIONS OF SLAVERY

Clearly the circumstances of a plantation slave, laboring under a tropical sun in the sugar cane fields and with the threat of the lash ever present, were radically different from the circumstances of a slave who advised a sultan of the Ottoman Empire on high government policy, or who ruled a province or led an army into battle. Even within a given society, such as the antebellum South in the United States, the circumstances of slaves varied from the classic plantation field hand to urban slaves who often led day-to-day lives not very different from those of ordinary employees, often choosing both their own housing and their own employers, while paying a share of their earnings to their owners.[34] This practice of slaves hiring themselves out to various employers also existed among slaves in ancient Roman society[35] and, in more recent centuries, in Southeast Asia.[36]

While the descendants of slaves carried an indelible stigma for generations in some countries, the male offspring of the Ottoman sultan's harem became his heirs, including his successors as sultan in the Ottoman Empire. In Southeast Asia, Chinese immigrants—overwhelmingly male—often took local slave women as concubines, in some cases selling them again in later years when the men returned to China, taking their children with them. In other cases, where the original intention to return to China faded away over the years, the concubines might become the wives of those men who remained. Among European men sojourning in Southeast Asia, it was more common to set the women free when the men returned to Europe alone.[37]

Clearly, slavery has existed in a very wide range of modifications, so much so that some scholars have spent much time trying to determine where slavery ended and other forms of bondage and dependency began, especially in non-Western societies where words and practices varied in ways not easy to discern.[38] Rather than attempt the impossible task of exploring all the modifications of slavery, we can examine the characteristics of a few disparate forms of the institution.

The simplest and purest form of slavery is that of the laborer working under the immediate and complete control and direction of some overseer with the arbitrary power of summary punishment. This was the fate of

millions of slaves throughout the Western Hemisphere, where the harshness of their conditions was such that few slave populations reproduced
themselves, and most had to be replenished with new captives from
Africa. Literally working slaves to death has been a practice recurring in
a number of very disparate settings, such as in the building of infrastructure in Iraq or in the Nazi slave labor camps in World War II. In some
societies in Asia, Africa, and the Western Hemisphere, slaves were deliberately killed as human sacrifices.[39] In ancient Rome, slave gladiators
killed each other in the coliseum for the amusement of the spectators,
and in other societies around the world slave owners arbitrarily killed
slaves, sometimes in sadistic ways, with impunity.[40]

It seems almost inconceivable that slaves could have ranged from this
abject level of debasement and dehumanization to wealthy and powerful
men who ruled over free populations and commanded armies. In between
were slaves who were craftsmen, teachers, doctors and, in at least one case,
a black captain of a Mississippi riverboat with a racially mixed crew in the
antebellum South.[41]

Both within and between societies, there was a systematic relationship
between the kinds of work that slaves did and the way they were treated—a
fact with wider and deeper implications for the use of power in general.
Although slaves were subject to the virtually unlimited arbitrary power of slave
owners in many societies—often de facto, even in societies which recognized
no such right de jure—many slave owners nevertheless found it expedient to
use other incentives than force, including money, autonomy, and even the
granting of civil or military power, to get slaves to carry out responsibilities of a
higher and more demanding nature. Nothing could more clearly indicate the
limited ability of even unbridled power to accomplish all its objectives.

Where those objectives were simply the growing and processing of
sugar or cotton, or the mining of salt or other minerals, then pure, stark,
and brutal slavery was sufficient to accomplish these objectives. But
where the work required somewhat more individual attention and discretion, as in the growing and processing of tobacco or the performing of
domestic chores, some relaxation of the strictest slavery became apparent. Ironically, slaves in poorer societies in Southeast Asia were often
treated more mildly than in more advanced, commercial, and industrial
societies[42] where mass production agriculture or mining absorbed vast
numbers of regimented slaves. It was not a difference between European
and Asian slavery, as such, that was crucial, but rather the nature of the
work. Manacled skeletons of men have been found in a Burma mine and

human sacrifice was a practice among various Asian peoples, with those sacrificed being more likely to be recent captives rather than slaves of long service.[43] Among the Circassian women who were prized as concubines in the harems of the Ottoman Empire, their treatment was sufficiently mild to cause mothers to deliberately train their daughters for this role and to sell them into bondage in the harems of wealthy Ottoman men, from which they often emerged later with advantageous marriages having been arranged for them by their owners.[44] As higher and higher levels of responsibility and discretion were required of slaves, they were treated less and less like slaves, so that this status became virtually nominal for those who held wealth and power as advisers or viceroys of Ottoman rulers, for example.

Not all societies permitted slaves to rise to high positions, and in many societies it was taboo to permit slaves to use arms. Weapons, like money or education, were a two-edged sword: They increased the range and value of the tasks that could be performed by slaves, while at the same time providing means to facilitate their escape. The nature of the social, military, and other circumstances determined where the point of balance might be for a given slave-owning society. In the Western Hemisphere, for example, education was in many places explicitly forbidden by law.

To make some sense of the vast numbers and almost chaotic varieties of slavery, it will be necessary to analyze in some systematic way the economic and social incentives and constraints within which slavery existed, the social consequences of this institution, and some of the broader implications of its existence and demise.What must be explained is not the rise of slavery, which pre-dates history, but why it ended and why it varied as it did during its existence.


## PURE SLAVERY

Before considering some of the modifications of slavery, and the reasons for those modifications, it is necessary to look at simple *unmodified* slavery, to see which of its characteristics and limitations made modification useful to the slave-owning societies—and under what conditions. While 100 percent pure, unmodified slavery may never have existed, any more than 100 percent pure capitalism, socialism, or feudalism ever existed, the concept is a useful starting point. Moreover, for many of the slaves who toiled in the sugarcane and cotton fields of the Western Hemisphere, what they experienced was in fact painfully close to 100 percent pure slavery.

## The Economics of Slavery

Like all economic institutions and activities, slavery had costs and benefits. While the benefits of slavery went predominantly to people who were not slaves, and the costs were paid predominantly by people subjected to bondage, there were also costs to the capture of slaves and more costs to the maintenance of slavery as a system. Moreover, these costs were different when the enslaved population was racially distinct from the free population.

In ancient Rome, individual Romans might be reduced to slavery as punishment for transgressions, but ordinarily slaves were non-Romans captured in battle or acquired in trade. Similarly, in a later era, it was common for the Ottoman Empire to enslave Europeans or Africans, as it was common for some African tribes to enslave others, or for people in Asia to enslave both non-Asians and Asians belonging to a different race or class from themselves. In short, except for debt-bondage or bondage as punishment, the process of enslavement has generally been one of enslaving outsiders of one sort or another, whether by race, religion, nationality, or other characteristics. For centuries in Europe, it was considered legitimate for the Christians of Western Europe to enslave "pagans" from the Balkans or Eastern Europe, and it was long after all of Europe became Christian that the Catholic Church finally insisted on an end to the pretense that European slaves were pagans.[45] In short, the choice as to which outsiders to enslave was not a matter of racial ideology, but was based on pragmatic considerations as to availability, including both the military and legal obstacles to their enslavement.

In ancient times, to attempt to raid the Roman Empire to acquire Romans as slaves was likely to prove costly in both immediate terms of armed resistance and in terms of provoking retaliatory raids and warfare from Rome. Such considerations not only determined which groups were more likely to become slaves and which were more likely to be slave masters as of a given time, but also suggest why continued enslavement of particular populations became less common with the rise of powerful nation states. Turkish enslavement of peoples in the Caucasus continued until the Caucasus was conquered by the Russians and incorporated into the Russian Empire.[46] Isolated slave raids might occur afterwards, but for the Ottoman Empire to attempt mass enslavement of subjects of the Russian Empire was to risk war.

The consolidation of nation-states around the world reduced the number of places from which people could be captured and enslaved. Long after it was no longer feasible for one nation-state to challenge another by attempting to enslave its people, free-lance pirates and similar marauders on land were not deterred by such considerations and continued to make raids to acquire slaves in Southeast Asia, for example, particularly in remote and backward regions beyond the effective control of either indigenous or colonial governments. These pirates were sometimes Chinese, sometimes Arabs, sometimes Malays, or members of other groups from within or outside the region.[47] Similarly, armed Arab free-lance marauders moved into Central Africa in the nineteenth century and established their own settlements, acquiring slaves and other forms of wealth as tribute from the surrounding African communities.[48] While pirates and comparable free-lance operators on land were active in the capture of people for enslavement, the actual trading of slaves in the marketplace was often done by merchant peoples who treated slaves as simply an additional form of merchandise.

Around the world, the slave trade was conducted by merchant peoples, such as the Venetians, Greeks, and Jews in Europe,[49] the overseas Chinese in Southeast Asia,[50] or by the Arabs who played both the merchant and marauder roles in Africa,[51] though even here the same individual seldom handled the slave from initial capture to final sale.[52] When Italian merchants began displacing Jewish merchants in the eastern Mediterranean and the Black Sea in medieval times, they also began displacing Jews in the Black Sea slave trade.[53] Another great merchant people— Gujaratis from India—often financed the African slave trade, though they did not usually conduct it.[54] The Yao, a Central African tribe noted for being the leading traders of ivory in their region, likewise became the leading traders of slaves in that region.[55] Neither a national policy nor a racial ideology was necessary for enslavement to take place. All that was necessary was the existence of vulnerable people, whoever and wherever they might be—and regardless of whether they were racially similar or different from those who victimized them. Slavery flourished in ancient Greece and Rome without any racial ideology.[56]

Vulnerable people were enslaved around the world and down through history. Sailors from Magellan's ships left stranded in Southeast Asia were sold into slavery by the local people.[57] In Spain, the Moors sometimes enslaved Spaniards and the Spaniards sometimes enslaved Moors, depending upon what the opportunities and the alternatives were.[58] The various peoples living in the drainage basins of the Caspian Sea and Black Sea likewise captured one another to sell as slaves during the Middle Ages.[59] In ancient times, Roman soldiers enslaved enemy captives and expected to be enslaved themselves if captured[60]—and, in fact, Romans enslaved in Carthage were repatriated after the war against Hannibal.[61] An estimated 97,000 Jews were enslaved by the Romans as a result of war.[62] Germans, Gauls, and Celts were also enslaved by the Romans.[63] Enslavement was based on self-interest and opportunity, not ideology.

Peoples regularly subjected to slave raids might indeed be despised, and treated with contempt both during their enslavement and after their emancipation, but that was not what caused them to be enslaved in the first place. Although there was no religious basis for racism in the Islamic world, the massive enslavement of sub-Saharan Africans by Arabs and other Moslems was followed by a racial disdain toward black people in the Middle East—but this racial disdain *followed*, rather than preceded, the enslavement of black Africans, and had not been apparent in the Arabs' previous dealings with Ethiopians.[64] In the West as well, racism was promoted by slavery, rather than vice versa. Both in North America and in South Africa, racist rationales for slavery were resorted to only after religious rationales were tried and found wanting.[65] But that is not to say that either rationale was in fact the reason for enslavement. In many other societies, no rationale was considered necessary.

Africa remained prey to other nations, long after mass enslavement was no longer viable in many other parts of the world, because it remained vulnerable longer. Africa was, and is, the least urbanized continent and long contained many smaller, weaker, and more isolated peoples, who were prey to more powerful African tribes, such as the Ashanti and the Yao, as well as to Arab slave raiders. Many of the peoples victimized by the Arabs in Central Africa had lived isolated from the outside world and were easy prey for marauders with firearms, who seized their goods and such people as they wished, leaving behind famine brought on by looted granaries and diseases spread by caravans.[66] Europeans became mass traders of African slaves largely by purchase from Africa's more powerful tribes and empires. A particularly high cost prevented most Europeans (the Portuguese being an exception) from capturing Africans directly—the extreme vulnerability of Europeans to African diseases during the era of slavery. Before the use of quinine became widespread, the average life expectancy of a European in the interior of sub-Saharan Africa was less than one year.[67] Most European slave traders therefore purchased Africans who had already been captured by others, typically by other Africans.

The costs of slavery did not end with capture. There were various kinds of costs to maintaining the system, including the prevention of escape by those enslaved. Moreover, these costs had to be minimized, for the system was economically viable only so long as these costs did not exceed the benefits to the slave owners. Thus, while slaves could be manacled and chained while in transit, this was seldom practical when they were at their destinations and at work. Even to have them continuously surrounded by armed guards was not always economically feasible, and in fact this was seldom, if ever, done in the antebellum South. Nor was it common in the Ottoman Empire or in Southeast Asia. Instead, social and psychological means of control were used, backed up by brutal force against those individuals for whom these means did not suffice.

Maintaining ignorance among slaves was one way of reducing the cost of maintaining slavery, particularly in societies where the work performed by slaves required no education. By ignorance is not meant here simply the absence of formal education—important as that sometimes was in deterring escape from the most brutal kinds of slavery, without incurring high costs of having armed guards—but also an ignorance of the local geographical region. Enslaving people on their own home grounds was more likely to lead to successful attempts at escape than where they were enslaved far from familiar surroundings. Thus, when the Dutch controlled Java, they preferred to import slaves from outside Java—and preferably of diverse origins, to reduce the likelihood of conspiracies.[68] When the British bought local slaves in Banten and tried to use them in a factory there, they found themselves losing their workforce through escapes.[69] Conversely, Malay and Indonesian slaves were sometimes transported thousands of miles away to South Africa[70] at a time when Africans were being transported thousands of miles to the Western Hemisphere. It was not literally impossible for foreigners to enslave people in their own homelands, as some indigenous peoples were enslaved in the Western Hemisphere, for example, but it was sufficiently more costly to be the exception rather than the rule.[71]

When costs are defined as economists conceive costs—as foregone benefits—then there were additional and less visible costs to slave owners and to slave-owning societies, but very large costs nonetheless. In a system of relatively unmodified slavery, such as prevailed in the Western

Hemisphere, the kinds of work done by slaves was limited by the need to maintain close control of a slave population that in some countries outnumbered the free population. The need to prevent escape and organized rebellion, and the maintenance of subordination in order to get the work done, precluded using slaves in a wide variety of otherwise productive activities requiring education, dispersal, or the use of money or arms. These foregone opportunities to develop and exploit the talents and potentialities of slaves, in ways that were done in other slave societies under different conditions, represented very large costs to the non-slave population, not only during the era of slavery, but even in the post-emancipation era, when millions of uneducated people were freed without the means of contributing as much as they could have to the larger society, as well as to their own maintenance and well-being.

In short, pure unmodified slavery reduced the productivity of people with given capabilities, as well as reducing the capabilities that could be developed from people with given potentialities. Moreover, since each generation is raised by the generation before it, later free descendants of the enslaved population would be similarly handicapped in their own development, not only to their own detriment but also to the detriment of the larger society in which they lived.

Race-based slavery had still more costs. Obviously the cost of maintaining slavery and preventing escapes would be lower if the slaves were isolated individuals with no connection to one another and no incentives to aid one another against the slave owners. Just as the Dutch in Java preferred slaves of diverse origins, so in parts of the Western Hemisphere, Africans from a mixture of tribes, speaking different languages, were preferred for the same reasons. In the United States, however, as the most distant of the slave plantation societies from Africa, the higher cost of importing new slaves led to a largely native-born black population as early as colonial times, and this population consisted of families and people who knew each other, and who spoke the same language. Moreover, the free black population had varying degrees of racial solidarity with the slaves, and in various ways could make the maintenance of the slave system more costly.

The most obvious way in which free blacks could impose costs on the slave system was by directly helping slaves escape. Some free blacks did this, as did some sympathetic whites, either individually or in an organized fashion through the so-called "underground railroad" that enabled slaves to escape from the South to the free states. Other deliberate actions, such as encouraging escapes or supplying information on escape routes, also raised the cost of the slave system. Moreover, free blacks raised the cost of maintaining slavery by their very existence, whether or not they took any active role in undermining it. Slaves seeing other members of their own race enjoying freedom were of course more likely to be disgruntled, creating morale and productivity problems, even if this discontent did not lead to escape.

Slaveholders were of course well aware of all this and tried to make the areas in the vicinity of slave plantations inhospitable to free blacks. All sorts of discriminatory legislation and practices sought to reduce the freedom of free blacks, to humble them publicly (by making them get off the sidewalks to make way for white pedestrians, for example), and otherwise make their lives less attractive to blacks still held in bondage. Such restrictions and harassments were far more common in those parts of the South dominated by slave plantations than in Southern cities or in other regions of the South where plantations were less common.[72] Had such policies reflected nothing but pure and simple racism, they might have been expected to be either uniform or to vary in a pattern unrelated to slave plantations. But in fact the special harshness of restrictions on free blacks in the regions where antebellum slave plantations were concentrated had the desired effect of causing them to relocate away from such regions, to move toward the cities and toward the upper South and the North. The net result was that, while the geographic center of the slave population tended to move southwestward at an average rate of nearly 50 miles per decade for nearly a century,[73] toward land more suitable for cotton production, the "free persons of color" were almost evenly split between North and South, with their proportions in the Deep South declining.[74]

One of the ways in which free blacks inadvertently raised the cost of slavery was by acting as a source of literacy to slaves. Most free blacks in the United States were literate in 1850,[75] despite being excluded from public schools in many parts of the country, and despite being forbidden to establish their own schools in much of the South. Since ignorance was a key part of the slave security system in a plantation-slave society, any access to knowledge was seen as a threat to the subordination inherent in slavery, as a source of discontent, and as an aid to escape. Therefore, this particular system of slavery had to pay a high price in lost productivity by keeping slaves ignorant. The Southern society as a whole also had to pay a price in restricting the education of a quarter of a million or more free blacks, even if these restrictions were not as effective as they wished.

While knowledge that would be useful in making escapes was repressed, slavery made investment in the *manual* skills of slaves more profitable than similar investments by an employer of free labor. After an employer incurs the costs of training an employee in some manual craft, that employee can later decide to go work elsewhere, causing the original employer to lose some of the benefits of his investment in training. Even if the employee remains, part of the investment can be lost meeting demands for higher wages, reflecting the greater value of the worker— and not meeting those demands would of course increase the incentives for the employee to go work for someone else. Neither of these problems existed for slaveholders, since slaves were in no position to demand wages, nor could most of them choose to work for someone else. Moreover, if the slave were to be sold later, he could be sold for a higher price as a skilled craftsman, thereby recouping the investment.

The net result of these incentives was that manual skills were common among the enslaved black population of the South, where plantations were more or less self-sufficient little worlds of their own, requiring a variety of skills. Moreover, these skills carried over into the occupations of many "free persons of color" during the era of slavery and afterward. Black craftsmen were long common in the South, as was the case in other parts of the Western Hemisphere, and skilled slaves of various racial backgrounds were common in other slave societies around the world, ancient and modern.[76] Very wide ranges of skills and talents were cultivated among various classes of slaves, especially in those societies where the demographic or other circumstances made organized slave revolts less likely. In addition to administrative, political, and military skills developed among male slaves in the Ottoman Empire, those female slaves who were used as concubines for elite men were often trained in music and in social skills. In short, a society with massive plantations manned by slaves of a different race (and often larger numbers) than themselves operated with more restricted options than a society where the free population had less reason to fear for its own safety and had less need to maintain strict and brutal control to get its work done. Societies with slave populations of racially and linguistically heterogeneous origins, often predominantly female, obviously had far wider options in the occupational use of slaves and the degree to which they could be educated and their talents exploited.

Whether or not specialized skills were involved, slaves were a capital investment in slave societies in general. That is, the current market value of slaves reflected an anticipated future stream of income (or value in kind) from their services. This market value, however, varied enormously from one part of the world to another, and the treatment of slaves tended to vary with this market value. The cost of a slave in the American South was about thirty times the cost of a slave on the coast of Africa, for example.[77] Part of this differential reflected the cost of transportation, including the risk of death en route, and part reflected the fact that slaves in the United States were sufficiently familiar with their tasks and roles as to be more valuable workers than new slaves who would require training. In a country much closer to Africa, such as Brazil, where slave prices were accordingly cheap[78] slaves might be worked to death and then replaced by new arrivals, but this was too costly to be done in the United States. On the contrary, it was common for Southern slaveholders to hire white workers, often Irish immigrants, to do work considered too dangerous for slaves.[79]

The greater capital value of slaves in the United States was also reflected in the lower infant mortality rates among children born to slave women in the South, as compared to infant mortality rates among children born to slave women in the Caribbean or South America. The cost of lower infant mortality rates was a reduced workload for the mother, both before and after giving birth, and some provision for the care of the child during the years when his consumption exceeded any economic contribution that he could make to the slaveholder. In countries where new adult male slaves from Africa were more readily available, these costs were less often incurred.

Given the different economic circumstances of slavery in different countries, it is not surprising that the infant mortality rate among black slaves in the West Indies was several times as high as in the American South,[80] or that the Brazilian plantation slave population was overwhelmingly male, with the few females often being kept locked up at night to prevent their getting pregnant.[81] The more humane laws in Latin American slave societies have led many to conclude that the treatment of slaves was better there than in societies lacking such legal protection of slaves, such as the United States.[82] However, laws are by no means the only constraint on the treatment of slaves, nor a priori the most effective constraint. For a slave to presume to avail himself of such laws was to risk devastating punishment, whether in North or South America—or in the

Middle East or Asia, for that matter. Economics often had much more influence on the treatment of slaves.

Slave prices were responsive to supply and demand, like the prices of inanimate merchandise or the prices of livestock. In Southeast Asia, the prices of male and female slaves were very similar before the arrival in the Straits Settlements of large numbers of predominantly male Chinese immigrants in the eighteenth century. These Chinese men then created an increased demand for female slaves as concubines. Thereafter, in the late eighteenth and early nineteenth centuries, the prices of female slaves rose to become two or three times the prices of male slaves of the same age. European men living in the same region paid even higher prices for the more attractive of the slave women.[83] In the Ottoman Empire, there was a hierarchy of slave prices, reflecting the varying demands and supplies. Because slaves were so often used for domestic purposes, rather than for heavy labor, in the Ottoman Empire, far more women than men were taken as slaves from Africa—so much so as to leave sexually unbalanced societies in parts of East Africa.[84] African women were more likely to be used as housekeepers, while European women, and especially Circassian women, were more likely to be concubines. Slave prices reflected these conditions: Males were generally sold for less than females and African females for less than Circassian females.[85] The large exception was the price of eunuchs, which tended to be the highest of all,[86] given that many men failed to survive castration and the prices of the survivors had to cover the cost of all those sacrificed.

In other ways as well, the slave market exhibited the same economic principles as other markets. In Southeast Asia, when a demand for field laborers became more pronounced, slave raids became more common, to supply that demand.[87] In West Africa, the traditional practice among some warrior tribes of slaughtering male captives and enslaving the women and children—a practice common among other conquerors in other places—changed after the development of a European demand for male slaves for use in the Western Hemisphere made the enslavement of males profitable, with the traditional practice resuming after the suppression of the Atlantic slave trade.[88] When the price of sugar declined in the 1840s, there was a decline in the exports of slaves from Mozambique,[89] these slaves being largely destined for Brazil and other sugar-producing areas, which now had a lower demand for slaves. After the British navy began patrolling the Indian Ocean to suppress the slave trade there, slaves began to be shipped in older and cheaper vessels, which would represent less of a loss if intercepted and confiscated by the British.[90] In short, the basic principles of economics operated in the international markets for slaves.

Values and costs are not independent abstractions. Something represents a value or a cost *to some particular individuals*, and only when those individuals are decision-makers do these values and costs affect outcomes. The value of a slave's life to the slave himself is quite different from its value to a plantation owner, for example, and that in turn is different from its value to an overseer with limited tenure on a given plantation. Thus slaves on plantations run by overseers, with the owner absent, were more likely to be overworked and their long-term maintenance neglected, like the long-term maintenance of buildings, equipment, and livestock. The overseer's incentive was to maximize output during his tenure, whether because he received a share of the proceeds or because his record for "results" was a long-term capital asset for him in seeking his next job.

When the plantation owner lived on the plantation himself, his incentives included maintaining his own long-term capital assets, principally the slaves, but also the buildings, equipment, and livestock. And since the owner employed the overseer, his interests overrode those of the overseer—to the extent that the owner was in a position to know what was going on. Absentee owners, of course, had no such access to knowledge. One reason for the far higher infant mortality among blacks on West Indian slave plantations was that the owners of these plantations typically lived in London. While the children born to slaves might be a capital asset to the plantation owner in London, they represented only a reduction in plantation profits to the overseer on the scene.

## The Economics of Freedom

When people are viewed as capital assets, and when their potential productivity is reduced by the need to maintain slavery as a relatively unmodified system, then the purely economic value of that asset can differ considerably according to whether a given individual works as a slave or a free worker. Even in the absence of a desire for freedom, the capital value of the same individual would tend to be higher as a free worker than as a slave, simply because a wider range of economic options is available for the use of free labor. Since capital assets in general tend to move through the marketplace from their lower-valued uses to their higher-valued uses, why did slaves not become free through the ordinary functioning of economic incentives?

Since others can own the value of an individual as a slave but only the given individual himself can own the capital value of his work as a free person, economic logic would lead to each individual's becoming the highest bidder for himself, since his higher value as a free worker would enable him to bid more than his value as a slave. The poverty of the slave was not an insurmountable obstacle, since various credit institutions have enabled slaves to purchase their own freedom in both ancient and modern slave societies.[91] Self-purchase was common in ancient Greece and Rome, often happened in Latin America, and happened sometimes in the Islamic countries and in the antebellum southern United States.[92] Government intervention, however, prevented mass self-emancipation through self-purchase in the marketplace in the antebellum South, where state governments increasingly restricted all forms of manumission of slaves, as did authorities in various other slave societies, ancient and modern.[93]

Such government intervention reflected the fact that, while the sale of freedom might be mutually beneficial to the slave and the slave owner, there were substantial external costs to the surrounding society. Given the repression of the slaves' development in the antebellum South, their presence as members of a free society would impose direct costs on that society, as well as indirect costs to maintaining the slave system for those remaining in bondage. Accordingly, in the decades leading up to the Civil War, the ability of a slaveholder to free his own slaves was progressively restricted by law, to prevent his externalizing the cost of slavery by freeing people who had not been prepared for freedom.

Even those antebellum Southerners convinced of the wrongness of slavery, such as Congressman John Randolph of Roanoke, were baffled by the dilemma as to what to do about it, since it was part of the world into which they had been born, making the question as to whether it should have been instituted in the first place a moot point for those now making decisions. While Congressman Randolph opposed the abolitionists politically, fearing a race war if slavery were abolished instead of being allowed to die out,[94] his will not only freed his own slaves but bought land for them to live on in the free state of Ohio.[95] Others tried to deal with the dilemma by plans to send freed slaves "back to Africa," though in fact most of these slaves had never seen Africa and neither had their parents or grandparents.


## MODIFIED SLAVERY

Even during the era of plantation slavery in the Western Hemisphere, there was work more complicated or more subtle than the routine drudgery of the sugarcane or cotton fields, and to get this work done by slaves required modifications of slavery itself. Sheer brute force was sufficient to get routine work done, where its performance was easily monitored by an overseer armed with a whip, and able to administer punishment on the spot, but not all work was so easily monitored, and for this kind of work some of the incentives of a non-slave economy were introduced.

The most obvious example of this different kind of work would be domestic service, where the alacrity, attentiveness, and pleasantness of the servants were at least as important as the mere physical performance of the chores themselves. The care of small children, as well as adjustments to the varying moods of the slaveholder and other members of his family, were things not easily defined or mechanically monitored, though obviously very important. Moreover, the constant administration of punishment could disturb the tranquility and harmony of the slaveholder's own family, quite aside from backlashes from domestic slaves in a position to retaliate secretly in ways that might range up to arson or poison.

It was a common feature of slave systems, whether in the antebellum South, in Southeast Asia, or in the Ottoman Empire, that domestic slaves were treated better than plantation slaves. In regions of the world where it was not feasible to grow plantation crops, slavery might often take forms very much modified from the pure slavery associated with mass-production, routine tasks. Where the slaves were of different races from one another—black slaves and white slaves in the Ottoman Empire being classic examples—racial solidarity among the slaves was less of a factor to be considered, especially in societies where other social divisions were more salient than race, such as religion in Islamic countries. Throughout the Caribbean and South America, racial solidarity was systematically undermined by making many legal and social distinctions among the African-ancestry population, according to their degree of racial mixture with whites.[96] In continental North America, the white population was sufficiently larger and more dominant over the black population that such divide-and-conquer strategies were unnecessary.

Given the virtually unlimited power of slave owners over slaves in the Western Hemisphere—including in practice the power of life and death, since the death of a slave from brutal punishment was unlikely to lead to a conviction for murder—it is remarkable how many incentives other than punishment were resorted to, in order to get particular kinds of non-routine work done by slaves. The implications of this reach beyond slavery, for this pattern suggests the limitations of what can be accomplished by power alone.

Power is inherently limited by knowledge. As already noted, an overseer could run a plantation in such a way as to maximize his own interests, at the expense of the interests of the absentee owner. Similarly, domestic servants who took care of the babies, the food, and the household of slave owners could likewise secretly retaliate through theft, arson, or poison. More fundamentally, from an economic standpoint, what an overseer could monitor was work performance, but not work potential. Punishment required norms, and these norms had to be set at levels that were feasible. Otherwise, slaves whose punishment was inevitable because of their inability to meet the norms had little incentive even to try. But other slaves who were capable of doing more than these lowest-common-denominator norms had no incentives to do so under pure slavery. Modifications of slavery were ways of eliciting more of the hidden potential of slaves. A woman with a talent for dealing with children might become a trusted and privileged "mammy" on a Southern slave plantation or a man with a gift for military operations might become a soldier or even an officer in the armies of the Ottoman Empire. Pay, bonuses, and privileges were ways of extracting more from slaves than could be extracted by force alone, for these were essentially ways of inducing slaves to reveal their hidden capabilities. In resorting to these non-slave incentives, however, the benefits to the individual slaveholder could conflict with the needs of maintaining slavery as a system—and in particular a system that was pervasively a plantation system of virtually pure slavery.

Just as the examples of free blacks undermined the acceptance or resignation of slaves to their lot in life, so the examples of privileged slaves contributed to discontent among the masses still dealt with as beasts of burden. A given slaveholder might consider it to his own advantage to indulge his house servants in learning to read and write, but literacy could spread readily, not only to his field hands but also to slaves on other plantations in the vicinity, making escapes easier and costly precautions and recapture efforts necessary. Accordingly, numerous laws were passed in the antebellum South to prevent individual slaveholders from benefiting themselves by actions which imposed costs on the slave society as a whole. Laws against teaching slaves to read and write were an obvious example, but there were many others. Laws regulating urban slavery were especially numerous, and especially ineffective, as the same laws were passed again and again in the same communities,[97] the local authorities apparently being unaware that what they were trying to forbid had already been forbidden years earlier, but without effect.

Urban slaves were usually domestic servants and, because they were in cities, had wider access to uncontrolled contacts with others than on plantations. One symptom of this freer movement was that urban slaves were more successful in making permanent escapes than were slaves on plantations. Because most plantation slaves were not kept under armed guard, temporary escapes were relatively easy and relatively frequent in the antebellum South, but their lack of knowledge of the wider world—their inability to read, much less to read a map—meant that most escapees were readily recaptured and then punished. Despite the existence of the "underground railroad," most of the slaves who escaped permanently came from within a hundred miles of a non-Southern state in which they could find freedom.[98]

Urban slaves were much more likely to be able to read or write, since it was costlier to monitor their movements and activities in a city. Moreover, they were more likely to have social contacts among free blacks in the cities. This not only led to more escapes, it led to better treatment, in order to forestall escapes. It was this better treatment, which included allowing slaves relatively free movement around Southern cities and even social interactions with whites in drinking establishments frequented by prostitutes,[99] that outraged Southern white public opinion, for such behavior undermined the racial subordination which made slavery possible at relatively low cost. Accordingly, laws requiring slaveholders to maintain tighter control of their slaves were passed in cities across the South—and were ineffective in these cities, because both the slaveholders and the slaves had incentives to behave otherwise, and policing numerous urban residences was not feasible for city governments. The net result, as Frederick Douglass put it, was that the urban slave "was almost a free citizen."[100] Douglass knew this from personal experience as an urban slave, before he escaped to the North to become a leader of his people. The line between slavery and freedom was particularly tenuous for those urban slaves who worked for an employer and simply paid the slaveholder a share of their wages. Such slaves might live separately from the slaveholder's home and even change employers at will.

Perhaps the most striking indication of the erosion of racial lines in urban settings was the much higher proportion of mulatto babies born to black women in antebellum Southern cities, as compared to black women on plantations. An estimated 1 to 2 percent of the babies born to planta- tion slave women were fathered by white men,[101] compared to nearly half in the cities.[102] Southern cities of that era had a chronic surplus of white men over white women and a chronic surplus of black women over black men.[103] Similar sexual imbalances have led to mixed offspring in many other times and societies, so the antebellum South was not exceptional in this. If most of the slave women who gave birth to racially mixed babies were simply raped by their owners, then such babies would undoubtedly have been more common on the plantations, where white control was greatest, rather than in the cities, where it was more lax.

Not all modifications of slavery in the antebellum South were due to urban residence. Some modifications were due to the nature of the work itself. Slaves working in lumbering—which required both disper- sion and initiative, unlike plantation work—were given more freedom and financial incentives, with no slave-driving by overseers even being attempted.[104] Similarly, slaves working in diving operations in the Car- olina swamps—where the skill, discretion, and initiative of the diver were crucial—likewise had slave-driving replaced by financial incen- tives.[105] Virginia tobacco factories also used financial incentives and greater personal freedom to get work done that required attentiveness and intelligence, though the lax treatment of these slaves caused a polit- ical backlash from other white Southerners, who saw this as undermining the slave system as a whole.[106]

In parts of the world where plantation slavery was more rare, there was less concern that modifications of slavery for some would undermine the more rigorous discipline of the plantation slaves of others. In much of the Ottoman Empire, for example, where slavery was usually domestic slav- ery rather than a system of crop production, the treatment of slaves was generally more lenient than in plantation societies, and a wider range of occupations were open to them under modifications of slavery that extended all the way to using slaves as both civil and military officials.

The women of the harems were slaves, with Circassian women from the

Caucasus being particularly prized as concubines and African women being used more often for domestic chores.[107] The treatment of the Circassian women was sufficiently good that mothers in the Caucasus often voluntarily turned their daughters over to wealthy Ottoman men for their harems, after which these women could be freed and advantageous marriages arranged for them. A concubine who gave birth to a son for her owner might even be freed and become his wife.[108] The wealthiest and most powerful slaves were the eunuchs who could rise to high positions in the Ottoman government if their skills and talents warranted. Often they were put into positions of high trust in preference to a normal man, who might become ambitious to overthrow the rulers and establish his own dynasty—the latter option obviously not being open to eunuchs.

In short, modifications of slavery were both widespread and far-reaching in the Ottoman Empire. Some have attributed the generally better treatment of slaves in this region to a more humane Islamic code. However, the Arabs' treatment of newly captured slaves en route to their destinations in North Africa and the Middle East was at least as harsh and cruel as that of slaves crossing the Atlantic en route to bondage in the Western Hemisphere. Indeed, the mortality rate of slaves crossing the Sahara was much higher than that of slaves on the dreadful and dangerous Atlantic crossing.[109] The treatment of these slaves was considered appalling by observers ranging from the Christian missionary-explorer David Livingstone to the battle-hardened military ruler Mohammed Ali.[110] Yet these Arabs were Moslems, just as were those who eventually bought these slaves and typically treated them better. Nor was ill treatment confined to the period of transit under slave traders. It was said that no slave survived in the Ottoman Empire's Sahara salt mines for more than five years.[111]

The dimensions of treatment are many and all slaves were not treated alike, even in a given society. African women in the Islamic lands were less likely to be freed than European women and had little to look forward to, except drudgery as long as they lived, without even a family life of their own. More African women than men were enslaved in the Islamic world,[112] just the opposite of the situation among Africans taken in bondage to the slave societies of the Western Hemisphere,[113] and these women were typically restricted from having sexual contact with men. The net result was that relatively few black children were born in the Middle East—and few of those born survived to adulthood.[114] Thus, despite the fact that even more vast millions of slaves were taken from

Africa to the Islamic countries of the Middle East and North Africa over the centuries than to the Western Hemisphere,[115] there is no such black population surviving in these Islamic nations today as the 60 million people of African ancestry living in the Western Hemisphere.

The treatment of slaves in Southeast Asia was generally considered mild,[116] in keeping with the use of slaves primarily for domestic purposes in that part of the world. However, in assessing the treatment of slaves, and especially in comparing that treatment as between Western and non-Western societies, considerable caution is necessary. Because of the moral revulsion against slavery that developed in the West, and especially in Anglo-Saxon countries, a large polemical literature emerged, both attacking and defending slavery. Biographies and testimonies of escaped slaves made a major impact, as did the novel *Uncle Tom's Cabin*, which caused Abraham Lincoln to refer to its author as "the little lady who started the civil war" and which caused Queen Victoria to weep as she read it. Such literature and such powerful emotional, moral, and political reactions were peculiar to Western civilization. Neither the morality of slavery nor the treatment of slaves was an issue of such magnitude in non-Western societies. As a result, there is much less firsthand information on the actual treatment of slaves in non-Western societies. What happened in the privacy of slave-holding households was inherently less observable than what happened in the fields on slave plantations. In some parts of Asia, for example, slaves were expected to prostrate themselves before their masters at home.[117] Among fellow-Africans enslaved by the Mende, it was the practice to "cringe up and place their hands one on each side of their master's hand, and draw them back slowly without the fillip while the head is bowed." In a traditional African society where age was accorded great respect, aged slaves were treated as if they were still not yet adults.[118] In the Middle East, wives of slave owners could be brutal to slave concubines who were, or seemed likely to become, his favorite—and who could, under Islamic law, become another wife whose children would be entitled to share the inheritance. Such slaves might be beaten, mutilated, or forcibly aborted against their will.[119] How often this happened will never be known. Nor can anyone ever know how concubines felt about being made available to male visitors. Yet the statements of non-Western slave masters that slaves were treated "like members of the family" have been uncritically accepted by scholars who would never accept similar self-serving statements from slaveholders in the antebellum South.

## THE END OF SLAVERY

After lasting for thousands of years, slavery was destroyed over most of the planet in a period of about one century, and over virtually all of the planet within two centuries. The destruction of this ancient and world-wide institution was all the more remarkable because it was accomplished in the face of determined opposition and cunning evasion at every level, from the individual slaveholders to the heads of nations and empires. Moreover, the impetus for the destruction of slavery came not from any of the objective, material, or economic factors so often assumed to be dominant in history, but from a moral revulsion against slavery which began in the late eighteenth century in the country which was the largest slave-trading nation of its day, with highly profitable slave-plantation colonies—Great Britain.

Slavery was so deeply entrenched and seemingly impregnable when the anti-slavery political crusade began among evangelical Christians in eighteenth-century Britain that the most fervent crusaders among them hoped only to be able to stop the continued enslavement and international trading of human beings. Any thought that the very institution of slavery itself could be abolished was considered Utopian. Yet the mobilization of public opinion in Britain against the slave trade produced such powerful and enduring political pressures that successive generations of British governments found themselves forced to push the anti-slavery effort further and further toward its logical conclusion—first to abolish the international slave trade, then to abolish slavery throughout the British Empire, and finally to pressure, bribe, and coerce other nations into abolishing slavery as well.

The Quakers were the first organized religious group in Britain to repudiate the institution of slavery and to impose on their members a requirement that they not hold any slaves. But the larger political effort to get the slave trade banned by government was led by others inspired by the Quakers' example. This worldwide political revolution against slavery began with a small and rather conservative group of evangelicals within the Church of England, staid people who distanced themselves from the emotionalism of the Methodists and whose principal leader, William Wilberforce, was such a relentless opponent of the radical ideas arising from the French Revolution that he sought to have those ideas stamped out in England by government censorship. Among the other members of the inner "Clapham Sect" that began the crusade against the slave trade was the very reserved and dignified Henry Thornton, wealthy banker and a landmark figure in the development of monetary economics. Yet these were the leaders of a movement whose achievement was one of the most revolutionary in the history of the human race. Seldom was there a group of revolutionaries that so defied stereotypes, in a crusade that defied the odds.

Repeatedly and resoundingly defeated in Parliament on bills to abolish the slave trade, Wilberforce, Thornton, and their supporters persisted for 20 years, until finally—on February 27, 1807—the House of Commons passed such a bill, 283 to 16.[120] It was a remarkable victory from a mass mobilization of public opinion—and, once mobilized, this public opinion proved to be so strong, so tenacious, so enduring, and ultimately so irresistible, that the anti-slavery crusade was swept along beyond its original goals of stopping the international trade in human beings to abolishing slavery itself throughout the British Empire, and eventually throughout the world. Once the moral issue seized the public's imagination in Britain, its support spread far beyond the particular religious group that initiated the antislavery drive. Socially, it extended across class lines from the rich to the poor, from the working class to the titled nobility.[121] In an age before mass communication, mass transit, or mass movements, people were astonished to see petitions arrive in Parliament with tens of thousands of signatures, demanding an end to the slave trade. At one point, Parliament received more than 800 petitions within a month, containing a total of 700,000 signatures.[122]

The anti-slavery movement proved to be as unrelenting as it was widespread. British missionaries fueled the public's outrage with their reports from Africa itself, reports widely disseminated by a powerful missionary lobby in London. Not all government officials favored the anti-slavery cause by any means, and some in both the civil and military establishments resented the extra burdens put upon them by this cause, as well as the complications that the anti-slavery crusade made in British foreign relations. But the political pressures forced successive British governments to continue their worldwide opposition to slavery. Though slavery did not exist in Britain itself, it became such a factor in British domestic politics that candidates for political office felt a need to declare where they stood on the issue. By the mid-1820s, being pro-slavery was considered a political liability.[123]

British warships were sent on patrol off West Africa, boarding not only

British ships to inspect them for slaves, but also boarding the ships of some other nations who had "voluntarily" granted them this right. By the early 1840s, Britain began to urge the Ottoman Empire to abolish the slave trade within its dominions. The initial response of the Ottoman sultan was described by the British ambassador:

> ... I have been heard with extreme astonishment accompanied with a smile at a proposition for destroying an institution closely inter-woven with the frame of society in this country, and intimately connected with the law and with the habits and even the religion of all classes, from the Sultan himself on down to the lowest peasant.[124]

Britain was far in advance of most of the rest of the world in its opposition to slavery. However, its example inspired abolitionists in the United States, and the French government later abolished slavery in its own empire and then sent its navy on patrol in the Atlantic to help intercept slave-trading ships. Eventually, opposition to slavery would spread throughout Western civilization, even to despotic governments like that of czarist Russia, which stamped out slavery among its Central Asian subjects. The European-offshoot societies of the Western Hemisphere all abolished slavery before the end of the nineteenth century, and the spread of Western imperialism to Asia and Africa brought slavery under pressure around the world.

Outside of Western civilization, the anti-slavery effort was opposed and evaded, especially in the Islamic world. Repeated pressure on the Ottoman Empire led its government to decree a ban on the slave trade within its domains in 1847, even though this ban led—as expected—to discontent and revolt among Ottoman subjects. However, mindful of the opposition within, Ottoman authorities were not very active at trying to stamp out the slave trade. Eventually, the British government threatened to begin boarding Ottoman ships in the Mediterranean to search for slaves, unless the Ottomans themselves began enforcing the ban on the forbidden slave trade.[125] Nor was the Ottoman Empire the only foreign government to feel the pressure of British anti-slavery policy. In 1873, British warships anchored off Zanzibar and threatened to blockade the island unless the slave market there closed down.[126] It closed.

A sharp distinction is apparent between the ending of slavery in Western civilization and in non-Western regions. By 1888, slavery had been abolished throughout the Western Hemisphere. Yet the struggle to end slavery, or even the slave trade, continued on into the twentieth century in Africa, Asia, and the Middle East. The British added naval patrols in the Indian Ocean and the Persian Gulf after the Ottoman Empire's formal ban on slave trading provided the legal cover for such intervention. Yet slave trading continued on land until after European imperialism took control of most of the African continent. Only then could the attempt be made to stamp out slavery itself. The difference between the Western and the non-Western worlds as regards the ending of slavery is perhaps epitomized in the words used to describe the process—"emancipation," a once-and-for-all process in the Western Hemisphere, and "the decline of slavery" in Africa, Asia, and the Middle East, where it was a more protracted process that lasted well into the twentieth century.

Even after Western hegemony extended into many nations of Asia, Africa, and the Middle East, slavery continued in remote regions of Borneo, Burma, Cambodia, and other parts of Southeast Asia.[127] Among the Islamic nations of North Africa and the Middle East, the abolition of slavery came especially late, with Saudi Arabia, Mauritania, and the Sudan continuing to hold slaves on past the middle of the twentieth century.[128] Mauritania officially abolished slavery on July 5, 1980—though its own officials admitted that the practice continued after the ban.[129]

Non-Western societies never developed the crusading zeal which led to the destruction of slavery wherever European power extended. Nevertheless, the national stigma of slavery eventually became a factor in the restriction or abolition of slavery in non-Western countries which did not wish to appear before the world—meaning largely the European world—as backward or uncivilized. Thus the king of Burma took the lead in officially outlawing slavery in that country in the nineteenth century,[130] though it continued to exist on into the twentieth century.[131] Siam began to crack down on slavery in the late nineteenth century, under the influence of foreign opinion.[132] The rise of nationalism among Southeast Asian countries in general gave an impetus to the effort to stamp out slavery in the twentieth century, in order to gain respect from the world's leading nations, which meant Western nations.[133] In the Philippines, at the beginning of the twentieth century, an American report on the continuation of slavery there was seen by Filipino leaders as a blow against their efforts to gain independence.[134] Even within the Islamic world, which retained the institution of slavery longest, Westernized elites began to oppose slavery,[135] whether out of conviction or out of embarrassment. In short, slavery was ultimately destroyed morally, though the chief instrument of this destruction was the overwhelming military power of the West, combined with the prestige of Western civilization, based at this juncture in history on its economic, scientific, and technological achievements. Ironically, after anti-Western views became fashionable among Western intellectuals in the late twentieth century, desperate expedients of rhetoric were resorted to, in order to depict the destruction of slavery by European civilization as somehow serving the economic interests of European powers.[136]

## THE AFTERMATH OF SLAVERY

### The Economic Legacy

What was accomplished by the enslavement of untold millions of human beings in countries around the world? No doubt particular projects here and there were the fruits of slave labor, but it would be difficult to make the more general case that slavery advanced the economic level of those societies in which it existed on a mass scale.

The American South, for example, was by no means the most economically dynamic region of the country, either during or after the era of slavery. It was in fact the poorest. Brazil, which imported several times as many slaves as the United States, remained a relatively backward country until the large-scale European immigration that began after the era of slavery was over. The slave societies of North Africa and the Middle East, which absorbed even more millions of slaves than the Western Hemisphere, lagged conspicuously behind the technological and economic level of the West, both during and after the end of slavery—until oil, not slaves, raised their standards of living in the modern era. In Europe, it was the nations in the western region of the continent, where slavery was abolished first, that led the continent and the world into the modern industrial age.

In many parts of the world, slaves were luxuries, or at least domestic amenities, rather than capital investments intended to yield a profit. A large retinue of slaves was a display of wealth and power, whether in ancient Rome,[137] China,[138] Africa,[139] Thailand,[140] Tibet,[141] or elsewhere. In regions where slaves were part of a lifestyle—and this included much of the Islamic world—it can hardly be surprising that slavery did not create any notable economic development. That was not its role. Moreover, even in societies where slaves were intended to produce profits for slave owners, it is by no means apparent that those profits played any major role beyond the current consumption of those slave owners. Some have attempted to claim that profits from slavery provided the investments that made the industrial revolution possible in Britain.[142] But even if all the profits from slavery had been invested in British industry, this would have come to less than 2 percent of Britain's domestic investments during that era.[143] Moreover, neither in Britain nor the Western Hemisphere was there any evidence that slave owners were such dedicated capitalists as to invest all or most of their incomes. Contemporary observers frequently character- ized slave owners as self-indulgent or ostentatious consumers,[144] often in debt. Finally, when the total cost of Britain's naval and military efforts against the slave trade for more than a century are added up, they are com- parable to all the profits ever made by Britain from the slave trade in ear- lier times.[145] In the United States, it is also questionable whether all the profits from slavery exceeded the enormous cost of fighting the Civil War—a war that would not have had to be fought if there were no slavery, even if its purposes were conceived in other immediate terms by those on both sides. Many other slave societies which sustained no such staggering costs also had no comparable profits from which these costs could be sub- tracted. Appalling as it may be to think of untold millions of human beings sacrificed for no larger purpose than the transient aggrandizement of oth- ers, that is what the historical record suggests.

Among the many negative aftermaths of slavery has been a set of coun- terproductive attitudes toward work, among both the slaves and their descendants and the non-slave members of slave societies and their descendants. "Work is for Negroes and dogs" is a Brazilian expression[146] that captures a spirit bred by slavery and not unknown in the American South or among the whites in South Africa. Nor is this a purely racial phenomenon. Descendants of the slave-owning and slave-trading Ashanti tribe of West Africa have exhibited similar disdain for work.[147] Free women in Burma were unwilling to do disagreeable work which had become associated with slaves.[148] There were similar reactions by the Egyptian lower classes against doing work associated with slaves and by the white lower classes in the antebellum southern United States against doing work associated with blacks, slave or free.[149] Similarly in Malaya, where manual labor was associated with slavery, an observer in Malacca said: "You will not find a native Malay who will carry on his back his own or any man's property, however much you may offer him for doing so." In Aceh, even those too poor to own slaves would hire a slave to carry things for them, "scorning to do it themselves."[150] A seventeenth-century observer in Sumatra found all the heavy work in Atjeh being performed by slaves from India, with the local people developing an aversion to performing even simple tasks:

> No Atjehnese would carry any load if he could help it; if he had no slave of his own he would hire that of another, even if it was only to fetch the rice from a place a hundred steps away.[151]

What was involved here was not mere laziness, but a positive sense of being above various kinds of work performed by slaves, or an aversion to any kind of toil or working under the direction of others, because these too were reminiscent of slavery. What a historian of medieval Spain called "a puerile pride in idleness"[152] has not been confined to that country or to that era. Adam Smith commented on the disdain toward work in ancient slave societies.[153] By contrast, immigrants from non-slave societies have arrived in various parts of the Western Hemisphere, often financially destitute but without such handicaps in their attitudes toward work, and have risen above the native-born white populations of former slave societies, often through very different work habits, often commented on by contemporary observers. Selective migration and other factors may well have contributed to the ability of destitute immigrants to overtake native-born whites in the Western Hemisphere. But patterns of disdain toward work in slave societies around the world, going back to ancient times, are at least suggestive.

## The Cultural Legacy

While some have seen the slavery of ancient times as a necessary foundation for the leisured life of a Greek elite that produced Socrates, Plato, Aristotle, the great dramatists, and such physical splendors as the Acropolis and the Parthenon, it is painfully obvious that no such contributions to world civilization came out of the antebellum Southern United States, out of Brazil, or out of the slave-holding whites of South Africa. It would be hard to think of any cultural figure of world stature, in any field, who came out of any of these modern societies during the centuries when slavery flourished in them. The contributions of Islamic civilization to Western culture and to world civilization in mathematics, astronomy, philosophy, and other fields were more substantial[154] but these contributions largely antedated the Islamic conquests in sub-Saharan Africa or in southeastern Europe, from which the Ottoman Empire received such large supplies of slaves.

In Asia, the relationship between slavery and cultural achievements was equally tenuous. Bondage was particularly prominent in Southeast Asia, rather than in the great civilization of China, from which both Asian and Western societies derived so much, technologically and culturally. Moreover, in Asia as in the Islamic Middle East, slaves were more often an item of expense for domestic purposes or for personal aggrandizement, rather than a source of profits.

Nations and empires which were wealthy and powerful often used that wealth and power to acquire slaves, among other luxuries and signs of glory, but that is wholly different from saying that the slaves created the wealth and power. Even for ancient Greece, the case that slavery was the source of their greatness is by no means unequivocal. While slavery existed in Homeric Greece, the numbers were limited and later, in Plato's time, a wealthy man might own 50 slaves[155]—a number suggesting a retinue of servants, attendants, and craftsmen, rather than a source of riches. Spartans lived off their helots, but it is Athens whose contributions to world civilization are still recognized after two millennia. In the Roman republic and early empire, slavery was not as large a factor as in the later empire, after wars and conquests had brought many slaves under Rome's dominion.[156] In a world where the capture of a city often led to the slaughter of the men and the enslavement of the women and children, the growth of the empire and an increase in the number of slaves was not unexpected. And though plantation slavery flourished in parts of the Roman Empire,[157] that is not the same as saying that Rome's power and cultural development depended on slaves.

## Moral Issues

For more than a century, economists have debated whether slavery was profitable in the United States. However, the terms of that debate have tended to be narrowly focused on the profitability of slavery to the individual slave owners during the antebellum era, but the social effects of slavery extend far more broadly in space and time. The moral dimensions of slavery are likewise a more complex issue than often assumed. Once the institution was in existence—and its origins antedate history—the issue was no longer whether slavery should have been created in the first place, but what the options were to all the generations born into a world where it was a fact of life. Those who criticize the writers of the Constitution of the United States for "condoning" slavery by their silence on the subject have a valid point only if its abolition was in fact an option open to them at the time, in a new country struggling for survival. A much larger and more powerful United States was shaken to its foundations by the Civil War, generations later. Had the United States split over the issue of slavery when the constitution was written in 1787, it is by no means clear that the North would have prevailed militarily, or that either region would have survived. Moreover, none of this would have ended slavery, but only sacrificed a nation for some futile phrases.

As it was, the moral consciousness aroused by the struggle for a free society in fact led to laws in the North abolishing slavery—no doubt a small and not always consequential act, as slavery was never as widespread in the North, and Northern slave owners had the option to sell their slaves to the South. Nevertheless, some people received their freedom as a result of the antislavery feelings and abolitionist laws of that period. More important, in the longer view of history, these abolitionist statutes were a first step toward the abolition of slavery in the United States and were in the vanguard of a far more general revulsion against slavery that would sweep across Western civilization in the century that followed.

Those who see in history the working out of economic forces, and especially of economic self-interest, have struggled desperately to fit the abolition of slavery into that framework of preconceptions. Yet the plain fact is that slavery was thriving economically, as far as the slave owners were concerned, when the moral forces of the age brought this ancient institution under political pressures that overwhelmed both the domestic moneyed interest in slavery and foreign nations' fierce resistance to imposed changes in their whole way of life. That this moral crusade began in eighteenth-century Britain, the largest slave-trading nation of the age, with thriving slave-plantation colonies in the Caribbean, further confounds the argument from economic forces and economic self-interest.

An amalgam of moral and economic arguments has been used to urge "reparations" to present-day descendants of slaves in the United States. The economic portions of these arguments are the weakest. If the purpose of reparations is to share equitably the economic contributions of slavery to the present economy, then it would first be necessary to establish that there were in fact net benefits. If the country is on net balance worse off economically because of the historical existence of slavery on its soil, then there are no benefits to share, equitably or otherwise.

A more plausible case for reparations is as compensation for the sufferings and degradations of millions of human beings during the centuries of slavery. Tempting as it may be to glide from uncompensated sufferings in the past to reparations to descendants in the present, the heritability of guilt is a principle without foundation and dangerously divisive in any society. If the heritability of guilt were accepted *as a principle*—not just as a talking point to secure immediate political objectives—then this generation of Jews would be justified in putting this generation of Germans in concentration camps. No one believes that—not Jews, not Germans, nor any other sane adults. No society could survive historical compensation as a general principle. Doing justice among contemporaries is more than enough challenge.

The principle of compensation has yet another side. To say that one has been compensated is to say that things have been set right. But nothing within human power can ever set right the sufferings and degradations of millions of human beings, all over this planet, for thousands of years. Slavery can neither be forgotten nor forgiven, certainly not by those who never suffered it personally—and certainly not in exchange for money or other benefits. Such a political deal would rank with the cynical sale of indulgences in the Middle Ages.

## The Mythology of Slavery

The history of slavery, like so much other history, has been sucked into the vortex of current ideological passions, and distorted in the process. The enormous disproportion between the vast literature on the enslavement of Africans in the Western Hemisphere and the sparse literature on all other slavery in all other societies around the world is just one symptom of this distortion. Moreover, the habit of considering only slavery in the Western Hemisphere, or perhaps only slavery in the United States, has led to theories and conclusions about slavery in general which are plausible only within a limited context—and not necessarily valid even there. To explain the enslavement of Africans by Europeans by things peculiar to Africans or Europeans[158] is to ignore the glaring fact that slavery was a worldwide institution, among the most disparate races and cultures, going back untold thousands of years. Clearly other factors must have been at work to explain the existence of slavery elsewhere—and once those other factors are acknowledged, it becomes mere dogmatism to insist that factors peculiar to Europeans and Africans, and to the period of the African slave trade, must have been responsible for slavery in the Western Hemisphere.

Another distortion of history is to assume a priori that social problems afflicting contemporary blacks in the United States are a "legacy of slavery." Broken families, lower rates of marriage, and lower rates of labor force participation have been included among the social phenomena explained and excused on grounds of a "legacy of slavery." In reality, most black children were raised in two-parent homes even during the era of slavery and for generations thereafter,[159] blacks had higher rates of marriage than whites in the early twentieth century,[160] and higher rates of labor force participation in every census from 1890 to 1950.[161] Whatever may be the real causes of the very different patterns among blacks in the world of today must be sought in the twentieth century, not in the era before emancipation.

One of the incidental but revealing aspects of the attempt to project current attitudes and assumptions back into the past has been the practice among some American blacks of changing their family names as a means of rejecting a heritage of slavery and the "slave names" supposedly given to their ancestors by their owners. In reality, slave owners in the antebellum South not only did not give surnames to slaves, but actually forbad slaves to have surnames.[162] Surnames implied a set of family relationships which had no legal sanction and whose existence was at variance with the slave owner's authority to buy and sell slaves or otherwise dispose of them individually as he saw fit. Slaves could be punished even for using such expressions as "my sister" or "my mother."[163] Nor was this hostility toward family ties peculiar to the antebellum South. Slaves in China and parts of the Middle East likewise had no surnames.[164] Only relatively recently in Western history have hereditary surnames been used for any but the elite, beginning in the Middle Ages,[165] and in Japan surnames were authorized for common people only in 1870.[166]

Far from having surnames given to them by slave owners, slaves in the United States gave themselves *clandestine* surnames with which to identify and dignify their forbidden family relationships. These surnames were never used in the presence of whites and, in fact, even after emancipation blacks born during the era of slavery hesitated to tell white people their surnames.[167]

The enduring tragedy of Africans enslaved in the Western Hemisphere was that they were introduced to the culture of the societies in which they and their descendants would live only at the lowest levels of that culture. Forming a substantial proportion of populations in many parts of the hemisphere—in some countries, a large majority of the population— African-origin people were seen as a potential danger by the whites and were accordingly denied access to education and other means of acquiring higher levels of Western civilization. Despite obstacles put in the way of their acquiring the culture of the society around them, blacks nevertheless acquired literacy at a remarkable rate. Most free blacks in the United States were literate as of 1850 and, half a century after emancipation, so were three quarters of the entire black population,[168] most of whom had been either illiterate former slaves or their descendants.

The importance of reaching higher levels of Western culture was demonstrated by that portion of the African-origin population of the United States that was free before the Civil War, and who had greater access to education and other cultural exposure at higher levels than the plantation field hands. Such "free persons of color" and their descendants continued to predominate among the elite of the Negro population, well into the twentieth century.[169] Their cultural headstart had enduring consequences.

Despite the desperate efforts of freed blacks to educate themselves after the Civil War,[170] and to find family members who had been sold during slavery and sent elsewhere,[171] a segment of today's black and white intelligentsia excuses contemporary blacks who disdain education as "acting white" or who abandon their families—both patterns being represented as being a "legacy of slavery," though blacks born under slavery or living immediately after emancipation did not exhibit this pattern to the extent seen today. For many critics of Western society, exempting blacks from the requirements of civilized life is a way of striking a blow against the West, regardless of its consequences for the black community. Whether forbidden to achieve higher levels of civilization during the era of slavery or excused from achieving those levels in the late twentieth century, blacks have been handicapped either way.

## IMPLICATIONS

The staggering sweep of slavery over thousands of years, and the enormous variety of forms it assumed at different times and places, are almost as remarkable as the scant amount of moral concern it aroused until the late eighteenth century in Britain and the United States. How and why this particular juncture in history produced a moral revulsion against slavery is much less clear than the confluence of circumstances which permitted this moral revulsion to drive a policy which resulted in the stamping out of slavery across most of the planet in a period of a century and a half. The mobilization of this moral concern into a political force that was both powerful and tenacious was historic in its consequences because of the military predominance of the countries in which these anti-slavery movements developed. More specifically, it was European imperialism which stamped out slavery over most of the world. Even in parts of the world which retained their independence or autonomy, the indelible stigma that slavery acquired in European eyes made abolition a policy to be pursued for the sake of national respectability, even in societies which had no strong feelings against slavery itself.

The irony of our times is that the destruction of slavery around the world, which some once considered the supreme moral act in history, is little known and less discussed among intellectuals in either Western or non-Western countries, while the enslavement of Africans by Europeans is treated as unique—and due to unique moral deficiencies in the West. Moreover, what is and is not considered to be a legacy of slavery is too often determined by what advances the ideological visions of today, rather than what accords with the record of history.

Attempts to explain the choice of which peoples to enslave, or the treatment of those already enslaved, on racial or other ideological grounds fail to account for the racially indiscriminate enslavement of whatever peoples were available for capture at particular places and times in history. It was not a change in ideology but such historical developments as the growth of powerful nations and empires which successively removed various peoples in Europe and Asia from the ranks of those whom it was feasible to enslave. Africa south of the Sahara remained vulnerable longer and its peoples paid a terrible price as a result, though other peoples in isolated and vulnerable backwaters in Asia continued to pay a similarly terrible price, long after the descendants of African slaves were emancipated in the Western Hemisphere.

The treatment of slaves also reflected economic and social realities, rather than being simply a function of racial or other ideological beliefs. Plantation slaves were treated worse than domestic slaves in societies around the world, regardless of the race of the slaves or the slave owners, and regardless of the prevailing beliefs. In societies where the enslaved population was large enough to be a potential threat, harsher treatment and greater restrictions (including restrictions on literacy) were imposed. Even in colonies under the same colonial rule, such as the Dutch Caribbean colonies of Surinam and Curaçao, slaves were treated much more harshly where the demographic and occupational patterns were the kind that tended to lead to harsh and brutal treatment elsewhere in the world. Surinam had plantation slavery, absentee owners, and a white population outnumbered several times over by the black slaves, and exceeded in size even by the small class of "free persons of color." Curaçao, however, did not have the kind of climate required to grow plantation crops, so its slaves were mostly domestic, were treated more mildly than the slaves in Surinam, and were one of the rare slave populations in the Western Hemisphere to have a natural rate of increase, whereas in Surinam the slave population followed the more usual Caribbean pattern by failing to reproduce itself. Manumission was far more common in Curaçao, where the instruments of torture used on slaves in Surinam were unknown. Although the slaves in both places were of the same race, and the slave owners in both places shared the same racial and cultural backgrounds, the different circumstances of the two Dutch colonies lead to very different results.[172] Circumstantial realities, not ideologies, were the crucial differences between the two colonies.

Slavery and racial ideologies have indeed been related in many societies around the world, but to say that slavery was based on race is to put the cart before the horse. Where those who were enslaved were of a different race, that race has been despised, whether in Western or non-Western societies, and whether the slave or the slave owner had the lighter complexion. Slavery has therefore left a legacy of attitudes toward race, as toward work, and both sets of attitudes have handicapped former slave societies, long after the institution of slavery itself has been destroyed. Slavery has, however, left little legacy of economic investment, especially in countries where slaves were a source of personal services, amenities, and public display, rather than a source of wealth. Even in countries where slavery was intended to be a source of production, as in the Western Hemisphere, the lifestyles of the slave owners often prevented either an economic or a cultural legacy from being left to the wider society.

Slavery's most important legacy may be a painful insight into human nature and into the terrible consequences of unbridled power, as well as the inherent limitations of power as a means of accomplishing goals, even when those goals are pursued "at all costs." Perhaps the most important moral legacy of slavery is a keener appreciation of freedom.

# CHAPTER 8

# RACE AND HISTORY

*In history a great volume is unrolled for our instruction, drawing the materials of future wisdom from the past errors and infirmities of mankind. It may, in the perversion, serve for a magazine, furnishing offensive and defensive weapons . . . and supplying the means of keeping alive, or reviving, dissensions and animosities, and adding fuel to civil fury.*

—Edmund Burke[1]

History is not destiny. Much of it consists of mistakes which need not be repeated and crimes which need not be tolerated again. As Burke suggested, history is mankind's painfully purchased experience, now available free or merely for the price of attention and reflection.

History shows patterns, even if it does not provide formulas. Its facts are especially needed when dealing with racial beliefs and issues, where powerful emotions reign, and where prejudice and bias have often been the norm. If nothing else, history can help dissolve the provincialism of time and place, and the hypocrisy of *selective* moral indignation.

Both causal explanations and moral judgements can change, when the emotionally compelling issues of the present are seen against the larger background of the history of similar events in other regions of the planet and in other regions of time. Yet, although the past can shed a powerful light on the present, what we seek in the past is also influenced by what we confront in the present. Each successive generation may have need of a different mixture of the many things available from the vast storehouse of history. Nevertheless, history cannot be simply the handmaiden of the present. Even to have contemporary relevance, history must have its own independence of the present, for the value and validity of history depend on its integrity as a record of what happened, not what we wish had happened, or what a theory would have us believe should have happened.

When considering the history of race and culture, we must consider not only the broad patterns discernible in the complex interactions of that history; we must also consider the pitfalls and limitations of history itself.

## PATTERNS IN HISTORY

A history which spans thousands of years, encompassing the rise and fall of empires and of peoples, makes it difficult—if not impossible—to believe in the permanent superiority of any race or culture. Equally, such a history—full of cultural diffusions, transfers, imitations, influences and inspirations from one society to another—makes it hard to believe that all the different ways of meeting human needs are equally effective, when those involved have gone to such trouble to seek better ways of doing things from other lands and other peoples.

When firearms have displaced bows and arrows over vast regions of the planet, when a numbering system originating in India has displaced all sorts of other numbering systems among all sorts of peoples on every continent, when printing and paper from China have likewise spread their dominion more widely, more irresistibly, and more permanently across the world than any of the greatest conquerors of all time, then cultural relativism seems less like a principle and more like a fetish, if not mere squeamishness. Certainly the peoples of the world have borrowed extensively from each other's cultures over centuries and millennia.[2] This began with the earliest known civilization, that of the Sumerians of the Tigris-Euphrates valley, which diffused outward to surrounding peoples, as did the ancient civilizations of Egypt, the Indus valley of India, and the Yellow River valley in China.[3]

The a priori dogma that all cultures are equal ignores the plain fact that cultures do not present a static tableau of differences, but rather a dynamic process of competition. Cultures compete most obviously in warfare, for the outcomes of wars of conquest can determine what language the descendants of the combatants will speak for centuries to come, what concepts will organize their thoughts, and what values will shape their moral universe. At a minimum, cultures are more effective and less effective in military terms. Wars, however, are only one of the ways in which cultures compete. More continuously and more pervasively, they compete in the many practical ways in which cultures serve a spectrum of human purposes, from the growing of food to trying to understand the motions of the stars. Agricultural methods and astronomy are just two of the many features borrowed by one culture from another. Horsemanship, mathematics, art, science, philosophy, foods, and music are just some of the innumerable things which not only supplement but displace the features of one culture with those of another.

Whatever the nature of cultural competition, whether it is warfare or international trade, scientific breakthroughs or the spread of popular music, competition means winners and losers—not merely a static display of "multicultural diversity" as tribal symbolism and multiprovincialism. Some may lament that colorful local fabrics in non-Western societies have been superseded by mass-produced cloth from the factories of Europe or the United States. They may regret seeing traditional local drinks replaced by carbonated sodas, or indigenous musical instruments put aside while people listen to American popular songs on Japanese-made portable radios. Those who deplore such things are also deploring the very process of cultural diffusion by which the human race has advanced for thousands of years. It would be contrary to all experience if there were no losses accompanying the gains. What is cheap and showy may attract a certain interest by its novelty, but competition is a process of trial and error, of sorting and weeding out. To demand that human beings be right on the first try in each individual decision is to demand that they not be human beings.

Cultural competition has been an integral part of the history of racial and ethnic groups around world. Emigrants have moved across mountains and oceans because what they had to offer was more valuable somewhere else than it was where they were born. It was not the material wealth that they brought with them—often pathetically small—which was crucial, but the cultural characteristics or human capital that enabled them to create new wealth for themselves and for the society around them at their many destinations. Unfortunately, one of the most recurrent patterns in history is that the passive beneficiaries of a growing prosperity created by foreigners have often been among the bitterest enemies of those foreigners who supplied the missing skills, organization, and other human capital that made it all possible. Where the creators of wealth receive, on average, somewhat more of it than the passive beneficiaries, the latter may feel that the former have benefitted at their expense, "exploiting" them in some undefined way, rather than seeing that wealth-creation is not a zero-sum game. Accusations of this sort have been hurled at the Chinese in Southeast Asia, the Indians in East Africa, and numerous other groups who have created whole new industries and higher standards of living for all, in countries around the world. Such misconceptions about both history and economics have not been confined to the unlettered masses, but have often been prevalent among the intelligentsia as well. Indeed, intellectuals have often taken the lead in spreading such misconceptions and whipping up such resentments.

Much as history has to contribute to understanding such social phenomena as wealth creation, history has itself become a target of desperate attack by those for whom the truth threatens devastating consequences to their visions, their egos, or their projects. A whole new class of intellectuals has arisen to supply a history geared to what people currently wish to believe, rather than to the record of the past. There are, of course, honest differences in the interpretation of history. But there are also dishonest differences. To allow those with a purely instrumental view of history to erase the national memory, or to record over it the ideological fashions of the day, is to discard an anchor in reality, and to set sail with light ballast and a reckless optimism.

Patterns in history do not mean that everything is the same, that nothing is unique in any way. But even to know how things are unique, they must first be compared. History offers more sweeping comparisons, across far more varied circumstances, than those of the contemporary world.

History cannot be ignored because it will not be ignored. Contemporary controversies almost invariably engender passionate appeals to history, or to presumed history, or to the presumed effects of history. Years before the beginning of the Second World War, Winston Churchill noted how one man's warped view of history was producing in Nazi Germany "currents of hatred so intense as to sear the souls of those who swim upon them."[4] Misconceptions of history took a toll measured in millions of lives and in the devastation of a continent.

Facts are the foundation of history, but an understanding of causation is the structure that rises on that foundation, and for which that foundation was built. "With all your getting, get understanding," was the Biblical injunction that still strikes a chord after two thousand years and in a secular society.

Today, two contending ways of trying to understand history focus, respectively, on internal causation and external causation. Both must be understood, though current tendencies in the "social sciences" are to emphasize the external and ignore the internal or cultural characteristics of peoples, or even to condemn the very attention paid to internal characteristics. Many attempts to explain history, or to explain contemporary events, emphasize the circumstances surrounding a people, a generation, or a racial or ethnic group. The Marxian theory that economic circumstances shape the way people think and act is just one of these theories of external causation. Internal theories range from those which claim a genetic basis for group achievements to the theories of Max Weber, who argued that differing religious beliefs were a major factor in different economic performances by Protestant and Catholic societies.

In the bitter disputes which turn on the roles of internal and external causation, those who suggest cultural or even demographic factors behind socioeconomic differences are accused of "blaming the victim" by those who see causation in terms of such immediate external factors as economic deprivation or social oppression. Since all of the factors cited on both sides can in fact be found in the contemporary world, as well as in history, a categorical victory for either side seems unlikely. The real question is: How much does the external environment explain, and which particular features of that environment?

To say, for example, that peoples are to some extent creatures of their environment is to say only that genetic factors do not explain everything. It is hard to imagine who would have thought otherwise. Even those who believe in the importance of cultural patterns know that those cultures did not develop in a vacuum. the real question is: How is environment conceived? There is a vast difference between saying that people are the creatures of the society immediately around them and saying that groups with different cultural heritages react very differently to the same current environment and the same objective opportunities.

Even the geographical environment can have radically different meanings. It is easy to understand how the availability of natural resources— including climate and fertile soil, as well as minerals, flora and fauna— provides greater or lesser opportunities to peoples indigenous to different parts of the world. What may not be so obvious, but may nevertheless be of at least equal importance, is how the contours of the land and the presence or absence of navigable waterways have shaped or limited the *cultural* opportunities to develop the capabilities for dealing with the given endowment of natural resources. The cave man, after all, had all the natural resources available to the most technologically advanced societies today. History is full of the stories of poor societies with rich natural resources, which were developed only after foreigners gained control of those resources, whether through economic, political, or military means.

In short, peoples whose skills and values have been shaped by different external factors in the past tend today to have different internal cultural patterns with which to confront the opportunities and challenges presented by the external conditions of the present. For example, Jewish and Italian immigrants arrived in the United States during the same era, equally destitute, and often lived in the same run-down and crowded neighborhoods, while their children sat side by side in the same schools. Yet they responded very differently to the educational system, including the availability of free higher education in New York City, and they rose up the socioeconomic ladder at different rates, through different occupational channels and in different industries. Even those individual Jews and Italians who became wealthy and prominent typically did so in different ways. Nor was this pattern peculiar to the United States. The same differences could be seen between Jews and Italians in Australia or Argentina. That the Jews made clothing while the Italians made wine, whether in the United States, Argentina, or Australia, can hardly be coincidental—especially since these same groups were prominent in these same industries in Europe before immigrating to these European offshoot societies.

In short, different peoples have lived in different cultural universes, rooted in different histories, evolved from different imperatives. Understanding the nature and scope of the cultural universe is essential to understanding differences in the ways in which different peoples confront the same challenges and opportunities in the external world of the present.

## THE CULTURAL UNIVERSE

Among the many ways in which cultures differ are their sheer size. They also differ, of course, in particular characteristics and some of those characteristic differences have already been explored, as regards particular racial and ethnic groups, or particular nations. However, even for a given nation or given racial or ethnic groups, cultural changes over time have often been dramatic. In particular, the emergence of the modern way of thinking as a worldwide phenomenon, among the educated elites at least, has been a remarkable development of the twentieth century. Three crucial aspects of the cultural universe will be explored here: (1) the effects of the size of the cultural universe on its development, (2) the role of natural, and especially geographical, factors in shaping cultures, and (3) the modern expansion of that universe to worldwide dimensions, at least as regards certain core scientific and logical processes, and the technology flowing from them.

## The Size of the Cultural Universe

The history of cultures suggests that population size matters greatly. Small, isolated groups of people have seldom, if ever, been in the vanguard of progress—technologically, intellectually, economically, or otherwise. This does not mean that population size is all-determining—otherwise China and India would be the leading nations of the contemporary world—but it does mean that severe limits face peoples who are both small and isolated from larger cultural developments elsewhere. Scientific breakthroughs have not come from small islands, whether in the South Pacific, the North Atlantic, the Caribbean, or the Indian Ocean.

Where geography creates population "islands" on land—the Scottish highlanders, the *Montagnards* of Vietnam, the Kandyan Sinhalese in Sri Lanka, or peoples who find only isolated patches of agriculturally viable land, as in parts of Southern Italy or of sub-Saharan Africa—there have been conspicuous cultural lags behind others who were either in contact with more of their own people or with other cultures more accessible by rivers, harbors, or plains. Minorities living in linguistic or cultural islands, like the Volga Germans in czarist Russia or the Ulster Scots in Appalachia, may maintain the level of cultural development with which they began their isolated existence but seldom keep pace with the further advance of their home country, or with the progress of compatriots living elsewhere as immigrants in touch with a wider world.

It is not simply that encapsulated minorities are offshoot societies, for large offshoot societies such as the United States may surpass the scientific or other advances of the mother country. Rather, it is the cultural isolation of the encapsulated minority that is salient. Similarly, it is not merely raw population size alone that is crucial. A vast nation, made up of isolated peasant communities, may represent no very large cultural universe, when the peasants of one village have little or no contact with the peasants in a village 50 miles away.

Mountains and highlands have been major factors in both cultural fragmentation and cultural retardation. As the eminent French historian Fernand Braudel put it:

The mountains are as a rule a world apart from civilizations, which are an urban and lowland achievement. Their history is to have none, to remain almost always on the fringe of the great waves of civilization, even the longest and most persistent, which may spread over great distances in the horizontal plane but are powerless to move vertically when faced with an obstacle of a few hundred metres.[5]

However detrimental mountains and highlands may have been to the cultural development of those who lived in them, however much the upland may have "persistently lagged behind the plain,"[6] in Braudel's words, nevertheless mountains have had some positive cultural effects on those living below. Mountains are not only barriers to invaders, they also promote the continuous flow of rivers because the melting of vast amounts of snow on mountain ranges feeds water into streams and rivers, making them less dependent on rainfall. Where there are no mountain ranges, as in tropical Africa, river flow varies radically between wet and dry seasons. Given the important role of navigable waterways, both economically and culturally mountains are also important for helping to maintain the flow of those waterways.

While geography and other factors have insulated some peoples from the cultural worlds of others, history has spread the Jews far and wide among many cultures and relocated them many times during the centuries of their wanderings as a people without a homeland. For no other group have cross-cultural experiences been more inescapable. The backwardness of isolated peoples has had as its counterpoint the remarkable historic achievements of the Jews—a relatively small group of people, spread thinly around the world, and yet so prominent in so many countries and in so many fields that it hardly seems credible that there are fewer Jews in the entire world than there are Kazakhs or Sri Lankans.

Historic differences within world Jewry only reinforce the general conclusion that cross-cultural experiences have been associated with cultural achievements. Where the Jews have been enabled—or forced—to maintain small separate communities in cultural backwaters such as the villages of Eastern Europe or of Yemen, for example, there they have lagged far behind the achievements of other Jews exposed to the wider world of either Islamic or European civilization, such as the Jews in medieval Spain or modern Germany and the United States. The history of Sephardic Jews illustrates the same thesis in a different way. Once the elite of world Jewry during the centuries of their "golden age" in Spain, when they stood at the cultural crossroads of Islamic and European civilizations, the Sephardim who migrated in large numbers into the Ottoman Empire after their expulsion from Spain in 1492 were initially very successful in their new settings. But as they lost their contacts with the rising civilization of Europe in later centuries, their initial prominence in the Ottoman Empire eroded away. By the time the modern state of Israel was formed, the Sephardic Jews who came there from North Africa and the Middle East lagged substantially behind the Ashkenazic Jews from Europe and the Western Hemisphere in income, occupation, education, and other common socioeconomic indicators. But this contrast within Israeli society did not correspond to any backwardness of Sephardic Jews in the lands of Western Europe or the Western Hemisphere, where they had suffered no such isolation.

The cultural advantages of coastal peoples, as compared to their respective compatriots in the interior hinterlands, or of metropolitan peoples as compared to their respective compatriots in the provinces, have long been noted by observers in many parts of the world. Words like "provincial," "tribal," or "peasant" carry connotations of backwardness—and correctly so, when they refer in fact to isolated groups. Even groups with special prominence in the development of world civilization have sometimes achieved that prominence only after emerging from cultural isolation—the Ashkenazic Jews of modern Europe after emerging into the post-ghetto era, the eighteenth-century Scots, or the Japanese after their isolation from the outside world was ended in the nineteenth century. These examples add support to the more general thesis that the size of the cultural universe sets limits to the level of cultural achievement within it.

Just as the extraordinary achievements of the Jews lend support to the thesis that the size of the cultural universe is fundamental to cultural progress, so this conclusion has grim implications for organized attempts to Balkanize societies in the name of cultural "identity" or of "multiculturalism," as in late twentieth-century America, Britain, Canada, or Australia, for example. Quite aside from ideological hidden agendas behind these efforts, the organized, government-subsidized cultural fragmentation of a nation artificially recreates the effects of natural geographic barriers which have constricted the cultural universe for so many peoples, with such tragic results, in various parts of the world.

This is not to claim that the opposite policy of government-imposed assimilation, such as "Russification" under the czars, has been widely successful. Both kinds of organized efforts and government policies have in practice made groups more culturally defensive and antagonistic toward one another. Where individuals and groups have been more free to retain as much of their own cultures as they saw fit, or to take from other cultures what they wished, the mutual absorption of cultural features has been considerable—and, more important, peaceful. Many of the benefits derived by the United States from its tens of millions of immigrants over the years have been due to its attraction as a place where people would be freer from religious, cultural, and other persecutions. Many came to preserve a way of life that, in fact, they or their descendants gradually abandoned as they became absorbed into an American culture in which their special contributions were now part of a larger mosaic.

While the cultural universe sets limits to group achievements, individual achievements in some fields are far less dependent upon the cultural exposure of the groups from which leading individuals come. In writing, sports, politics, and entertainment, where the individual's talent counts for more, many individuals of national or even world stature come from groups not noted for scientific, economic, or technological achievements. An incisive writer like V. S. Naipaul, legendary athletes like Pele in Brazil or Willie Mays in the United States, or innumerable Irish writers, athletes, entertainers, and politicians in various countries around the world, exemplify such individual achievements. Indeed, groups less able to achieve in fields with large cultural prerequisites may channel more of their talents and energies into fields where purely individual abilities are decisively important. While there are also great individual feats in science, technology, or other fields of higher culture—so that Edison, Einstein, or Beethoven were not mere creatures of their environments—nevertheless their genius required a major cultural foundation on which to build.

In short, cultures differ not only in specific features or in their relative effectiveness for particular purposes, but also in their scope. Islam, for example, has provided a common cultural framework for interaction across vast regions of North Africa, the Middle East, the Indian subcontinent, and in lands as far away as Malaysia and Indonesia. Within this vast Islamic world, groups ranging in size from tribes to nation-states, differing in lifestyle from Saharan nomads to Malay farmers or Ottoman scholars, in race from Albanians to West African Negroes, have all been part of a cultural pattern which facilitated social interactions ranging from trade to migrations to the building of empires. By contrast, the culture of Japan has remained largely confined to Japan. While Islamic, as well as Christian, nations have fought each other, it is also true that the wider hegemony made possible by a common cultural pattern can facilitate pacification among disparate groups otherwise likely to be at war, or at least withdrawn from contact with those whose cultural patterns are incomprehensible. Here too, culture has practical consequences, in this case as an integrating force where diversity might otherwise exceed the bounds of the mutually tolerable.

The Islamic culture provided a framework, not only for Islamic peoples, but also for Christians and Jews living in the Ottoman Empire or in medieval Spain, for example. For administrative convenience, the Ottoman Empire agglomerated a number of Christian ethnic groups into an Orthodox community where they had a certain autonomy. Thus the Christian Orthodox community was also a large cultural community, extending the Greek culture well beyond the Ottoman Greeks to Bulgarians, Albanians, and others encompassed by the Orthodox community as recognized by the Ottoman authorities. This Greek cultural hegemony was shattered in the later, declining, phases of the Ottoman Empire, as ethnic minority intellectuals arose among the Orthodox to promote specifically Bulgarian, Albanian, etc., cultures within the predominantly Greek Orthodox community. In many other settings as well, a newly rising intellectual class has fragmented the cultural universe, whether these were Latvians or Czechs rebelling against German cultural hegemony in the nineteenth century, or Maoris rebelling against British cultural hegemony in New Zealand, or the aborigines in Australia, among many others in the twentieth century. Language separatism—a bitter issue from Sri Lanka to Quebec—has been only one aspect of this fragmentation of the cultural universe.

Among the forces operating powerfully in the opposite direction have been economic forces, more specifically the international integration of economic activities. Airline flights spanning the globe require a common language in which pilots and control towers can communicate with one another, in circumstances where a misunderstanding can mean instant death to hundreds of passengers. It is less important that English has been chosen for that language than that *some* language be agreed upon and learned by all those with life-and-death responsibilities. In international commerce and finance as well, the stakes are very large when multibillion-dollar investments ride on mutual understandings. Here too, English has been chosen as a *lingua franca*, even when all those involved may be people whose native languages are not English.

Intellectuals have often seen language issues, like other issues, in largely invidious terms—as implicit assertions of the "superiority" of English to Spanish or French, or of one people to another. But language, like other features of a culture, exists to accomplish some purpose, not merely to be symbolic or invidious. A more widely diffused language accomplishes its purpose more fully, regardless of the relative merits of various languages as such, or of the peoples among whom those languages have arisen. In the same way, a scientific or business ethos more widely diffused around the world facilitates international scientific and economic cooperation. Just as cultures are consequential, rather than being merely symbolic, so the size of the cultural universe is consequential in itself, aside from the particular merits of the particular cultural features themselves.

## Geographical Influences

While the influence of the geographical settings in which peoples evolve has been widely recognized to one degree or another, there is a great difference between saying that natural resources affect economic development and saying that navigable waterways affect the size of the cultural universe. The difference is between focussing on the external opportunities available to a given people and focussing on what cultural resources those people have within themselves as a result of the setting in which they have evolved.

Geographical influences do not mean geographical determinism, for however much the contours of the land, its mineral wealth, the availability of navigable waterways, and the climatic and epidemiological environment may limit the options of people developing in a given geographical region, these people make choices within those limits, and the intrusions of the ideas, technologies, emigrants, or armies from other regions add to the complexity of the process and the uncertainty of the ultimate outcome. Nevertheless, geographical factors are among many other factors which virtually preclude equal economic and technological progress among peoples from the many and varied regions of the world, for the various continents and regions are by no means equally supplied with the factors that make for either economic progress or cultural integration.

It is relatively easy to understand the historic implications of the vast deposits of petroleum in the Middle East, the iron ore deposits of Western

Europe, the tin in Malaysia, or the gold in South Africa. What may not be so obvious, but of equal or greater importance, is the crucial importance of navigable waterways to transport these and other natural resources, and the products resulting from them, to different regions of the Earth—creating wider cultural interactions in the process.

The enormous importance of rivers and harbors to economic and cultural development is indicated by the fact that nearly all the world's great cities have developed on rivers or harbors. This reflects in part the vast differences in costs between transporting goods by water and transporting them by land. For example, in mid-nineteenth-century America, before the transcontinental railroad was built, San Francisco could be reached both faster and cheaper from a port in China than it could be reached over land from the banks of the Missouri.[7] In the city of Tiflis in the Caucasus, it was cheaper to import kerosene from Texas, across 8,000 miles of water, than to get it over land from Baku, less than 400 miles away.[8] In Africa, even in the twentieth century, the cost of shipping an automobile from Djibouti to Addis Ababa (342 miles) has been estimated as being the same as the cost of shipping it from Detroit to Djibouti (7,386 miles).[9] Similarly, in nineteenth-century Japan, before roads were improved and railroads built, it was said to cost as much to transport goods 50 miles over land within Japan as to transport them from Europe to Japan.[10] Huge transportation costs shrink the economic universe, severely limiting how far given goods can be carried, and severely limiting which goods have sufficient value condensed into a small size and weight (gold or diamonds, for example) to be feasible to transport over land for substantial distances. These same high transportation costs shrink the cultural universe as well.

The various continents and regions of the world are by no means equally supplied with rivers and harbors. Although Africa is more than twice the size of Europe, the African coastline is shorter than the European coastline, whose twists and turns produce harbors and inlets all around the continent, while the relatively smooth coastline of Africa offers far fewer places where ships can anchor in a harbor, sheltered from the rough waters of the open sea. Moreover, there are entire nations in Africa—Libya and South Africa, for example—without a single navigable river. This reflects in part the low and irregular rainfall over many parts of the continent, filling rivers and streams to a navigable depth only intermittently.[11] Moreover, just as rainfall patterns limit the navigability of rivers with respect to time, so the many rapids and waterfalls of Africa limit the distances over which rivers can be navigated, even when they have sufficient water. Because many of Africa's rapids and waterfalls occur not far inland,[12] even large rivers may provide no practicable access for large-scale commerce from the sea. The Zaire River, for example, is 2,900 miles long and has a volume of water second only to that of the Amazon, but it has rapids and waterfalls near the sea, thus preventing oceangoing ships from reaching one of the largest networks of navigable rivers in the world.[13] Thus, the Zaire River and its tributaries are prevented from being the kinds of navigable waterways which have played so important a role in the development of other lands.

Across Europe and Asia—and, later, the Western Hemisphere and Australia—man's dependence on waterways has been demonstrated again and again in the sites of leading cities, from London to Bombay and from Sydney to Rio de Janeiro. These ports became not only economic centers but also cultural centers and centers of progress in general, as cities have led the progress of civilization.[14] Africa's most famous civilization likewise arose, thousands of years ago, within a few miles on either side of its longest navigable river, the Nile. The two largest cities on the continent today—Cairo and Alexandria—are both on the Nile. However, a general lack of navigable waterways to facilitate economic and cultural interchanges has in Africa been reflected in a general dearth of large cities, on what remains the world's least urbanized continent.[15] Except for the Nile, Africa's rivers that are even seasonally navigable tend to be concentrated in equatorial West Africa.[16] Here too, larger, more advanced, and more enduring polities were established than in many other regions of the continent. The general importance of waterways may be suggested by the fact that, at the beginning of the nineteenth century, four-fifths of the world's population lived in coastlands. The modern development of artificially powered, non-waterborne transportation—motor vehicles, railroads, and airplanes—reduced that coastal concentration but, as late as 1975, two-thirds of the world's population still lived in coastal regions.[17] In Africa, the coastal plain averages only 20 miles in width and is often backed by steep upsweeps of land which make road and rail construction difficult, as well as making Africa's rivers plunge over plateau edges.[18]

Geography is not all-determining, but it can set the limits of human possibilities narrowly or widely. For much of sub-Saharan Africa, it has set those limits narrowly. Not only were economic activities restricted by the high cost of transportation; more fundamentally, human interactions in general were narrowly circumscribed, resulting in such cultural barriers as numerous language differences and tribalism. Although Africans are less than 10 percent of the human race, their many languages are one-third of all the languages in the world,[19] one index of their cultural fragmentation. The great number of languages and dialects in Africa, besides being a symptom of this cultural fragmentation, constitute as well a severe handicap in themselves, inhibiting effective economic or political consolidation of numerous separate peoples. Waterways extend the boundaries of cultural interchange, but in much of Africa they did not extend those cultural boundaries very far. For the peoples of sub-Saharan Africa, the most formidable barrier to cultural interchanges with the other peoples and cultures of the world was the Sahara Desert itself, which is larger than the continental United States. It was not until the second millennium of the Christian era that the central rain forest of Africa and the land south of it were much influenced by the civilizations which had arisen in other parts of the world[20]—and, until the sixteenth century, the influence of these civilizations was conveyed only through Islamic intermediaries.[21]

While the geographical influences that affect the cultural development of a people may attract less attention than such direct influences on economic development as mineral resources, land fertility, and the like, these latter are by no means always as decisive as they might seem. For example, an eighteenth-century observer in Chile made an assessment that would apply to many other countries in other parts of the world:

> . . . here it never thunders nor hails. The country is laden with mines of all the known metals, the climate is benign, the fields fertile and irrigated. There are good ports and excellent fishing, all the plants and animals of Europe flourish, none have degenerated and some have improved. There are no beasts, no insects, no poisonous snakes . . . nor many of the plagues of other countries. . . . In this privileged land beneath a benign and limpid sky, there should be a numerous population, a vast commerce, flourishing industry, and important arts. But instead, this most fertile kingdom in America is the most miserable.[22]

Conversely, Japan, virtually destitute of all natural resources, nevertheless became one of the leading industrial nations of the world and its expatriates in Brazil dominated the growing of various agricultural produce in the southern region of that country. In Europe likewise, Switzerland has become one of the most prosperous countries of the continent and the world, despite lacking almost all natural resources.[23] If, as these and other examples might suggest, it is the skills and cultural patterns of a people which are crucial, then it becomes more understandable why a global redistribution of peoples, whether through emigration or conquest, should produce such dramatic economic changes as those following the Europeanization of the Western Hemisphere.

Geographical settings which seem very favorable in presenting a spontaneous abundance of food, or lands and streams easily farmed and fished, may prove to be less favorable in the long run than natural settings in which people must develop in themselves discipline, work habits, and frugality merely in order to survive. Peoples whose cultures were shaped under the severe discipline of exacting geographical and climatic conditions have often been able to flourish when transplanted into more favorable settings, and to surpass indigenous peoples whose cultures evolved under these favorable circumstances. People used to a struggle for survival in the less favored parts of southern China rose from poverty-stricken beginnings as coolie laborers in colonial Malaya to surpass the Malays, whose geographical lot in life was much more favorable in the sense of their ease of producing a livelihood.[24] Much the same story could be told of the immigrants to Fiji from India,[25] as well as other immigrant groups in other parts of the world. Something similar has happened when peoples from geographically less favored regions of the same country—Ibos from southern Nigeria or Tamils from northern Ceylon—flourished when artificially more favorable opportunities were presented by a new culture brought by conquerors and colonizers, cultural opportunities which their geographically more favored compatriots were not as quick to exploit.

On a national scale, those European countries facing the turbulent and stormy north Atlantic—notably Britain, France, Spain, and Portugal—ultimately developed the technological skills and seagoing experience to become the world's leading naval powers in the modern age of exploration and imperialism. But those nations and empires whose naval forces developed earlier in the much calmer waters of the Mediterranean—where most sailing was in sight of land[26]—never became naval powers able to challenge the upstarts of Western Europe on the high seas of the world. In short, neither on land or at sea are short-run advantages necessarily long-run advantages.

Europe, Asia, and Africa have been the sources of the major cultural features of the modern world's population, not only because they contain such a large proportion of that population, but also because the cultures of much of the rest of the world, and especially of the Western Hemisphere, derive from cultures which first developed on these three continents. While geography has not by itself determined European, Asian, or African cultures, it has set limits within which each continent and region has worked out its own destiny, and those limits and these destinies have varied substantially between and within continents.

On the great Eurasian land mass, where a majority of the human race has lived for most of recorded history, some of the geographical contrasts between the European and the Asian portions of this super-continent have been as large as the racial or historical contrasts within these two regions. For example, Asia has suffered far more from floods, droughts, earthquakes, and famines than Europe has. Many of the great epidemic diseases which have struck sporadically in Europe have been endemic in Asia,[27] which has been called an "epicentre of viral outbreaks."[28] Its diseases have spread through both animal and human populations, and crop diseases have likewise originated in Asia,[29] where agriculture itself originated. Worm infestations have sapped the energy of humans in parts of China, India, and the Middle East.[30]

On the other hand, the soil of much of Asia has, on the whole, been more fertile than that of Europe, and has historically supported much larger population densities.[31] The monsoons of East Asia and the hot summers accompanying them are favorable for producing rice, which supports more people on given land than does wheat, the principal cereal grown in Europe.[32] Because the main population centers of Asia are farther south than those of Europe—even a relatively northern capital in Asia like Tokyo is farther south than Rome or Madrid, much less London and Paris—the Asian climates, combined with the ample rainfall, often permit two crops a year to be grown in much of the continent, compared to one crop per year in most of Europe.[33]

It is both unnecessary and impossible to determine the net advantages of the two regions of Eurasia. What is clear—and important—is that particular features of the natural environment vary enormously as between Europe and Asia, as they do within each continent as well. It would take an almost miraculous coincidence for all these factors to balance out in such a way as to cause the peoples of these two regions of the world to achieve similar technological, organizational, or economic levels continuously throughout history. Insofar as cultural development is influenced at all by the natural environment within which it takes place, nature becomes one of many influences tending to make societies and groups within societies unequal in their achievements as of any given time.

The geography of Europe is such that no place on the continent, outside of Russia, is more than 500 miles from the sea.[34] By contrast, much of tropical Africa is farther than that from the nearest sea, and parts of it are more than a thousand miles from the sea.[35] Moreover, many African communities located closer to the sea, as the crow flies, are in reality less accessible to it than are European communities located a like distance from open waters. To be located a hundred miles from the Mediterranean across the sands of the Sahara is not the same as being located a hundred miles from the open sea in a river port on the Rhine or the Seine. In Africa there are very few analogues to the Rhine or the Seine—or many other European rivers. Unlike much of South America or some other Third World regions, much of sub-Saharan Africa lacks both objective geographical opportunities (such as fertile land and ample rainfall) and the geographical conditions favorable to developing the cultural patterns enabling people to make the most of whatever economic opportunities exist. To the difficulties of water transport in much of Africa must be added the devastating effects of the tsetse fly on animals and humans alike, making the use of animals in transportation or farming virtually impossible in many parts of the continent below the Sahara.

While Europe's many navigable waterways made possible its long-distance transportation of common, bulky, and low-valued commodities such as grain, to a greater extent than in Asia,[36] so in sub-Saharan Africa the unavailability of water or animal transport over substantial regions limited both the distance of trade and the range of commodities which were high enough in value to repay the expensive use of human carriers.

Geographical features interact. Mountains affect the flow of rivers. Where there are large mountain ranges which collect vast amounts of snow, the melting of that snow feeds water into the streams and rivers, maintaining their flow even during periods of low rainfall. Put differently, in a vast region without mountain ranges, such as sub-Saharan Africa, river flow is entirely dependent on rainfall and varies drastically between wet and dry seasons. Land features affect water flow in yet another important way. A region of vast high plateaus, such as tropical Africa or Tibet, has streams and rivers that must descend large vertical distances on their way to the sea. This means that they must have steeper gradients en route than rivers which flow across coastal plains, and are therefore less navigable, or not navigable at all, because of rapids and waterfalls. This in turn means that much cargo that is transported by waterways in other parts of the world must, in such regions, be transported by land or not transported at all.

Land transport not only differs vastly from water transport in cost, but also imposes its own requirements. In the great desert regions, for example, the distances between sources of water—compared to the distance a camel can travel without water—determine which routes across the trackless sands or dry steppes are feasible and which are not. In turn, these routes and their traffic determine which of the oases have enough economic activity passing through them to become permanent settlements. Settlements at the crossroads of several routes through the desert—Samarkand in Central Asia, for example—could grow to be large cities,[37] much as river and harbor ports grew into urban centers in other parts of the world.

Even the political histories of the three continents were constrained by their natural environments. The great mounted hordes of conquerors who could sweep across the vast open reaches of Central Asia, the Middle East, and North Africa to establish their empires could not do so in heavily forested early Europe, where the barrier of trees and the absence of adequate grazing lands set a more formidable limit to these mounted warriors than the military defenses of the early Europeans themselves. In parts of Asia, the need for such huge communal projects as irrigated agriculture, to take advantage of the monsoon rain patterns, required a collective regimentation under political control.

None of these broad geographical differences among continents implies that there is uniformity within a given continent. Even within a given country such as China, the Yangtze River basin receives twice as much rainfall annually as the basin of the Yellow River, whose shifting course and catastrophic floods have caused it to be called "China's sorrow." The volume and depth of water in the Yangtze is such that a 10,000-ton ship can go hundreds of miles up the river from the sea and smaller vessels another thousand miles beyond that.[38] Meanwhile, Tibet has been largely cut off from the rest of the world by the mountains around it. Similarly in Europe, where the course of the Gulf Stream as it heads north through the Atlantic produces warmer weather in the western portion of the continent than at similar latitudes on the east coast of North America—London has a milder winter than New York, though hundreds of miles farther north—the climatic effect of the Gulf Stream has less and less influence in areas more distant from it in the eastern portion of the continent, where rivers are frozen more days per year as one proceeds from west to east. Moreover, the meager rainfall in much of southern Europe has meant that rivers navigable by oceangoing vessels are much rarer there than in northern and western Europe. Parts of the Balkans isolated by mountains and lacking river access to the sea remained at Third World levels of development until late in history, when the technology of the rest of Europe was finally able to reach them.

During the European industrialization of the nineteenth century, every one of the early industrial regions had the benefit of navigable waterways.[39] Where that advantage was lacking—as in parts of Eastern Europe and Mediterranean Europe, and especially in the Balkans, economic development lagged far behind that in such countries as Britain, France, and Germany. The standard of living in the less favored parts of Europe was much more like the standards of living in non-European countries than like those in the more advanced parts of the continent.[40] The fossil fuels which were largely lacking in southern Europe,[41] for example, often could not be brought into the interior by water—the only economically feasible way of delivering them. Although urban growth was dramatic in nineteenth-century Europe, few towns developed in the Balkans.[42] As roads and railroads developed and were improved in the more developed parts of Europe, they remained virtually unknown in the Balkans, so that people living in Balkan villages were isolated from people in other villages less than 20 miles away.[43] Before 1860, not a mile of railroad track was built south of the Sava and the Danube.[44] The mountains along the Adriatic coast, marked by short and widely spaced river valleys,[45] were yet another reason for human settlements to be separate from one another, and to have separate cultural development. In general, the Balkan mountains fractured the peninsula culturally as well as isolating it economically,[46] thereby contributing to the tribalistic divisions and lethal hatreds which have long characterized the Balkans. Although the Balkans were rich in natural harbors, there were few rivers to connect these harbors to the hinterlands, which were often cut off by mountains.[47] While much of nineteenth-century Europe not only grew economically but became interconnected with other nations within the continent and overseas, much of eastern and southeastern Europe remained "self-sufficient"[48]—which is to say, isolated, poor, and backward.

As people from eastern and southern Europe immigrated to the Western Hemisphere or to Australia, the backwardness of their regions became as apparent among them there as in Europe itself, when they began to compete for jobs with people from more fortunate parts of the continent, or with the descendants of such people. Whether in the Western Hemisphere or in Australia, eastern Europeans and southern Europeans tended to have to take the lowest level, lowest paid jobs, which were often the hardest, dirtiest, and sometimes most dangerous jobs. This is apparent, not only in comparisons of emigrants from different nations, but also in comparisons between emigrants from culturally different regions of the same country, such as northern and southern Italians. Conditions in southern Italy were in many ways similar to those in the Balkans, Spain, or the less fortunate parts of eastern Europe, while northern Italy, and especially the region of the Po River valley, had geographical and industrial conditions much more like those of northwestern Europe. It was not simply that peoples from different parts of Europe were richer or poorer. They differed more fundamentally in the extent to which they had the kinds of skills, experience, work habits, and general aptitude which developed in modern industrial and commercial societies, and which would be in demand in other modern industrial and commercial societies, such as the United States or Australia. These patterns were not simply a result of such subjective factors as others' stereotypes, perceptions, or racism, but in fact reflected historical realities, however much additional penumbra of prejudice may have developed around these realities, or remained resistant to change after the realities themselves changed with the assimilation and rising skill levels of the newcomers.

To say that the peoples of Mediterranean Europe have in modern times lagged behind the peoples of the northern and western parts of the continent is not to say that they are inherently less able races. For most of recorded history, the cultures of the peoples of Mediterranean Europe were clearly in advance of the cultural level in the rest of the continent. It is only within the past few centuries that their positions have been reversed. It was in southeastern Europe that the great civilizations of ancient Greece and Rome arose, at a time when much of Europe to the north consisted of illiterate tribal societies. It was in the ancient Mediterranean countries that crops were first grown by Europeans, metals first smelted, and towns first built on the continent.[49] Ancient Greece is estimated to have been 3,000 years ahead of Lapland in cultural development.[50] While the navigable waterways of Mediterranean Europe were primarily coastal, rather than rivers, these coastal waterways put Greeks, Romans, and other southern Europeans in touch with some of the most advanced civilizations of ancient and medieval times, in the Middle East and in Asia. The fact that the northern and western parts of Europe had the key natural resources needed for an industrial revolution meant nothing at a time when human development in general was nowhere near the level required for an industrial revolution.

What constitutes a natural resource depends on what human beings know how to use. Even highly fertile land was often not usable at a time when farm implements able to turn heavy soils were not yet available, so that intrinsically less fertile land was in fact more productive when it was light enough to be farmed with the implements of the times.[51] Similarly, in ancient times, crops could be more readily grown on the hillsides of river valleys, where gravity automatically drained away excess water,[52] at a time when human beings had not yet mastered the techniques of artificial drainage, whereas in later eras the flat or gently rolling lands of the northwestern European plains became prime agricultural land[53]—as did the land of southern China, after more advanced people from northern China moved down into that region and provided the drainage and other agricultural techniques needed to bring out its productivity.[54] In Europe, the plains were often not only unproductive but also deadly breeders of disease in the ages before they were drained—an arduous process which itself took a toll in sickness and death.[55] For much earlier eras of human evolution, it has been suggested that Africa may have provided an optimal environment for the survival of the human species, before that species reached a level of cultural development at which it could produce the kind of clothing and shelter necessary to survive in the colder climates of Europe and Asia[56]—and then make use of the advantages of those continents. In short, what is a geographical advantage or disadvantage varies over time and depends on the cultural development that has already taken place in a given geographical setting. One continent or region has not been permanently optimal for human development.

Where the land in a given location will not permanently support human life, there cannot be permanent human settlements, unless the produce of the land can be supplemented with the produce of the sea, as in some coastal regions of the Mediterranean.[57] Otherwise, the exhaustion of a given land's productivity must be followed by a movement of people to some other land, at least until the first land has recovered it ability to sustain human life. Where the land is used for growing crops, slash-and-burn agriculture may be practiced, with the burnt vegetation serving as fertilizer for restoring the exhausted soil. Where the land is used for grazing animals, then it is the exhaustion of grasses and scrub which determines when the shepherds and their flocks must move on—or when particular kinds of animals must move on, to be succeeded by other animals better able to subsist on the meager leavings. These joint movements of people and their animals may take the form of long-run movements of whole nomadic communities, with their belongings, or the seasonal movements called transhumance,[58] in which shepherds leave their families behind in permanent dwellings while they lead their animals away to distant pastures. The latter pattern is much more like the eking out of subsistence from both the land and the sea, only in this case combining herding and agriculture to make a living. But where such combinations are not available and the land will not permanently support human life, then permanent villages, towns, and cities are not possible—which is to say, that the people in such geographical settings must forego not only the economic benefits of urban life, but also the cultural development which has historically accompanied urban development in countries around the world. More of their own human potential must remain undeveloped.

Whatever the limits placed on cultural and economic development by geographical or other factors, it cannot be supposed that every group or every society reaches those limits. China, for example, sent ships on voyages of exploration that reached the east coast of Africa, more than half a century before Columbus' historic voyage reached the Western Hemisphere. Yet China's voyages—longer than those of Columbus, and in a navy more advanced than those of contemporary Europe[59]—did not lead to historic changes because China did not choose to establish colonies overseas nor even to continue its explorations. China's cultural and political imperatives were simply different from those of European powers, so that it began an era of deliberate isolation from the rest of the world before Europe began its era of overseas expansion.[60] A century later, Japan likewise chose the path of isolation,[61] and in the twentieth century it chose the path of war, which ultimately led to its own cities and industries being devastated. The limits of a society's options do not determine what that society will choose to do within those limits.

## The Modern World Culture

Among the educated elites at least, in various national cultures around the world, there is a certain vision of the world, and a certain set of logi-

cal procedures for dealing with that world, held more or less in common—and at the same time radically different in many respects from the
visions, assumptions, and thought processes of people anywhere in the
world more than a few centuries ago. The thought of human beings walk-
ing on the moon, for example, would have been staggering to most Europeans, Asians, or Africans five centuries ago. So would the microscopic
world and its enormous range of effects on human health and life. Even
something as mundane as a clock had sweeping ramifications, including
not only a new precision in the concept of time and the emergence of the
notion of punctuality, but also a new impetus to the development of all
sorts of complex, geared machinery which is now taken for granted
throughout the modern world. The concept of our planet spinning on its
axis and circling in an orbit around the sun is a concept that is now the
common property of mankind, but just four centuries ago—not long in the
history of the human race—men were burned at the stake for espousing
such ideas.

Much of what has become a world culture, or a set of beliefs and intellectual procedures superimposed on innumerable national and group cultures, originated in medieval and modern European civilization, though
drawing upon concepts and products from other civilizations. By the end
of the twentieth century, these once peculiarly European concepts had
become as familiar in Japan as in England or France, and the further
elaboration and development of this world scientific and technological
culture often came from non-Europeans, as well as from those who were
the biological descendants of the people who first created this new mental
vision and its physical products. Yet the world of scientific empiricism,
now so much taken for granted by races and cultures all over the planet,
would have been shocking everywhere in premodern times, not only
because of its particular discoveries and products, but simply because of
its way of looking at things. The development of this particular way of
looking at things was a long and painful process, not just because of the
intellectual or technological difficulties involved, but also because of
fierce opposition from the learned and the ignorant alike, from the populace and the powerful. Learned men who refused to look through Galileo's
telescope understood—or at least sensed—that what they might see were
not merely the physical phenomena of astronomical bodies, but the end of
the world as they knew it.

While the modern era is often dated from the time of Columbus' first
voyage to the Western Hemisphere, connecting two halves of the planet

with one another and ultimately making their physical and cultural resources available to all, perhaps the voyage of Magellan's ship around the world from 1519 to 1522 was an even more significant point from which to date the revolutions within the human mind that have produced the modern world. Not only did this voyage prove that the world was round, as it set out to do, but also proved more than it intended. When the ship returned to Spain, its log showed that the day was a Saturday—but when the crew went ashore, they discovered that it was Sunday. Scholars called in to explain this baffling discrepancy concluded that it indicated that the Earth was spinning on its axis.[62] The king ordered the log burned. He understood that the issue was not just about an isolated fact, but was a question of undermining part of the foundation under a whole superstructure of beliefs supporting existing institutions, societies, and ways of life. Copernicus, having determined that the Earth was spinning on its axis even before Magellan's voyage, delayed publication of his work until he was on his deathbed because he too understood the implications for the world—and for himself. Decades later, Giordano Bruno paid with his life for publicly supporting the ideas of Copernicus.

European civilization was not unique in fearing the social implications of scientific advances. In the era of the great Chinese dynasties, astronomy was treated as a state secret.[63] So too was a clock that the Chinese developed that was more advanced than any contemporary clock in the Western world, but which did not develop as far as Western clocks, which were publicly known and therefore had many people adding improvements to them over the years.[64] Other Chinese inventions—porcelain, gunpowder, paper, and printing—were likewise more fully exploited in Europe than in China itself, by European capitalists who were freer of the kinds of social and political constraints faced by entrepreneurs in Chinese society.[65]

As in Europe, so in non-Western societies, many peoples' conceptions of the world had themselves in the center of it.[66] What was common in the premodern era was not simply an ignorance of various scientific facts, but an absence of a canon of scientific empiricism—and the presence of a belief that ancient authorities and sacred texts were more reliable sources of information and understanding. In European civilization, the great authority of Aristotle's a priori conclusions about the physical world hobbled scientific empiricism for centuries. So did Galen's surmises about the human body, which not only antedated the dissection of cadavers but served as a deterrent to such dissection.

Copernicus, Galileo, Harvey, Darwin, and Einstein, among others, had to run a gauntlet of criticism and hostility for upsetting or destroying the familiar world inside people's minds. But once they succeeded in supplanting the old mental world with a new one, this new vision became that of educated people far beyond the confines of European civilization. At least a portion of every society became part of a worldwide culture. Race and culture were by no means always co-extensive before, but they became progressively less so as the modern culture spread across the Earth.

Although the modern culture began in European society, it was initially as antithetical to the beliefs of that society as to any other. It was cosmopolitan also in its elements—in its mathematical foundations in a numbering system from India, in knowledge of optics and astronomy from the Mediterranean world, in the very paper on which this was written, from China. To say that the modern vision or culture first developed in Europe is no more than to acknowledge its historical origins. To do so is not to be Euro-centric but to be world-centric about a common culture of the modern era.

## THE MORAL DIMENSIONS OF HISTORY

Causation and morality are separate concerns, whether in history or in contemporary matters. What is most morally revolting, or morally inspiring, about a given situation may not be what is the most important causal factor. But, while causation may be independent of morality, moral issues often cannot be independent of causation. Colonial Malay society was neither causally nor morally responsible for the fact that Chinese immigrants arrived destitute and illiterate, and so took jobs which the Malays spurned. But generations later, when an independent Malaysia restricted the educational and occupational opportunities of the Chinese by law, that was a chosen policy for whose consequences the Malay government was both causally and morally responsible.

Some seem to argue as if any historical or contemporary source of unhappiness which a government could have prevented is something for which it should be held morally accountable—regardless of whether the government or the society created the source of the unhappiness. This ignores the crucial fact that what the government has the resources to prevent in isolation or *seriatim* vastly exceeds what the government has the resources to prevent *simultaneously*. It ignores scarcity, the crucial and defining factor in economics. Given scarcity, innumerable sources of unhappiness that could be prevented should not be prevented, because to do so would require neglecting other and more urgent problems. Arguments may well be made in particular cases as to which are the most urgent problems, but that is very different from arguing moral culpability for a society which does not prevent every individually preventable evil.

Misplaced specificity has plagued both moral and causal arguments. Seldom are either racial oppressions or the crimes of conquerors peculiarities of particular oppressors or particular conquerors. This in no way reduces the moral responsibility of oppressors or conquerors, but it does undermine the selective indignation of observers who condemn a particular society for evils common to societies around the world, and trace that evil to some unique characteristic of that society. To explain the enslavement of Africans by Europeans by things peculiar to Africans or Europeans[67] is to ignore the obvious fact that slavery was a worldwide institution, among the most disparate races and cultures, going back untold thousands of years. The same approach which treats sins common to the human race as peculiarities of "our society" often also makes the fatal error of confusing victimhood with virtue, by lining up on the side of the victim, instead of lining up on the side of a moral principle. Yet nothing has been more common in history than for victims to become oppressors when they gain power, whether among the successor states of the Habsburg Empire and the Ottoman Empire after World War I or among the successor states of the European overseas colonial empires in Asia and Africa after World War II.

Misplaced specificity has likewise plagued attempts to understand the sources of many intergroup conflicts. The hatred and contempt often found in history between peoples of different skin color have been found as well between groups physically indistinguishable from one another, but deeply divided by religious bigotry or national animosities. To those caught up in racial hostility, skin color may indeed be crucial. But to an observer, historian, or analyst, such patterns of behavior may differ in no essential way from the behavior of those motivated by differences of creed, nationality, caste, or any of the other divisions of the human race. The oppressions, harassments, and humiliations visited on Jews in parts of the Middle East are all too similar to the treatment of the untouchables in India or of blacks in the worst parts of the American South during the worst periods of American history.

It is difficult to survey the history of racial or ethnic relations without being appalled by the inhumanity, brutality, and viciousness of it all. There is no more humane or moral wish than the wish that this could all be set right somehow. But there are no more futile or dangerous efforts than attempts to redress the wrongs of history. These wrongs are not to be denied. Wrongs in fact constitute a major part of history, in countries around the world. But while the victims of these wrongs may live on forever as symbols, most have long ago died as flesh-and-blood human beings. So have their persecutors, who are as much beyond the reach of our vengeance as the victims are beyond our help. This may be frustrating and galling, but that is no justification for taking out those frustrations on living human beings—or for generating new strife by creating privileges for those who are contemporary reminders of historical guilt.

After territorial irredentism has led nations to slaughter each other's people over land with virtually no value in itself, merely because it once belonged in a different political jurisdiction at a time before any living person's memory, what is to be expected from instilling the idea of *social* irredentism, growing out of historical wrongs? What can any society hope to gain by having some babies in that society born into the world with a priori grievances against other babies born into that same society on the same day?

The biological or cultural continuity of a people does not make guilt inheritable. Nor can the particular economic and social consequences of particular past actions necessarily be isolated or quantified in the lives of contemporaries—not when innumerable other influences have intervened in the meantime. Moreover, no group was a tabula rasa to begin with. Yet a vast literature in many countries confidently attributes intergroup economic "gaps" or statistical disparities in occupational "representation" to particular historical evils, often with little or no examination of the specifics of history, or of contemporary demographic, cultural, or other differences. In keeping with this approach, statistical theories of random events are often applied to group differences, not only in intellectual speculation but also in courts of law—as if people were random events, rather than members of groups with pronounced, enduring, and highly disparate cultural patterns.

## THE INTEGRITY OF HISTORY

For history to contribute to human understanding, its own integrity as history must be respected. A history that is essentially a projection into the past of current theories and assumptions cannot be a test of those theories and assumptions. A search of the past for group image-enhancement cannot be called history either, nor can a record of the past purged of whatever may be currently embarrassing or whatever is vetoed by contemporary group spokesmen, for whatever reason. Still less can a contemporary's presumption of speaking from the perceptions of others in the past be called history. The limitations of one's own perceptions are unavoidable, though much of value can be done within those limitations, through honest endeavor and competing interpretations. But the pretense of viewing history from someone else's perspective[68] is only a conscripting of the dead for current ideological exploitation. To be a partisan of a subjugated people today is not to share the outlook of their ancestors who were conquered—and whose bitterness may have reflected disappointment at not being the ones able to subjugate and oppress their enemies. The idea that subjugation and oppression are wrong, in and of themselves, is unfortunately relatively new as a widespread belief.

History as balm for wounded egos is likewise suspect. What was said of Irish American immigrants during their difficult adjustment era in America could have been said of many groups in many countries:

> ... by 1916 Irish nationalism in America had little to do with Ireland. It was a hodgepodge of fine feeling and bad history with which the immigrants filled a cultural void.[69]

In the very different setting of Sri Lanka, both the Sinhalese majority and the Tamil minority have likewise created their own fictitious histories. The Sinhalese insist on their "Aryan" racial purity—Hitler's theories enjoyed a vogue among them during the 1930s—despite archaeological and anthropological evidence to the contrary. The Tamils' "history" had Tamils discovering America, centuries before Columbus, and a Tamil as one of the three wise men who journeyed to Bethlehem.[70] In the United States, extravagant group myths have become a common part of the output of college ethnic studies programs.[71]

Even when there is an authentic history of former greatness, it may prove to be more of a hindrance than a help to current progress. No nation has had a longer history of cultural preeminence in the world than China. Yet this past glory has itself been one of the major obstacles to China's modernization. Back in the late 1890s, after suffering disastrous and humiliating military defeats from much smaller Japan, China continued to train its soldiers in such obsolete exercises as archery on horseback, and required them to pass promotions examinations which included quoting a classic work on war from the fourth century B.C.[72] The dramatic contrast between the prosperity of the overseas Chinese and the poverty of the Chinese in their native land may in part reflect the difference between people forced to compete in modern terms overseas and those long handicapped by a backward-looking culture (or, more recently, by ideological dogmatism) at home. The complacency of the Ottoman Empire toward the rising European civilization, which they had so often bested on the battlefield and in cultural realms as well, was an important factor in their ultimately falling behind the growing power of the Europeans—and then falling prey to them, politically, militarily, and culturally.[73] Former greatness, even when real, is no magic key to future progress.

It is easier to find historical examples of upstart nations which emerged from obscurity to move to the forefront of world civilization—Scotland and Japan, for example—than to find nations which recovered their lost greatness of centuries past. However much pragmatists may flatter themselves on their instrumental use of history, it is difficult to see how a mythical glorious past can produce any more contemporary success than a real one. Such myths seem more likely to produce a romantic distraction from the hard, unglamorous work on which real achievements are built.

Even the more modest claim that history should teach "mutual respect" for different cultures is suspect. There is much in the history of all peoples that does not deserve respect. How much in which peoples' histories is a very large question that no one can answer for others with different values. More fundamentally, respect is earned, not conferred. It is not a door prize. Equal respect is a contradiction in terms, since the very concept of respect implies an inequality of esteem and regard. All may be entitled to common decency but not all can receive a higher relative ranking. For history to aim at mutual respect or equal regard is to prejudge facts and preempt other people's value judgements, while prostituting the integrity of history itself. Much that is admirable may emerge from the histories of many peoples and the study of their cultures. But this can only be determined after the fact in specific instances. To impose blanket conclusions a priori is not history but dogmatism, and to impose them on others is not education but intimidation, violating the very "mutual respect" that is supposedly being promoted.

History, like literature and law, has become a target of efforts to empty it of intrinsic meaning. While we all know from Einstein, and from Marx before him, that the position of the observer is an integral part of the data, neither of them said that it was the *only* part of the data, or that either science or history could be reduced to an exercise in solipsism or politics. Indeed, the very attempt to escape, evade, or delegitimize the record of the past is inadvertently a perverse tribute to the power of history—and to the great danger that history represents to any ideological house of cards. Conversely, to those seeking understanding, rather than confirmation of preconceptions, history is of enormous value, and nowhere more so than in assessing heated contemporary claims and counterclaims involving race.

## Verbal Abstractions

History requires generalizations—about "the British," "the Japanese," or "the Arabs," for example. For some purposes and within some limits, this may be as harmless as it is inescapable. Yet historical generalizations have pitfalls over and above the pitfalls of generalizations about contemporaries. Across vast spans of time, "the British" refer to radically different people, living under radically different circumstances. Above all, moral responsibility cannot attach to an inter-temporal abstraction, when deeds are done by flesh-and-blood people at particular times and places. "The British" were the world's leading slave-traders in the eighteenth century—and the most implacable and relentless enemies of slave-trading in the nineteenth and twentieth centuries. These facts do not contradict each other, or cancel each other, nor is it necessary to attempt a net balance for "the British." Both facts are realities of history, and it is only our use of a single inter-temporal abstraction called "the British" for a changing collection of people with changing ideas and commitments that makes the facts seem inconsistent.

Much the same story could be told of "the Moslems" who, in medieval and early modern times, often provided a haven for the Jews and played a major role in the intellectual development of the Jews during the same eras—despite the seething hostility of much of the Islamic world toward the Jews in the twentieth century, culminating in repeated attempts to destroy the state of Israel. Aboriginal peoples, both in the Western Hemisphere and in Australia, have been at some places and times targets of systematic extermination attempts and at other periods of history have been subsidized and given legal privileges. Looking beyond deliberate policies to the wider social and cultural effects of one people on another, the picture is even more mixed, confused, or contradictory—especially if we insist on giving a literal, monolithic meaning to such inter-temporal abstractions as "the white man" or "the Asians."

## Statistical Abstractions

The study of history has been enriched by a growing availability of statistics, including statistics on racial and ethnic groups, and by a growing sophistication in the analytical techniques and electronic equipment used to analyze these statistics. Like most human opportunities, like science itself, these opportunities can easily be misused to make matters worse, rather than better, whether deliberately or inadvertently.

Perhaps the greatest pitfall in the use of statistics is a failure to pay attention to the mundane but fundamental question as to how the particular numbers in question were generated in the first place. The more exciting and prestigious part of the work is the display of technical virtuosity in analysis and the derivation of conclusions with important intellectual or policy implications. Yet none of this has any validity unless the numbers themselves are valid for the purposes for which they are used.

Many statistics which serve as the starting point for very sophisticated analyses are either inaccurate or ill-defined for the purposes for which they are used, or too often both. An example already discussed in Chapter 6 are the IQ scores of people of Chinese and Japanese ancestry. Obsolete tests, IQ norms decades out of date, and wholly unrepresentative populations used to establish norms, generated IQ scores very different from what they turned out to be when these factors were finally recognized and corrected. In the meantime, a whole literature had been spawned by invalid statistics, uncritically accepted and used as a basis for speculative theories and sweeping policy recommendations.

IQ statistics are by no means unique. Economic statistics, immigration statistics, and statistics on innumerable other social variables are subject to huge variations, according to how they are defined, collected, and used. The number of Germans in Australia is ten times greater by some definition of "Germans" than by other definitions.[74] The same has been true of the number of Chinese in various countries in Southeast Asia,[75] depending on whether persons of Chinese ancestry or Chinese citizenship are intended—and each of these criteria has further complications, depending on how one categorizes people of partial Chinese ancestry or dual citizenship, both of whom have been quite numerous in the region.

Immigration statistics can be very treacherous, not only because of innumerable inaccuracies in the processes by which such statistics are generated, but also because of inherent difficulties in trying to use definitions which are relevant to the analysis at hand and which, at the same time, will correspond to categories actually available from the official statistics. For example, if one counts all the people who immigrated from Russia as Russians, then many Germans, Poles, and other non-Russian peoples will be statistically transformed into Russians and any conclusions derived from such statistics will be correspondingly invalid. For some countries and some periods of history, a majority of the emigrants from a given country were *not* members of the majority population in that country. Conversely, most of the Germans who immigrated to Canada in the nineteenth century did not come from Germany but from Russia.[76] Later, most of the Japanese who immigrated to Bolivia did not come from Japan[77] and most of the mainland Greeks who immigrated to Australia did not come from Greece.[78]

The economic fate of a particular immigrant group in a particular country is not always easy to determine, even in general terms, despite an abundance of statistics. In the United States, for example, Mexican Americans are either (1) rising economically, like other immigrant groups before them, or (2) are stagnating or retrogressing—depending on whether all Mexican Americans are lumped together statistically, or whether those who were born in the United States are distinguished from those who are still arriving and beginning at the bottom.[79] The same is true of black West Indians in the United States who, in the 1970 Census data, could be separated into those born in the U. S. and those who were not—while in the 1980 Census all were lumped together. The fact that the 1980 data present a more grim picture of West Indians has been seized upon by some to deny conclusions based on the 1970 data,[80] where the offspring of West Indian black immigrants surpassed white Americans in income.[81]

These and other pitfalls in statistics obviously do not mean that statistical data should not be used. Blind disbelief is as dangerous as uncritical acceptance. Both laymen and high-powered analysts must ask the same question: *Where and how did these numbers originate and how are they defined?* Sometimes, especially in controversies over public policy, the political origin as well as the statistical origin must be considered. In 1991, for example, much media attention was given to two statistical facts, presented in tandem: (1) black Americans received much less pre-natal care than white Americans and (2) black Americans had much higher infant mortality rates than white Americans. The conclusion widely drawn, and in fact actively promoted by organizations seeking larger government funding of prenatal care, was that one of these facts was the cause of the other. Statistics in the very same study, however, showed that Mexican Americans received even less prenatal care than blacks and had infant mortality rates no higher than those of whites.[82] The invalid inference that lack of prenatal care caused higher infant mor-tality was an example of what might be called "Aha!" statistics. Starting with a certain presupposition, one may say "Aha!" when encountering statistics consonant with that presupposition. Often, however, one could just as easily have started with the opposite presupposition and found occasion to say "Aha!" from the same set of data.

If statistics are to be used to produce a deeper understanding of his-tory, rather than to support presuppositions, then the dull and tedious task of scrutinizing definitions and analyzing the processes by which numbers are generated must be performed as thoroughly as the more interesting and rewarding task of applying high-powered statistical tech-niques.

## Independence and Integrity

The difficulties of maintaining the integrity of history as an indepen-dent record of the past is no proof that it cannot be done, nor an excuse for abandoning the effort, much less for condoning the substitution of other goals. Perfection in this is no more likely than perfection in any other human endeavor, but neither has perfection been necessary in other endeavors.

Even a particular historical survey may achieve a certain indepen-dence of its author, much as children eventually become independent of their parents. Others may find different lessons in that history or see things that never occurred to the author. Certainly the application of whatever insights history provides will vary with time and place. Ulti-mately, however, the whole point of history is not immediate practical application but understanding. History cannot solve today's problems, but it can expose fallacies which make matters worse, or which make resolutions harder to see or to achieve. Above all, history offers understanding—not in the psychological sense of maudlin patronage, but in the sense of a clear-sighted view of reality, its limitations and its possibilities. Nowhere is such understanding more important than among peoples from different racial, ethnic, or cultural backgrounds.

# NOTES

## EPIGRAPH

1. Oscar Handlin, "Introduction," *The Positive Contributions by Immigrants* (Paris: United Nations Educational, Scientific and Cultural Organization, 1960), p. 13.

## PREFACE

1. Thomas J. Archdeacon, "Hansen's Hypothesis as a Model of Immigrant Assimilation," *American Immigrants and Their Generations: Studies and Commentaries on the Hansen Thesis After Fifty Years* (Urbana: University of Illinois Press, 1990), p. 51.
2. Ibid.
3. Thomas Sowell, *Race and Economics* (New York: David McKay Co., Inc., 1975), p. v.

## CHAPTER 1: A WORLD VIEW

1. Stephen Steinberg, *The Ethnic Myth: Race, Ethnicity, and Class in America* (New York: Atheneum, 1981), pp. 99–103.
2. Aryeh Schmuelevitz, *The Jews of the Ottoman Empire in the Late Fifteenth and the Sixteenth Centuries: Administrative, Economics, Legal and Social Relations as Reflected in the Responsa* (Leiden, the Netherlands: E. J. Brill, 1984), p. 138; Bernard Lewis, *The Jews of Islam* (Princeton: Princeton University Press, 1984), pp. 132, 133; Moses Rischin, *The Promised City: New*

*York's Jews, 1870–1914* (Cambridge, Mass.: Harvard University Press, 1967), pp. 61–68; Judith Laikin Elkin, *Jews of the Latin American Republics* (Chapel Hill: University of North Carolina Press, 1980), pp. 114–115; Howard M. Sachar, *Diaspora: An Inquiry Into the Contemporary Jewish World* (New York: Harper & Row, 1985), pp. 250, 254, 287.

3. Orlando Patterson, "Context and Choice in Ethnic Allegiance: A Theoretical Framework and Caribbean Case Study," *Ethnicity: Theory and Experience*, edited by Nathan Glazer and Daniel P. Moynihan (Cambridge, Mass.: Harvard University Press, 1981), p. 327.

4. Yuan-li Wu and Chun-hsi Wu, *Economic Development in Southeast Asia: The Chinese Dimension* (Stanford: Hoover Institution Press, 1980), pp. 30, 51; S. W. Kung, *Chinese in American Life: Some Aspects of Their History, Status, Problems and Contributions* (Seattle: University of Washington Press, 1962), pp. 22, 23.

5. Victor Wolfgang van Hagen, *The Germanic People in America* (Norman: Oklahoma University Press, 1976), p. 326; Alfred Dolge, *Pianos and Their Makers* (Covina, Calif.: Covina Publishing Company 1911), pp. 172, 264; Edwin M. Good, *Giraffes, Black Dragons, and Other Pianos: A Technological History From Cristofori to the Modern Concert Grand* (Stanford: Stanford University Press, 1982), p. 137n; W. D. Borrie, "Australia," *The Positive Contributions by Immigrants*, edited by Oscar Handlin (Paris: United Nations Educational, Scientific and Cultural Organization, 1960), p. 94.

6. K. L. Filion, *Fiji's Indian Migrants: A History to the End of Indenture in 1920* (Melbourne: Oxford University Press, 1962), pp. 130–133; Agehananda Bharati, *The Asians in East Africa: Jayhind and Uhuru* (Chicago: Nelson-Hall Company, 1972), pp. 11, 17; J. S. Mangat, *A History of the Asians in East Africa: c. 1886 to 1945* (Oxford: Oxford University Press, 1969), pp. 49, 95; Floyd and Lillian O. Dotson, *The Indian Minority of Zambia, Rhodesia, and Malawi* (New Haven: Yale University Press, 1968), pp. 12, 28, 33.

7. Robert F. Foerster, *The Italian Emigration of Our Times* (New York: Arno Press, 1969), pp. 195, 206, 207, 211, 213, 214, 215, 220, 222, 325, 419.

8. Ibid., pp. 257–259; *The Great Palace of the Moscow Kremlin*, translated by M. Wilkinson (Leningrad: Aurora Art Publishers, 1981), p. 9.

9. William R. Brock, *Scotus Americanus: A Survey of the Sources for Links Between Scotland and America in the Eighteenth Century* (Edinburgh: Edinburgh University Press, 1982), pp. 119–120.

10. Bernard Lewis, *The Jews of Islam* (Princeton: Princeton University Press, 1984), pp. 129, 132, 133.

11. Ingeborg Fleischauer, "The Germans' Role in Tsarist Russia: A Reappraisal," *The Soviet Germans: Past and Present*, edited by Edith Rogovin Frankel (New York: St. Martin's Press, 1986), pp. 17–18.

12. William Chase Greene, *The Achievement of Rome: A Chapter in Civilization* (New York: Cooper Square Publishers, Inc., 1973), p. 85.

13. P. T. Bauer, *Reality and Rhetoric: Studies in the Economics of Development* (Cambridge, Mass.: Harvard University Press, 1984), p. 7.

14. See Thomas Sowell, "Three Black Histories," *Essays and Data on American Ethnic Groups*, edited by Thomas Sowell and Lynn D. Collins (Washington, D.C.: The Urban Institute, 1978), pp. 7–64.

15. The Scots of Ulster County, Ireland, who settled along hundreds of miles of Appalachia, had a different history on both sides of the Atlantic from that of the Scots from the Scottish lowlands, as the latter did also from the highland Scots. The Ulster Scots "developed habits of thought and conduct differentiating them from the Scots at home." Maldwyn Allen Jones, "Scotch-Irish," *Harvard Encyclopedia of American Ethnic Groups*, edited by Stephan Thernstrom, et al. (Cambridge, Mass.: Harvard University Press, 1980), p. 896. For social and cultural histories of these various subgroups of Scots see James G. Leyburn, *The Scotch-Irish* (Chapel Hill: University of North Carolina Press, 1962); Rory Fitzpatrick, *God's Frontiersmen: The Scots-Irish Epic* (London: George Weidenfeld and Nicolson, 1989); Duane Meyer, *The Highland Scots of North Carolina: 1732–1776* (Chapel Hill: University of North Carolina Press, 1961); William R. Brock, *Scotus Americanus: A Survey of the Sources for Links Between Scotland and America in the Eighteenth Century* (Edinburgh: Edinburgh University Press, 1982); Gordon Donaldson, "Scots," *Harvard Encyclopedia of American Ethnic Groups*, pp. 908–916. See also David Hackett Fischer, *Albion's Seed: Four British Folkways in America* (New York: Oxford University Press, 1989), pp. 605–782.

16. Yasuo Wakatsuki, "Japanese Emigration to the United States," *Perspectives in American History*, 1979 (Volume XII), pp. 430–434, 465–470.

17. Raphael Patai, *The Jewish Mind* (New York: Charles Scribner's Sons, 1977), pp. 122–125.

18. Geoffrey Blainey, *Triumph of the Nomads: A History of Ancient Australia* (South Melbourne: The Macmillan Co. of Australia, 1982), p. vi.

19. See, for example, Irowokawa Daikichi, *The Culture of the Meiji Period*, translated and edited by Marius B. Jansen (Princeton: Princeton University Press, 1988), Chapter II.

20. John R. Harris, "Movements of Technology Between Britain and Europe in the Eighteenth Century," *International Technology Transfer: Europe, Japan and the USA, 1700–1914*, edited by David J. Jeremy (Brookfield, Vt.: Edward Elgar Publishing Company, 1991), p. 14.

21. Bruno Lasker, *Human Bondage in Southeast Asia* (Chapel Hill: University of North Carolina Press, 1950), p. 16.

22. David J. Jeremy and Darwin H. Stapleton, "Transfers Between Culturally-Related Nations: The Movement of Textile and Railroad Technologies Between Britain and the United States, 1780–1840," *International Technology Transfer: Europe, Japan and the USA, 1700–1914*, edited by David J. Jeremy, pp. 31–48; Takeshi Yuzawa, "The Transfer of Railway Technologies From Britain to Japan, With Special Reference to Locomotive Manufac-

ture," Ibid., pp. 199–218; Tetsuro Nakaoka, "The Transfer of Cotton Manu-
facturing Technology From Britain to Japan," Ibid., pp. 181–198; Gregory
Clark, "Why Isn't the Whole World Developed? Lessons From Cotton
Mills," *Journal of Economic History*, March 1987, p. 142; W. O. Henderson,
*The Rise of German Industrial Power: 1834–1914* (Berkeley: University of
California Press, 1975), p. 44; Mark Jefferson, *Peopling the Argentine
Pampa* (Port Washington, N.Y.: Kennikat Press, 1971), p. 137; Winthrop R.
Wright, *British-Owned Railways in Argentina: Their Effect on the Growth of
Economic Nationalism, 1854–1948* (Austin: University of Texas Press,
1974), pp. 5, 19, 23; Neena Vreeland et al., *Area Handbook for Malaysia*,
third edition (Washington, D.C.: U.S. Government Printing Office, 1977),
pp. 301–302; Dharma Kumar, *The Cambridge Economic History of India*,
Vol. 2 (Hyderabad: Orient Longman, Ltd., 1984), pp. 737–761; T. O. Lloyd,
*The British Empire: 1558–1983* (Oxford: Oxford University Press, 1984), p.
239; Daniel R. Headrick, *The Tools of Empire: Technology and European
Imperialism in the Nineteenth Century* (New York: Oxford University Press,
1981), pp. 180–191, 195.

23. Donald L. Horowitz, *Ethnic Groups in Conflict* (Berkeley: University of Cali-
fornia Press, 1985), p. 677; Myron Weiner, "The Pursuit of Ethnic Equality
Through Preferential Policies: A Comparative Public Policy Perspective,"
*From Independence to Statehood: Managing Ethnic Conflict in Five African
and Asian States*, edited by Robert B. Goldmann and A. Jeyaratnam Wilson
(London: Frances Pinter, 1984), p. 64; Cynthia Enloe, *Police, Military and
Ethnicity: Foundations of State Power* (New Brunswick, N.J.: Transaction
Books, 1980), pp. 37, 163, 164.

24. See, for example, Irowokawa Daikichi, *The Culture of the Meiji Period*,
translated and edited by Marius B. Jansen (Princeton: Princeton University
Press, 1988), Chapter II.

25. Hattie Plum Williams, *The Czar's Germans: With Particular Reference to the
Volga Germans* (Lincoln, Neb.: American Historical Society of Germans
From Russia, 1975), p. 163.

26. W. D. Borrie, *Italians and Germans in Australia* (Melbourne: Australian
National University, 1954), p. 221; Eric N. Baklanoff, "External Factors in
the Economic Development of Brazil's Heartland: The Center-South,
1850–1930," *The Shaping of Modern Brazil*, edited by Eric N. Baklanoff
(Baton Rouge: Louisiana State University Press, 1969), p. 30; Frederick C.
Luebke, "A Prelude to Conflict: The German Ethnic Group in Brazilian
Society, 1890–1917," *Ethnic and Racial Studies*, January 1983, p. 3; Terry
G. Jordan, *German Seed in Texas Soil* (Austin: University of Texas Press,
1982), p. 108; Fred C. Koch, *The Volga Germans: In Russia and the Ameri-
cas, From 1763 to the Present* (University Park: Pennsylvania State Univer-
sity Press, 1978), pp. 214–215, 227, 230; Richard Sallet, *Russian-German
Settlements in the United States*, translated by LaVern J. Rippley and
Armand Bauer (Fargo, N.D.: North Dakota Institute for Regional Studies,

1974), pp. 42–62; George F. W. Young, *Germans in Chile: Immigration and Colonization, 1849–1914* (Staten Island, N.Y.: The Center for Migration Studies, 1974), Chapters II, III, IV; Hans Juergen Hoyer, "Germans in Paraguay, 1881–1945," Ph.D. dissertation, American University, 1973, pp. 46, 49, 51–56.

27. Orlando Patterson, "Context and Choice in Ethnic Allegiance: A Theoretical Framework and Caribbean Case Study," *Ethnicity: Theory and Experience*, edited by Nathan Glazer and Daniel P. Moynihan (Cambridge, Mass.: Harvard University Press, 1981), p. 327.

28. Pierre L. van den Berghe, "Asian Africans Before and After Independence," *Kroniek van Afrika* (The Netherlands), 1975, No. 6 (New Series), p. 199.

29. Ibid., p. 201.

30. Ibid., p. 200.

31. Charles A. Price, *Southern Europeans in Australia* (Canberra: Australian National University, 1979), pp. 140, 162, 198.

32. See, for example, Illsoo Kim, *New Urban Immigrants: The Korean Community in New York* (Princeton: Princeton University Press, 1981), p. 258; Pyong Gap Min, *Ethnic Business Enterprise: Small Business in Atlanta* (New York: Center for Migration Studies, 1988), pp. 33–34; Ivan Light and Edna Bonacich, *Immigrant Entrepreneurs: Koreans in Los Angeles, 1965–1982* (Berkeley: University of California Press, 1988), pp. 318–319.

33. Karl Stumpp, *The German-Russians: Two Centuries of Pioneering* (Bonn: Edition Atlantic-Forum, 1966), pp. 140–141; Albert Bernhardt Faust, *The German Element in the United States* (New York: Arno Press, 1969), pp. 131–139, 148; I. Harmstorf, "German Settlement in South Australia Until 1914," *The Australian People: An Encyclopedia of the Nation, Its People and Their Origins,* edited by James Jupp (North Ryde, N.S.W.: Angus and Robertson, 1988), p. 482; T. Lynn Smith, *Brazil: People and Institutions* (Baton Rouge: Louisiana State University Press, 1972), p. 134.

34. Donald L. Horowitz, *Ethnic Groups in Conflict* (Berkeley: University of California Press, 1985), pp. 169–175; Mahatir bin Mohamad, *The Malay Dilemma* (Kuala Lumpur: Federal Publications, 1970), passim. It may seem as though this implies acceptance of self-reported conclusions in this case but not in the case of survey research. However, much survey research inquires into things desired (becoming a doctor, owning a home, etc.) or behavior valued (hardwork, reliability, etc.) rather than the actual characteristics of one's group behavior pattern.

35. See, for example, Solomon Grayzel, *A History of the Jews: From the Babylonian Exile to the Present, 5728–1968* (New York: New American Library, 1968), p. 342; John William Henderson, et al., *Area Handbook for Burma* (Washington, D.C.: U.S. Government Printing Office, 1971), p. 238.

36. See, for example, Roy E. H. Mellor, *Europe: A Geographical Survey of the Continent* (New York: Columbia University Press, 1979), especially Chapter 1.

37. P. T. Bauer, *Reality and Rhetoric: Studies in the Economics of Development*

(Cambridge, Mass.: Harvard University Press, 1984), p. 7.

38. Kernial Singh Sandhu, *Indians in Malaya: Immigration and Settlement* (Cambridge: Cambridge University Press, 1969), p. 261.

39. Cecil Clementi, *The Chinese in British Guiana* ("The Argosy" Company Ltd., 1915), p. 224.

40. Sidney Pollard, "Labour in Great Britain," *The Cambridge Economic History of Europe*, Vol. VII: *The Industrial Economies: Capital, Labour, and Enterprise*, Part I: *Britain, France, Germany, and Scandinavia*, edited by Peter Mathias and M. M. Postan (Cambridge: Cambridge University Press, 1978), p. 157.

41. See, for example, Ronald C. Newton, *German Buenos Aires, 1900–1933: Social Change and Cultural Crisis* (Austin: University of Texas Press, 1977), p. 9; Gino Germani, "Mass Immigration and Modernization in Argentina," *Studies in Comparative Development*, Vol. 2 (1966), p. 167, 170; Laura Randall, *An Economic History of Argentina in the Twentieth Century* (New York: Columbia University Press, 1978), p. 116; Jean Roche, *La Colonisation Allemande et Le Rio Grande do Sul* (Paris: Institut des Hautes Études de L'Amérique Latine, 1959); J. F. Normano and Antonello Gerbi, *The Japanese in South America: An Introduction Survey With Special Reference to Peru* (New York: Institute of Pacific Relations, 1943), pp. 38–39; Robert Foerster, *The Italian Emigration of Our Times* (New York: Arno Press, 1969), Chapters XIII, XIV, XV, XVI; Winthrop R. Wright, *British-Owned Railways in Argentina: Their Effect on the Growth of Economic Nationalism, 1854–1948* (Austin: University of Texas Press, 1974).

42. Roger P. Bartlett, *Human Capital: The Settlement of Foreigners in Russia 1762–1804* (Cambridge: Cambridge University Press, 1979), pp. 132, 144, 158–164; John P. McKay, *Pioneers for Profit: Foreign Entrepreneurship and Russian Industrialization 1885–1913* (Chicago: University of Chicago Press, 1970), pp. 34, 35, 48, 144; Arcadius Kahan, "Notes on Jewish Entrepreneurship in Tsarist Russia," *Entrepreneurship in Imperial Russia and the Soviet Union*, edited by Gregory Guroff and Fred V. Carstensen (Princeton: Princeton University Press, 1983), pp. 104–124.

43. David Lamb, *The Africans* (New York: Random House, 1982), pp. 214–217, 295.

44. Stephen Steinberg, *The Ethnic Myth: Race, Ethnicity, and Class in America* (New York: Atheneum, 1981), pp. 79–81, 93–103; Joel Perlmann, *Ethnic Differences: Schooling and Social Structure Among the Irish, Italians, Jews and Blacks in an American City 1880–1935* (New York: Cambridge University Press, 1988), p. 204.

45. "Race, Class, and Scores," *New York Times*, October 24, 1982, Section 4, p. 9; College Entrance Examination Board, *Profiles, College-Bound Seniors, 1981* (New York: College Entrance Examination Board, 1982), pp. 27, 36, 45, 55.

46. For a general survey of these developments, see Jason Schneider, "How the

Japanese Camera Took Over," *Modern Photography*, July 1984, pp. 56ff.

47. John P. McKay, *Pioneers for Profit*, pp. 193, 257.

48. David J. Jeremy and Darwin H. Stapleton, "Transfers Between Cultur-ally-Related Nations: The Movement of Textile and Railroad Technolo-gies Between Britain and the United States, 1780–1840," *International Technology Transfer: Europe, Japan and the USA, 1700–1914*, edited by David J. Jeremy (Brookfield, Vt.: Edward Elgar Publishing Company, 1991), p. 35.

49. Charles K. Hyde, "Iron and Steel Technologies Moving Between Europe and the United States Before 1914," Ibid., pp. 52–53.

50. David J. Jeremy and Darwin H. Stapleton, "Transfers Between Culturally-Related Nations," Ibid., p. 42.

51. Charles K. Hyde, "Iron and Steel Technologies Moving Between Europe and the United States Before 1914," Ibid., p. 54.

52. David J. Jeremy and Darwin H. Stapleton, "Transfers Between Culturally-Related Nations," Ibid., pp. 40–41.

53. Ibid., p. 32.

54. Irowokawa Daikichi, *The Culture of the Meiji Period*, p. 7.

55. David J. Jeremy and Darwin H. Stapleton, "Transfers Between Culturally-Related Nations," *International Technology Transfer: Europe, Japan and the USA, 1700–1914*, edited by David J. Jeremy (Brookfield, Vt.: Edward Elgar Publishing Company, 1991), pp. 32, 34, 35; John R. Harris, "Movements of Technology Between Britain and Europe in the Eighteenth Century," Ibid., pp. 12–13, 15, 16, 18, 20, 21, 22, 23.

56. Tetsuro Nakaoka, "The Transfer of Cotton Manufacturing Technology From Britain to Japan," Ibid., p. 183.

57. Ibid., p. 188.

58. Ibid., p. 193.

59. Ibid., p. 194.

60. Takeshi Yuzawa, "The Transfer of Railway Technologies From Britain to Japan, With Special Reference to Locomotive Manufacture," Ibid., pp. 205, 206.

61. Ibid., p. 212.

62. Simon Ville, "Shipping Industry Technologies," Ibid., p. 80.

63. Richard Pipes, *Russia Under the Old Regime: The History of Civilization* (New York: Charles Scribner's Sons, 1974), pp. 196, 218; Antony C. Sutton, *Western Technology and Soviet Economic Development, 1930 to 1945* (Stan-ford: Hoover Institution Press, 1971), pp. 11, 13.

64. David J. Jeremy, "Introduction: Some of the Larger Issues Posed by Tech-nology Transfer," *International Technology Transfer: Europe, Japan and the USA, 1700–1914*, edited by David J. Jeremy (Brookfield, Vt.: Edward Elgar Publishing Company, 1991), p. 1.

65. Tetsuro Nakaoka, "The Transfer of Cotton Manufacturing Technology From Britain to Japan," Ibid., p. 184.

66. John R. Harris, "Movements of Technology Between Britain and Europe in the Eighteenth Century," Ibid., p. 10.

67. W. Montgomery Watt, *The Influence of Islam on Medieval Europe* (Edinburgh: Edinburgh University Press, 1972), pp. 22–26, 30–43, 58–71.

68. Simon Ville, "Shipping Industry Technologies," *International Technology Transfer: Europe, Japan and the USA, 1700–1914*, edited by David J. Jeremy (Brookfield, Vt.: Edward Elgar Publishing Company, 1991), pp. 80, 90.

69. Winthrop R. Wright, *British-Owned Railways in Argentina*, pp. 267–268.

70. Seymour Martin Lipset, "Values, Education, and Entrepreneurship," *Elites in Latin America*, edited by Seymour Martin Lipset and Aldo Solari (New York: Oxford University Press, 1967), p. 25.

71. Seymour Martin Lipset, *Revolution and Counter-revolution: Change and Persistence in Social Structures*, revised edition (Garden City, N.Y.: Anchor Books, 1970), pp. 109–110.

72. Seymour Martin Lipset, "Values, Education, and Entrepreneurship," *Elites in Latin America*, edited by Seymour Martin Lipset and Aldo Solari, pp. 20–21.

73. Carl K. Fisher, "Facing Up to Africa's Food Crisis," *Foreign Affairs*, Fall 1982, p. 166.

74. Ibid., p. 170.

75. Yuan-li Wu and Chun-hsi Wu, *Economic Development in Southeast Asia*, p. 57. See also Donald R. Snodgrass, *Inequality and Economic Development in Malaysia* (Kuala Lumpur: Oxford University Press, 1980), pp. 249–250.

76. Gordon P. Means, *Malaysian Politics* (New York: New York University Press, 1970), p. 20; see also Been-lan Wang, "Government Intervention in Ethnic Stratification: Effects on the Distribution of Students Among Fields of Study," *Comparative Education Review*, Vol. 21 (1977), p. 123; Victor Purcell, *The Chinese in Southeast Asia*, 2nd edition (Kuala Lumpur: Oxford University Press, 1980), p. 227.

77. Wolfgang Kasper, et al., *Fiji: Opportunity From Adversity?* (St. Leonards, Australia: Centre for Independent Studies, 1988), p. 129.

78. Derek T. Healey, "Development Policy: New Thinking About an Interpretation," *Journal of Economic Literature*, September 1972, p. 771.

79. Ibid., p. 771n.

80. James Fallows, "Indonesia: An Effort to Hold Together," *The Atlantic*, June 1982, p. 22.

81. Donald L. Horowitz, *Ethnic Groups in Conflict*, p. 114.

82. Gunnar Myrdal, *Asian Drama: An Inquiry Into the Poverty of Nations* (New York: Vintage Books, 1972), p. 295.

83. Ibid., p. 296.

84. Maurice Pinard and Richard Hamilton, "The Class Base of the Quebec Independence Movement: Conjectures and Evidence," *Ethnic and Racial Studies*, January 1984, pp. 19–54.

85.  Marc Galanter, *Competing Equalities: Law and the Backward Classes in India* (Delhi: Oxford University Press, 1984), p. 63.

86.  Alec Nove and J. A. Newth, *The Soviet Middle East: A Communist Model for Development* (New York: Frederick A. Praeger, 1967), p. 80.

87.  Sammy Smooha and Yochanan Peres, "The Dynamics of Ethnic Inequalities: The Case of Israel," *Studies of Israeli Society*, Vol. I: *Migration, Ethnicity and Community*, edited by Ernest Krausz (New Brunswick, N.J.: Transaction Books, 1980), p. 173.

88.  George H. Brown, Nan L. Rosen, and Susan T. Hill, *The Condition of Education for Hispanic Americans* (Washington, D.C.: National Center for Educational Statistics, 1980), p. 119. See also Manuel P. Servín, "The Post–World War II Mexican-American, 1925–1965: A Non-Achieving Minority," *The Mexican-Americans: An Awakening Minority*, edited by Manuel P. Servín (Beverly Hills: Glencoe Press, 1970), p. 156; Ellwyn R. Stoddard, *Mexican Americans* (New York: Random House, 1973), pp. 133–134.

89.  Paul Compton, "The Conflict in Northern Ireland: Demographic and Economic Considerations," *Economic Dimensions of Ethnic Conflict: International Perspectives*, edited by S. W. R. de A. Samarasinghe and Reed Coughlan (London: Pinter Publishers, 1991), p. 42.

90.  Sue E. Berryman, *Who Will Do Science: Trends, and Their Causes, in Minority and Female Representation Among Holders of Advanced Degrees in Science and Mathematics* (New York: The Rockefeller Foundation, 1983), p. 10.

91.  Seymour Martin Lipset, *Revolution and Counter-revolution*, pp. 83–84.

92.  Ibid.; C. R. Boxer, *The Portuguese Seaborne Empire: 1415–1825* (New York: Alfred A. Knopf, 1969), p. 88; Carl Degler, *Neither Black Nor White: Slavery and Race Relations in Brazil and the United States* (New York: Macmillan Publishing Co., Inc., 1971), p. 245.

93.  Seymour Martin Lipset, "Values, Education, and Entrepreneurship," *Elites in Latin America*, edited by Seymour Martin Lipset and Aldo Solari, pp. 20–21.

94.  Jaime Vicens Vives, "The Decline of Spain in the Seventeenth Century," *The Economic Decline of Empires*, edited by Carlo M. Cipolla (London: Methuen & Co., 1970), p. 127.

95.  William H. McNeill, *The Rise of the West: A History of the Human Community* (Chicago: University of Chicago Press, 1991), p. 667.

96.  Norman R. Stewart, *Japanese Colonization in Eastern Paraguay* (Washington, D.C.: National Academy of Sciences, 1967), p. 153.

97.  Harry Leonard Sawatsky, *They Sought a Country: Mennonite Colonization in Mexico* (Berkeley: University of California Press, 1971), p. 365.

98.  Frederick C. Luebke, *Germans in the New World: Essays in the History of Immigration* (Urbana: University of Illinois Press, 1990), pp. 94, 96; Carl Solberg, *Immigration and Nationalism: Argentina and Chile, 1890–1914* (Austin: University of Texas Press, 1970), Chapter 1; George F. W. Young,

"Bernardo Philippi, Initiator of German Colonization in Chile," *Hispanic American Historical Review*, August 1971, p. 490; Fred C. Koch, *The Volga Germans: In Russia and the Americas, From 1763 to the Present* (University Park: Pennsylvania State University Press, 1978), pp. 231–233.

99. See, for example, Herbert Stein and Murray Foss, *An Illustrated Guide to the American Economy* (Washington, D.C.: The American Enterprise Institute, 1992), pp. 12–13.

100. Donald L. Horowitz, *Ethnic Groups in Conflict*, p. 114.

101. William McGowan, *And Only Man Is Vile: The Tragedy of Sri Lanka* (New York: Farrar, Straus & Giroux, 1992), p. 13. See also pp. 113, 287.

102. Ibid., p. 341.

103. Ibid., p. 288.

104. See, for example, Ibid., pp. 291–292.

105. See Ibid., p. 292.

106. Thomas Sowell, "Race and I.Q. Reconsidered," *Essays and Data on American Ethnic Groups*, edited by Thomas Sowell and Lynn D. Collins, p. 219.

107. Edwin R. Reubens, "Low-level Work in Japan Without Foreign Workers," *International Migration Review*, Winter 1981, pp. 749–757.

108. See, for example, William McGowan, *And Only Man Is Vile*, pp. 94, 288.

109. See Hugh D. Hudson, Jr., *The Rise of the Demidov Family and the Russian Iron Industry in the Eighteenth Century* (Newtonville, Mass.: Oriental Research Partners, 1986), passim, especially pp. 44, 48, 117, 119–120.

110. Ibid., pp. 119–120. Ping-ti Ho, "Economic Decline and Institutional Factors in the Decline of the Chinese Empire," *The Economic Decline of Empires*, edited by Carlo M. Cipolla, p. 275; William H. McNeill, *The Rise of the West: A History of the Human Community* (Chicago: University of Chicago Press, 1991), p. 520.

111. Arthur Hertzberg, *The French Enlightenment and the Jews: The Origins of Modern Anti-Semitism* (New York: Columbia University Press, 1990), p. 80; William H. McNeill, *The Rise of the West*, p. 679.

112. Charles O. Hucker, *China's Imperial Past* (Stanford: Stanford University Press, 1975), Chapter 11, 12, passim; Jaime Vicens Vives, "The Decline of Spain in the Seventeenth Century," *The Economic Decline of Empires*, edited by Carlo M. Cipolla, pp. 121, 126–128.

113. Jaime Vicens Vives, "The Decline of Spain in the Seventeenth Century," *The Economic Decline of Empires*, edited by Carlo M. Cipolla, pp. 130–136, 143, 190.

114. See Chapter 2 of this book.

115. Bernard Lewis, "Some Reflections on the Decline of the Ottoman Empire," *The Economic Decline of Empires*, edited by Carlo M. Cipolla, p. 226; Robert Mantran, "Foreign Merchants and the Minorities in Istanbul during the Sixteenth and Seventeenth Centuries," *Christians and Jews in the Ottoman Empire: The Functioning of a Plural Society*, edited by Benjamin

Braude and Bernard Lewis, Vol. I: *The Central Lands* (New York: Holmes and Meier Publishers, Inc., 1982), pp. 127–137; Charles Issawi, "The Transformation of the Economic Position of the *Millets* in the Nineteenth Century," Ibid., pp. 261–285.

116. Yuan-li Wu and Chun-hsi Wu, *Economic Development in Southeast Asia*, pp. 30–31, 34, 36; Haraprasad Chattopadhyaya, *Indians in Africa: A Socio-Economic Study* (Calcutta: Bookland Private Ltd., 1970), pp. 262–263, 394.

117. O. R. Dathorne, Jr., *The Black Mind: The History of African Literature* (Minneapolis: University of Minnesota Press, 1974), p. 309; see also Edward A. Jones, *Voices of Negritude* (Valley Forge, Pa.: Judson Press, 1971), p. 14.

118. Geoffrey Moorhouse, *India Britannica* (New York: Harper & Row, 1983), p. 243.

119. J. F. Normano and Antonello Gerbi, *The Japanese in South America: An Introduction Survey With Special Reference to Peru* (New York: Institute of Pacific Relations, 1943), p. 62.

120. Robert N. Kearney, *Communalism and Language in the Politics of Ceylon* (Durham: Duke University Press, 1967), pp. 80–81.

121. Donald L. Horowitz, *Ethnic Groups in Conflict*, p. 72; "Both Islam and Christianity are vital and growing religions in Africa today. In the worldwide gatherings of both faiths, African representatives are an increasingly important section. At the same time the observance of traditional religious rituals is probably decreasing, although some young university-educated people are advocating a deliberate return to traditional culture, including its religious aspects. It is doubtful whether the majority of Africans will ever take this seriously." Jocelyn Murray, ed., *Cultural Atlas of Africa* (New York: Facts on File Publications, 1981), p. 35. See also Ashis Nandy, "The Making and Unmaking of Political Cultures in India," *Daedelus*, Winter 1973, pp. 127–128.

122. Ken Adachi, *The Enemy That Never Was: A History of the Japanese Canadians* (Toronto: McClelland & Stewart Ltd., 1976), p. 362.

123. This was pointed out long ago by Marcus Lee Hansen in *The Problem of the Third Generation Immigrant* (Rock Island, Ill.: Augustana Historical Society, 1938), pp. 9–10.

124. "Racism 'Not Changed' Says Professor," *The Press* (Christchurch, New Zealand), September 23, 1988, p. 6.

## CHAPTER 2: MIGRATION AND CULTURE

1. Albert Hourani, "Introduction," *The Lebanese in the World: A Century of Emigration*, edited by Albert Hourani and Nadim Shehadi (London: I. B. Taurus & Co., Ltd., 1992), p. 3; Roger Owen, "Lebanese Migration in the Context of World Population Movements," Ibid., p. 33.

2. Donald Fleming and Bernard Bailyn, "Introduction," *Perspectives in American History*, Vol. III (1973), pp. v–vi.

3.  Philip Taylor, *The Distant Magnet: European Emigration to the U.S.A.* (New York: Harper & Row, 1971), p. ix.

4.  J. S. Mangat, *History of the Asians in East Africa, 1896–1965* (Oxford: The Clarendon Press, 1969), pp. 7, 10, 58, 85, 86, 89, 90, 139; Allison Butler Herrick, et al., *Area Handbook for Uganda* (Washington, D.C.: U.S. Government Printing Office, 1969), p. 266.

5.  See, for example, Victor Purcell, *The Chinese in Southeast Asia*, second edition (Kuala Lumpur: Oxford University Press, 1980), pp. 7, 83, 128, 195, 540; Yuan-li Wu and Chun-hsi Wu, *Economic Development in Southeast Asia: The Chinese Dimension* (Stanford: Hoover Institution Press, 1980), pp. 30, 51, 71, 85; S. W. Kung, *Chinese in American Life: Some Aspects of Their History, Status, Problems, and Contributions* (Seattle: University of Washington Press, 1962), pp. 22, 23.

6.  Emilio Willems, "Brazil," *The Positive Contributions by Immigrants*, edited by Oscar Handlin, et al. (Paris: United Nations Educational, Scientific and Cultural Organization, 1960), p. 123.

7.  Thomas Sowell, *The Economics and Politics of Race: An International Perspective* (New York: William Morrow, 1983), p. 52; Eric N. Baklanoff, "External Factors in the Economic Development of Brazil's Heartland: The Center-South, 1850–1930," *The Shaping of Modern Brazil*, edited by Eric N. Baklanoff (Baton Rouge: Louisiana State University Press, 1969), p. 31.

8.  Warren Dean, *The Industrialization of São Paulo* (Austin: University of Texas Press, 1969), p. 50.

9.  Ibid., p. 54.

10. Gino Germani, "Mass Immigration and Modernization in Argentina," *Studies in Comparative Development*, Vol. 2 (1966), p. 172.

11. Ronald C. Newton, *German Buenos Aires, 1900–1933: Social Change and Cultural Crisis* (Austin: University of Texas Press, 1977), p. 9.

12. Gino Germani, "Mass Immigration and Modernization in Argentina," *Studies in Comparative Development*, Vol. 2 (1966), p. 167; Thomas Weil, et al., *Area Handbook for Argentina* (Washington, D.C.: U.S. Government Printing Office, 1974), p. 75.

13. Ronald C. Newton, *German Buenos Aires, 1900–1933*, p. 19.

14. Gino Germani, "Mass Immigration and Modernization in Argentina," *Studies in Comparative Development*, Vol. 2 (1966), p. 170; Laura Randall, *An Economic History of Argentina in the Twentieth Century* (New York: Columbia University Press, 1978), p. 116.

15. Mark Jefferson, *Peopling the Argentine Pampa* (Port Washington, N.Y.: Kennikat Press, 1971), p. 76.

16. Gino Germani, "Mass Immigration and Modernization in Argentina," *Studies in Comparative Development*, Vol. 2 (1966), p. 178.

17. Eric N. Baklanoff and Jeffrey T. Brannon, "Forward and Backward Linkages in a Plantation Economy: Immigrant Entrepreneurship and Indus-

trial Development in Yucatan, Mexico," *Journal of Developing Areas*, October 1984, pp. 84–94.

18. Pablo Macera and Shane J. Hunt, "Peru," *Latin America: A Guide to Economic History 1830–1930,* edited by Roberto Cortis Conde and Stanley J. Stein (Berkeley: University of California Press, 1977), p. 565.

19. Carl Solberg, *Immigration and Nationalism: Argentina and Chile, 1890–1914* (Austin: University of Texas Press, 1970), p. 40; George F. W. Young, *Germans in Chile: Immigration and Colonization, 1849–1914* (New York: Center for Migration Studies, 1974), pp. 111–114.

20. George F. W. Young, *Germans in Chile*, p. 115.

21. Carl Solberg, *Immigration and Nationalism*, p. 63.

22. Gino Germani, "Mass Immigration and Modernization in Argentina," *Studies in Comparative Development*, Vol. 2 (1966), pp. 171–172.

23. See, for example, Watt Stewart, *Chinese Bondage in Peru: A History of the Chinese Coolie in Peru, 1849–1874* (Durham: Duke University Press, 1951), Chapter V; C. Harvey Gardiner, *The Japanese and Peru: 1873–1973* (Albuquerque: University of New Mexico Press, 1975), pp. 25–30.

24. See Chapters 3 and 8.

25. See, for example, Gino Germani, "Mass Immigration and Modernization in Argentina," *Studies in Comparative Development*, Vol. 2 (1966), pp. 173–174; Eric N. Baklanoff, "External Factors in the Economic Development of Brazil's Heartland: The Center-South, 1850–1930," *The Shaping of Modern Brazil*, edited by Eric N. Baklanoff, p. 30; Eugene W. Ridings, "Foreign Predominance Among Overseas Traders in Nineteenth-Century Latin America," *Latin American Research Review*, Vol. 20, No. 2 (1985), p. 18.

26. Eugene W. Ridings, "Foreign Predominance Among Overseas Traders in Nineteenth-Century Latin America," *Latin American Research Review*, Vol. 20, No. 2 (1985), p. 8.

27. Ibid., p. 5.

28. Ibid., p. 3.

29. Ibid., pp. 5–6.

30. Ibid., p. 5.

31. Gino Germani, "Mass Immigration and Modernization in Argentina," *Studies in Comparative Development*, Vol. 2 (1966), p. 170.

32. Rosemary Thorp and Geoffrey Bertram, *Peru 1890–1977: Growth and Policy in an Open Economy* (New York: Columbia University Press, 1978), p. 35.

33. Eugene W. Ridings, "Foreign Predominance Among Overseas Traders in Nineteenth-Century Latin America," *Latin American Research Review*, Vol. 20, No. 2 (1985), p. 12.

34. Ibid., pp. 12, 13, 15, 18.

35. Ibid., p. 12.

36. Victor Purcell, *The Chinese in Southeast Asia*, second edition (Kuala

Lumpur: Oxford University Press, 1980), pp. 282–285; Kernial Sandhu Singh, *Indians in Malaya: Some Aspects of Their Immigration and Settlement (1786–1957)* (Cambridge: Cambridge University Press, 1969), pp. 10, 48–56.

37. M. C. Madhavan, "Indian Emigrants: Numbers, Characteristics, and Economic Impacts," *Population and Development Review*, September 1985, p. 457.

38. Ibid., p. 465.

39. George K. Weissenborn, "Three Hundred Years of German Presence in Canada," *Language and Society*, Spring 1983, p. 16.

40. Harry Leonard Sawatzky, *They Sought a Country: Mennonite Colonization in Mexico* (Berkeley: University of California Press, 1971), p. 331.

41. Charles A. Price, *Southern Europeans in Australia* (Melbourne: Australian National University, 1979), p. 106.

42. James L. Tigner, "Japanese Immigration Into Latin America," *Journal of Interamerican Studies and World Affairs*, November 1981, p. 466.

43. Mostafa N. Nagi, "Determinants of Current Trends in Labor Migration and the Future Outlook," *Asian Labor Migration: Pipeline to the Middle East*, edited by Fred Arnold and Nasra M. Shah (Boulder: Westview Press, 1986), p. 48.

44. Fred Arnold and Nasra M. Shah, "Asia's Labor Pipeline: An Overview," Ibid., p. 3.

45. Ibid., p. 6.

46. Ibid., p. 7.

47. Hugh Tinker, *The Banyan Tree: Overseas Emigrants From India, Pakistan, and Bangladesh* (Oxford: Oxford University Press, 1977), pp. 51–52.

48. Nathaniel H. Leff, *The Brazilian Capital Goods Industry 1929–1964* (Cambridge, Mass.: Harvard University Press, 1968), p. 17.

49. See, for example, Hattie Plum Williams, *The Czar's Germans: With Particular Reference to the Volga Germans* (Lincoln, Neb.: American Historical Society of Germans From Russia, 1975), pp. xi–xii, 97; Fred C. Koch, *The Volga Germans: In Russia and the Americas, From 1763 to the Present* (University Park: Pennsylvania State University Press, 1978), pp. xi, xv, 1, 146, 159; Adam Giesinger, *From Catherine to Khrushchev: The Story of Russia's Germans* (Lincoln, Neb.: American Historical Society of Germans From Russia, 1974), pp. 48, 55; Richard Sallett, *Russian-German Settlements in the United States* (Fargo, N.D.: North Dakota Institute for Regional Studies, 1974), pp. 3, 106. As against this testimony, there is the curt dismissal of the idea that German culture remained intact in Russia by James W. Long, *From Privileged to Dispossessed: The Volga Germans, 1860–1917* (Lincoln: University of Nebraska Press, 1988), p. xi. His evidence offered is sparse and inconclusive. See Ibid., pp. 50–54, 69–70, 159, 169–172, 175, 176–177. Moreover, even Long refers to the persistence of the German language among Germans in Russia into the twentieth century. Ibid., pp. 226–241.

50. Albert Hourani, "Introduction," *The Lebanese in the World*, edited by Albert Hourani and Nadim Shehadi, pp. 8–9.

51. Charles A. Price, *Southern Europeans in Australia*, pp. 162–164.

52. Samuel L. Baily, "The Adjustment of Italian Immigrants in Buenos Aires and New York," *American Historical Review*, April 1983, p. 291; Robert F. Foerster, *The Italian Emigration of Our Times* (New York: Arno Press, 1969), p. 393; Dino Cinel, *From Italy to San Francisco: The Immigrant Experience* (Stanford: Stanford University Press, 1982), p. 28; John E. Zucchi, *Italians in Toronto: Development of a National Identity 1875–1935* (Kingston, Ontario: McGill-Queen's University Press, 1988), pp. 41, 53–55, 58.

53. Robert C. Ostergren, "Prairie Bound: Migration Patterns to a Swedish Settlement on the Dakota Frontier," *Ethnicity on the Great Plains*, edited by Frederick C. Luebke (Lincoln: University of Nebraska Press, 1980), pp. 84–88.

54. Albert Hourani, "Introduction," *The Lebanese in the World*, edited by Albert Hourani and Nadim Shehadi, p. 7.

55. Humbert S. Nelli, *The Italians in Chicago, 1880–1930: A Study in Ethnic Mobility* (New York: Oxford University Press, 1970), p. xiii; Luciano J. Iorizzo and Salvatore Mondello, *The Italian-Americans* (New York: Twayne Publishers, Inc., 1971), pp. 88–89; Gino Germani, "Mass Immigration and Modernization in Argentina," *Studies in Comparative Development*, Vol. 2 (1966), p. 175; John E. Zucchi, *Italians in Toronto*, pp. 5–7, 34, 193.

56. Charles A. Price, *Southern Europeans in Australia*, p. 243.

57. See, for example, H. H. Ben-Sasson, "Diaspora Configuration and Jewish Occupational Patterns at the Beginning of the Middle Ages," *A History of the Jewish People*, edited by H. H. Ben-Sasson (Cambridge, Mass.: Harvard University Press, 1976), p. 398.

58. Albert Hourani, "Introduction," *The Lebanese in the World*, edited by Albert Hourani and Nadim Shehadi, p. 8.

59. Magnus Morner, *Adventurers and Proletarians: The Story of Migrants in Latin America* (Pittsburgh: University of Pittsburgh Press, 1985), p. 13.

60. John R. Harris, "Movements of Technology Between Britain and Europe in the Eighteenth Century," *International Technology Transfer: Europe, Japan and the USA, 1700–1914*, edited by David J. Jeremy (Brookfield, Vt.: Edward Elgar Publishing Co., 1991), pp. 15, 22; David J. Jeremy and Darwin H. Stapleton, "Transfers Between Culturally-Related Nations: The Movement of Textile and Railroad Technologies Between Britain and the United States, 1780–1840," Ibid., p. 32; Simon Ville, "Shipping Industry Technologies," Ibid., p. 80; Takeshi Yuzawa, "The Transfer of Railway Technologies From Britain to Japan, With Special Reference to Locomotive Manufacture," Ibid., pp. 210–211, 214–215; W. O. Henderson, *The Rise of German Industrial Power: 1834–1914* (Berkeley: University of California Press, 1975), p. 44; Mark Jefferson, *Peopling the Argentina Pampa*, p. 137.

61. John R. Harris, "Movements of Technology Between Britain and Europe in the Eighteenth Century," *International Technology Transfer*, edited by David J. Jeremy, pp. 14, 15; David J. Jeremy and Darwin H. Stapleton, "Transfers Between Culturally-Related Nations: The Movement of Textile and Railroad Technologies Between Britain and the United States, 1780–1840," Ibid., pp. 40, 41–42; Simon Ville, "Shipping Industry Technologies," Ibid., pp. 80–81.

62. Anthony DePalma, "Foreigners Flood U.S. Graduate Schools," *New York Times*, November 29, 1990, p. A14; "Characteristics of Recipients of Doctorates 1988," *The Chronicle of Higher Education*, September 5, 1990, p. 18.

63. Sergio Diaz Briquets, *International Migration Within Latin America and the Caribbean: An Overview* (Staten Island, N.Y.: Center for Migration Studies, 1983), p. 28.

64. Ibid., p. 6.

65. Ibid., p. 11.

66. Ibid., p. 5.

67. Seth Rosenfeld, "Hong Kong Gang Muscles Into Bay Area," *San Francisco Examiner*, November 25, 1991, pp. 1ff.

68. In Australia, this political phenomenon has been aptly referred to as "the burgeoning multicultural subsidy industry." Wolfgang Kasper, "The Case for Sustained Immigration," *IPA Review*, Vol. 44, No. 44 (1991), p. 54.

69. Julian Simon, *The Economic Consequences of Immigration* (Cambridge, Mass.: Basil Blackwell, Inc., 1991), pp. 230–232.

70. Ibid., p. 238.

71. Ibid., pp. 105–128. However, Simon omits the costs of special assistance to refugees. Ibid., p. 112.

72. B. McGuie, "Lebanese Asylum Applicants in Denmark 1985–1988: Political Refugees or War Emigrants?" *The Lebanese in the World*, edited by Albert Hourani and Nadim Shehadi, pp. 661–662. Conversely, Lebanese immigrants and refugees have been more welcome in France, where the public perception, at least, seems to be that the Lebanese are self-supporting and do not become public charges. See Amir Abdul-Karim, "Lebanese Business in France," Ibid., pp. 692–693.

73. Jean-Francois Revel, *The Flight From Truth: The Reign of Deceit in the Age of Information* (New York: Random House, 1991), p. 77.

74. Constanza Montana, "Hispanic Communities in U.S. Are Divided by Influx of Mexicans," *Wall Street Journal*, October 21, 1986, pp. 1ff.

75. Alan Riding, "Europe's Growing Debate Over Whom to Let Inside," *New York Times*, December 1, 1991, p. 2.

76. See, for example, Craig R. Whitney, "Europeans Look for Ways to Bar Door to Immigrants," *New York Times*, December 29, 1991, pp. 1ff; Judith Miller, "Strangers at the Gate," *New York Times Magazine*, September 15, 1991, pp. 33ff; Robert Birrell, "Closing the Door on Immigration," *IPA Review*, Vol. 44, No. 4 (1991), pp. 50–55.

77. See, for example, Thomas Sowell, "The High Cost of 'Identity,'" *Forbes*, August 5, 1991, p. 69.

78. Lennox A Miller, *Southeast Asia* (Minneapolis: University of Minnesota Press, 1964), p. 111.

79. H. L. van der Laan, *The Lebanese Traders in Sierra Leone* (The Hague: Mouton, 1975), p. 136; Alixa Naff, "Lebanese Immigration Into the United States," *The Lebanese in the World*, edited by Albert Hourani and Nadim Shehadi, p. 148.

80. Hagen Koo and Eui-Young Yu, *Korean Immigration to the United States: Its Demographic Pattern and Social Implications for Both Societies* (Honolulu: East-West Center, 1981), p. 11; Ivan Light and Edna Bonacich, *Immigrant Entrepreneurs: Koreans in Los Angeles, 1965–1982* (Berkeley: University of California Press, 1988), pp. 168, 170, 172; Illsoo Kim, *New Urban Immigrants: The Korean Community in New York* (Princeton: Princeton University Press, 1981), pp. 114, 115.

81. Haraprasad Chattopadhyaya, *Indians in Africa* (Calcutta: Bookland Private Ltd., 1970), p. 264.

82. Neil Leighton, "Lebanese Emigration: Its Effect on the Political Economy of Sierra Leone," *The Lebanese in the World*, edited by Albert Hourani and Nadim Shehadi, p. 583.

83. Pyong Gap Min, *Ethnic Business Enterprise: Korean Small Business in Atlanta* (New York: Center for Migration Studies, 1988), p. 82. See also p. 93.

84. Alixa Naff, "Lebanese Immigration Into the United States: 1880 to the Present," *The Lebanese in the World*, edited by Albert Hourani and Nadim Shehadi, p. 148.

85. Antonio S. Tan, "The Changing Identity of the Philippine Chinese, 1946–1984," *Changing Identities of the Southeast Asian Chinese Since World War II*, edited by Jennifer Cushman and Wang Gungwu (Hong Kong: Hong Kong University Press, 1988), p. 192.

86. Charles Issawi, "The Historical Background of Lebanese Emigration: 1800–1914," *The Lebanese in the World*, edited by Albert Hourani and Nadim Shehadi, p. 31; Baha Abu-Laban, "The Lebanese in Montreal," Ibid., p. 237; Ignacio Klich, "Criollos and Arabic Speakers in Argentina: An Uneasy Pas de Deux, 1888–1914," Ibid., p. 273; Clark S. Knowlton, "The Social and Spatial Mobility of the Syrian and Lebanese Community in São Paulo, Brazil," Ibid., pp. 293, 302; Estela Valverde, "Integration and Identity in Argentina: The Lebanese of Tucuman," Ibid., pp. 315, 316, 317, 318; David Nicholls, "Lebanese of the Antilles: Haiti, Dominican Republic, Jamaica, and Trinidad," Ibid., p. 342, 352; Trevor Batrouney, "The Lebanese in Australia, 1880–1989," Ibid., p. 421; H. Laurens van der Laan, "Migration, Mobility and Settlement of the Lebanese in West Africa," Ibid., p. 532; Said Boumedouba, "Change and Continuity in the Relationship Between the Lebanese in Senegal and Their Hosts," Ibid., p. 551; Neil O.

Leighton, "Lebanese Emigration: Its Effect on the Political Economy of Sierra Leone," Ibid., pp. 581, 586.

87.  Eric E. Hirshler, "Jews From Germany in the United States," *Jews From Germany in the United States*, edited by Eric E. Hirshler (New York: Farrar, Straus and Cudahy, 1955), pp. 37, 66; Alixa Naff, "Lebanese Immigration Into the United States: 1880 to the Present," *The Lebanese in the World*, edited by Albert Hourani and Nadim Shehadi, p. 148.

88.  See, for example, P. T. Bauer, *West African Trade: A Study of Competition, Oligopoly and Monopoly in a Changing Economy* (Cambridge: Cambridge University Press, 1954), Chapter 2.

89.  Hugh Tinker, *The Banyan Tree: Overseas Emigrants From India, Pakistan, and Bangladesh* (Oxford: Oxford University Press, 1977), p. 143.

90.  Bayley R. Winder, "The Lebanese in West Africa," *Comparative Studies in Society and History*, Vol. IV (1962), p. 310; H. L. van der Lann, *The Lebanese Traders in Sierra Leone* (The Hague: Mouton, 1975), p. 222; Said Boumedouha, "Change and Continuity in the Relationship Between the Lebanese in Senegal and Their Hosts," *The Lebanese in the World*, edited by Albert Hourani and Nadim Shehadi, p. 556.

91.  L. A. Peter Gosling, "Chinese Crop Dealers in Malaysia and Thailand: The Myth of the Merciless Monopsonistic Middleman," *The Chinese in Southeast Asia*, edited by Linda Y. C. Lim and L. A. Peter Gosling, Vol. I: *Ethnicity and Economic Activity* (Singapore: Maruzen Asia, 1983), pp. 134–135, 144–145.

92.  See, for example, Virginia Thompson and Richard Adloff, *Minority Problems in Southeast Asia* (New York: Russell & Russell, 1970), p. 85; Donald R. Snodgrass, *Inequality and Economic Development in Malaysia* (Kuala Lumpur: Oxford University Press, 1980), p. 212.

93.  Donald L. Horowitz, *Ethnic Groups in Conflict*, pp. 117–118.

94.  Arthur Hertzberg, *The French Enlightenment and the Jews: The Origins of Modern Anti-Semitism* (New York: Columbia University Press, 1960), p. 88; Victor Purcell, *The Chinese in Southeast Asia*, second edition (Kuala Lumpur: Oxford University Press, 1980), pp. 197, 203, 443–444.

95.  H. L. van der Lann, *The Lebanese Traders in Sierra Leone*, p. 226.

96.  Victor Purcell, *The Chinese in Southeast Asia*, second edition, p. 450.

97.  Illsoo Kim, *New Urban Immigrants*, p. 119.

98.  A study of Korean businessmen in New York found that they "were contemptuous of the extravagant life styles of blacks and Puerto Ricans, from whom they want to maintain a social distance," even though these were among their principal customers. Illsoo Kim, *New Urban Immigrants*, p. 138. Although their businesses tended to be in inner city neighborhoods, the Koreans themselves tended to live in predominantly white neighborhoods. Ibid., pp. 143, 258. The same was true of Koreans in Atlanta and similar patterns were found in Los Angeles, where Koreans tended to live either in their own neighborhood or in the non-ghetto areas of the city and

suburbs. Pyong Gap Min, *Ethnic Business Enterprise*, pp. 70, 125; Ivan Light and Edna Bonacich, *Immigrant Entrepreneurs*, pp. 6, 207.

99. Alixa Naff, "Lebanese Immigration Into the United States: 1880 to the Present," *The Lebanese in the World*, edited by Albert Hourani and Nadim Shehadi, p. 157.

100. Illsoo Kim, *New Urban Immigrants*, p. 138.

101. Ibid., pp. 143, 258; Pyong Gap Min, *Ethnic Business Enterprise*, pp. 70, 125; Ivan Light and Edna Bonacich, *Immigrant Entrepreneurs*, pp. 6, 207.

102. Hugh Tinker, *The Banyan Tree*, p. 143.

103. H. L. van der Lann, *The Lebanese Traders in Sierra Leone*, pp. 42–43.

104. Yuan-li Wu, "Chinese Entrepreneurs in Southeast Asia," *American Economic Review*, May 1983, pp. 113–114.

105. Janet L. Abu-Lughod, *Before European Hegemony: The World System A.D. 1250–1350* (New York: Oxford University Press, 1989), pp. 16–17.

106. Nizar Motani, "The Ugandan Civil Service and the Asian Problem, 1894–1972," *Expulsion of a Minority: Essays on Ugandan Asians*, edited by Michael Twaddle (London: The Athlone Press, 1975), p. 101.

107. Myron Weiner, *Sons of the Soil: Migration and Ethnic Conflict in India* (Princeton: Princeton University Press, 1978), pp. 128–129.

108. Rita Cruise O'Brien, "Lebanese Entrepreneurs in Senegal: Economic Integration and the Politics of Protection," *Cahiers d'Etudes Africaines*, Vol. 15, No. 57 (1975), p. 103.

109. Dr. Omotosho Ogunniy, "Human Resource Flows in Relation to Integration and National Unity," *Journal of Business and Social Studies* (December 1970), p. 177. This journal is published at the University of Lagos, Nigeria.

110. Myron Weiner, *Sons of the Soil*, pp. 128–129.

111. Didier Bigo, "The Lebanese Community in the Ivory Coast: A Non-native Network at the Heart of Power?" *The Lebanese in the World*, edited by Albert Hourani and Nadim Shehadi, p. 524.

112. Pyong Gap Min, *Ethnic Business Enterprise*, p. 111.

113. Hugh Tinker, *The Banyan Tree*, p. 132.

114. Donald L. Horowitz, *Ethnic Groups in Conflict*, p. 666; Donald M. Nonini, "The Chinese Truck Transport 'Industry' of a Peninsular Malaysia Market Town," *The Chinese in Southeast Asia*, Vol. I: *Ethnicity and Economic Activity*, edited by Linda Y. C. Lim and L. A. Peter Gosline, p. 195.

115. See, for example, *Mid-term Review of Fourth Malaysia Plan 1981–1985* (Kuala Lumpur: Government Press, 1984), p. 17.

116. Donald L. Horowitz, *Ethnic Groups in Conflict*, p. 666.

117. Rita Cruise O'Brien, "Lebanese Entrepreneurs in Senegal: Economic Integration and the Politics of Protection," *Cahiers d'Etudes Africaines*, Vol. 15, No. 57 (1975), p. 113.

118. "Old Uneconomic Policy," *The Economist*, March 11, 1989, p. 40.

119. Hugh Tinker, *The Banyan Tree*, p. 126.

120. See Illsoo Kim, *New Urban Immigrants*, p. 111. See also Hagen Koo and

Eui-Young Yu, *Korean Immigration to the United States*, p. 7; Ivan Light and Edna Bonacich, *Immigrant Entrepreneurs*, pp. 207–208, 225–226.

121. Edna Bonacich, "A Theory of Middleman Minority," *American Sociological Review*, October 1973, pp. 585, 588.

122. Ibid., p. 585.

123. Ibid., p. 590.

124. Pierre van den Berghe, "Asian Africans Before and After Independence," *Kroniek van Afrika* (New Series), no. 6 (1975), pp. 198–199.

125. Ibid., p. 201.

126. Ibid., p. 204.

127. P. T. Bauer, *West African Trade: A Study of Competition, Oligopoly and Monopoly in a Changing Economy* (Cambridge: Cambridge University Press, 1954), p. 27.

128. Ibid., p. 25.

129. R. A. Radford, "The Economic Organisation of a P.O.W. Camp," *Economica*, November 1945, p. 199.

130. Thomas Sowell, *Ethnic America: A History* (New York: Basic Books, 1981), p. 99.

131. Judith Laikin Elkin, *Jews of the Latin American Republics* (Chapel Hill: University of North Carolina Press, 1980), p. 229.

132. Victor Purcell, *The Chinese in Southeast Asia*, 2nd edition, p. 343; Judith Strauch, "The Political Economy of a Chinese-Malaysian New Village: Highly Diversified Insecurity," *The Chinese in Southeast Asia*, edited by Y. C. Lim and L. A. Peter Gosling, Vol. I, p. 207.

133. Hugh Tinker, *The Banyan Tree*, p. 105.

134. Wolfgang Kasper, et al., *Fiji: Opportunity From Adversity?* (St. Leonards, Australia: Centre for Independent Studies, 1988), p. 3.

135. Hugh Tinker, *The Banyan Tree*, p. 39.

136. John Train, "A Talk With Leon Louw," *Harvard Magazine*, September–October, 1993, p. 23.

137. William B. Mitchell, et al., *Area Handbook for Guyana* (Washington, D.C.: U.S. Government Printing Office, 1969), pp. 167–168.

138. Avraham Shama and Mark Iris, *Immigration Without Integration: Third World Jews in Israel* (Cambridge, Mass.: Schenkman Publishing Company, 1977), p. 39.

139. Sammy Smooha, *Israel: Pluralism and Conflict* (Berkeley: University of California Press, 1978), pp. 128–129.

140. Avraham Shama and Mark Iris, *Immigration Without Integration*, pp. 10, 19.

141. Benjamin Pinkus, "From the October Revolution to the Second World War," *The Soviet Germans: Past and Present*, edited by Edith Rogovin Frankel (New York: St. Martin's Press, 1986), p. 61.

142. See Bernard Lewis, *The Jews of Islam* (Princeton: Princeton University Press, 1984), pp. 130, 175–176.

## CHAPTER 3: CONQUEST AND CULTURE

1.  John Stuart Mill, "Considerations on Representative Government," *Collected Works of John Stuart Mill*, Vol. XIX: *Essays on Politics and Society*, edited by J. M. Robson (Toronto: University of Toronto Press, 1977), p. 571.

2.  See, for example, Lord Kinross, *The Ottoman Centuries: The Rise and Fall of the Turkish Empire* (New York: William Morrow, 1977), pp. 74, 77, 109, 131, 187; Edward Gibbon, *The Decline and Fall of the Roman Empire* (New York: The Modern Library, no date), Vol. III, pp. 774–775.

3.  L. H. Gann and Peter Duignan, *Burden of Empire: An Appraisal of Western Colonialism in Africa South of the Sahara* (Stanford: Hoover Institution Press, 1977), p. 140.

4.  Harold E. Driver, *Indians of North America*, second edition (Chicago: University of Chicago Press, 1975), p. 471.

5.  Alvin M. Brandon, *The American Heritage Book of Indians* (New York: American Heritage Publishing Co., Inc., 1961), p. 77.

6.  Edward Gibbon, *The Decline and Fall of Roman Empire*, Vol. II, pp. 374, 593, 621, 790; Ibid., Vol. III, pp. 249, 624.

7.  N. J. G. Pounds, *An Historical Geography of Europe* (Cambridge: Cambridge University Press, 1990), p. 89.

8.  David C. Lindberg, "The Transmission of Greek and Arabic Learning to the West," *Science in the Middle Ages*, edited by David C. Lindberg (Chicago: University of Chicago Press, 1978), pp. 52–90.

9.  William H. McNeill, *The Rise of the West: A History of the Human Community* (Chicago: University of Chicago Press, 1991), pp. 102–109.

10. I. M. Stead, *Celtic Art in Britain Before the Roman Conquest* (Cambridge, Mass.: Harvard University Press, 1985), p. 4.

11. John Wacher, *The Coming of Rome* (New York: Charles Scribner's Sons, 1980), p. 76; F. E. Halliday, *An Illustrated Cultural History of England* (New York: Crescent Books, 1967), p. 17.

12. John Burke, *Roman England* (New York: W. W. Norton, 1984), pp. 13, 16, 25; John Wacher, *The Coming of Rome*, p. 39; F. E. Halliday, *An Illustrated Cultural History of England*, pp. 19–22.

13. Winston S. Churchill, *A History of the English-Speaking Peoples*, Vol. I: *The Birth of Britain* (New York: Bantam Books, 1974), p. 28.

14. F. E. Halliday, *An Illustrated Cultural History of England*, p. 25. See also C. J. Arnold, *Roman Britain to Saxon England* (Bloomington: Indiana University Press, 1984), pp. 58, 66, 71.

15. C. J. Arnold, *Roman Britain to Saxon England*, pp. 38, 150.

16. N. J. G. Pounds, *An Historical Geography of Europe: 1800–1914* (Cambridge: Cambridge University Press, 1990), pp. 70, 71, 86.

17. James Campbell, "The End of Roman Britain," *The Anglo-Saxons*, edited by James Campbell (Ithaca: Cornell University Press, 1982), p. 19.

18. Karl Polanyi, *The Great Transformation: The Political and Economic Origins*

*of Our Time* (Boston: Beacon Press, 1957), p. 45.

19.  N. J. G. Pounds, *An Historical Geography of Europe: 1800–1914*, p. 146.

20.  Geoffrey Moorhouse, *India Britannica* (New York: Harper & Row, 1983), pp. 180–193, 202, 243, 253, 269.

21.  Jorge Heine, "A People Apart," *The Wilson Quarterly*, Spring 1980, pp. 125, 129.

22.  "Divided They Stand," *The Economist*, February 2, 1985, pp. 4–18.

23.  L. H. Gann, "Changing Patterns of a White Élite: Rhodesian and Other Settlers," *Colonialism in Africa, 1870–1960*, Vol. II: *The History and Politics of Colonialism 1914–1960*, edited by L. H. Gann and Peter Duignan (Cambridge: Cambridge University Press, 1982), p. 135.

24.  See, for example, Harold E. Driver, *Indians of North America*, 2nd edition (Chicago: University of Chicago Press, 1975), pp. 471–472.

25.  L. H. Gann and Peter Duignan, "Introduction," *Colonialism in Africa: 1870–1960*, edited by L. H. Gann and Peter Duignan, Vol. I: *The History and Politics of Colonialism 1870–1914* (Cambridge: Cambridge University Press, 1981), p. 17.

26.  Robert Cornevin, "The Germans Before 1918," Ibid., p. 403.

27.  Myron Weiner and Mary Fainsod Katzenstein, *India's Preferential Policies: Migrants, the Middle Class, and Ethnic Equality* (Chicago: University of Chicago Press, 1981), p. 71.

28.  Chandra Richard de Silva, "Sinhala-Tamil Ethnic Rivalry: The Background," *From Independence to Statehood: Managing Ethnic Conflict in Five African and Asian States*, edited by Robert B. Goldmann and A. Jeyaratnam Wilson (London: Frances Pinter, 1984), p. 115.

29.  James Coleman, *Nigeria: Background to Nationalism* (Berkeley: University of California Press, 1971), p. 134.

30.  Ibid., p. 142.

31.  Donald L. Horowitz, *Ethnic Groups in Conflict* (Berkeley: University of California Press, 1985), pp. 448, 451.

32.  "The Ibo, who today play an important part in Nigerian trade, were in an almost savage state as recently as 1910." P. T. Bauer, *West African Trade: A Study of Competition, Oligopoly and Monopoly in a Changing Economy* (Cambridge: Cambridge University Press, 1954), p. 7.

33.  James S. Coleman, *Nigeria: Background to Nationalism* (Berkeley: University of California Press, 1971), p. 142; Donald L. Horowitz, *Ethnic Groups in Conflict* (Berkeley: University of California Press, 1985), pp. 448, 451; Northern Nigeria, *Statistical Yearbook 1965* (Kaduna: Ministry of Economic Planning, 1965), pp. 40–41; Robert Nelson and Howard Wolpe, *Nigeria: Modernization and Politics of Communalism* (East Lansing: Michigan State University Press, 1971), p. 127; Bernard Nkemdirim, "Social Change and the Genesis of Conflict in Nigeria," *Civilizations*, Vol. 25, Nos. 1–2 (1975), p. 94; Okwudiba Nnoli, *Ethnic Politics in Nigeria* (Enugu, Nigeria: Fourth Dimension Publishers, 1978), p. 64.

34. S. J. Tambiah, "Ethnic Representation in Ceylon's Higher Administrative Service, 1870–1946," *University of Ceylon Review*, April–July 1955, p. 130.

35. W. Ivor Jennings, "Race, Religion and Economic Opportunity in the University of Ceylon," *University of Ceylon Review*, November 1944, p. 2.

36. Chandra Richard de Silva, "Sinhala-Tamil Ethnic Rivalry: The Background," *From Independence to Statehood: Managing Ethnic Conflict in Five African and Asia States*, edited by Robert B. Goldmann and A. Jeyaratnam Wilson (London: Frances Pinter, 1984), p. 16. See also Chandra Richard de Silva, "Sinhala-Tamil Relations and Education in Sri Lanka: University Admissions Issue—The First Phase," Ibid., p. 136.

37. Chandra Richard de Silva, "Sinhala-Tamil Relations and Education in Sri Lanka," Ibid., p. 138.

38. Alec Nove and J. A. Newth, *The Soviet Middle East: A Communist Model for Development* (New York: Frederick A. Praeger, 1967), p. 83.

39. R. G. Collingwood, *Roman Britain and the English Settlements* (Oxford: Oxford University Press, 1987), p. viii.

40. William H. McNeill, *The Rise of the West: A History of the Human Community* (Chicago: University of Chicago Press, 1991), pp. 217, 229.

41. Scottish universities, for example, were ahead of the English universities in science and technology. The world's first university chair in engineering was founded in Glasgow in 1840. By 1871, nearly half the ships built in the United Kingdom were built in Scotland. Newly industrializing nineteenth-century Japan looked to Scotland for its science and engineering, and many of the ships for the new Japanese navy were built in Scottish shipyards. (Olive and Sydney Checkland, *Industry and Ethos: Scotland 1832–1914* [Edinburgh: Edinburgh University Press, 1989], pp. 20, 147, 148, 149.) The Scots also surpassed the English in agricultural techniques during the eighteenth century. (G. M. Trevelyan, *English Social History: A Survey of Six Centuries* [New York: Viking Penguin, Inc. 1986], p. 463.)

42. William R. Brock, *Scotus Americanus: A Survey of the Sources for Links Between Scotland and America in the Eighteenth Century* (Edinburgh: Edinburgh University Press, 1982), pp. 114–115.

43. Peter Salway, *Roman Britain* (Oxford: Oxford University Press, 1984), p. 15.

44. N. J. G. Pounds, *An Historical Geography of Europe* (Cambridge: Cambridge University Press, 1990), p. 67.

45. Bernard Lewis, *The Arabs in History* (New York: Harper & Row, 1967), pp. 14, 137.

46. William H. McNeill, *The Rise of the West: A History of Civilization* (Chicago: University of Chicago Press, 1991), p. 229.

47. Ibid., pp. 492–494, 576–577.

48. Ibid., pp 243–244.

49. Jaime Vicens Vives, "The Decline of Spain in the Seventeenth Century," *The Economic Decline of Empires*, edited by Carlo M. Cipolla (London: Methuen & Co., 1970), pp. 121, 126–128; Bernard Lewis, "Some Reflec-

tions on the Decline of the Ottoman Empire," Ibid., pp. 229–230.

50. Janet L. Abu-Lughod, *Before European Hegemony: The World System A.D. 1250–1350* (New York: Oxford University Press, 1989), p. 182.

51. Bernard Lewis, "Some Reflections on the Decline of the Ottoman Empire," *The Economic Decline of Empires*, edited by Carlo M. Cipolla, pp. 229–230.

52. J. H. Elliott, "The Decline of Spain," Ibid., p. 178. See also Jaime Vicens Vives, "The Decline of Spain in the Seventeenth Century," Ibid., p. 123.

53. Jane S. Gerber, *The Jews of Spain: A History of the Sephardic Experience* (New York: The Free Press, 1992), p. x.

54. Fernand Braudel, *The Mediterranean and the Mediterranean World in the Age of Phillip II*, translated by Sian Reynolds (New York: Harper & Row, 1976), Volume II, p. 795.

55. Christopher Hibbert, *The English: A Social History 1066–1945* (New York: W. W. Norton, 1987), p. 121.

56. Gerhard Simon, *Nationalism and Policy Toward the Nationalities in the Soviet Union: From Totalitarian Dictatorship to Post-Stalinist Society*, translated by Karen Forster and Oswald Forster (Boulder: Westview Press, 1991), pp. 248–249.

57. Hélène Carrère d'Encausse, *Decline of an Empire* (New York: Harper & Row, 1979), p. 170.

58. T. C. Smout, *A History of the Scottish People, 1560–1830* (New York: Charles Scribner's Sons, 1969), pp. 31–32, 34, 333.

59. Frank Barlow, "Who Are the English?" *The English World: History, Character, and People*, edited by Robert Blake (New York: Harry N. Abrams, Inc., 1982), p. 56.

60. "Introduction," *Colonialism in Africa 1870–1960*, edited by Peter Duignan and L. H. Gann, Vol. IV: *The Economics of Colonialism* (Cambridge: Cambridge University Press, 1975), p. 11.

61. Harold D. Nelson, et al., *Nigeria: A Country Study* (Washington, D.C.: U.S. Government Printing Office, 1982), p. 26; Lance E. Davis and Robert A. Huttenback, *Mammon and the Pursuit of Empire: The Political Economy of British Imperialism, 1860–1912* (Cambridge: Cambridge University Press, 1987), pp. 6–7, 10, 301–303.

62. L. H. Gann and Peter Duignan, "Reflections on Imperialism and the Scramble for Africa," *Colonialism in Africa 1870–1960*, Volume I, edited by L. H. Gann and Peter Duignan, p. 112.

63. Ibid., p. 107.

64. Ibid.

65. L. H. Gann, "Economic Development in Germany's African Empire, 1884–1914," *Colonialism in Africa 1870–1960*, Volume IV, edited by Peter Duignan and L. H. Gann, p. 218.

66. L. H. Gann and Peter Duignan, "Reflections on Imperialism and the Scramble for Africa," *Colonialism in Africa 1870–1960,* Volume I, edited by L. H. Gann and Peter Duignan, p. 113.

67. Sir Frederick Pedler, "British Planning and Private Enterprise in Colonial Africa," *Colonialism in Africa 1870–1960*, Volume IV, edited by Peter Duignan and L. H. Gann, p. 95.

68. L. H. Gann, "Economic Development in Germany's African Empire, 1884–1914," Ibid., pp. 248–249.

69. Peter Duignan and L. H. Gann, "Economic Achievements of the Colonizers: An Assessment," Ibid., p. 679.

70. L. H. Gann, "Economic Development in Germany's African Empire, 1884–1914," Ibid., p. 250.

71. Peter Duignan and L. H. Gann, "Economic Achievements of the Colonizers: An Assessment," Ibid., p. 682.

72. Ibid., p. 684.

73. L. H. Gann and Peter Duignan, *Burden of Empire*, p. 247.

74. "Introduction," *Colonialism in Africa 1870–1960*, edited by Peter Duignan and L. H. Gann, Volume IV, pp. 10, 20–21, 24; Charles Wilson, "The Economic Role and Mainsprings of Imperialism," Ibid., p. 68; Sir Frederick Pedler, "British Planning and Private Enterprise in Colonial Africa," Ibid., pp. 102, 120; L. H. Gann, "Economic Development in Germany's African Empire, 1884–1914," Ibid., pp. 239–240; Jan S. Hogendorn, "Economic Initiative and African Cash Farming: Pre-Colonial Origins and Early Colonial Developments," Ibid., pp. 296–297; Simon E. Katzenellenbogen, "The Miner's Frontier, Transport and General Economic Development," Ibid., p. 399.

75. L. H. Gann, "Economic Development in Germany's African Empire, 1884–1914," Ibid., p. 239.

76. Richard J. Hammond, "Some Economic Aspects of Portuguese Africa in the Nineteenth and Twentieth Centuries," Ibid., p. 262.

77. Robert Cornevin, "The Germans in Africa Before 1918," *Colonialism in Africa 1870–1960*, Volume I, edited by L. H. Gann and Peter Duignan, p. 388.

78. Geoffrey Blainey, *The Causes of War*, third edition (New York: The Free Press, 1988), p. 198.

79. Peter Duignan and L. H. Gann, "Economic Achievements of the Colonizers: An Assessment," *Colonialism in Africa 1870–1960*, Volume IV, edited by Peter Duignan and L. H. Gann, p. 694.

80. Adam Smith, *The Wealth of Nations* (New York: The Modern Library, 1937).

81. See the classic study by Robert Conquest, *Harvest of Sorrow: Soviet Collectivization and the Terror-Famine* (New York: Oxford University Press, 1986).

82. Peter Duignan and L. H. Gann, "Economic Achievements of the Colonizers: An Assessment," *Colonialism in Africa 1870–1960*, Volume IV, edited by Peter Duignan and L. H. Gann, p. 261.

83. E. L. Jones, *The European Miracle: Environments, Economies and Geopolitics in the History of Europe and Asia*, second edition (Cambridge: Cambridge University Press, 1987), pp. 35–36.

84. Henry F. Dobyns, *Native American Historical Demography: A Critical Bibliography* (Bloomington: Indiana University Press, 1976), p. 37.

85. Edward H. Spicer, "American Indians," *Harvard Encyclopedia of American Ethnic Groups*, edited by Stephan Thernstrom, et al. (Cambridge, Mass.: Harvard University Press, 1981), p. 59.

86. Ibid., p. 58.

87. Richard B. Sheridan, "Mortality and Medical Treatment of Slaves in the British West Indies," *Race and Slavery in the Western Hemisphere: Quantitative Studies*, edited by Stanley L. Engerman and Eugene D. Genovese (Princeton: Princeton University Press, 1975), p. 285.

88. Noble David Cook, *Demographic Collapse: Indian Peru, 1520–1620* (Cambridge: Cambridge University Press, 1981), p. 116.

89. John Hemming, *Red Gold: The Conquest of the Brazilian Indians* (London: Macmillan, Ltd., 1978), p. 492.

90. William H. McNeill, *The Rise of the West: A History of the Human Community* (Chicago: University of Chicago Press, 1991), pp. 571–572, 578, 601, 656.

91. S. Ettinger, "The Modern Period," *A History of the Jewish People*, edited by H. H. Ben-Hasson (Cambridge, Mass.: Harvard University Press, 1976), pp. 953–957; Ezra Mendelsohn, *The Jews of East Central Europe Between the World Wars* (Bloomington: Indiana University Press, 1983).

92. N. J. G. Pounds, *An Historical Geography of Europe: 1800–1914* (Cambridge: Cambridge University Press, 1988), p. 102.

## CHAPTER 4: RACE AND ECONOMICS

1. Robert F. Foerster, *The Italian Emigration of Our Times* (New York: Arno Press, 1969), pp. 314, 335.

2. Eric Woodrum, et al., "Japanese American Economic Behavior: Its Types, Determinants and Consequences," *Social Forces*, June 1980, pp. 1237, 1238; Daniel O. Price, *Changing Characteristics of the Negro Population* (Washington, D.C.: U.S. Government Printing Office, 1969), p. 45.

3. Arcadius Kahan, "Notes on Jewish Entrepreneurship in Tsarist Russia," *Entrepreneurship in Imperial Russia and the Soviet Union*, edited by Gregory Guroff and Fred V. Carstensen (Princeton: Princeton University Press, 1983), p. 124; Irving Howe, *World of Our Fathers* (New York: Harcourt Brace Jovanovich, 1976), p. 82.

4. Walter E. Williams, *South Africa's War Against Capitalism* (New York: Praeger Publishers, 1989), pp. 100–106. See also Merle Lipton, *Capitalism and Apartheid: South Africa, 1910–84* (Totawa, N.J.: Rowman & Allanheld, 1985), passim.

5. Thomas Sowell, *Preferential Policies: An International Perspective* (New York: William Morrow, 1990), pp. 24–31.

6. Robert Higgs, *Competition and Coercion: Blacks in the American Economy*

*1865–1914* (Cambridge: Cambridge University Press, 1977), pp. 47–49.

7. Robert Higgs, "Landless by Law: Japanese Immigrants in California Agriculture to 1941," *Journal of Economic History*, March 1978, pp. 207–209.

8. W. E. B. DuBois, *The Philadelphia Negro* (New York: Shocken Books, 1967), p. 323.

9. Ibid., p. 395.

10. Luciano J. Iorizzo, "The Padrone and Immigrant Distribution," *The Italian Experience in the United States*, edited by S. M. Tomasi and M. H. Engel (Staten Island, N.Y.: Center for Migration Studies, Inc., 1970), pp. 43–75; Charles A. Price, *Southern Europeans in Australia* (Melbourne: Oxford University Press, 1963), pp. 63–64; John E. Zucchi, *Italians in Toronto: Development of a National Identity 1875–1935* (Kingston: McGill-Queen's University Press, 1988), pp. 46–48, 53; R. Pascoe, "Italian Settlements Until 1914," *The Australian People: An Encyclopedia of the Nation, Its People and Their Origins*, edited by James Jupp (North Ryde, N.S.W., Australia: Angus & Robertson Publishers, 1988), p. 597.

11. See, for example, Jacob Riis, *How the Other Half Lives* (Cambridge, Mass.: Harvard University Press, 1970), pp. 80–81, 83; Moses Rischin, *The Promised City: New York's Jews 1870–1914* (Cambridge, Mass.: Harvard University Press, 1962), pp. 61–68.

12. Agehananda Bharati, *The Asians in East Africa: Jayhind and Uhuru* (Chicago: Nelson-Hall Co., 1972), pp. 8–9.

13. P. T. Bauer, *Reality and Rhetoric: Studies in the Economics of Development* (Cambridge, Mass.: Harvard University Press, 1984), p. 7.

14. See, for example, Marvin Koster and Finis Welch, "The Effects of Minimum Wages on the Distribution of Changes in Aggregate Employment," *American Economic Review*, June 1972, pp. 323–332; Thomas G. Moore, "The Effect of Minimum Wages on Teenage Unemployment Rates," *Journal of Political Economy*, July/August 1971, pp. 897–902.

15. Thomas Sowell, *Minimum Wage Escalation* (Stanford: Hoover Institution Press, 1977), p. 4 (Reprint of Testimony Before the Subcommittee on Human Resources, U.S. Senate Committee on Labor and Public Welfare, August 3, 1977).

16. Walter E. Williams, *Youth and Minority Unemployment* (Stanford: Hoover Institution Press, 1977), p. 14.

17. George M. Fredrickson, *White Supremacy: A Comparative Study in American and South African History* (New York: Oxford University Press, 1981), p. 233.

18. Charles H. Young and Helen R. Y. Reid, *The Japanese Canadians* (Toronto: University of Toronto Press, 1938), p. 49.

19. P. T. Bauer, "Regulated Wages in Under-Developed Countries," *The Public Stake in Union Power*, edited by Philip D. Bradley (Charlottesville: University of Virginia Press, 1959), p. 332.

20. U.S. Bureau of the Census, *Historical Statistics of the United States: Colonial Times to 1957* (Washington, D.C.: U.S. Government Printing Office, 1961), p. 72.

21. Christopher Hibbert, *The English: A Social History 1066–1945* (New York: W. W. Norton, 1987), p. 509.

22. Roi Ottley and William J. Weatherby, *The Negro in New York: An Informal Social History 1626–1940* (New York: Praeger Publishers, 1967), pp. 36–37.

23. S. Enders Wimbush and Alex Alexiev, *The Ethnic Factor in the Soviet Armed Forces* (Santa Monica, Calif.: The Rand Corporation, 1982), pp. 15, 16, 20, 22, 36; John Hope Franklin, *From Slavery to Freedom: A History of Negro Americans* (New York: Vintage Books, 1969), pp. 580–591; Morris J. MacGregor, *Integration of the Armed Forces 1940–65* (Washington, D.C.: U.S. Government Printing Office, 1981), Chapters 2, 3, 4.

24. Virginia Thompson and Richard Adloff, *Minority Problems in Southeast Asia* (New York: Russell & Russell, 1970), p. 12.

25. T. R. Davenport, *South Africa: A Modern History*, second edition (Toronto: University of Toronto Press, 1980), p. 348.

26. William B. Mitchell, et al., *Area Handbook for Guyana* (Washington, D.C.: U.S. Government Printing Office, 1969), p. 39.

27. Thomas Sowell, "Three Black Histories," *Essays and Data on American Ethnic Groups*, edited by Thomas Sowell and Lynn D. Collins (Washington, D.C.: The Urban Institute, 1978), pp. 16–18.

28. See, for example, Albert D. Kirwan, *Revolt of the Rednecks* (New York: Harper & Row, 1965).

29. Walter E. Williams, *South Africa's War Against Capitalism* (New York: Praeger Publishers, 1989), pp. 97, 126; Pierre L. van den Berghe, *South Africa: A Study in Conflict* (Berkeley: University of California Press, 1965), p. 205.

30. Herbert Northrup, *Organized Labor and the Negro* (New York: Kraus Reprint, 1971), p. 22.

31. Robert F. Foerster, *The Italian Emigration of Our Times*, pp. 145, 147, 166, 167–168, 185, 186; Lucio Sponza, *Italian Immigrants in Nineteenth Century Britain: Realities and Images* (Leicester: Leicester University Press, 1988), pp. 195–196.

32. See, for example, Virginia Yans-McLaughlin, *Family and Community: Italian Immigrants in Buffalo, 1880–1930* (Ithaca: Cornell University Press, 1977), pp. 47–48, 176–177; Constance Cronin, *The Sting of Change: Sicilians in Sicily and Australia* (Chicago: University of Chicago Press, 1970), pp. 162–163.

33. Jacob Riis, *How the Other Half Lives*, pp. 70–71, 84.

34. Blacks in the South, for example, were not the focus of nineteenth-century housing reformers to nearly the same extent as European immigrants in Northern urban slums. Yet housing improvements for Southern blacks were at least as dramatic over a period of a generation, from the time of emancipation to the end of the nineteenth century. Thomas Sowell, *Markets and Minorities* (New York: Basic Books, 1981), pp. 78–79.

35. Jacob A. Riis, *How the Other Half Lives*, pp. 13–14.

36. Oliver MacDonagh, "The Irish Famine Emigration to the United States," *Perspectives in American History*, Vol. X (1976), p. 403.

37. Louis Wirth, *The Ghetto* (Chicago: University of Chicago Press, 1956), pp. 204–205.

38. J. C. Furnas, *The Americans* (New York: G. P. Putnam's Sons, 1969), p. 63; George Potter, *To the Golden Door: The Story of the Irish in Ireland and America* (Westport, Conn.: Greenwood Press, 1960), p. 169.

39. David M. Katzman, *Before the Ghetto* (Urbana: University of Illinois Press, 1975), p. 73; Gilbert Osofsky, *Harlem: The Making of a Ghetto* (New York: Harper Torchbooks, 1968), pp. 45, 120; Stephen Birmingham, *Certain People: America's Black Elite* (Boston: Little, Brown and Co., 1977), pp. 185–186.

40. David Lowenthal, *West Indian Societies* (New York: Oxford University Press, 1972), p. 157.

41. Charles A. Price, *Southern Europeans in Australia* (Canberra: Australian National University, 1979), pp. 293–294.

42. Robert N. Kearney, *Communalism and Language in the Politics of Ceylon* (Durham, N.C.: Duke University Press, 1967), p. 27.

43. See, for example, E. Franklin Frazier, "The Negro Family in Chicago," *E. Franklin Frazier on Race Relations: Selected Writings*, edited by G. Franklin Edwards (Chicago: University of Chicago Press, 1968), pp. 119–141; E. Franklin Frazier, "Negro Harlem: An Ecological Study," Ibid., pp. 142–160; Louis Wirth, *The Ghetto*, pp. 241–261.

44. Louis Wirth, *The Ghetto*, Chapters XI, XII.

45. Oscar Handlin, *Boston's Immigrants* (New York: Atheneum, 1970), p. 114; George Potter, *To the Golden Door*, p. 181.

46. Thomas Sowell, *Markets and Minorities*, pp. 72–73.

47. Ibid., pp. 70–71.

48. Ibid., p. 71.

49. Allan H. Spear, *Black Chicago: The Making of a Negro Ghetto, 1890–1920* (Chicago: University of Chicago Press, 1967), p. 168; E. Franklin Frazier, *The Negro in the United States* (New York: The Macmillan Co., 1971), pp. 284–285; Florette Henri, *Black Migration: Movement North, 1900–1920* (New York: Anchor Books, 1976), pp. 96–97; Gilbert Osofsky, *Harlem*, p. 44; Ivan H. Light, *Ethnic Enterprise in America* (Berkeley: University of California Press, 1972), Figure 1 (after p. 100); St. Clair Drake and Horace R. Cayton, *Black Metropolis* (Chicago: University of Chicago Press, 1970), Vol. I, pp. 66–67, 73–76.

50. Thomas Sowell, *Markets and Minorities*, pp. 69–70.

51. P. T. Bauer, *West African Trade: A Study of Competition, Oligopoly and Monopoly in a Changing Economy* (Cambridge: Cambridge University Press, 1954), p. 102.

52. Edna Bonacich, "A Theory of Middleman Minorities," *American*

    *Sociological Review*, October 1973, p. 590.

53. See, for example, P. T. Bauer, *West African Trade*, Chapter 12.

54. John P. McKay, *Pioneers for Profit: Foreign Entrepreneurship and Russian Industrialization, 1885–1913* (Chicago: University of Chicago Press, 1970), p. 139.

55. Virginia Thompson and Richard Adloff, *Minority Problems in Southeast Asia*, pp. 8, 85.

56. Donald R. Snodgrass, *Inequality and Economic Development in Malaysia* (Kuala Lumpur: Oxford University Press, 1980), p. 213.

57. Yuan-li Wu, "Chinese Entrepreneurship in Southeast Asia," *American Economic Review*, May 1983, p. 115.

58. David Caplovitz, *The Poor Pay More* (New York: The Free Press, 1967), passim.

59. Ronald P. Grossman, *The Italians in America* (Minneapolis: Lerner Publications Company, 1975), pp. 34–35.

60. Neil O. Leighton, "Lebanese Emigration: Its Effect on the Political Economy of Sierra Leone," *The Lebanese in the World: A Century of Emigration* (London: I. B. Tauris & Co., Ltd., 1992), p. 583.

61. Fred C. Koch, *The Volga Germans: In Russia and the Americas, From 1763 to the Present* (University Park: Pennsylvania State University Press, 1978), p. 215.

62. Ivan H. Light, *Ethnic Enterprise in America: Business and Welfare Among Chinese, Japanese, and Black* (Berkeley: University of California Press, 1972), p. 46; Walter E. Williams, "Some Hard Questions on Minority Businesses," *The Negro Educational Review*, April–July 1974, pp. 128–129.

63. Paulette Thomas, "Federal Data Detail Pervasive Racial Gap in Mortgage Lending," *Wall Street Journal*, March 31, 1992, p. 1.

64. U.S. Bureau of the Census, *Current Population Reports*, Series P-23, No. 173, *Population Profile of the United States: 1991* (Washington, D.C.: U.S. Government Printing Office, 1991), p. 20.

65. Jacob Riis, *How the Other Half Lives*, pp. 6n, 80–81.

66. Thomas Sowell, *The Economics and Politics of Race: An International Perspective* (New York: William Morrow, 1983), pp. 200–201.

67. As an example of this kind of reasoning, see Lester C. Thurow, *Poverty and Discrimination* (Washington, D.C.: Brookings Institution, 1969), pp. 2, 130–134.

68. William Tucker, *The Excluded Americans: Homelessness and Housing Policies* (Washington, D.C.: Regnery Gateway, 1990), p. 92.

69. Thomas Sowell, *Preferential Policies: An International Perspective* (New York: William Morrow, 1990), pp. 23–24, 29, 48, 51, 59.

70. Thomas Sowell, *Race and Economics* (New York: David McKay, 1975), pp. 166–167.

71. Ibid., p. 168.

## CHAPTER 5: RACE AND POLITICS

1. Donald L. Horowitz, *Ethnic Groups in Conflict* (Berkeley: University of California Press, 1985), p. xi.

2. See for example, Walter E. Williams, *The State Against Blacks* (New York: McGraw-Hill Book Co., 1982).

3. Donald L. Horowitz, *Ethnic Groups in Conflict*, pp. 172–173; Victor Purcell, *The Chinese in Southeast Asia*, second edition (Kuala Lumpur: Oxford University Press, 1980), p. 545n.

4. Bernard Lewis, *The Jews of Islam* (Princeton: Princeton University Press, 1984), pp. 134–135; Jane S. Gerber, *The Jews of Spain: A History of the Sephardic Experience* (New York: The Free Press, 1992), pp. 164–165.

5. T. C. Smout, *A History of the Scottish People, 1560–1830* (London: Collins Clear-Type Press, 1969), p. 113; L. H. Gann and Peter Duignan, *Burden of Empire: An Appraisal of Western Colonialism in Africa South of the Sahara* (Stanford: Hoover Institution Press, 1967), p. 248.

6. See, for example, Janet L. Abu-Lughod, *Before European Hegemony: The World System A.D. 1250–1350* (New York: Oxford University Press, 1989), pp. 49, 158, 164, 177.

7. Ray E. Mellor and E. Alistair Smith, *Europe: A Geographical Survey of the Continent* (New York: Columbia University Press, 1979), p. 99.

8. Hugh Tinker, *The Banyan Tree: Overseas Emigrants From India, Pakistan, and Bangladesh* (Oxford: Oxford University Press, 1977), p. 126.

9. Charles Assawi, "The Transformation of the Economic Position of the *Millets* in the Nineteenth Century," *Christians and Jews in the Ottoman Empire: The Functioning of a Plural Society*, edited by Benjamin Braude and Bernard Lewis, Vol. I: *The Central Lands* (New York: Holmes & Meier Publishers, Inc., 1982), pp. 261–285.

10. Peter Gunst, *The Origins of Backwardness in Eastern Europe: Economics and Politics From the Middle Ages Until the Early Twentieth Century*, edited by Daniel Ghirot (Berkeley: University of California Press, 1989), pp. 63–66.

11. Walter E. Williams, "Why the Poor Pay More: An Alternative Explanation," *Social Science Quarterly*, September 1973, pp. 375–379.

12. Jack Chen, *The Chinese of America* (New York: Harper & Row, 1980), p. 137; Charles A. Coppel, *Indonesian Chinese in Crisis* (Kuala Lumpur: Oxford University Press, 1983), pp. 2–3, 58–61; Ben J. Wattenberg, *The Real America* (New York: Doubleday, 1974), p. 117.

13. Donald L. Horowitz, *Ethnic Groups in Conflict*, pp. 191–192; Virginia Thompson and Richard Adloff, *Minority Problems in Southeast Asia* (New York: Russell & Russell, 1955), p. 9.

14. Adam Clymer, "Displeasure With Carter Turned Many to Reagan," *New*

*York Times*, November 9, 1980, p. A28; Ronald Smothers, "Election Results Troubling Blacks," *New York Times*, November 9, 1984, p. A20; E. J. Dionne, Jr., "Democratic Strength Shifts to West," *New York Times*, November 13, 1988, p. A32; Donald L. Horowitz, *Ethnic Groups in Conflict*, pp. 322–324; John A. A. Ayoade, "Ethnic Management in the 1979 Nigerian Constitution," *Canadian Review of Studies in Nationalism*, Spring 1987, p. 140.

15. Robert N. Kearney, *Communalism and Language in the Politics of Ceylon* (Durham: University of North Carolina Press, 1967), p. 27; Walter Schwarz, *The Tamils of Sri Lanka* (London: Minority Rights Group, 1988), p. 6.

16. Robert N. Kearney, *Communalism and Language in the Politics of Ceylon*, Chapters V, VI.

17. Robert N. Kearney, "Language and the Rise of Tamil Separatism in Sri Lanka," *Asian Survey*, May 1978, p. 525.

18. Robert N. Kearney, *Communalism and Language in the Politics of Ceylon*, p. 27.

19. Ibid., p. 29.

20. Donald L. Horowitz, *Ethnic Groups in Conflict*, pp. 429–433.

21. Gordon P. Means, "Ethnic Preference Policies in Malaysia," *Ethnic Preference and Public Policy in Developing States* (Boulder: Lynne Riemer Publishers Inc., 1986), p. 103.

22. Donald L. Horowitz, *Ethnic Groups in Conflict*, pp. 334–342.

23. See Ibid., pp. 293–349.

24. L. H. Gann and Peter Duignan, *Why South Africa Will Survive* (London: Croom Helm, 1981), pp. 122–125.

25. Cynthia T. Enloe, *Police, Military and Ethnicity: Foundation of State Power* (New Brunswick, N.J.: Transaction Books, 1980), p. 143; Donald L. Horowitz, *Ethnic Groups in Conflict*, p. 444.

26. Donald L. Horowitz, *Ethnic Groups in Conflict*, p. 545n.

27. Alexander R. Alexiev and S. Enders Wimbush, "The Ethnic Factor in the Soviet Armed Forces," *Ethnic Minorities in the Red Army: Asset or Liability?* edited by Alexander R. Alexiev and S. Enders Wimbush (Boulder: Westview Press, Inc., 1988), p. 151.

28. Donald L. Horowitz, *Ethnic Groups in Conflict*, pp. 447–449; Gordon P. Means, "Ethnic Preference Policies in Malaysia," *Ethnic Preference and Public Policy in Developing States*, pp. 105–106. For a more general survey of ethnic representation in military forces, see Cynthia T. Enloe, *Police, Military and Ethnicity*.

29. Donald L. Horowitz, *Ethnic Groups in Conflict*, pp. 457–459, 467–470.

30. Ibid., pp. 447–449.

31. Ibid., pp. 448, 451–452.

32. Ibid., pp. 467–469.

33. Ibid., p. 475; S. Karene Witcher, "With 'God on My Side,' Coup Leader Attempts to Regain Fiji's Paradise Lost," *New York Times*, October 23, 1988, Section I, p. 22.

34. Donald L. Horowitz, *Ethnic Groups in Conflict*, pp. 485, 487.

35. Kevin O'Connor, *The Irish in Britain* (London: Sidgwick and Jackson Ltd., 1972), p. 83.

36. Thomas Sowell, *Ethnic America: A History* (New York: Basic Books, 1981), p. 174.

37. Sammy Smooha, *Israel: Pluralism and Conflict* (Berkeley: University of California Press, 1978), pp. 108, 190.

38. Adam Giesinger, *From Catherine to Khrushchev: The Story of Russia's Germans* (Lincoln, Neb.: American Historical Society of Germans From Russia, 1974), pp. 143–144, 262–263; Frederick C. Luebke, "The German Ethnic Group in Brazil: The Ordeal of World War II," paper presented to the 1982 Annual Meeting of the American Historical Association, pp. 9–10, 12, 14; Frederick C. Luebke, *Germans in Brazil: A Comparative History of Cultural Conflict During World War I* (Baton Rouge: Louisiana State University Press, 1987), Chapters 5, 7; Jean Roche, *La Colonisation Allemande et le Rio Grande do Sul* (Paris: Institut des Hautes Études de L'Amérique Latine, 1959), p. 539; Ian Harmstorf and Michael Cigler, *The Germans in Australia* (Melbourne: Australasian Educa. Press Pty. Ltd., 1985), pp. 129–133, 172–173; Charles A. Price, *German Settlers in South Australia* (Melbourne: Melbourne University Press, 1945), p. 68.

39. Richard Sallet, *Russian-German Settlements in the United States*, translated by LaVern J. Rippley and Armand Bauer (Fargo: North Dakota Institute for Regional Studies, 1974), p. 3; John A. Armstrong, "Mobilized Diaspora in Tsarist Russia," *Soviet Nationality Policies and Practices*, edited by Jeremey R. Azrael (New York: Praeger Publishers, 1978), pp. 95–96; Adam Giesinger, *From Catherine To Khrushchev: The Story of Russia's Germans* (Lincoln, Neb.: American Historical Society of Germans From Russia, 1974), pp. 311, 313–314.

40. Benjamin Bruade and Bernard Lewis, "Introduction," *Christians and Jews in the Ottoman Empire*, Vol. I: *The Central Lands* (New York: Holmes & Meier Publishers, Inc., 1982), p. 29.

41. Robert Mantran, "Foreign Merchants and the Minorities in Istanbul During the Sixteenth and Seventeenth Centuries," Ibid., pp. 132, 135; Kemal H. Karpat, "Millets and Nationality: The Roots of the Incongruity of Nation and State in the Post-Ottoman Era," Ibid., p. 165; Charles Issawi, "The Transformation of the Economic Position of the Millets in the Nineteenth Century," Ibid., pp. 272, 273; A. Üner Turgay, "Trade and Merchants in Nineteenth-Century Trabzon: Elements of Ethnic Conflict," Ibid., pp. 291, 293, 296–297, 298, 299; Steven Rosenthal, "Minorities and Municipal Reform in Istanbul, 1850–1870," Ibid., pp. 370, 382; Feroz Ahmad, "Unionist Relations With the Greek, Armenian, and Jewish Communities of the Ottoman Empire, 1908–1914," Ibid., pp. 404, 406; Ibid., Samir Khalaf, "Communal Conflict in the Nineteenth Century," Vol. II: *The Arabic-Speaking Lands*, p. 121; Dominique Chevallier, "Non-Muslim Communities in Arab Cities,"

Ibid., 162; Thomas Phillip, "Image and Self-Image of the Syrians in Egypt: From the Early Eighteenth Century to the Reign of Muhammad Ali," Ibid., 169.

42. Frederick C. Luebke, *Germans in the New World: Essays in the History of Emigration* (Urbana: University of Illinois Press, 1990), pp. 127–128; Charles A. Price, *German Settlers in South Australia* (Melbourne: Melbourne University Press, 1945), Chapter VI; G. Kinne, "Nazi Stratagems and Their Effects on Germans in Australia up to 1945," *Journal of the Royal Australia Historical Society*, June 1980, pp. 1–19.

43. Bringing wives and children to the United States was not the same economic burden as the men's returning to China. Family members working in the American economy after arrival could undoubtedly repay the cost of passage more readily than a husband working in the much poorer Chinese economy after returning home.

44. Jack Chen, *The Chinese of America*, p. 53; S. W. Kung, *Chinese in American Life: Some Aspects of Their History, Status, Problems, and Contributions* (Seattle: University of Washington Press, 1962), 66.

45. Yasuo Watatsuki, "Japanese Emigration to the United States, 1866–1924," *Perspectives in American History*, Vol. XII (1979), p. 452.

46. Lionel Demery, "Asian Labor Migration: An Empirical Assessment," *Asian Labor Migration: Pipeline to the Middle East* (Boulder: Westview Press, Inc., 1986), pp. 41–42.

47. Leo Suryadinata, *China and the ASEAN States: The Ethnic Chinese Dimension* (Singapore: Singapore University Press, 1985), pp. 38–43.

48. Ibid., pp. 35–37, 45–49.

49. See, for example, Hugh Tinker, *The Banyan Tree*, pp. 68, 124, 125, 149.

50. Quoted in Anirudha Gupta, "India and the Asians in East Africa," *Expulsion of a Minority: Essays on Ugandan Asians* (London: The Athlone Press, 1975), p. 129.

51. Hugh Tinker, *The Banyan Tree*, p. 28.

52. Thomas Sowell, "Ethnicity in a Changing America," *Daedalus*, Winter 1978, pp. 220–235.

53. Myron Weiner, *Sons of the Soil: Migration and Ethnic Conflict in India* (Princeton: Princeton University Press, 1978), p. 112.

54. Myron Weiner and Mary Fainsod Katzenstein, *India's Preferential Policies: Migrants, the Middle Classes, and Ethnic Equality* (Chicago: University of Chicago Press, 1981), p. 98.

55. Charles A. Coppel, *Indonesian Chinese in Crisis* (Kuala Lumpur: Oxford University Press, 1983), pp. 82–85, 110–111, 164.

56. Donald V. Smiley, "French-English Relations in Canada and Consociational Democracy," *Ethnic Conflict in the Western World*, edited by Milton J. Esman (Ithaca: Cornell University Press, 1977), p. 118.

57. Ibid., p. 187.

58. Myron Weiner and Mary Fainsod Katzenstein, *India's Preferential Policies*,

pp. 132–133; Myron Weiner, *Sons of the Soil*, pp. 285–286; Ezra Mendelsohn, *The Jews of East Central Europe Between the World Wars* (Bloomington: Indiana University Press, 1983), pp. 167, 232; Donald V. Smiley, "French-English Relations in Canada and Consociational Democracy," *Ethnic Conflict in the Western World*, edited by Milton J. Esman, p. 186. See also Gary B. Cohen, *The Politics of Ethnic Survival: Germans in Prague, 1861–1914* (Princeton: Princeton University Press, 1981), p. 28; Donald L. Horowitz, *Ethnic Groups in Conflict*, pp. 224–226.

59. Myron Weiner, *Sons of the Soil*, pp. 271–272.

60. P. T. Bauer, *West African Trade: A Study of Competition, Oligopoly and Monopoly in a Changing Economy* (Cambridge: Cambridge University Press, 1954), p. 40.

61. Myron Weiner, *Sons of the Soil*, p. 285.

62. Ibid., pp. 285–288.

63. Ibid., p. 273.

64. See, for example, Raymond Sestito, *The Politics of Multiculturalism* (St. Leonards, Australia: The Centre for Independent Studies, 1982).

65. Lennox A. Mills, *Southeast Asia* (Minneapolis: University of Minnesota Press, 1964), p. 130.

66. Donald L. Horowitz, *Ethnic Groups in Conflict*, p. 666.

67. See Ibid., pp. 216–226, 236–243.

68. Robert Weisbrot, *The Jews of Argentina: From the Inquisition to Perón* (Philadelphia: The Jewish Publication Society of America, 1979), pp. 198–199.

69. Pierre L. van den Berghe, "Asian Africans Before and After Independence," *Kroniek van Afrika* (The Netherlands), New series, No. 6 (1975), p. 202.

70. Bernard Lewis, *Race and Slavery in the Middle East* (Princeton: Princeton University Press, 1990), p. vi.

71. David Brion Davis, *The Problem of Slavery in Western Culture* (Ithaca: Cornell University Press, 1966), p. 30.

72. J. Fox, "'For Good and Sufficient Reasons': An Examination of Early Dutch East India Company Ordinances on Slaves and Slavery," *Slavery, Bondage and Dependency in Southeast Asia*, edited by Anthony Reid (New York: St. Martin's Press, 1983), pp. 256–257.

73. William L. Westermann, *The Slave Systems of Greek and Roman Antiquity* (Philadelphia: The American Philosophical Society, 1955), p. 18.

74. Leo Elisabeth, "The French Antilles," *Neither Slave Nor Free: The Freedman of African Descent in the Slave Societies of the New World*, edited by David W. Cohen and Jack P. Greene (Baltimore: Johns Hopkins University Press, 1972), pp. 140–141.

75. H. Hoetink, "Surinam and Curaçao," *Neither Slave Nor Free*, edited by David W. Cohen and Jack P. Greene, p. 63.

76. See for example, Eric Williams, *Capitalism and Slavery* (New York: Russell & Russell, 1961). The thesis of this work has been so effectively demolished

by others that these critiques need only be cited: Stanley L. Engerman, "The Slave Trade and Capital Formation in the Eighteenth Century: A Comment on the Williams Thesis," *Business History Review*, Winter 1972, pp. 431–443; Roger Anstey, "Capitalism and Slavery: A Critique," *Economic History Review*, Second series, August 1968, pp. 307–320.

77. For example, David Brion Davis, *The Problem of Slavery in the Age of Revolution 1770–1823* (Ithaca: Cornell University Press, 1975), where it is asserted: "The anti-slavery movement, like Smith's political economy, reflected the needs and values of the emerging capitalist order" (p. 350). Such sweeping, undefined, and *untestable* statements abound as an alternative to Eric Williams's straightforward—and demonstrably false—hypothesis. For reasons unknown, Professor Davis insists on discussing Adam Smith at some length in this connection, even though (1) his ignorance of Smith is painfully apparent in his depiction of him as a spokesman for landowners (p. 348) and a believer in "a natural identity of interests" among classes (p. 350), and (2) in Professor Davis' repeated citations of the *secondary literature* on Smith, all of it at least 20 years old when Davis' own book was published. Anyone who takes seriously the claims that Smith was a spokesman for landowners or for capitalists, or believed in a natural identity of interests among classes need only read Smith himself to be disabused of such notions. See Adam Smith, *An Inquiry Into the Nature and Causes of the Wealth of Nations* (New York: The Modern Library, 1977), pp. 49, 66–67, 98, 128, 249–250, 460–461, 537, 783.

78. Illsoo Kim, *New Urban Immigrants: The Korean Community in New York* (Princeton: Princeton University Press, 1981), p. 140.

79. R. Bayly Winder, "The Lebanese in West Africa," *Comparative Studies in Society and History*, Vol. 4 (1967), pp. 309–310.

80. Ibid., p. 307.

81. Eligio R. Padilla and Gail E. Wyatt, "The Effects of Intelligence and Achievement Testing in Minority Group Children," *The Psychosocial Development of Minority Group Children*, edited by Gloria Johnson Powell, et al. (New York: Brunner/Mazel Publishers, 1983), p. 418.

82. Robert A. Wilson and Bill Hosokawa, *East to America: A History of the Japanese in the United States* (New York: William Morrow, 1980), p. 123.

83. Harry Leonard Sawatsky, *They Sought a Country: Mennonite Colonization in Mexico* (Berkeley: University of California Press, 1971), p. 365.

84. Donald L. Horowitz, *Ethnic Groups in Conflict*, p. 178.

## CHAPTER 6: RACE AND INTELLIGENCE

1. Eligio R. Padilla and Gail E. Wyatt, "The Effects of Intelligence and Achievement Testing in Minority Group Children," *The Psychosocial Development of Minority Group Children*, edited by Gloria Johnson Powell, et al. (New York: Brunner/Mazel Publishers, 1983), p. 418.

2. "Most psychologists working in the test field have been guilty of a *naming fallacy* which easily enables them to slide mysteriously from the score in the test to the hypothetical faculty suggested by the name given to the test." Carl C. Brigham, "Intelligence Tests of Immigrant Groups," *Psychological Review*, March 1930, p. 159.

3. A. Harry Passow, et al., *The National Case Study: An Empirical Comparative Study of Twenty-One Educational Systems* (Stockholm: Almqvist & Wiksell International, 1970), p. 20.

4. Philip E. Vernon, *The Abilities and Achievements of Orientals in North America* (London: Academic Press, 1982), p. 69.

5. "Race, Class, and Scores," *New York Times*, October 24, 1982, Section 4, p. 9; College Entrance Examination Board, *Profiles, College-Bound Seniors, 1981* (New York: College Entrance Examination Board, 1982), pp. 32, 41, 51, 60, 70.

6. Computed from *Profiles, College-Bound Seniors, 1981*, pp. 32, 41, 51, 60, 70.

7. Ibid.

8. Philip E. Vernon, *The Abilities and Achievements of Orientals in North America*, pp. 123, 124.

9. Ibid., p. 126.

10. Robert Klitgaard, *Elitism and Meritocracy in Developing Countries: Selection Policies for Higher Education* (Baltimore: Johns Hopkins University Press, 1986), p. 122.

11. H. J. Butcher, *Human Intelligence: Its Nature and Assessment* (New York: Harper & Row, 1968), pp. 234–235.

12. Carl Brigham, *A Study of American Intelligence* (Princeton: Princeton University Press, 1923), p. 119.

13. Thomas Sowell, "Race and I.Q. Reconsidered," *Essays and Data on American Ethnic Groups*, edited by Thomas Sowell and Lynn D. Collins (Washington, D.C.: The Urban Institute, 1978), pp. 207–209.

14. Florette Henri, *Black Migration: Movement North, 1900–1920* (Garden City, N.Y.: Anchor Books, 1976), p. 71; Thomas Sowell, *Ethnic America: A History* (New York: Basic Books, 1981), pp. 210–211.

15. Sammy Smooha, *Israel: Pluralism and Conflict* (Berkeley: University of California Press, 1978), p. 162; Ernest van den Haag, *The Jewish Mystique* (New York: Stein and Day Publishers, 1969), pp. 21–22.

16. H. J. Eysenck, *The IQ Argument* (New York: The Library Press, 1971), p. 123.

17. Philip E. Vernon, *Intelligence and Cultural Environment* (London: Methuen & Co., 1969), p. 155; Lester E. Wheeler, "A Comparative Study of the Intelligence of East Tennessee Mountain Children," *Journal of Educational Psychology*, May 1942, pp. 322, 324; H. Gordon, *Mental and Scholastic Tests Among Retarded Children* (London: Board of Education Pamphlet No. 44), p. 38.

18. Robert Klitgaard, *Elitism and Meritocracy in Developing Countries*, pp. 119, 124.

19. Ibid., p. 19.

20. Lillian Belmont and Francis A. Marolla, "Birth Order, Family Size, and Intelligence," *Science*, December 14, 1973, p. 1096. But see also Phillip R. Kunz and Evan T. Peterson, "Family Size, and Academic Achievement of Persons Enrolled in High School and the University," *Social Biology*, December 1973, pp. 454–459; Phillip R. Kunz and Evan T. Peterson, "Family Size, Birth Order, and Academic Achievement," *Social Biology*, Summer 1977, pp. 144–148.

21. Arthur R. Jensen, "Cumulative Deficit in I.Q. of Blacks in the Rural South," *Developmental Psychology*, Vol. 13, No. 3 (1977), pp. 184–191. Although Professor Jensen is identified with the hereditary explanation of mental test differences, in this case he suggests that the differences in level and pattern among blacks in the two areas compared is probably environmental.

22. Robert Klitgaard, *Elitism and Meritocracy in Developing Countries*, pp. 36–37.

23. Robert Klitgaard, *Choosing Elites* (New York: Basic Books, 1985), p. 10.

24. Between 1981 and 1991, blacks, Mexican Americans, American Indians, and Asian Americans all had increases in both verbal and mathematical Scholastic Aptitude Test scores. Puerto Ricans' verbal scores remained the same as a decade earlier but their math scores rose by 10 points. Whites' average verbal score declined one point while their average mathematical score rose by 6 points. College Entrance Examination Board, *Profiles, College-Bound Seniors, 1981*, pp. 32, 41, 51, 60, 70, 79; College Entrance Examination Board, *College-Bound Seniors: 1992 Profile of SAT and Achievement Test Takers* (New York: College Entrance Examination Board, 1991), p. 6. Measuring from the beginning of the tabulation of various ethnic scores separately in 1976, all these ethnic groups had higher mathematics scores in 1991 and only Puerto Ricans and Asians had slightly lower verbal scores. Blacks made the largest gains on both tests. College Entrance Examination Board, *College-Bound Seniors: 1992 Profile of SAT and Achievement Test Takers*, p. v.

25. Philip E. Vernon, *Intelligence and Cultural Environment*, pp. 42–43, 85, 101–102.

26. Ibid., p. 173.

27. Philip E. Vernon, *The Abilities and Achievements of Orientals in North America*, pp. 121–122.

28. John C. Loehlin, Gardner Lindzey, and J. N. Spuhler, *Race Differences in Intelligence* (San Francisco: W. H. Freeman and Co., 1975), p. 183.

29. Daniel B. Hier, M.D., and William F. Crowley, M.D., "Spatial Ability in Androgen-Deficient Men," *The New England Journal of Medicine*, May 20, 1982, pp. 1202–1205. See also Jerome Kagan, M.D., "The Idea of Spatial Ability," Ibid., pp. 1225–1226. See also Sandra Blakeslee, "Man's Test

Scores Linked to Hormones," *New York Times*, November 14, 1991, p. A11.

30. Morris Kline, *Mathematics in Western Culture* (Middlesex, England: Penguin Books, Ltd., 1953), pp. 150–169.

31. John C. Loehlin, Gardner Lindzey, and J. N. Spuhler, *Race Differences in Intelligence*, pp. 179–181.

32. Bertha Boody, *A Psychological Study of Immigrant Children at Ellis Island* (Baltimore: The Williams and Wilkins Co., 1926), p. 67.

33. H. H. Goddard, "The Binet Tests in Relation to Immigration," *Journal of Psycho-Asthenics*, December 1913, p. 110; Leon J. Kamin, *The Science and Politics of I.Q.* (New York: John Wiley & Sons, 1974), p. 6.

34. Mandel Sherman and Cora B. Key, "The Intelligence of Isolated Mountain Children," *Child Development*, Vol. 3, No. 4 (1932), p. 284.

35. Arthur R. Jensen, "How Much Can We Boost IQ and Scholastic Achievement?" *Harvard Educational Review*, Winter 1969, p. 81.

36. Philip E. Vernon, *Intelligence and Cultural Environment*, p. 145.

37. Ibid., pp. 157–158.

38. Ibid., p. 168.

39. Ibid., p. 104.

40. Ibid., p. 103.

41. Robert M. Yerkes, *Psychological Examining in the United States Army*, Memoirs of the National Academy of Sciences, Volume 15 (Washington, D.C.: Government Printing Office, 1921), p. 705.

42. Philip E. Vernon, *Intelligence and Cultural Environment*, p. 101.

43. Ibid., p. 155.

44. John C. Loehlin, Gardner Lindzey, and J. N. Spuhler, *Race Differences in Intelligence*, p. 137.

45. James R. Flynn, "Massive I.Q. Gains in 14 Nations: What I.Q. Tests Really Measure," *Psychological Bulletin*, Vol. 101, No. 2 (1987), pp. 171–191, passim, especially p. 185.

46. Cf. Carl Brigham, *A Study of American Intelligence* (Princeton: Princeton University Press, 1923), pp. 80, 121.

47. Ibid., p. 190.

48. Rudolph Pintner, *Intelligence Testing: Methods and Results* (New York: Henry Holt and Co., 1931), p. 453; Ernest van den Haag, *The Jewish Mystique* (New York: Stein and Day Publishers, 1969), pp. 19–20.

49. Carl C. Brigham, "Intelligence Test of Immigrant Groups," *Psychological Review*, March 1930, p. 165.

50. Thomas Sowell, "Race and I.Q. Reconsidered," *Essays and Data on American Ethnic Groups*, edited by Thomas Sowell and Lynn D. Collins, p. 210.

51. Ibid., p. 207.

52. Audrey Shuey, *The Testing of Negro Intelligence* (New York: Social Science Press, 1966), pp. 308–355, 357. See also H. J. Eysenck, *The IQ Argument*, p. 92.

53. Sandra Scarr and Richard A. Weinberg, "I.Q. Test Performance of Black

Children Adopted by White Families," *American Psychologist*, October 1976, pp. 731–733. For a critique of this study, see Arthur R. Jensen, *Straight Talk About Mental Tests* (New York: The Free Press, 1981), pp. 223–224.

54. Audrey M. Shuey, *The Testing of Negro Intelligence*, pp. 489–490; Thomas Sowell, "Race and I.Q. Reconsidered," *Essays and Data on American Ethnic Groups*, edited by Thomas Sowell, p. 217.

55. H. J. Butcher, *Human Intelligence*, p. 252.

56. Diane Ravitch, *The Schools We Deserve: Reflections on the Educational Crises of Our Time* (New York: Basic Books, 1985), p. 63.

57. Robert Klitgaard, *Elitism and Meritocracy in Developing Countries*, p. 29.

58. Ibid., pp. 16, 31.

59. Earlier controversies centered on differences between immigrants from southern and eastern Europe, as compared to northern and western Europe.

60. College Entrance Examination Board, *College-Bound Seniors: 1992 Profile of SAT and Achievement Test Takers*, p. v.

61. Mark Snyderman and Stanley Rothman, *The IQ Controversy, the Media and Public Policy* (New Brunswick, N.J.: Transaction Books, 1988), p. 285.

62. Arthur R. Jensen, "How Much Can We Boost IQ and Scholastic Achievement?" *Harvard Educational Review*, Winter 1969, pp. 1–123.

63. Ibid., p. 117.

64. Ibid., pp. 116–117.

65. Ibid., p. 117.

66. John C. Loehlin, Gardner Lindzey, and J. N. Spuhler, *Race Differences in Intelligence*, p. 127.

67. James R. Flynn, "Massive I.Q. Gains in 14 Nations: What I.Q. Tests Really Measure," *Psychological Bulletin*, Vol. 101, No. 2 (1987), passim.

68. Arthur R. Jensen, "The Race × Sex × Ability Interaction," *Intelligence: Genetic and Environment Factors*, edited by Robert Cancro (New York: Grune and Stratton, 1971), pp. 116–118; Arthur R. Jensen, "How Much Can We Boost IQ and Scholastic Achievement?" *Harvard Educational Review*, Winter 1969, pp. 32, 67.

69. Thomas Sowell, "Race and I.Q. Reconsidered," *Essays and Data on American Ethnic Groups*, edited by Thomas Sowell and Lynn D. Collins, p. 222.

70. Clifford Kirkpatrick, *Intelligence and Immigration* (Baltimore: The Williams and Wilkins Co., 1926), pp. 26–27.

71. Sandra Scarr and Richard A. Weinberg, "I.Q. Test Performance of Black Children Adopted by White Families," *American Psychologist*, October 1976, p. 731.

72. Thomas Sowell, "Race and I.Q. Reconsidered," *Essays and Data on American Ethnic Groups*, edited by Thomas Sowell and Lynn D. Collins, p. 222.

73. Arthur R. Jensen, "How Much Can We Boost IQ and Scholastic Achievement?" *Harvard Educational Review*, Winter 1969, pp. 46–54. See also Arthur R. Jensen, *Straight Talk About Mental Tests*, pp. 102–107.

74. Philip E. Vernon, *The Abilities and Achievements of Orientals in North America*, p. 123.

75. Arthur R. Jensen, "How Much Can We Boost IQ and Scholastic Achievement?" *Harvard Educational Review*, Winter 1969, pp. 82–84.

76. College Entrance Examination Board, *Profiles, College-Bound Seniors, 1981*, pp. 27, 36, 46, 55. By 1985, American Indians and Mexican Americans from families earning $50,000 a year edged ahead of Asian Americans from families earning $6,000 or less. However, the low-income Asian Americans continued to score higher on the quantitative SAT than children from the other groups from families earning $40,000 and $50,000. Leonard Ramist and Solomon Arbeiter, *Profiles, College-Bound Seniors, 1985* (New York: College Entrance Examination Board, 1986), pp. 27, 37, 47, 57.

77. Thomas Sowell, "Assumptions Versus History in Ethnic Education," *Teacher College Record*, Fall 1981, pp. 42–45, 46.

78. Barbara Lerner, "The War on Testing: David, Goliath & Gallup," *The Public Interest*, Summer 1980, pp. 119–147.

79. For example, Robert Klitgaard, *Choosing Elites* (New York: Basic Books, 1985), pp. 104–131; Stanley Sue and Jennifer Abe, *Predictors of Academic Achievement Among Asian Students and White Students* (New York: College Entrance Examination Board, 1988), p. 1; Robert A. Gordon and Eileen Rudert, "Bad News Concerning IQ Tests," *Sociology of Education*, July 1979, pp. 174–190; Frank L. Schmidt and John E. Hunter, "Employment Testing: Old Theories and New Research Findings," *American Psychologist*, October 1981, pp. 1128–1137; T. Anne Cleary, "Test Bias: Predictions of Grades of Negro and White Students in Integrated Colleges," *Journal of Educational Measurement*, Summer 1966, pp. 115–124; J. C. Stanley and A. L. Porter, "Correlation of Scholastic Aptitude Test Scores With College Grades for Negroes vs. Whites," *Journal of Educational Measurement*, 1969, pp. 199–218. This is only a sampling of a much larger literature reaching similar conclusions.

80. Robert Klitgaard, *Choosing Elites*, pp. 104–115; Stanley Sue and Jennifer Abe, *Predictors of Academic Achievement Among Asian Students and White Students*, p. 1; Robert A. Gordon and Eileen E. Rudert, "Bad News Concerning IQ Tests," *Sociology of Education*, July 1979, p. 176; Frank L. Schmidt and John E. Hunter, "Employment Testing," *American Psychologist* October 1981, p. 1131; Arthur R. Jensen, "Section of Minority Students in Higher Education," *University of Toledo Law Review*, Spring–Summer 1970, pp. 440, 443; Donald A. Rock, "Motivation, Moderators, and Test Bias," Ibid., pp. 536, 537; Ronald L. Flaughter, *Testing Practices, Minority Groups and Higher Education: A Review and Discussion of the Research* (Princeton: Educational Testing Service, 1970), p. 11; Arthur R. Jensen, *Bias in Mental Testing* (New York: The Free Press, 1980), pp. 479–490.

81. Robert Klitgaard, *Elitism and Meritocracy in Developing Countries*, pp. 77, 84.

82. Ibid., p. 147.

83. Robert Klitgaard, *Choosing Elites*, pp. 160–164.

84. Leonard Ramist and Solomon Arbeiter, *Profile, College-Bound Seniors, 1985*, pp. 27, 37, 47, 57.

85. Barbara Lerner, "The War on Testing," *The Public Interest*, Summer 1980, pp. 119–147.

86. Suma Chitnis, "Positive Discrimination in India With Preference to Education," *From Independence to Statehood: Managing Ethnic Conflict in Five African and Asian States*, edited by Robert B. Goldmann and A. Jeyaratnam Wilson (London: Frances Pinter, 1984), p. 36; George H. Brown, et al., *The Condition of Education for Hispanic Americans* (Washington, D.C.: National Center for Education Statistics, 1980), pp. 118–119.

87. Sammy Smooha and Yochanan Peres, "The Dynamics of Ethnic Inequalities: The Case of Israel," *Studies of Israeli Society: Migration, Ethnicity and Community*, edited by Ernest Krausz (New Brunswick, N.J.: Transaction Books, 1980), p. 173.

88. This is true both theoretically and empirically. See Thomas Sowell, "Race and I.Q. Reconsidered," *Essays and Data on American Ethnic Groups*, edited by Thomas Sowell and Lynn D. Collins, pp. 220–222.

89. Ibid., p. 222.

90. College Entrance Examination Board, *Profiles, College-Bound Seniors, 1981*, pp. 60, 79.

91. Robert Klitgaard, *Choosing Elites*, p. 175.

92. Leonard Ramist and Solomon Arbeiter, *Profiles, College-Bound Seniors, 1985*, pp. 32, 42, 52, 62, 72.

93. Robert Klitgaard, *Choosing Elites*, p. 160.

94. Ibid., p. 162.

95. Robert Klitgaard, *Elitism and Meritocracy in Developing Countries*, pp. 84–85.

96. See, for example, Suma Chitnis, "Measuring Up to Reserved Admissions," *Reservation: Policy, Programmes and Issues*, edited by Vimal P. Shah and Binod C. Agrawal (Jaipur, India: Rawat Publications, 1986), pp. 37–42.

97. Thomas Sowell, *Preferential Policies: An International Perspective* (New York: William Morrow, 1990), pp. 109–110.

98. Robert Klitgaard, *Choosing Elites*, Chapter 4.

99. James R. Flynn, *Asian Americans: Achievement Beyond IQ* (Hillsdale, N.J.: Lawrence Erlbaum Associates, 1991), pp. 3–5.

100. Ibid., p. 14, Chapter 2.

101. Philip E. Vernon, *The Abilities and Achievements of Orientals in North America*, p. 28.

102. James R. Flynn, *Asian Americans*, pp. 1, 74, 99.

103. Ibid., p. 61.

104. Ibid., p. 76.

105. Ibid., p. 61.

106. See, for example, Robert Klitgaard, *Choosing Elites*, pp. 212–218, 225–226.

107. Edwin Markham, *The Man With the Hoe and Other Poems* (New York: Doubleday & McClure Co., 1899), pp. 15–18.

108. Judith Laikin Elkin, *The Jews of Latin American Republics* (Chapel Hill: University of North Carolina Press, 1980), Chapter 6.

109. Albert Bernhardt Faust, *The German Element in the United States* (New York: Arno Press, 1969), pp. 441–442.

110. Edward B. Fiske, *Selective Guide to Colleges, 1982–1983* (New York: Times Books, 1982), pp. 20, 53, 237.

111. Thomas Sowell, *Preferential Policies*, pp. 48–51, 84–85, 96–101, 107–112, 115–116.

## CHAPTER 7: RACE AND SLAVERY

1. David Eltis, "Europeans and the Rise and Fall of African Slavery in the Americas: An Interpretation," *American Historical Review*, December 1993, p. 1400.

2. See, for example, William L. Westermann, *The Slave Systems of Greek and Roman Antiquity* (Philadelphia: The American Philosophical Society, 1955), pp. 1, 24, 74–75; Bernard Lewis, *Race and Slavery in the Middle East* (New York: Oxford University Press, 1990), pp. 3–5; Ehud R. Toledano, *The Ottoman Slave Trade and Its Suppression* (Princeton: Princeton University Press, 1982), pp. 272–274.

3. Orlando Patterson, *Slavery and Social Death: A Comparative Study* (Cambridge, Mass.: Harvard University Press, 1982), pp. 406–407.

4. W. Montgomery Watt, *The Influence of Islam on Medieval Europe* (Edinburgh: Edinburgh University Press, 1972), p. 19; Bernard Lewis, *Race and Slavery in the Middle East*, p. 11.

5. Daniel Evans, "Slave Coast of Europe," *Slavery and Abolition*, May 1985, p. 53, note 3.

6. Lord Kinross, *The Ottoman Centuries: The Rise and Fall of the Turkish Empire* (New York: William Morrow, 1977), p. 221.

7. Ibid., p. 223.

8. Bernard Lewis, *The Muslim Discovery of Europe* (New York: W. W. Norton, 1982), pp. 191–192.

9. Richard Hellie, *Slavery in Russia: 1450–1725* (Chicago: University of Chicago Press, 1982), pp. 21–22.

10. Adam Smith, *An Inquiry Into the Nature and Causes of the Wealth of Nations* (New York: Modern Library, 1937), p. 365.

11. Lord Kinross, *The Ottoman Centuries*, pp. 188–189.

12. Bernard Lewis, *Race and Slavery in the Middle East*, pp. 11–12.

13. Hattie Plum Williams, *The Czar's Germans: With Particular Reference to*

*the Volga Germans* (Lincoln, Neb.: American Historical Society of Germans From Russia, 1975), p. 117.

14. R. W. Beachey, *The Slave Trade of Eastern Africa* (New York: Harper & Row, 1976), pp. 122, 166.

15. Liu Chia-chu, "The Creation of the Chinese Banners by the Early Ch'ing," *Chinese Studies in History*, Summer 1981, p. 50.

16. Jim Warren, "Who Were the Balangingi Samal? Slave Raiding and Ethnogenesis in Nineteenth-Century Sulu," *Journal of Asian Studies*, May 1978, p. 481; James Franis Warren, *The Sulu Zone 1768–1898: The Dynamics of External Trade, Slavery and Ethnicity in the Transformation of a Southeast Asian Maritime State* (Singapore: Singapore University Press, 1981).

17. Mark Naidis, "The Abolitionists and Indian Slavery," *Journal of Asian History*, Vol. 15, No. 2 (1981), p. 147.

18. Anthony Reid, "Introduction," *Slavery, Bondage and Dependency in Southeast Asia*, edited by Anthony Reid (New York: St. Martin's Press, 1983), pp. 29–30.

19. Ibid., p. 32; A. van der Kraan, "Bali: Slavery and the Slave Trade," Ibid., pp. 315–340.

20. Anthony Reid, "Introduction," Ibid., p. 27; I. Mabbett, "Some Remarks on the Present State of Knowledge About Slavery in Angkor," Ibid., pp. 44, 54; V. Matheson and M. B. Hooker, "Slavery in the Malay Texts: Categories of Dependency and Compensation," Ibid., p. 205; K. Endicott, "The Effects of Slave Raiding on the Aborigenes of the Malay Peninsula," Ibid., pp. 216–245; T. Bigalke, "Dynamics of the Torajan Slave Trade in South Sulawesi," Ibid., p. 343; Bruno Lasker, *Human Bondage in Southeast Asia* (Chapel Hill: University of North Carolina Press, 1950), pp. 17–18, 19, 44.

21. R. W. Beachey, *The Slave Trade of Eastern Africa*, pp. 183–184.

22. Harold D. Nelson, *Nigeria: A Country Study* (Washington, D.C.: Government Printing Office, 1982), p. 16.

23. Daniel Evans, "Slave Coast of Europe," *Slavery and Ambition*, May 1985, p. 42.

24. Ibid., p. 45.

25. Ralph A. Austen, "The Trans-Saharan Slave Trade: A Tentative Census," *Uncommon Market: Essays in the Economic History of the Atlantic Slave Trade*, edited by Henry A. Gemery and Jan S. Hogendorn (New York: Academic Press, 1979), pp. 68–69.

26. Philip D. Curtin, "Epidemiology and the Slave Trade," *Political Science Quarterly*, June 1968, pp. 190–216.

27. Reginald Coupland, *The Exploitation of East Africa 1856–1890: The Slave Trade and the Scramble* (Evanston: Northwestern University Press, 1967), p. 148.

28. Allan G. B. Fisher and Humphrey J. Fisher, *Slavery and Muslim Society in Africa: The Institution in Saharan and Sudanic Africa and the Trans-Saharan Trades* (London: C. Hurst & Co., 1970), pp. 97–148; William Gervase Clarence-Smith, "The Economics of the Indian Ocean and Red Sea Slave

Trades in the 19th Century: An Overview," *The Economics of the Indian Ocean Slave Trade in the Nineteenth Century*, edited by William Gervase Clarence-Smith (London: Frank Cass and Co., 1989), p. 14; Lewis H. Gann and Peter Duignan, *The Burden of Empire: An Appraisal of Western Colonialism in Africa South of the Sahara* (Stanford: Hoover Institution Press, 1967), p. 154.

29. David Eltis, "Free and Coerced Transatlantic Migrations: Some Comparisons," *American Historical Review*, April 1983, pp. 254–255.

30. Bernard Lewis, *Race and Slavery in the Middle East*, p. vi; R. W. Beachey, *The Slave Trade of Eastern Africa* (New York: Harper & Row, 1976), p. vii.

31. This is the thesis of David Brion Davis, *Slavery and Human Progress* (New York: Oxford University Press, 1984), especially Part One.

32. As suggested Ibid., pp. 58, 61–62, 67–68, 73.

33. Janet J. Ewald, "The Nile Valley System and the Red Sea Slave Trade, 1820–1880," *The Economics of the Indian Ocean Slave Trade in the Nineteenth Century*, edited by William Gervase Clarence-Smith, p. 85; William Gervase Clarence-Smith, "The Economics of the Indian Ocean and Red Sea Slave Trades in the 19th Century: An Overview," Ibid., p. 8; Thomas M. Ricks, "Slaves and Slave Traders in the Persian Gulf, 18th and 19th Centuries: An Assessment," Ibid., p. 64; Murray Gordon, *Slavery in the Arab World* (New York: New Amsterdam Books, 1989), pp. 52, 94; Bruno Lasker, *Human Bondage in Southeast Asia* (Chapel Hill: University of North Carolina Press, 1950), pp. 21–22; William L. Westermann, *The Slave Systems of Greek and Roman Antiquity* (Philadelphia: The American Philosophical Society, 1955), pp. 5, 94; V. Matheson and M. B. Hooker, "Slavery in the Malay Texts: Categories of Dependency and Compensation," *Slavery, Bondage and Dependency in Southeast Asia*, edited by Anthony Reid (New York: St. Martin's Press, 1983), p. 187.

34. Richard C. Wade, *Slavery in the Cities: The South 1820–1860* (London: Oxford University Press, 1964), pp. 38–54.

35. William L. Westermann, *The Slave Systems of Greek and Roman Antiquity* (Philadelphia: The American Philosophical Society, 1955), p. 12.

36. Anthony Reid, "Introduction," *Slavery, Bondage and Dependency in Southeast Asia*, edited by Anthony Reid, p. 14.

37. Ibid., p. 26.

38. See, for example, Anthony Reid, "Preface," Ibid., p. xv; Anthony Reid, "Introduction," Ibid., pp. 1–14, 36; I. Mabbett, "Some Remarks on the Present State of Knowledge About Slavery in Angkor," Ibid., pp. 47–48; M. Aung Thwin, "Athi, Kyun-Taw, Kpaya-Kyun: Varieties of Commendation and Dependence in Pre-Colonial Burma," Ibid., pp. 67–73; Mo Hoadley, "Slavery, Bondage and Dependency in Pre-Colonial Java: The Cirebon-Priangan Region, 1700," Ibid., 91–93, 97–99; B. Terwiel, "Bondage and Slavery in Early Nineteenth Century Siam," Ibid., pp. 127–130, 132, 134.

39. Bruno Lasker, *Human Bondage in Southeast Asia*, p. 26; Orlando Patterson,

*Slavery and Social Death: A Comparative Study* (Cambridge, Mass.: Harvard University Press, 1982), p. 191; Harold E. Driver, *Indians of North America*, second edition (Chicago: University of Chicago Press, 1975), p. 325.

40. Orlando Patterson, *Slavery and Social Death*, pp. 190–192.

41. John Hebron, "Simon Gray Riverman: A Slave Who Was Almost Free," *Mississippi Valley Historical Review*, December 1962, pp. 472–484.

42. Bruno Lasker, *Human Bondage in Southeast Asia*, p. 17.

43. Ibid., p. 22; Anthony Reid, "Introduction," *Slavery, Bondage and Dependency in Southeast Asia*, edited by Anthony Reid, pp. 24–25.

44. See, for example, Ehud R. Toledano, *The Ottoman Slave Trade and Its Suppression* (Princeton: Princeton University Press, 1982), pp. 18, 59, 80, 171.

45. Daniel Evans, "Slave Coast of Europe," *Slavery and Ambition*, May 1985, pp. 45–46, 48–49.

46. Bernard Lewis, *Race and Color in Islam: An Historical Enquiry* (New York: Oxford University Press, 1990), p. 72.

47. Bruno Lasker, *Human Bondage in Southeast Asia*, pp. 17–18.

48. Francois Renault, "The Structures of the Slave Trade in Central Africa in the 19th Century," *The Economics of the Indian Ocean Slave Trade in the Nineteenth Century*, edited by William Gervase Clarence-Smith, pp. 146–165.

49. Bernard Lewis, *The Muslim Discovery of Europe* (New York: W. W. Norton, 1982), p. 189; Daniel Evans, "Slave Coast of Europe," *Slavery and Abolition*, May 1985, p. 46; Murray Gordon, *Slavery in the Arab World* (New York: New Amsterdam Books, 1989), p. 107; Solomon Grayzel, *A History of the Jews: From the Babylonian Exile to the Present, 5728–1968* (New York: New American Library, 1968), pp. 280–281; David Brion Davis, *Slavery and Human Progress*, pp. 91–93; Lord Kinross, *The Ottoman Centuries: The Rise and Fall of the Turkish Empire* (New York: William Morrow, 1977), p. 146.

50. A. van der Kraan, "Bali: Slavery and the Slave Trade," *Slavery, Bondage and Dependency in Southeast Asia*, edited by Anthony Reid (New York: St. Martin's Press, 1983), pp. 328, 330; Bruno Lasker, *Human Bondage in Southeast Asia* (Chapel Hill: University of North Carolina Press, 1950), p. 17.

51. William Gervase Clarence-Smith, "The Economics of the Indian Ocean and Red Sea Slave Trades in the 19th Century: An Overview," *The Economics of the Indian Ocean Slave Trade in the Nineteenth Century*, edited by William Gervase Clarence-Smith, p. 12; Francois Renault, "The Structures of the Slave Trade in Central Africa in the 19th Century," Ibid., pp. 146, 150–152.

52. William L. Westermann, *The Slave Systems of Greek and Roman Antiquity* (Philadelphia: The American Philosophical Society, 1955), p. 59.

53. David Brion Davis, *Slavery and Human Progress*, p. 93.

54. William Gervase Clarence-Smith, "The Economics of the Indian Ocean and Red Sea Slave Trades in the 19th Century: An Overview," *The Economics of*

*the Indian Ocean Slave Trade in the Nineteenth Century,* edited by William
Gervase Clarence-Smith, pp. 11–12.

55.  Edward A. Alpers, *Ivory and Slaves: Changing Patterns of International
     Trade in East Central Africa to the Later Nineteenth Century* (Berkeley: Uni-
     versity of California Press, 1975), pp. 58–62, 94, 104, 229–230.

56.  William L. Westermann, *The Slave Systems of Greek and Roman Antiquity,*
     p. 23.

57.  Charles McKew Parr, *So Noble a Captain: The Life and Times of Ferdinand
     Magellan* (New York: Thomas Y. Crowell Company, 1953), p. 368.

58.  Richard Fletcher, *Moorish Spain* (New York: Henry Holt and Co., 1992), p.
     136.

59.  Richard Hellie, *Slavery in Russia: 1450–1725* (Chicago: University of
     Chicago Press, 1982), p. 21.

60.  William L. Westermann, *The Slave Systems of Greek and Roman Antiquity*
     (Philadelphia: The American Philosophical Society, 1955), p. 59.

61.  Ibid., p. 61.

62.  Ibid., p. 85.

63.  Ibid., p. 63.

64.  Bernard Lewis, *Race and Slavery in the Middle East,* especially Chapters 2,
     3, 5. Middle Eastern racism toward darker peoples is also noted in Orlando
     Patterson, *Slavery and Social Death: A Comparative Study* (Cambridge,
     Mass.: Harvard University Press, 1982), p. 176.

65.  George M. Frederickson, *White Supremacy: A Comparative Study in Ameri-
     can and South African History* (New York: Oxford University Press, 1981),
     pp. 76–85.

66.  Francois Renault, "The Structures of the Slave Trade in Central Africa
     in the 19th Century," *The Economics of the Indian Ocean Slave Trade in
     the Nineteenth Century,* edited by William Gervase Clarence-Smith, pp.
     150, 152.

67.  See L. H. Gann and Peter Duignan, "Introduction," *Colonialism in Africa,
     1870–1960,* Vol I: *The History and Politics of Colonialism* (Cambridge:
     Cambridge University Press, 1981), p. 1; L. H. Gann and Peter Duignan,
     *Burden of Empire* (Stanford: Hoover Institution Press, 1977), p. 151.

68.  S. Abeyasekere, "Slavery and Slave Trade in South Sulawesi, 1660s–1800s,"
     *Slavery, Bondage and Dependency in Southeast Asia,* edited by Anthony
     Reid, p. 286.

69.  Anthony Reid, "'Closed' and 'Open' Slave System in Pre-Colonial Southeast
     Asia," Ibid., p. 173.

70.  Bruno Lasker, *Human Bondage in Southeast Asia* (Chapel Hill: University
     of North Carolina Press, 1950), p. 24.; A. van der Kraan, "Bali and the Slave
     Trade," *Slavery, Bondage and Dependency in Southeast Asia,* edited by
     Anthony Reid, p. 331.

71.  Orlando Patterson, *Slavery and Social Death,* pp. 110–111.

72.  See, for example, Thomas Sowell, "Three Black Histories," *Essays and Data*

*on American Ethnic Groups* (Washington, D.C.: The Urban Institute, 1978), pp. 16–17.

73. Bureau of the Census, *Negro Population: 1790–1915* (Washington, D.C.: Government Printing Office, 1918), p. 41.

74. Ibid., p. 55. While the number of slaves in Mississippi more than doubled between 1840 and 1860, the number of "free persons of color" was nearly halved during the same period. In Arkansas the number of slaves increased fivefold between 1840 and 1860, while the number of "free persons of color" fell by more than two-thirds. Ibid., p. 57.

75. E. Franklin Frazier, *The Negro in the United States* (New York: The Macmillan Co., 1971), p. 74.

76. Eugene Genovese, "The Slave States of North America," *Neither Slave Nor Free*, edited by David W. Cohen and Jack P. Greene (Baltimore: Johns Hopkins University Press, 1972), pp. 266–267; A. J. R. Russell-Wood, "Colonial Brazil," Ibid., p. 88; William L. Westermann, *The Slave Systems of Greek and Roman Antiquity*, pp. 5, 13, 64, 68, 73, 74, 92, 114, 156; William Gervase Clarence-Smith, "The Economics of the Indian Ocean and Red Sea Slave Trades in the 19th Century: An Overview," *The Economics of the Indian Ocean Slave Trade in the Nineteenth Century*, edited by William Gervase Clarence-Smith, pp. 4, 8; Timothy Fernyhough, "Slavery and the Slave Trade in Southern Ethiopia in the 19th Century," Ibid., p. 106; Bruno Lasker, *Human Bondage in Southeast Asia*, p. 35; Anthony Reid, "Introduction," *Slavery, Bondage and Dependency in Southeast Asia*, edited by Anthony Reid, p. 22; S. Abeyasekere, "Slaves in Batavia: Insights From a Slave Register," Ibid., p. 301.

77. David Eltis, "Free and Coerced Transatlantic Migrations: Some Comparisons," *American Historical Review*, April 1983, p. 262.

78. Richard B. Sheridan, "Mortality and the Medical Treatment of Slaves in the British West Indies," *Race and Slavery in the Western Hemisphere: Quantitative Studies*, edited by Stanley L. Engerman and Eugene D. Genovese (Princeton: Princeton University Press, 1975), p. 287; Thomas Sowell, *The Economics and Politics of Race: An International Perspective* (New York: William Morrow, 1983), p. 95.

79. Thomas Sowell, *Markets and Minorities* (New York: Basic Books, 1981), p. 92.

80. Compare U. B. Phillips, *American Negro Slavery* (Baton Rouge: Louisiana State University Press, 1969), p. 62; Robert W. Fogel and Stanley L. Engerman, *Time on the Cross* (Boston: Little, Brown and Co., 1974), p. 123.

81. Carl Degler, *Neither Black Nor White* (New York: Macmillan Publishing Co., 1971), p. 64.

82. See, for example, Frank Tannenbaum, *Slave and Citizen: The Negro in the Americas* (New York: Alfred A. Knopf, 1946).

83. Anthony Reid, "Introduction," *Slavery, Bondage and Dependency in Southeast Asia*, edited by Anthony Reid, p. 27.

84. Patrick Manning, "Contours of Slavery & Social Change in Africa," *American Historical Review*, October 1983, p. 844.

85. Allan G. B. Fisher and Humphrey J. Fisher, *Slavery and Muslim Society in Africa: The Institution in Saharan and Sudanic Africa and the Trans-Saharan Trade* (London: C. Hurst & Co., 1970), p. 165; Bernard Lewis, *Race and Slavery in the Middle East*, p. 13.

86. Abdussamad H. Ahmad, "Ethiopian Slave Exports at Matamma, Massawa and Tajura c. 1830 to 1885," *The Economics of the Indian Ocean Slave Trade in the Nineteenth Century*, edited by William Gervase Clarence-Smith, p. 98; Bernard Lewis, *Race and Slavery in the Middle East*, p. 13.

87. Bruno Lasker, *Human Bondage in Southeast Asia*, p. 62.

88. Orlando Patterson, *Slavery and Social Death: A Comparative Study* (Cambridge, Mass.: Harvard University Press, 1982), pp. 121–122.

89. Gwyn Campbell, "Madagascar and Mozambique in the Slave Trade of the Western Indian Ocean 1800–1861," *The Economics of the Indian Ocean Slave Trade in the Nineteenth Century*, edited by William Gervase Clarence-Smith, p. 185.

90. Ibid., p. 172. See also Marina Carter and Hubert Gerbeau, "Covert Slaves and Coveted Coolies in the Early 19th Century Mascareignes," Ibid., p. 202.

91. See, for example, William L. Westermann, *The Slave Systems of Greek and Roman Antiquity*, p. 7; A. J. R. Russell-Wood, "Colonial Brazil," *Neither Slave Nor Free*, edited by David W. Cohen and Jack P. Greene (Baltimore: Johns Hopkins University Press, 1972), p. 91; Mavis Campbell, "The Price of Freedom: On Forms of Manumission," *Review Interamericana*, Summer 1976, pp. 244–250.

92. William L. Westermann, *The Slave Systems of Greek and Roman Antiquity* (Philadelphia: The American Philosophical Society, 1955), pp. 18–19, 25, 35, 83; David W. Cohen and Jack P. Greene, "Introduction," *Neither Slave Nor Free*, edited by David W. Cohen and Jack P. Greene (Baltimore: Johns Hopkins University Press, 1972), p. 7; Frederick P. Bowser, "Colonial Spanish America," Ibid., p. 24–26, 31–32, 34; A. J. R. Russell-Wood, "Colonial Brazil," Ibid., pp. 86, 88, 91, 96, 125; Jerome S. Handler and Arnold A. Sio, "Barbados," Ibid., pp. 225–226; Richard Roberts and Suzanne Miers, "The End of Slavery in Africa," *The End of Slavery in Africa*, edited by Suzanne Miers and Richard Roberts (Madison: University of Wisconsin Press, 1988), p. 23; Richard C. Wade, *Slavery in the City* (New York: Oxford University Press, 1964), p. 49; Ira Berlin, *Slaves Without Masters* (New York: Pantheon Books, 1974), pp. 153–157.

93. William L. Westermann, *The Slave Systems of Greek and Roman Antiquity*, p. 18; David W. Cohen and Jack P. Greene, "Introduction," *Neither Slave Nor Free*, edited by David W. Cohen and Jack P. Greene, p. 7, 8, 11; H. Hoetink, "Surinam and Curaçao," Ibid., p. 63; Leo Elisabeth, "The French Antilles," Ibid., pp. 140–145; Eugene D. Genovese, "The Slave States of North America," Ibid., p. 259; J. Fox, "'For Good and Sufficient Reasons':

An Examination of Early Dutch East India Company Ordinances on Slaves and Slavery," *Slavery, Bondage and Dependency in Southeast Asia*, edited by Anthony Reid, pp. 256, 257; Ira Berlin, *Slaves Without Masters*, pp. 138–141. Legal "barriers against manumission" were by no means "distinctive characteristics" of "slavery in North America," as claimed by David Brion Davis, *The Problem of Slavery in Western Culture* (Ithaca: Cornell University Press, 1966), p. 30.

94. Russell Kirk, *John Randolph of Roanoke: A Study in American Politics* (Indianapolis: Liberty Press, 1978), pp. 372–373.

95. Ibid., p. 189. Yet David Brion Davis dismissed Randolph for "hypocrisy" for publicly condemning slavery in England in 1822. David Brion Davis, *The Problem of Slavery in the Age of Revolution* (Ithaca: Cornell University Press, 1975), p. 49.

96. Philip D. Curtin, *Two Jamaicas: The Role of Ideas in Tropical Colony, 1830–1865* (New York: Atheneum, 1970), pp. 45–46; David Lowenthal, *West Indian Society* (New York: Oxford University Press, 1972), p. 308; Thomas Sowell, *The Economics and Politics of Race*, p. 130.

97. See, for example, Richard C. Wade, *Slavery in the Cities: The South 1820–1860* (London: Oxford University Press, 1967), pp. 48–51, 64–66.

98. J. C. Furnas, *The Americans: A Social History of the United States 1587–1914* (New York: G. P. Putnam's Sons, 1969), pp. 400–401.

99. Richard C. Wade, *Slavery in the Cities: The South 1820–1860* (New York: Oxford University Press, 1967), pp. 85–87, 258–261.

100. Ibid., p. 110.

101. Robert W. Fogel and Stanley L. Engerman, *Time on the Cross* (Boston: Little, Brown and Co., 1974), p. 233.

102. Richard C. Wade, *Slavery in the Cities*, p. 124.

103. Ibid., pp. 24–25; David C. Rankin, "The Impact of the Civil War on the Free Colored Community of New Orleans," *Perspectives in American History*, Vol. XI (1977–1978), p. 381.

104. Frederick Law Olmstead, *The Cotton Kingdom* (New York: Modern Library, 1969), pp. 114–115.

105. Ibid., pp. 119–120.

106. Herbert S. Klein, *Slavery in the Americas: A Comparative Study of Virginia and Cuba* (Chicago: University of Chicago Press, 1967), p. 188; Frederick Law Olmstead, *A Journey in the Seaboard Slave States* (New York: New American Library, 1969), p. 127.

107. Bernard Lewis, *Race and Slavery in the Middle East: An Historical Enquiry* (New York: Oxford University Press, 1990), pp. 12, 56; Ehud R. Toledano, *The Ottoman Slave Trade and Its Suppression: 1840–1890* (Princeton: Princeton University Press, 1982), p. 8.

108. Ehud R. Toledano, "Slave Dealers, Women, Pregnancy, and Abortion: The Story of a Circassian Slave-girl in Mid-Nineteenth Century Cairo," *Slavery and Abolition*, May 1981, p. 54, 57.

109. Compare Ehud R. Toledano, *The Ottoman Slave Trade and Its Suppression*, p. 30; Roger Anstey, "The Volume and Profitability of the British Slave Trade, 1761–1807," *Race and Slavery in the Western Hemisphere: Quantitative Studies*, edited by Stanley L. Engerman and Eugene D. Genovese (Princeton: Princeton University Press, 1975), p. 25.

110. Reginald Coupland, *Exploitation of East Africa*, pp. 139–140; R. W. Beachey, *The Slave Trade of Eastern Africa*, p. 123.

111. Bernard Lewis, *Race and Slavery in the Middle East*, p. 14.

112. Patrick Manning, "Contours of Slavery and Social Change in Africa," *American Historical Review*, October 1983, p. 844.

113. Ibid.

114. Bernard Lewis, *Race and Slavery in the Middle East*, pp. 10, 56, 59, 65, 74, 84. Among 3,000 females slaves emancipated in Zanzibar in 1860, only 5 percent had ever borne children. Abdul Sheriff, *Slaves, Spices and Ivory in Zanzibar: Integration of an East African Commercial Empire Into the World Economy, 1770–1873* (London: James Curry, Ltd., 1987), p. 59.

115. Ralph Austen, "The Trans-Saharan Slave Trade: A Tentative Census," *The Uncommon Market: Essays in the Economic History of the Atlantic Slave Trade*, edited by Henry A. Gemery and Jan S. Hogendorn (New York: Academic Press, 1979), pp. 68–69.

116. Bruno Lasker, *Human Bondage in Southeast Asia* (Chapel Hill: University of North Carolina Press, 1950), pp. 17, 22, 27, 32, 36, 37, 44, 48, 50, 58, 286, 290.

117. I. Mabbett, "Some Remarks on the Present State of Knowledge About Slavery in Angkor," *Slavery, Bondage and Dependency in Southeast Asia*, edited by Anthony Reid (New York: St. Martin's Press, 1983), p. 45.

118. Orlando Patterson, *Slavery and Social Death: A Comparative Study* (Cambridge, Mass.: Harvard University Press, 1982), p. 83.

119. See, for example, Ehud R. Toledano, "Slave Dealers, Women, Pregnancy, and Abortion," *Slavery and Ambition*, May 1985, pp. 54–68.

120. Standish Meacham, *Henry Thornton of Clapham: 1760–1815* (Cambridge, Mass.: Harvard University Press, 1964), p. 1.

121. Stanley L. Engerman, "Some Implications of the Abolition of the Slave Trade," *The Abolition of the Atlantic Slave Trade: Origins and Effects in Europe, Africa, and the Americas* (Madison: University of Wisconsin Press, 1981), p. 7; James Walvin, "The Public Campaign in England Against Slavery, 1787–1834," Ibid., pp. 63–77.

122. James Walvin, "The Public Campaign in England Against Slavery, 1787–1834," Ibid., p. 68.

123. Ibid., p. 71.

124. Ehud R. Toledano, *The Ottoman Slave Trade and Its Suppression: 1840–1890* (Princeton: Princeton University Press, 1982), p. 93. See also the similar response of the Sultan of Zanzibar: R. W. Beachey, *The Slave Trade of Eastern Africa* (New York: Harper & Row, 1976), pp. 51–52.

125. Ehud R. Toledano, *The Ottoman Slave Trade and Its Suppression,* p. 127.

126. Reginald Coupland, *East Africa and Its Invaders, from the Earliest Times to the Death of Seyyid Said in 1856* (Oxford: The Clarendon Press, 1961), pp. 205–213.

127. Bruno Lasker, *Human Bondage in Southeast Asia,* p. 17.

128. Orlando Patterson, *Slavery and Social Death,* p. 159; Murray Gordon, *Slavery in the Arab World* (New York: New Amsterdam Books, 1989), p. xi.

129. Murray Gordon, *Slavery in the Arab World,* p. x. See also Eva Hoffman and Margot Slade, "Where Labor and Life Are Cheap," *New York Times,* August 30, 1981, Section 4, p. E7; Bernard D. Nossiter, "U.N. Gets A Report on African Slaves," *New York Times,* August 26, 1981, p. A11.

130. B. Terweil, "Bondage and Slavery in Early Nineteenth Century Siam," *Slavery, Bondage and Dependency in Southeast Asia,* edited by Anthony Reid (New York: St. Martin's Press, 1983), p. 133.

131. Bruno Lasker, *Human Bondage in Southeast Asia* (Chapel Hill: University of North Carolina Press, 1950), p. 46.

132. Ibid., p. 58.

133. Ibid., pp. 66–67.

134. Ibid., p. 38.

135. See, for example, Ehud R. Toledano, *The Ottoman Slave Trade and Its Suppression,* pp. 108, 171, 277–278.

136. The most blatant statement of this viewpoint was by Eric Williams, *Capitalism and Slavery* (New York: Russell & Russell, 1961), and it was devastated by Stanley Engerman, "The Slave Trade and British Capital Formation" and by Roger Anstey, "Capitalism and Slavery: A Critique," *Economic History Review,* Vol. XXI, 2nd Series (1968), pp. 307–329.

137. William L. Westermann, *The Slave Systems of Greek and Roman Antiquity,* p. 88.

138. James L. Watson, "Slavery as an Institution: Open and Closed Systems," *Asian and African Systems of Slavery,* edited by James L. Watson (Berkeley: University of California Press, 1980), p. 14; James L. Watson, "Transactions in People: The Chinese Market in Slaves, Servants, and Heirs," Ibid., p. 239.

139. Gill Shepherd, "The Comorians and the East African Slave Trade," Ibid., pp. 84–85.

140. Andrew Turton, "Thai Institutions of Slavery," Ibid., pp. 280–281.

141. Nancy E. Levine, "Opposition and Interdependence: Demographic and Economic Perspectives on Nyinba Slavery," Ibid., p. 213.

142. See, for example, Eric Williams, *Capitalism and Slavery* (New York: Russell & Russell, 1961), pp. vii–viii and passim.

143. Roger Anstey, "The Volume and Profitability of the British Slave Trade, 1675–1808," *Race and Slavery in the Western Hemisphere,* edited by Stanley L. Engerman and Eugene D. Genovese, pp. 22–23.

144. See, for example, Asa Briggs, *A Social History of England* (New York: Viking Press, 1983), p. 164.

145. David Eltis, *Economic Growth and the Ending of the Transatlantic Slave Trade* (New York: Oxford University Press, 1987), p. 97.

146. Pierre L. van den Berghe, *Race and Racism* (New York: John Wiley & Sons, 1978), p. 67. Also see Carl Degler, *Neither Black Nor White* (New York: Macmillan Publishing Co., 1971), p. 245.

147. David E. Apter, *Ghana in Transition* (Princeton: Princeton University Press, 1972), p. 62; R. W. Beachey, *The Slave Trade of Eastern Africa*, p. 131.

148. Bruno Lasker, *Human Bondage in Southeast Asia*, p. 43.

149. R. W. Beachey, *The Slave Trade of Eastern Africa*, p. 131; Ira Berlin, *Slaves Without Masters*, pp. 184, 234.

150. Anthony Reid, "'Closed' and 'Open' Slave Systems in Pre-Colonial Southeast Asia," *Slavery, Bondage and Dependency in Southeast Asia*, edited by Anthony Reid, p. 166.

151. Bruno Lasker, *Human Bondage in Southeast Asia*, p. 28. See also pp. 43, 65.

152. Jaime Vincens Vives, "The Decline of Spain in the Seventeenth Century," *The Economic Decline of Empires*, edited by Carlo M. Cipolla (London: Methuen & Co., 1970), p. 127.

153. Adam Smith, *An Enquiry Into the Nature and Causes of the Wealth of Nations* (New York: The Modern Library, 1937), pp. 647–648.

154. See, for example, W. Montgomery Watt, *The Influence of Islam on Medieval Europe* (Edinburgh: Edinburgh University Press, 1987).

155. William L. Westermann, *The Slave Systems of Greek and Roman Antiquity* (Philadelphia: The American Philosophical Society, 1955), pp. 2, 8.

156. Ibid., pp. 59–63.

157. Ibid., p. 42.

158. The remarkable thesis that European concepts of "progress" led to the enslavement of Africans is presented in David Brion Davis, *Slavery and Human Progress* (New York: Oxford University Press, 1984). See especially the title of Part One of that book: "How 'Progress' Led to the Europeans' Enslavement of Africans."

159. Herbert B. Gutman, *The Black Family in Slavery and Freedom, 1750–1925* (New York: Vintage Books, 1977), pp. 32, 45.

160. Henry Walker, "Black-White Differences in Marriage and Family Patterns," *Feminism, Children and the New Families*, edited by Sanford M. Dornbusch and Myra H. Strober (New York: The Guilford Press, 1988), p. 92.

161. U.S. Bureau of the Census, *Historical Statistics of the United States: Colonial Times to 1957* (Washington, D.C.: U.S. Government Printing Office, 1960), p. 72.

162. Herbert G. Gutman, *The Black Family in Slavery and Freedom*, pp. 231, 236, 238; Leon F. Litwack, *Been in the Storm So Long* (New York: Alfred A. Knopf, 1979), p. 238.

163. Herbert G. Gutman, *The Black Family in Slavery and Freedom*, pp. 217–218; Leon F. Litwack, *Been in the Storm So Long*, p. 238.

164. Orlando Patterson, *Slavery and Social Death*, pp. 55, 189.

165. "Names," *The New Encyclopedia Brittanica* (Chicago: Encyclopedia Brittanica, Inc., 1991), Vol. 24, p. 731.

166. John K. Fairbank, Edwin O. Reischauer, and Albert M. Craig, *East Asia:*

*Tradition and Transformation* (Boston: Houghton Mifflin Company, 1989), p. 509.

167. Herbert G. Gutman, *The Black Family in Slavery and Freedom*, pp. 230, 236–237.

168. Computed from *The Seventh Census of the United States: 1850* (Washington, D.C.: Robert Armstrong, public printer, 1853), pp. xliii, lxi.

169. See, for example, Thomas Sowell, "Three Black Histories," *Essays and Data on American Ethnic Groups*, edited by Thomas Sowell and Lynn D. Collins (Washington, D.C.: The Urban Institute, 1978), pp. 12–13.

170. See, for example, Leon F. Litwack, *Been in the Storm So Long*, pp. 68, 472–476; Booker T. Washington, W. E. B. DuBois, and James Weldon Johnson, *Three Negro Classics* (New York: Avon Books, 1965), pp. 44–45.

171. See, for example, Herbert G. Gutman, *The Black Family in Slavery and Freedom*, pp. 418–425.

172. H. Hoetink, "Surinam and Curaçao," *Neither Slave Nor Free*, edited by David W. Cohen and Jack P. Greene, pp. 59–83.

## CHAPTER 8: RACE AND HISTORY

1. Edmund Burke, *Reflections on the Revolution in France* (London: J. M. Dent & Sons, Ltd., 1967), p. 137.

2. William H. McNeill, *The Rise of the West: A History of the Human Community* (Chicago: University of Chicago Press, 1991), pp. xxvi, 48, 63, 68, 98, 102–103, 108, 148, 168, 229, 233, 250, 251, 252, 272–287, 298, 299, 330, 357, 361, 373–374, 379, 384, 390–391, 392, 398, 412, 419, 420, 437–438, 448n, 464, 465n, 469, 476, 477, 478, 479, 483, 485, 501, 506, 512, 530–531, 535, 536, 548, 550, 555, 558, 566, 578, 599, 600–601, 606, 633, 643, 646n, 651, 656, 660, 665, 666, 671, 674, 730, 776–777, 782, 787–788; John K. Fairbank, Edwin O. Reischauer, and Albert M. Craig, *East Asia: Tradition and Transformation*, revised edition (Boston: Houghton Mifflin Co., 1989), pp. 38, 77, 107, 112, 174, 243, 260, 300–302, 310, 324, 335, 354, 355, 429, 515, 530, 562–563; E. L. Jones, *The European Miracle: Environments, Economies and Geopolitics in the History of Europe and Asia*, second edition (Cambridge: Cambridge University Press, 1992), pp. xxi, 45, 54, 57–58, 60, 73, 83, 115–116, 179–180.

3. William H. McNeill, *The Rise of the West*, pp. 48, 63, 98, 145, 229, 477, 656.

4. Winston S. Churchill, *Great Contemporaries* (Chicago: University of Chicago Press, 1973), p. 267.

5. Fernand Braudel, *The Mediterranean and the Mediterranean World in the Age of Phillip II*, translated by Sian Reynolds (New York: Harper & Row, 1972), Volume I, p. 34.

6. Ibid., p. 35.

7. Jack Chen, *The Chinese of America* (San Francisco: Harper & Row, 1980), p. 65.

8. Daniel Yergin, *The Prize: The Epic Quest for Oil, Money, and Power* (New York: Simon & Schuster, 1990), p. 60.

9. William A. Hance, *The Geography of Modern Africa* (New York: Columbia University Press, 1964), p. 5.

10. John K. Fairbank, Edwin O. Reischauer, and Albert M. Craig, *East Asia: Tradition and Transformation*, revised edition (Boston: Houghton Mifflin Co., 1989), p. 515.

11. Margaret Sedeen, editor, *Great Rivers of the World* (Washington, D.C.: National Geographic Society, 1984), p. 24.

12. Ibid., Section 1.

13. Ibid., pp. 69–70; Daniel R. Headrick, *The Tools of Empire: Technology and European Imperialism in the Nineteenth Century* (New York: Oxford University Press, 1981), p. 196.

14. Even agricultural improvements have originated in the vicinity of major cities, such as Venice, Milan, and Florence in the sixteenth century. Fernand Braudel, *The Mediterranean and the Mediterranean World in the Age of Phillip II*, Vol. I, p. 84.

15. Jocelyn Murray, editor, *Cultural Atlas of Africa* (New York: Facts on File Publications, 1981), p. 73.

16. J. F. Ade Ajayi and Michael Crowder, editors, *Historical Atlas of Africa* (Essex: Longman Group Ltd., 1985), map facing Section 1.

17. E. L. Jones, *The European Miracle: Environments, Economies and Geopolitics in the History of Europe and Asia*, second edition (Cambridge: Cambridge University Press, 1987), p. 159.

18. William A. Hance, *The Geography of Modern Africa*, pp. 4–5.

19. H. J. de Blij and Peter O. Muller, *Geography: Regions and Concepts* (New York: John Wiley & Sons, Inc., 1992), p. 394.

20. William H. McNeill, *The Rise of the West*, p. 481.

21. Ibid., p. 650.

22. Arnold J. Bauer, "Industry and the Missing Bourgeoisie: Consumption and Development in Chile, 1850–1950," *Hispanic American Historical Review*, May, 1990, p. 227.

23. Ray H. Whitbeck and Olive J. Thomas, *The Geographic Factor: Its Role in Life and Civilization* (Port Washington, N.Y.: Kennikat Press, 1970), pp. 304–305.

24. For a Malay view of this phenomenon, see Mahathir bin Mohamad, *The Malay Dilemma* (Kuala Lumpur: Federal Publications, 1970), pp. 20–25.

25. Ralph R. Premdas, "The Political Economy of Ethnic Strife in Fiji and Guyana," *Ethnic Studies Report* (International Centre for Ethnic Studies, Sri Lanka), July 1991, pp. 34–37.

26. Fernand Braudel, *The Mediterranean and the Mediterranean World in the Age of Phillip II*, Vol. I, pp. 103–107.

27. E. J. Jones, *The European Miracle*, pp. 26–32.

28. Ibid., p. 31.

29. Ralph R. Premdas, "The Political Economy of Ethnic Strife in Fiji and Guyana," *Ethnic Studies Report* (International Centre for Ethnic Studies, Sri Lanka), July, p. 31.

30. Ibid., p. 19.

31. Ibid., p. 8.

32. Edwin O. Reischauer and John K. Fairbank, *A History of East Asian Civilization*, Volume I: *East Asia: The Great Tradition* (Boston: Houghton Mifflin Co., 1960), p. 12.

33. Ibid., pp. 10–12.

34. Ray H. Whitbeck and Olive J. Thomas, *The Geographic Factor*, p. 167.

35. L. Dudley Stamp, *Africa: A Study in Tropical Development* (New York: John Wiley & Sons, Inc., 1954), p. 5.

36. Ibid., p. xxvii.

37. Janet L. Abu-Lughod, *Before European Hegemony: The World System A.D. 1250–1350* (New York: Oxford University Press, 1989), pp. 176, 178.

38. Edwin O. Reischauer and John K. Fairbank, *A History of East Asian Civilization*, Volume I, pp. 20–21.

39. N. J. G. Pounds, *An Historical Geography of Europe: 1800–1914* (Cambridge: Cambridge University Press, 1988), pp. 492–493.

40. Ibid., p. 1.

41. Ibid., p. 43.

42. Ibid., pp. 132, 178–179.

43. Ibid., p. 430.

44. Ibid., pp. 457–458.

45. George W. Hoffman, "Changes in the Agricultural Geography of Yugoslavia," *Essays in the Geography of Eastern Europe*, edited by Norman J. G. Pounds (Bloomington: Indiana University Press, 1961), p. 113.

46. N. J. G. Pounds, *An Historical Geography of Europe: 1800–1914* (Cambridge: Cambridge University Press, 1988), p. 459.

47. Ibid., p. 485.

48. Ibid., p. 488.

49. Ibid., p. 16.

50. Ibid., p. 21.

51. Ibid., pp. 18–19.

52. William H. McNeill, *The Rise of the West*, pp. 22, 30.

53. Ibid., p. 452.

54. Ibid., p. 464.

55. Fernand Braudel, *The Mediterranean and the Mediterranean World in the Age of Phillip II*, Vol. I, pp. 6–75, 81–82.

56. Ibid., p. 4.

57. Ibid., p. 144.

58. Ibid., pp. 85–89.

59. See Daniel Boorstin, *The Discoverers* (New York: Harry N. Abrams, Inc., 1991), Vol. I, p. 273. See also "Cheng Ho," *Dictionary of Ming Biography:*

*1368–1644* (New York: Columbia University Press, 1976), Vol. I, p. 197; Janet L. Abu-Lughod, *Before European Hegemony*, pp. 320–321.

60.  William H. McNeill, *The Rise of the West*, pp. 526–527.

61.  Ibid., pp. 645–646 .

62.  William Manchester, *A World Lit Only by Fire: The Medieval Mind and the Renaissance* (Boston: Little, Brown and Co., 1992), pp. 290–291.

63.  Daniel Boorstin, *The Discoverers* (New York: Harry N. Abrams, Inc., 1983), Volume I, pp. 115, 117.

64.  Ibid., p. 154.

65.  William H. McNeill, *The Rise of the West*, pp. 468–469; E. J. Jones, *The European Miracle*, p. 189.

66.  Daniel Boorstin, *The Discoverers*, p. 154.

67.  The remarkable thesis that European concepts of "progress" led to the enslavement of Africans is presented in David Brion Davis, *Slavery and Human Progress* (New York: Oxford University Press, 1984). See especially the title of Part One of that book: "How 'Progress' Led to the Europeans' Enslavement of Africans."

68.  ". . . in the inevitable taking of sides which comes from selection and emphasis in history, I prefer to try to tell the story of the discovery of America from the viewpoint of the Arawaks, of the Constitution from the standpoint of the slaves, of Andrew Jackson as seen by the Cherokees, of the Civil War as seen by the New York Irish . . . " Howard Zinn, *A People's History of the United States* (New York: Harper & Row, 1980), p. 10.

69.  Nathan Glazer and Daniel Patrick Moynihan, *Beyond the Melting Pot* (Cambridge, Mass.: The M.I.T. Press, 1970), p. 241.

70.  William McGowan, *And Only Man Is Vile: The Tragedy of Sri Lanka* (New York: Farrar, Straus & Giroux, 1992), pp. 144, 172–173.

71.  See, for example, Dinesh D'Souza, *Illiberal Education: The Politics of Race and Sex on Campus* (New York: The Free Press, 1991), pp. 111–121.

72.  Victor Purcell, *The Boxer Uprising: A Background Study* (Cambridge: Cambridge University Press, 1963), pp. 30–31.

73.  Bernard Lewis, "Some Reflections on the Decline of the Ottoman Empire," *The Economic Decline of Empires*, edited by Carlo M. Cipolla (London: Methuen & Co., 1970), p. 229.

74.  Ian Harmstorf and Michael Cigler, *The Germans in Australia* (Melbourne: Australasian Educa. Press Pty. Ltd., 1985), pp. 164, 174.

75.  S. W. Kung, *Chinese in American Life: Some Aspects of Their History, Status, Problems, and Contributions* (Seattle: University of Washington Press, 1962), p. 9.

76.  Adam Giesinger, *From Catherine to Khrushchev: The Story of Russia's Germans* (Lincoln, Neb.: American Historical Society of Germans From Russia, 1974), pp. 230–234.

77.  James L. Tigner, "Japanese Immigration Into Latin America," *Journal of Interamerican Studies and World Affairs*, November 1981, p. 466.

78. H. Gilchrist, "Greek Settlement Until 1940," *The Australian People: An Encyclopedia of the Nation, Its People and Their Origins*, edited by James Jupp (North Ryde, N.S.W.: Angus & Robertson Publishers, 1988), pp. 508, 509, 510.

79. Linda Chavez, *Out of the Barrio: Toward a New Politics of Hispanic Assimilation* (New York: Basic Books, 1991), pp. 101–102.

80. See, for example, Reynolds Farley, "Does Preference Reinforce White Prejudice?" *Racism and Justice: The Case for Affirmative Action* (Ithaca: Cornell University Press, 1991), p. 60, which is of course like comparing apples and oranges, since the relative proportions of newly arriving West Indian immigrants and second-generation West Indians is not known for the later period. What is known is that, even in the earlier period, the *initial* incomes of newly arriving black immigrants were not only well below those of white Americans, but were even below the incomes of native-born black Americans, though the incomes of these immigrants eventually surpassed that of black Americans within their own lifetimes (Barry Chiswick, "The Economic Progress of Immigrants: Some Apparently Universal Patterns," *Contemporary Economic Problems: 1979*, edited by William Fellner [Washington, D.C.: The American Enterprise Institute, 1979], pp. 373–374).

81. Thomas Sowell, "Three Black Histories," *Essays and Data on American Ethnic Groups*, edited by Thomas Sowell and Lynn D. Collins (Washington, D.C.: The Urban Institute, 1978), p. 44.

82. U.S. Department of Health and Human Services, *Health United States 1990* (Washington, D.C.: U.S. Government Printing Office, 1991), pp. 8–9, 41, 58–59.

# INDEX